T0325480

Praise for *The Road to Luxury, 2e*

"Ashok Som and Christian Blanckaert have brilliantly outlined and share with us the new frontiers and opportunities in the luxury management. I find their development on the second hand, vintage, pre-loved opportunity for the luxury and fashion Maisons and Brands very interesting. As Jean-Louis Dumas said in his famous definition of luxury 'Luxury is what you repair.' It also what you transmit. A very inspired and inspiring book to read!"

—**Stanislas de Quercize**, former CEO of Cartier, Van Clef & Arpels & Richemont, France

"*The Road to Luxury* presents a thorough analysis of the luxury industry in a remarkably easy-to-read way. The authors evaluate the critical processes, skills and major players of luxury compared to those of other industries, skilfully identifying the key points that harness success. Professor Ashok Som has studied and worked with the major industry players and this clearly grants him a privileged and passionate perspective on the industry. The book is a good reference point for understanding the luxury industry's key drivers and making more informed decisions, which makes it as an ideal handbook for people who are currently working in the industry or who wish to understand what makes this industry special."

—**Stefano Rivera**, CEO, Scabal

"I found this book beautifully illustrated, very pleasant to read, and full of great ideas for managing the LEONARD operations worldwide in the years to come. I will keep the book within reach so I can consult it regularly to find inspiration."

—**Daniel Tribouillard**, Chairman of the Board, LEONARD Fashion

"*The Road to Luxury* is a must-read for anyone interested in the future of luxury, and how to find successful paths in its new environment. Christian Blanckaert and Ashok Som have combined the best of academic analysis and business expertise to give a unique perspective on how to predict, and create, the luxury of tomorrow."

—**Jonathan Siboni**, President, Luxurynsight

The Road to Luxury

The New Frontiers in Luxury Brand Management

Second Edition

Ashok Som
Christian Blanckaert

WILEY

Other Wiley Editorial Offices

John Wiley & Sons, 111 River Street, Hoboken, NJ 07030, USA
John Wiley & Sons, The Atrium, Southern Gate, Chichester, West Sussex, P019 8SQ, United Kingdom
John Wiley & Sons (Canada) Ltd., 5353 Dundas Street West, Suite 400, Toronto, Ontario, M9B 6HB, Canada
John Wiley & Sons Australia Ltd., 42 McDougall Street, Milton, Queensland 4064, Australia
Wiley-VCH, Boschstrasse 12, D-69469 Weinheim, Germany

Library of Congress Cataloging-in-Publication Data is Available:

Names: Som, Ashok, author. | Blanckaert, Christian, author.
Title: The road to luxury : the new frontiers in luxury brand management
    / Ashok Som, Christian Blanckaert.
Description: Second edition. | Singapore : Wiley, [2021] | Includes index.
Identifiers: LCCN 2021028320 (print) | LCCN 2021028321 (ebook) | ISBN
    9781119741312 (cloth) | ISBN 9781119741381 (adobe pdf) | ISBN
    9781119741367 (epub)
Subjects: LCSH: Luxuries–Marketing. | Luxury goods industry. | Brand name
    products–Management. | Branding (Marketing)
Classification: LCC HD9999.L852 S66 2021 (print) | LCC HD9999.L852
    (ebook) | DDC 658.8–dc23
LC record available at https://lccn.loc.gov/2021028320
LC ebook record available at https://lccn.loc.gov/2021028321

Cover Image: © bgblue/iStock/Getty Images
Cover Design: Wiley

Typeset in 11.5/14pt Bembo by Straive™, Chennai, India

Printed in Singapore
M111874_190721

We dedicate this book to
Wladimir, Amelie, and Zoya

Contents

Acknowledgments

The idea of the second edition of The Road to Luxury started to take shape as I witnessed double-digit growth of the personal luxury goods segment from 2015 to 2019. Four of the luxury companies—namely, LVMH, L'Oreal, Hermès, and Kering—were within the top six companies in the CAC40 index, with an all-time-high market cap. Each of these companies was witnessing spectacular growth. For this reason, the examples we had used in the first edition of the book was becoming outdated. Digitalization, sustainability and China were moot in most discussions. The idea finally crystallized at the beginning of the COVID-19 pandemic in early 2020. I started to organize my notes and interview managers and CEOs to understand how the new frontier of the luxury goods industry would look in the future. In March 2020 the market crashed and most of the companies lost 50% of their value. That was the moment I went back to the first chapter to be reminded that every 10 years such a calamity occurs and usually there is a sharp rebound. Over the rest of that year I reworked and revisited the book as I interacted with participants from the EMiLUX and the Masters in Management programs.

Prompted by my students, I created assignments such as case studies, which the students from the program wrote under my supervision. Those teaching materials were used in the program with great success and were adopted worldwide in other universities and business schools. I am grateful to the participants in this program for their insights and feedback. My work environment in a French *grande ecole* provided and sustained my interest in French and Italian luxury businesses. I appreciate the efforts of my colleague, manager and friends to discuss and debate the world of fashion and luxury trends. My sincere thanks to all of them.

I acknowledge the support of all my students, especially Zula Hu, Sandhya Rangan, Nikhil Anand, Shirin Sonal, Yu Cao, Arushi Chopra, Sushanta Das, Rashi Gupta, Hannes Gurzki, Naja Pape, Shiva Pappu, and Milan Rabold who supported me in my research as I wrote the two editions of this book. My sincere thanks to my students, Manuela Brische, Lilly Liu, Deepak Yachamaneni, Boris Gbahoué, Geraldine Carter, Stephanie Masson, Misha Gupta, Karyn Bell, Anna Nolting, Fernanda Harger, Nora Kato, Raghavendra Sheshamurthy, Nonika Vyas, Tina Huang, Sid Shetty, Priscilla Mark, Mario Sanz del Castillo, Lynn Chou, Lan Wu, Leonardo Banegas, Pajaree Kasemsant, and Salman Bukhari who spent their time revising and integrating my comments multiple times to make their work publishable. Also, my appreciation goes to Ruchi Shangari Dsouza, Debjani Roy, Daniel Tobar-Richter, Clara Gonzalez Goicoechea, Valerie Flexor, Jisook Anh, Mo Cheng, Wenjing Wang, Meng Li, Erik Lobatom, Kanika Holloway, Sophia Redford, Alessandro Cannata, Hui Xu and many others who worked diligently in my course on Managing the Global Corporation.

I unhesitatingly acknowledge the support and encouragement of Françoise Rey, who inspired me to try new concepts and creative ways of managing programs to keep on building my network in this industry. I express my sincere thanks to all my colleagues, especially Michel Baroni, Dean of Faculty, who was there to extend support in this endeavor whenever required.

I acknowledge the following companies: LVMH, Kering, Richemont, Chanel, Van Cleef and Arpels, Chaumet, Krug, MFK, and many others who enhanced my knowledge about the different sectors of the luxury business. Prashant Mishra from IIM Calcutta, India, with whose invitation I was appointed as Hindustan Unilever Visiting Faculty at IIM Calcutta to continue research in emerging brands.

Despite the best efforts of the contributors, I remain responsible for any shortcomings. Finally, I would like to acknowledge the efforts of my fourteen-year-old daughter, Mekhala-Zoya, who regularly reminded me not to waste my time during the pandemic on browsing Facebook but to complete my part of revising and rewriting the chapters before the ever-nearing deadlines.

Ashok Som

About the Authors

ASHOK SOM is Professor in the Management Department at ESSEC Business School. Professor Som is one of the pioneering thought leaders in designing organizations and an expert in Global Strategy. His book *Organization: Redesign and Innovative HRM* was published by Oxford University Press (2008) and *International Management: Managing the Global Corporation* by McGrawHill, UK (2009). At ESSEC, he is the Founding Director of the Executive Masters in Luxury Management (EMiLUX) that partners with the Parsons School of Design—The New School, New York; Accademia Costume and Moda, Italy; and previously with SDA Bocconi. He was the Founding Associate Dean of the full-time, one-year post-experience, Global MBA program; the founder of the India Research Centre; and the founder and Director of the Global Management Programs on Luxury and Retail Management (in partnership with the Indian Institute of Management [IIM], Ahmedabad). He received his PhD from IIM Ahmedabad; M.Sc and M.Tech from the Indian Institute of Technology, Kharagpur; and a bachelor's degree from Presidency University, Calcutta, India. He is passionate about case-based research and teaching. He was the winner of the EFMD Case Writing Competition 2008 in the Indian Management category. He won the Case Centre Award 2014 in the Entrepreneurship category. He is Adjunct Faculty at IIM Ahmedabad, (India), and Mannheim Business School (Germany), and Visiting Professor at IIM Calcutta (India), Auckland University of Technology (New Zealand), the Graduate School of Business, Keio University (Japan), and Tamkang University (Taiwan). His current research is on creative industries, focusing on the luxury industry. He is a regular speaker at international conferences and consults with European and Indian multinationals.

CHRISTIAN BLANCKAERT's resume establishes him as a global leader in luxury. He is currently senior advisor of EPI Group (J.M.Weston, Bonpoint, Champagnes Piper Heidseick and Charles Heidsieck), senior advisor of Eurazeo, Vilebrequin, Furla SPA. He is a board member of the Yves Rocher Group and Figaret. For several years he was President of Petit Bateau and a board member of Moncler. From 1996 to 2009, Blanckaert was the CEO of Hermes Sellier and Executive Vice President of Hermes International. From 1988 to 1996 he was President of Comité Colbert (a french organization that represents 70 French Luxury companies). During his career, Christian has been a consultant with the Boston-base consulting firm Harbridge House. He was the CEO of the do-it-yourself chain Bricorama, Chairman and CEO of Thomson Distribution, and Managing Director of the SCAC group.

Christian was also for many years Chairman of the board of the French National School of Decorative Arts (ENSAD) and Vice President of Action Again Hunger (ACF). Blanckaert was Mayor of Varengeville-sur-Mer for 21 years and is the author of several books: les chemins du luxe (Grasset 1996), Portraits en Clair Obscur (Balland, 2004), a biography of Roger Salengro (Balland 2001), Luxe (Éditions du Cherche-Midi, 2007), Luxe Trotter (Éditions du Cherche-Midi, 2012), Les 100 mots du Luxe (Les Presses Universitaires de France PUF, 2012), Argent, Fortunes et Luxe en Asie with JM Bouissou and J. Siboni (Picquier Éditions 2013). Instants Précieux (Allary Éditions, 2018). He is a visiting Professor at ESSEC, ESCP in Paris, Singapore and ESA in Beirut. Blanckaert graduated from the Institut d'Etudes Politiques de Paris, the Faculty of Law of Paris and has an MBA of INSEAD.

Prologue

The Pink Bag

I t had been sitting there, on the shelf, for ages.

Two years, three years—nobody knew exactly, but it was surely a "depreciated asset," as a slick city banker might say.

They could have hidden it away at the back of a store cupboard, but that would have been too sad, too harsh. The bag had become a fixture, a familiar friend of the store, and it sat there, doggedly, fixedly—probably for a long time.

This bag had personality. It was pink. Pink crocodile leather with a diamond clasp. Worth a small fortune. Yet still on the shelf.

From time to time, someone would move it to another spot.

It would be showcased, at the entrance, or to one side, or right in the middle, or at the back of the store.

It had attracted plenty of dust, watched thousands of customers pass by, as it waited in vain to catch someone's eye.

The pink crocodile bag filled the sales assistants with despair, but it was no use to think about it. They kept it, convinced that one day there would be a new turn of fate.

The pink bag had aged a little, the candy pink had begun to fade slightly, and the diamonds, which were polished every day, had lost some of their sparkle.

"We should take it off the shelf," said the leather section manager. "We can't keep it on sale," said the head sales manager. In short, the pink bag was a nuisance; its continual presence was annoying and it was beginning to stand out like a sore thumb.

The bag felt ashamed. What could be the reason for its failure? Its price, its color, its skin?

The sales assistants resorted to making jokes and calling it "unsellable," which is of course the worst insult for a handbag.

One Monday morning, a customer came across the bag, high up on its perch. The bag seemed rather aloof, almost condescending, as it looked down on the crowd of customers.

"May I have a look at it?" inquired the lady.

Excited, the sales assistant took down the bag, taking care to don her white gloves, so as not to scratch the crocodile leather. She announced the price, one hundred and ten thousand francs, and said rather clumsily, almost apologetically: "Madam, just look at the magnificent diamonds." The customer replied, "No, I think the bag itself is beautiful. The color is unique. I've never seen a pink quite like it." Gilberte, the sales assistant, couldn't believe her ears when the lady added, "I'll take it."

With a wave of her arms, a hand in the air, Gilberte did all she could to alert her colleagues.

"The pink bag has been sold!"

The news spread through the store like wildfire.

At the checkout, the bag was ready and waiting, all polished and packaged, magnificent in its superb orange box.

The sales assistant accompanied the customer to the checkout. "How would you like to pay?" she asked.

"American Express," replied the lady, confidently.

Normally, the transaction is accepted at the first try. But this time, the machine tried once, twice, three times . . . before the harassed cashier was obliged to announce, in hushed tones, "I'm sorry Madam, your card is refused."

"The swine!" cried the customer. "It's my husband's doing, we're divorcing and he's blocked the account. I'll come back tomorrow and pay cash."

A few shrugs and gesticulations later and the whole store heard the message that something was wrong.

The bag remained calmly in its box while its would-be owner stormed out.

Gilberte slowly removed the packaging, took the bag out of the orange box, and placed it back on the shelf.

At closing time, the bag was still there, shrouded in disappointment and surrounded by the sales team, who were muttering, "It's because of the color," and "It will never sell." In the end, the manager said, "We'll take it off sale tomorrow."

The story of the pink bag should have ended there.

The next day, around 11 a.m., a man stopped at the store, asked to see the bag, examined it lovingly, and bought it.

This time, the American Express card was accepted, the bag was sold; a victory for candy pink and a relief for Gilberte. The pessimists and the gigglers were both left speechless.

The story of the pink bag should have ended there. It had been purchased by its very own knight in shining armor.

That afternoon, something extraordinary happened.

Nobody had believed the lady when she said she would come back for the bag and pay cash. They had sold it without as much as a second thought for her.

And who was going to believe that divorce story, anyway?

Well, she turned up, all happy and smiling, and proudly placed 110,000 francs in notes on the desk.

"I've come to pick up my dream," she said.

The reactions among the sales assistants ranged from unease to sheer horror.

This was not going to be easy to explain. What could they say?

It was Gilberte who took the plunge. She explained the situation and promised to remedy it. And so, a second and last bag was made, identical to the first.

They say crocodiles will wait a long time to catch their prey.

Part I

UNDERSTANDING
THE LUXURY BUSINESS

Chapter 1

Introduction—Definition and Crisis of Luxury

L uxury has a long and fascinating history. This is apparent from artifacts of the Egyptian period of lavishness, from 1550 to 1070 B.C. The Italian Renaissance, an era of great painters, sculptors, and architects, through the course of the fourteenth through sixteenth centuries A.D., introduced another important wave of a lifestyle marked by luxury. This was followed by the reign of King Louis XIV of France (1638–1715), whose reign deepened the meaning of an authentic French lifestyle. Then came Charles Frederick Worth (1825–1895) of Great Britain, the designer who coined the concept of haute couture. Worth moved to Paris in 1846 to perfect and then commercialize his craft, holding the first fashion shows and launching the use of fashion labels. Coco Chanel (1883–1971) and Christian Dior (1905–1957) gave birth to modern trends and ideals, marked by the rise of New York City as a capital of luxury. Over the course of the 1960s and 1970s, the world saw the second Italian luxury revolution. Gucci and Bernard Arnault started applying the principles of strategic management to modern luxury by building the first multibrand conglomerate: the Louis Vuitton Moët Hennessy (LVMH) group. The latest chapter to this fascinating tale of luxury and high fashion is the information technology revolution, in which news about a new product spreads like wildfire, and how opinions pertaining to brands, products, and companies are shared at the click of a button. What is important to remember is that the history of the evolution of luxury is highly correlated to the evolution of society.

Changes in consumption in the luxury industry affect the ways countries evolve. The first stage is deprivation: despite being crushed by poverty, the population of a country maintains the desire to consume. The second stage is a new wave of prosperity: as the country witnesses economic growth, its middle class seeks to acquire luxuries that have high functional utilities, like washing machines, cars, and practical appliances. Then the wealthy and elite start buying luxury products. The third stage of development is the desire of consumers to show their wealth: mere possession is insufficient when luxury goods become a symbol of social status and bestow their owners with an aura of divinity. The fourth stage is that of being plentiful: in which most people in the nation are well-off and have sufficient resources; however, they have a need to fit in with their group. If someone is not carrying or wearing an appropriate social marker, they might find it hard to fit in with a particular group. The fifth and final stage is normalization: where luxury becomes a way of life. When people become used to this lifestyle, it becomes difficult for them to go back to their previous habits. Here luxury is more and more associated with personal tastes and pleasure, and not necessarily with wealth or status.

Issues of Defining Luxury

It is important to understand why certain brands are called luxury brands and what justifies the superior positioning they command. Luxury empires are not built by selling tasteful products at an exorbitant price. Luxury brands have been carefully crafted through meticulous strategies in marketing and brand building, making their mark in the consumer's subconscious and having the following main characteristics: brand strength, differentiation, exclusivity, innovation, product craftsmanship and precision, premium pricing, and high quality.

It is the differentiated quality of the material, design, and performance of a Patek Philippe watch that merits a 1,000% premium over a normal watch picked up from a general store. It is the craftsmanship that goes into the Kelly bag made by Hermès that justifies its exceptionally high price tag. It is only the brand strength of Louis Vuitton that can entice customers to preorder bags months in advance. It is attention to craftsmanship and nuances of details that help differentiate a luxury product.

Many misconceptions surround the luxury industry: (1) Do luxury and fashion mean the same thing? (2) Does a high price imply a luxury product? and (3) Does luxury imply perfection?

Luxury and fashion do not mean the same thing; they can coexist, but that's not always the case. Until the nineteenth century, only the very privileged few could afford to keep up with changing trends. So only those who could bear the cost of luxury could afford to make and follow fashion. However, the twenty-first century consumer doesn't need to be wealthy to be fashionable; being trendy no longer needs to be costly. For example, streetwear brands produced by H&M and Zara are fashionable and affordable. Haute couture is still the trendsetter but is not the only reference anymore. Luxury products used to be seen as an investment, which is not replaced that often, but now they have become more of a lifestyle choice. Many luxury houses try to release fashionable products along with their traditional luxury goods. For instance, Chanel offers fashionable products in order to keep up with the times and renew interest in their classic items.

A large price tag does not explicitly indicate that a product is a luxury good. Everyday products could trade up and charge a higher price. All luxury products are expensive, but not all expensive products are luxurious. This means that it is difficult to sell premium products as luxury goods—a phenomenon known as "premiumization" or "trading-up." Similarly, it is unwise to reposition a luxury brand as a premium product to extend its market. Automobile companies have tried to reposition products both ways and have failed, such as Mercedes with both the launch of the Smart car and its acquisition of Chrysler. However, the brand managed to strengthen its luxurious image through its portfolio of products, namely Maybach, AMG, and its venture into the pure electric vehicle industry. In the meantime, Porsche rose to become the most valuable luxury brand for the year 2020 through a brand value increase of 15.6% to USD33.91 billion. When one pays a tidy sum to procure a luxury brand, what does he or she pay for? Perfection? Not necessarily. In some ways, what defines the luxury brands are the creators and not the consumers. A luxurious product may thus be far from perfect. However, would these characteristics be questioned in times of a recession, when consumers become more cautious, have a limited budget, and spend less?

Crisis

Bling is over. Red carpet covered with rhinestones is out. I call it the new modesty.

—Karl Lagerfeld

There were several economic crises during the 1970s to 2020, starting with the oil crises in 1973 and 1979, the stock market crash in 1987, the 1992 Black Wednesday crash, and 1997's Asian financial crisis. The first 10 years of the twenty-first century also saw many crises. The stock markets collapsed in early 2000, following the dot-com bubble of the late 1990s. In 2001 the world watched as the terrorist attacks in New York and Washington took place, followed by the war in Afghanistan in 2001 and the invasion of Iraq in 2003. The early 2000s also saw a recession in many countries of the world, aggravated by the outbreak of SARS in Asia in 2003. In 2004, the tsunami in Asia killed hundreds of thousands. In 2007 the subprime mortgage crisis that began in the United States housing market spread all over the world and caused, among many other things, the collapse of Lehman Brothers and the European debt crisis of 2011, which continues to have effects such as the Cyprus bailout and political turmoil in Russia and Italy. In 2020 the outbreak of the coronavirus all around the globe has wiped billions off luxury companies' market value.

Crisis can take four forms: (1) endogenous (inner), such as economic and financial crises; (2) exogenous (outer), such as a political crisis; (3) natural disasters; and (4) mixed characteristics. An *economic crisis* is one where the real economy, of one country or worldwide, experiences a significant slowdown. The gross domestic product consumption stagnates or shrinks, along with investments, capacity utilization, household incomes, company profits, and inflation, while bankruptcies and unemployment rates rise. Figure 1.1 shows periods of shrinking GDP between 1950 and 2013, followed by negative GDP in the year 2020 using the examples of the world's biggest economy, the United States.

On the other hand, a *financial crisis* is a sudden devaluation of assets, such as stocks or currencies, which may or may not have an effect on the real economy. In itself, a financial crisis only leads to the destruction of paper wealth. It has been observed that there is a reciprocal relationship with other types of crises, such as economic crises and political crises, which is the reason why financial crises generally lead to increased levels of caution within politics and the real economy. Examples of such financial crises are the burst of the dot-com bubble, together with the September 11, 2001, and other terrorist attacks, the subprime crisis of 2007, and the ongoing Eurozone debt crisis facing the world, transforming from the private debt property bubble of 2008–2009 into the sovereign debt crisis of major banks and economies of Europe, in which the Dow

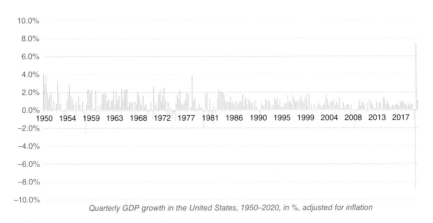

Quarterly GDP growth in the United States, 1950–2020, in %, adjusted for inflation

Figure 1.1   Quarterly GDP Growth in the United States, 1950–2020 (in percentage adjusted for inflation)

Jones has lost about 50% of its value. Other such crises that affected the world include the South American debt crisis of the 1980s, known as the "lost decade"; the Asian financial crisis of 1997; the Russian crisis of 1998; and the European debt crisis that started in 2010 and has taken an enormous toll up until the present moment.

Like financial crises, *political crises* may affect the economy and have an effect on industries, including the luxury industry. Examples of political crises are the Cuban Missile crisis, the Falklands crisis, the Iraqi invasion of Kuwait and the subsequent intervention by the United States in 1990, and the terrorist attacks in 2001. In 2011, the governments of Tunisia and Egypt were overthrown by revolutions and Libya saw a regime change after a civil war that was supported mainly by France and the United Kingdom. In 2013, the election results of Beppe Grillo's Five Star movement in Italy combined with the EU's decision on tax issues in Cyprus have fueled disbelief in the democratic problem-solving capacity of the EU and its members. In 2019, protests against the government in Hong Kong, a tax haven, forced luxury companies to close retail stores and shift their priority more to mainland China.

Natural disasters, such as the tsunami in Asia in 2004, the Tōhoku earthquake and tsunami that caused a meltdown at the Fukushima nuclear plant in Japan in 2011, and the typhoon Bhopa in the Philippines in 2012 had devastating effects on the local economies. The coronavirus pandemic was one such global health crisis, which created a global economic impact affecting most luxury markets worldwide.

The Luxury Industry

In the past, crises have had different impacts on various groups (be it luxury conglomerates or independent luxury houses) at different times; this could be attributed to the exogenous and endogenous characteristics of the economic cycles. Nonetheless, the 2009 financial crisis was global in nature and ultimately evolved into the Eurozone crisis in 2014. The luxury industry slowly recovered. Brexit was announced in 2016 and the US–China trade war started in 2018, which shredded any shade on luxury's future. The Hong Kong protests of 2019 forced luxury companies to close retail stores and cancel shows. If there was still optimism for growth, that was due to the China mainland market. However, at the beginning of 2020 it was surprisingly hit by the coronavirus, which soon evolved into a global pandemic. The luxury industry is probably one of the industries most affected, as all of its major markets were hit.

To understand this effect, luxury must first be divided into: (1) hard luxury, such as watches and jewelry; and (2) soft luxury, such as fashion. A more comprehensive definition of the luxury industry includes products and services such as wine and spirits, food, travel, hotels and spas, technology, and cars. Among the most well-known luxury brands are Louis Vuitton, Hermès, Gucci, Cartier, Porsche, Ralph Lauren, Rolex, Tiffany, Armani, Burberry, and Ferrari. In 2015 the worldwide market for luxury grew more than 11% over 2014 to a massive €245 billion. In 2019 the worldwide market for personal luxury goods grew over 7% in 2018 to a massive €281 billion, followed by a decline of over 22% in the year 2020.[1]

Luxury consumers changed, and so did the industry, with the rise of luxury multibrand conglomerates such as LVMH of Bernard Arnault, Kering of Francois Pinault, and Richemont of Johann Rupert, which were formed by the acquisition of traditional family-run brands. Other luxury brands (usually family-owned) that resisted being taken over by the aforementioned conglomerates also grew alongside the conglomerates. The family brands protected their brand heritage and DNA; in addition, they purchased their suppliers and integrated vertically. They focused on brand equity, investing heavily in international expansion while repurchasing franchises and licenses to gain more control over their retail operations.

Notably, over the past several years, more and more luxury companies have been trying to create synergies and omni-personal experiences by expanding product categories, acquiring or building more daughter brands. Very few remain as monobrands and focus on a single product line. Figure 1.2 depicts conglomerates that have a portfolio of brands selling different product categories (LVMH), conglomerates with many

---

[1]Statista, 2021. *Value of the global luxury goods market 2020 | Statista.* [online] Available at: <https://www.statista.com/statistics/266503/value-of-the-personal-luxury-goods-market-worldwide/>.

Figure 1.2 Where Conglomerates Fall in Different Brand and Product Categories

brands on one product category (Estée Lauder), companies with one brand and only one product category (Patek Philippe), and houses with one brand with many product categories (Chanel).

The oligopolistic nature of the luxury industry at first gave rise to intense competition among the handful of players. Then, consumer buying power became the most important driver for luxury brands to succeed. The disposable income of high-net-worth individuals has increased since 2010. As society became relatively more affluent, consumers with disposable income were "created" through advertising to establish an artificial demand for products beyond the individual's basic needs.

Reaction to the Crisis of Global Markets

On the one hand, the luxury industry is said to be recession-proof,[2] due to its non cyclical nature. This belief may be attributed in part to the

---

[2]Jean-Marc Bellaiche, Antonella Mei-Pochtler, and Dorit Hanisch, 2010, 1; Jean-Noel Kapferer and Olivier Tabatoni, 2010, 11.

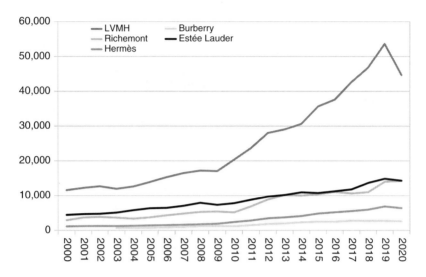

Figure 1.3   Revenues of the Main Players of the Luxury Industry, 2000–2020

change of consumer behavior in the United States and the broadening of the luxury consumer base, fueled by an increase in the disposable income of high-net-worth consumers. Another argument in favor of non cyclicality is the fact that luxury customers are generally the happy few who are less affected by economic crises, and whose spending patterns tend not to change.[3] Both arguments, to a certain extent, are supported by the quick recovery of the luxury industry after the financial crises of 2001 and 2009, and the health crisis of 2020. Figure 1.3 illustrates that over a 21-year period the main players in the luxury industry have been able to weather the effects of crises.

On the other hand, with democratization of the luxury goods industry, whereby companies create accessible products, the non cyclicality of the luxury industry has become a questionable proposition. Historically, in recessions there has always been a quick rebound. For example, during the financial recession that started in 2007, though the luxury sector lost about 10%, there was an immediate rebound in 2009. Reports from different consulting companies and industry associations, like Bain &

---

[3] *Forbes*, "Luxury Brands, Tiffany's, LVHM Still Report Sales Growth," 2011.

Company and the Italian luxury goods association, Altagamma, show that luxury sales slumped by 13% in 2011, due to the debt crisis; but, in 2013, it was about 5% when foreign tourism slowed down in Europe. In 2020, the coronavirus pandemic further pushed luxury brands to close stores and halt operations, shrinking the market size down by 23% on average across sectors. Figure 1.4 depicts the effects of these three recessions, showing that the luxury firms are not immune to the slowdown in growth and revenue that follows each crisis.

The economic crisis deeply affected the luxury world, but in a way that was somewhat predictable. For many years, luxury brands were undergoing constant growth and no one thought they could be affected by a world financial crisis. They thought quite the opposite, in fact. The general opinion was that these losses would soon be overshadowed by the perennial story of growth and profitability.

Sales figures from countries across the globe were interesting to observe in light of the above discussion. In fact, the crises of 2009, 2010–2013, and more recent ones have helped us to better understand the luxury world. Most interesting was the behavior of consumers. Countries that were considered to be the homes and strongholds of the luxury planet were affected.

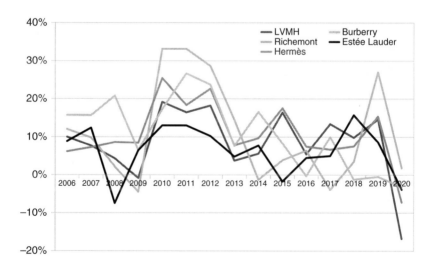

Figure 1.4 Revenues of the Main Players of the Luxury Industry as a percentage of the Previous Year, 2000–2020

Japan   Japan had been a star of luxury for 25 years, beginning in the 1980s. It represented 30% of sales for Hermès in 2005, at least 35–40% for Louis Vuitton, and up to 41% of the worldwide luxury goods market. Japan had always been a place where luxury shopping was considered to be an occasion. At the time of the global financial crisis, Japan represented about 50% of the clients of all key luxury brands. Up until 2005 luxury companies forged their futures with Japanese consumers in mind. For example, 94% of Japanese women in their twenties owned a Louis Vuitton handbag; 92% owned products from Gucci; more than 58% owned a Prada item, and over 51% possessed a product with a Chanel label on it. Traditionally, this market had been impervious to recession. Most major companies—LVMH, Hermès, Richemont, Kering, and Coach—made supernormal profits in Japan until 2009. Two local crises hit the Japanese economy: the earthquake and its resulting tsunami, and the Fukushima nuclear meltdown.[4] Since Japan accounted for a significant share of global luxury sales, the shares of LVMH, Hermès, and Burberry tumbled when the crisis hit.[5] Overall, the Japanese market retreated between 20% and 30%. LVMH witnessed declining sales by 6%. Salvatore Ferragamo reduced prices of its 42 items by 7–10% for the first time since it began operations in Japan. Chanel held a sale of clothes and other items. Distributors such as Seibu and Sogo merged to form Millenium, Isetan merged with Mitsukoshi, Takashimaya merged with Hankyu, and Daimaru merged with Matsuzakaya to survive. Clearly, Japan became a nightmare for most luxury brands, as consumers saw the stock market at a five-year low and hoped to reduce their consumption to prepare for rainy days in the future. For the first time in history, 2009 showed a decline of the luxury market in Japan. Given the aftermath of the tsunami and nuclear disaster that rocked Japan, it is not surprising that people did not feel like shopping.

In 2014, Japan registered between 5 and 16% of luxury sales. Chinese customers accounted for about 15% of former Japanese sales. Does that mean that Japan has become a nightmare? Based on an interview about sales outlook, conducted by McKinsey & Co. on 20 CEOs of luxury

---

[4]Kelly Wetherille, 2011.
[5]James Topham, 2011

companies who were based in Japan, 75% were optimistic about the future prospects of Japan's luxury market. The reality proved their optimism correct. According to Deloitte, Japan experienced positive growth in its luxury goods market in FY 2017, with an expectation that this growth would continue to 2022, presumably dashed by the pandemic.

Although temporarily interrupted by the coronavirus, which is a global challenge, Japan has been, and is more than ever, a key market: stable, mature, and full of promise. For brands like Van Cleef & Arpels, Cartier, Bottega Veneta, Hermès, Prada, Chanel, and others, Japan remains a strong and vital market. It is still the world's third-largest luxury market outside Europe, after the United States and China. Despite the uncertainty around the 2020 Olympic Games, it will surely have a positive effect on the Japanese luxury market when it is held, because it will bring international tourists, especially from China.

Europe   During the global financial crisis, Europe—the birthplace of luxury goods—surprised everybody. Europe had witnessed 40% or more of all luxury sales, but after the crisis it showed its resilience, with an average decline of only 5%. Compared to Europe, Asia-Pacific, mainly due to China, showed a growth of 20%. The luxury market in France in particular did not decline. Old Europe was again a market to cultivate during the period of financial turmoil. Brands that were present in small European cities reaped the benefit of their regional strategies. Hermès, Chanel, Louis Vuitton, Armani, and Tod's were among the companies that were not significantly affected due to their sales in Europe. This proved that Europe has been, and still is, the most important market for luxury; it may remain so, for two reasons. First, the cultural heritage of Europe is linked to luxury. Europeans love luxury goods and have the buying power to be the most stable luxury goods consumers in the world. Second, Europe remains the number-one destination for tourists, France in particular. This means that, though the luxury business was going through the global financial crisis, the continuous flow of tourists who spend a considerable proportion of their budget buying luxury goods offset the effects of the crisis. For example, the Chinese spent nearly 1,500 euros per person annually. At the Galeries Lafayette, 60% of the total business came from tourists, and within this 60%, between 60 and 80% were Chinese tourists.

Despite social turmoil offsetting high tourist spending, such as the Yellow Vests Movement in France, Europe's luxury market remained strong thanks to euro awakening. However, Europe has been the second most affected area of the coronavirus. As brands just finished up a month of spring/summer collections in Milan, Italy was put under lockdown. Brands were not only worried about not being able to manufacture in Italy, but also unable to sell due to the scale of the virus outbreak, let alone the sunk cost of the Milan shows and their inventory. France also followed the measure of lockdown. The luxury giant LVMH had to face a day-to-day crisis and even changed its perfume and cosmetic production line to produce hand sanitizer.

China   Asia overall, including Russia, China, India, Hong Kong, South Korea, and the Middle East, came to the rescue of most luxury brands after the global financial meltdown. During the recession phase, China became the winning horse that reported a growth of 20–30% for most luxury brands. Richemont was one brand that relied heavily on Asia-Pacific consumers to help buttress its sales. The same held true for Hermès, which also sold heavily in Asia. They were saved, although the crisis affected all the actors in the luxury sector, at each level. China alone during this period could show the difference it made to the top line of a luxury company. When the distributors of the United States and Japan nearly collapsed, when Neiman Marcus reported a 20% decline in sales, stores in Beijing and Shanghai were reporting sales growth of up to 30%. Businesses in mainland China, Hong Kong, and Macau were flourishing.

From an emerging luxury market to the biggest luxury market, China reported consistent growth and developed itself as an attractive destination to sell luxury. China saved many brands from sliding into the red. During this period, Kering witnessed double-digit growth in China. Richemont and Zegna, which were otherwise losing money, enjoyed healthy growth in China. Brands like YSL regretted not maintaining showrooms in mainland China. The Ferragamo family trusted Chinese women to continue demanding statement handbags, which they continued distributing despite an otherwise gloomy environment. Some brands, on the other hand, were apprehensive about the Chinese miracle. Patek Philippe was cautious with China as it felt that the country could impose sudden import duties or levy taxes, which could destroy the business instantaneously. According to a McKinsey report, China delivered more than half the global growth in luxury spending between 2012 and 2018 and was expected to deliver 65% of the world's additional spending up to 2025. However, the US–China trade war and Hong Kong protests made the overdependence on China's market alarming. Hong Kong used to be a tax haven for mainland luxury purchasers. Its international image and reputation also made it an interesting venue for luxury events. However, due to the protests in 2019, many brands decided to close their stores, or even announced their permanent departure. The protests are still going on as of today. In 2020, the coronavirus broke out in Wuhan, resulting in a nationwide shutdown. Most businesses closed. E-Commerce was the only remaining point-of-sale. In mid-March, the virus was basically under control and more and more commercial spaces were reopened. But how much the negative effect on China's economy will affect the luxury market is still to be seen. According to different reports, the reduction in international travel was bound to boost domestic luxury sales in Mainland China. One such evidence can be seen through the sales statistics of LVMH group, where Mainland China accounted for around 34.41% of total sales in the year 2020, compared to 30.16% in the year 2019.

United States The American market represents a great untapped potential for European luxury brands as only 17% of luxury goods sold in the United States are personal luxury goods, compared to 47% in Italy, 25% in Japan, and 25% in China. However, it is worth noticing that the US market alone drives 70% of Ralph Lauren's and 55% of Tiffany & Co's worldwide sales, whereas this market accounts for only 15–25% of the worldwide sales of most European brands, such as Hermès. Moreover, it can be observed that luxury sales are high in areas with a large Latin American population due to this group's appreciation of personal luxury goods. Thus, the American market offers a promising outlook for European brands if they manage to exploit the potential.

Over the years, the US market has always been open to brands that had the capacity to invest, to persevere, and to face conflicts. In 2019, in response to France passing a 3% tax on American digital companies such as Google and Facebook, Donald Trump threatened to place 100% tariffs on French goods, including wine and personal luxury goods. Despite it being only a threat, luxury stock fell 2% or more. Some companies leaped to stay on Trump's good side: LVMH opened a new Louis Vuitton factory in Texas, part of Chairman Bernard Arnault's efforts to hedge against trade tensions and build on the rapport he had established with the US president. LVMH agreed to buy Tiffany & Co. for $16.2 billion to expand its US footprint.

The US has remained a difficult market that requires a lot of time, energy, and resources. Luxury brands suffer in the United States. For example, Dior went in the wrong direction, running after licenses, opening everywhere—and subsequently losing money. Fred Segal, which opened in Los Angeles, could not meet its overhead costs and was acquired by LVMH. But the US market has strong potential in the long run in many cities other than the expensive centers such as New York, Los Angeles, and Miami. This is the reason why luxury brands should ask the question "To be or not to be in the United States"—Leonard Fashion answered "Not to be." They were right. Hermès, LV, Cartier, and Chanel succeeded in the United States, competing with Coach, Ralph Lauren, and Tiffany. US brands have hundreds of stores, a very different tactic from the European shopping experience. Americans do not yet have a taste for European luxury; they have a long way to go, and apart from two or three main cities, the interior of America is not ready to understand the French or Italian luxury worlds. It will take time and effort to develop a customer base. It is, however, a market full of promise. All the factors to succeed in the United States are there. It is a stable and rich country, and the only country where a great number of women are millionaires.

Africa   The North African market has also experienced crises, most notably the Egyptian revolution of 2011 and the Arab Spring. Burberry and Ferragamo stores were closed permanently, while the companies that remained open watched as sales declined up to 70%. One reason was that wealthy customers were the first to leave North Africa during the unrest. This was corroborated by the fact that occupancy in luxury hotels, such as the Four Seasons, Kempinski, Hyatt, and Sofitel, dropped by 30%. However, due to democratization or increasing accessibility of the luxury industry, perfume sales in Africa were increasing at a rate of 25%, due to licenses from Gucci and Dolce & Gabbana. It has also been predicted that distributor sales for perfume will reach $100 million in the coming decade. Niche brands have started to make their mark in Africa. For example, Vlisco, a luxury textile brand from Holland engaged in textile wax, has long been successful in Ghana. Soon the entire continent of Africa will be a promising market for luxury brands.

The Effect of a Crisis on the Luxury Industry

The luxury world was a place where no one expected to perish. And then suddenly Christian Lacroix rang its bell—investors collapsed in the face of the debts of the famous Lacroix. It had been the epitome of creative talent, so long supported by the LVMH Group, spoken about and recognized by the media. But all of a sudden Lacroix was abandoned, sold by LVMH to Falic in 2005, and finally declared bankrupt in 2009. It was a shock to the industry. Did that mean that talent was not enough to survive in the luxury world? More names of failing brands were heard, such as Roberto Cavalli and Escada in 2019. Their managers, coming from Louis Vuitton and Céline, were obliged to leave the company when the shareholders of Escada refused to inject the fresh capital required to turn around the company.

On the other hand, consider the resurrection of the legendary Italian haute couture house, Schiaparelli, known for the introduction in the 1920s of women's shorts, colored zip fastenings, and catwalk shows. After being shut down since World War II, it was repurchased in 2009 by Diego Della Valle and relaunched in 2012. Diego Della Valle, the chairman of Tod's Group, who also revived the famous brand Roger Vivier, has brought Schiaparelli back on the stage of the fashion business after more than 60 years. This is not the only case in the luxury world. The almost immortal vitality and endless potential of a luxury brand can never be compared to any other normal brands.

The 2009 financial crisis was a wake-up call for the luxury industry. All *métiers* were hit by the recession but not at the same level: each reacted in its own way. Watches showed the most profound weakness, decreasing in all markets to the tune of 20%, which scared the Swiss and most other brands. Jewelry followed, with a decrease of 15–20%. *Arts de la table* fell at least 20% or much more. Ready-to-wear for women and men fell 10–20% depending on the brands, and even perfumes fell between 7–15%. It affected L'Oréal, Estée Lauder, Clarins, and their competitors. The most resilient were leather goods, which explains the consistency of Louis Vuitton, Goyard, Hermès, and, within the brands, Chanel, Gucci, and Dior bags and other leather goods.

Overall, the watches and jewelry segment faced a mixed reaction. While the recession was known to hit the watch industry the worst, some people still invested in the Rolex brand at a time of crashing stock markets and devaluing currency. Luxury houses like LVMH were known to have fared better than the likes of Richemont, because LVMH, through Tag Heuer, invested in hard luxury versus Richemont, which focused on soft luxury. Brands like Hermès, Swatch, Chopard, Hublot, and De Beers faced declining profits, whereas Dior fared well in the watches and jewelry sector. However, industry figures depicted a decline of 31.9% in June 2009 and a slowdown in the summer of 2013 due to the unfavorable economic climate in Europe and in China. Swiss exports of watches declined, indicating it was an industry-wide phenomenon.

For the wine and spirits sector, brands like Diageo, Moët & Chandon, Pernod Ricard, and Remy Martin all reported a significant decline in profits. Diageo, which was more exposed to Ireland and Greece at the time they were saddled by the debt crisis, was the worst hit of all, indicating a strong negative impact on sales.

Luxury cosmetic and fragrance brands were hit by the recession, too. Estée Lauder and L'Oréal slid into the red, and undertook significant cost-cutting operations. The recession is hitting this segment in part because women tend to stock beauty products and perfumes. During times of recession, they usually fall back on the stock they have built over the years. However, some companies managed to stay profitable, including Sephora, Revlon, and Sally Beauty.

The crisis heavily affected smaller niche brands, especially in the field of *Arts de la table*. In 2009, Lalique, Daum, Baccarat, Cristalleries de Saint Louis, and many others suffered a great deal. On the other hand, the crises of 2009, 2011, 2013 and 2020 tested the resilience of the sector. The conglomerates experienced a slump in their books, compared to the growth they had witnessed over the course of the decade. Sales of brands such as Burberry, Armani, Cartier—including the whole Richemont Group—suffered. Hermès, Louis Vuitton, Bottega Veneta, Cartier,

Moncler, and Prada were probably the most successful survivors. More recent crises, such as the Yellow Vest Movement in France, Hong Kong's protests, and the coronavirus pandemic inflicted more dramatic harm on the luxury industry across sectors. Crises were real as far as the luxury world was concerned. The response of the luxury sector revealed to analysts, researchers, investors, and other stakeholders that luxury was also sensitive to the economic situation of the global world, just like every other sector. In fact, no one could pretend that luxury was invincible and rich investors realized that the niche aspect of luxury was fading away. This was in fact a consequence of the evolution of the luxury world. It was not just big and financially strong conglomerates, with millions of customers, who were hit by the crisis—small family-owned luxury players also faced the music. They were all affected by the crisis and the stock market's movements.

Strategic Response to Crisis

The strategic response to the crisis was not easy. It showed that the evolution of the luxury sector was still wide open. Transformations were taking place. Luxury could not be defined as it had been before. Brands had to reposition themselves during the crisis, adopting starkly opposing strategies.

Responses varied. A change in consumer behavior was observed during the recession, wherein consumers spent a lot more time comparing the prices of various fashion brands. Thus, the conversion of a potential customer into an actual customer required more time and resources. Before, a consumer would buy 10 products, but after the crisis it was observed that the consumer bought just one, and even then only after careful deliberation.

The broad strategies adopted by players during and after the recession involved two fundamental approaches: internal and external. Internal strategies were company-centric policies, established both to change and better business practices and company culture. External strategies targeted the consumer and focused on creating new and more effective ways to gain and maintain attention and the desire to buy. The internal strategies included cost-cutting, a greater focus on product quality, financial restructuring, and downsizing. As Bernard Arnault described it, "A natural tendency of companies during a crisis such as the one we are in now is to cut costs, drop prices, and stop expanding, because it has the most immediate impact on numbers."[6]

External strategies included expansion in terms of both product offering and geography, repositioning, up-scaling of the brand to tap the richer among the super-rich, or downscaling to recruit a larger customer group.

In response to the crisis, as a knee-jerk reaction, some luxury brands stopped hiring, reduced the number and size of their collections, rationalized media spending, and reduced headcounts. It was felt that dropping prices and cutting costs was the last resort. The press referred to it as cost containment. For example, Dolce & Gabbana slashed its prices by 10–20%. At the same time the company began a search for alternative low-cost stitching techniques and reduced spending on advertising, returning to the low rates of 20 years before. Stella McCartney closed its boutique in Moscow just 18 months after it was opened. Richemont closed 62 stores, mainly in the United States, while Burberry absorbed heavy charges on its Spanish stores. For example, in the 2009 crisis, Burberry unveiled a cost-cutting program which resulted in the closure of the Thomas Burberry collection. It hoped to generate infrastructure efficiencies by shutting down six stores and reducing the headcount by more than 1,000 people. All this cost Burberry $6.7 million, with the hope the company would generate savings of $77.8 million. In response to the slowdown of Asia, their key market, Burberry announced in September 2012 that it would suspend further hiring, lower its travel expenditure, cut marketing spending, and defer IT projects. Estée Lauder followed a four-pronged strategy with layoffs of about 2,000 employees, freezes in pay, discontinuations of non-profit-making brands, and cuts in discretionary capital expenditures of 25%.

Contrary to the cost containment approach, Bernard Arnault stated, "What we have learned in the many crises we have been through is that this (cutting costs) is a mistake, especially when it comes to luxury. . . . If you don't put your products on sale, consumers feel they are buying something that retains its value. . . . Even during tough times, we can

---

[6]Vanessa Friedman, interview with Bernard Arnault, 2009.

continue to invest and during the crisis I went through in the past 20 years, we always gained in market share."[7]

Different companies tried different strategies to reposition their brands. Christian Dior abandoned its logo and accessory product business as it pursued an up-scaling drive, in the hopes that the super-rich would not be affected by the crisis. Coach, which happened to be in the heart of the subprime crisis in the United States, felt that "normal" buying behavior among consumers had experienced a shift and consumer spending levels would never return to what they had been pre-crisis. Thus, an internal change in the company itself was required. Coach explored lower price options for the consumer, providing them with a larger range of accessible products. Driven by a similar thought process, Swatch and Ralph Lauren also launched products at lower price points. To reduce costs, some brands took their manufacturing operations to low cost regions of the world. Prada and Burberry shifted their manufacturing base to China for certain products. Louis Vuitton considered building a shoe factory in India.

During the crises in the decade of 2010, independent brands such as Armani, Burberry, Mission, and Roberto Cavalli suffered more than others. Some companies were sold; some scaled down their operations. For instance, Roberto Cavalli was sold to Vision Investments, the investment firm of the president of DAMAC Properties, Hussain Sajwani. Dolce & Gabbana scaled back their operations in Japan and are still trying to survive in China. As an LVMH executive summarized, "Before the crisis, we were putting a lot of energy into beautiful stores, but now we care a bit less about expanding our network and even more about design and price."[8]

However, some companies decided not to compromise on such factors. Bottega Veneta continued to manufacture its products in Italy and invested in its artisans to ensure that they continued to produce traditional, quality output. The idea was to ensure that their product was sufficiently exclusive to merit the premium price they intended to demand. One of the major winners from the crisis, Bottega Veneta, had a very different strategy: the company decided to not change its positioning at all. It held steady and stuck to what it was best at—finely crafted products

---

[7]Vanessa Friedman, interview with Bernard Arnault, 2009.
[8]*The Economist*, "The Substance of Style," 2009.

with clean, classic lines. This ensured that the brand was two steps ahead of its panic-stricken competitors. In early 2021, Bottega moved into online stealth mode.[9] It went dark on social media, choosing to be more inclusive—or more exclusive—with its own customers. It did it with silence. It deleted its accounts on all social media and removed its content from Weibo. It positioned itself as more upscale, exclusive, and elegant: sophistication with a distinctive stealth style, true to its DNA. It gained superstar status with this move, together with its fastest-selling squishy clutch bag named the Pouch. It is exactly the opposite strategy of Gucci, for whom millennials and Gen-Z made up a considerable proportion of its audience. Thus, Gucci had more of an inclusive approach toward its communications and followed the metrics on which brands measured their success in the digital age. IWC also practiced this philosophy. It utilized handmade craftsmanship, limited distribution, and impeccable service. Hermès manufactured its leather goods and silk products in France and Italy and did not resort to production in China. Not only did some companies try to deliver unmatched service quality, but they also standardized this service quality across continents. This ensured that a consumer walking into an outlet in New Delhi would not get a different experience from one walking into an outlet on Rodeo Drive or the Champs-Élysées. Ritz Carlton and HFS were brands that worked on the parameters of service excellence.

Continuing with the varied strategic response, some brands saw the crisis as an opportunity and expanded through: (1) widening or spreading to new geographies, and/or (2) launching new products. Notable among the geographical expanders (or base wideners) were Prada, Hermès, Bottega Veneta, and Christian Dior Couture.

For example, in the crisis of 2008–2009 Prada undertook its most aggressive investment plan. It hoped to get out of the crisis with a very strong distribution network. Having seen earnings slide by 22% in 2008, the company saw heavy increases in revenues and profits from 2009 onward. Hermès, like Prada, expanded during the crisis. Hermès opened stores in Manchester in England, Las Vegas, Japan, India, Wuxi in China, and Busan in South Korea during that period. Hermès was known for weathering the crisis rather gracefully.

---

[9]Bottega Veneta: Stealth Luxury.

During the recession some brands launched new and special products while simultaneously trimming their overall product lines. This resulted in fewer offerings and simultaneous price increases on both existing and new products, stimulating consumer demand and generating market interest, discontinuing low-margin products, and increasing prices in some product categories. Some companies ventured into new products and product lines (deepening), whereas others consolidated their brands under one umbrella. Burberry ventured into a new product line with a stand-alone children's store in Hong Kong, Bottega Veneta ventured into watches, and Versace launched a new fragrance, Gianni Versace Couture. Brioni reacted to the crisis by including more accessible items in its product range of suits, such as T-shirts. Coach kept the prices of its regular lines stable, but introduced new lines, such as the Poppy handbags, to cater to a less affluent segment. Estée Lauder moved away from a strategy that fostered competition among various brands. It believed in following a more synergistic and coordinated policy of brand interdependence rather than competition. Its aim was probably to make the consumer feel that its brands were complementary in nature rather than supplementary. By maintaining or increasing prices, for example, these brands segmented their consumers and were more likely to pick up market share after the recession. Francois-Henri Pinault, CEO of Kering, was of the opinion that "there's a new perception of luxury, a more discrete sophisticated luxury where notions of heritage and craft play a big role."[10]

During this period many consumers had to cut back on their purchases and many sensed that it was not appropriate to show off with obviously expensive products. It was something that only traditional, artisanal, and legitimate houses could uphold. Brands did not act at all but kept true to their values and their traditional offerings. These included Hermès, Harry Winston, IWC, Chanel, and Patek Philippe.

Some brands explored new channels to deliver their products to the customer. Gucci and Ralph Lauren adopted the QR code. This was an image that shoppers could scan and download through their camera phone to obtain more information about the product or make purchases via their phone. Cartier adopted advertising through mobile phones. Companies like LVMH and Gucci also adopted online retail as

---

[10]Dominique Ageorges, 2010.

an option for selling their products. This was quick to gain acceptance in Japan, where 20% of consumers make their purchases online.

Some brands diversified during the recession to strategic but complementary businesses or acquired greater control of their current businesses. From 2000 onwards, most if not all luxury brands, be it multibrand conglomerates or family houses, expanded horizontally into different traditional luxury categories. For example, Louis Vuitton expanded into fashion, high jewelry, and watches. Mont Blanc expanded into watches and jewelry. Chanel diversified into high jewelry. Salvatore Ferragamo expanded into fragrances and accessories. During the recession, Louis Vuitton, Bulgari, Armani, Missoni, and Trussardi diversified into a nontraditional luxury goods category with the opening of luxury hotels. Moreover, brands acquired greater control of their core businesses to integrate vertically, purchased key suppliers, and bought back licenses and franchises to increase efficiency, control their brand image, and generate superior margins.

Some companies tried to understand changing customer needs during the recession. For instance, Diageo noticed that people reduced their consumption of alcohol outside their homes. Thus, it launched pre-mixed cocktails such as Smirnoff Tuscan Lemonade for home consumption. Ritz Carlton coined Mystique, its CRM system, to keep a closer tab on the consumers' pulse. Taking this flexibility a step further, some companies let the consumer guide the company rather than the other way round (which has been the norm in luxury branding). For instance, the sales representatives of most brands were given free hand to contact their personal customers and close sales. So each salesperson acted like a shop able to sell any product in the catalogue. Sales representatives were encouraged to find local customers and reach out to them for their full customer journey.

Due to the profound impact that the coronavirus pandemic had on the luxury industry, most luxury houses had no choice but to rediscover new ways of working. With the ultra-high-end brick-and-mortar stores forced to close under national level lockdowns and restrictions on non-essential travel, both international and domestic, selling products was a challenge. Many luxury brands were seen diverting their focus toward philanthropic activities and working on their brand heritage. LVMH and Armani group addressed the shortage of medical supplies by converting their production facilities into factories for essential supplies. Bulgari and Dior were quick to switch their perfume facilities into hand sanitizer factories, reinforcing their commitment to saving lives and putting an end to the pandemic. Conglomerates like LVMH, Kering and Richemont were able to optimally utilize their financial and brand well-being to execute their strategies of strengthening their brand image and contribute to the society.[11] These are just a few of the many examples which indicated the emphasis on heritage, story, and brand values.

Conclusion

We need to be pessimistic in the short-term and optimistic in the long term.
—Bernard Arnault

In conclusion, different brands adopted different strategies in response to the crisis. None of the brands adopted a single universal strategy. They remained creative in their responses. Some succeeded, some did not. As the industry rebounded they adjusted. The bouquets of responses were meant to encompass different types of customer from different cultures and geographies. A global brand strategy was needed to convince several segments of clients—so different and interested by so many various luxury sectors. With the crisis it was seen that luxury lost its definition, the market remained totally open, and goods varied from premium, to super-premium, to ultimate luxury.

Formerly accessible to the few, the luxury industry started to become more accessible from 1985 onwards—three decades—with brand extensions such as perfume and eyewear attracting larger (and younger) consumers. The future of luxury would therefore be built on the capacity of brands to understand the scope of potential customers, fixing a strategy based on a specific language. There was no universal response, nor any universal language. Chanel speaks Chanel, Hermès speaks Hermès, and Gucci has its own vocabulary—the challenge is to keep the dream going, for everyone, after the crisis.

---

[11]LVMH, 2021. *At the Heart of the Fight Against Covid-19 Is the Manufacture of Masks and Gowns by Our Maisons—LVMH.* [online] Available at: https://www.lvmh.com/news-documents/news/lvmh-maisons-repurpose-facilities-to-make-face-masks-and-gowns-for-hospital-staff-helping-battle-covid-19-in-france/.

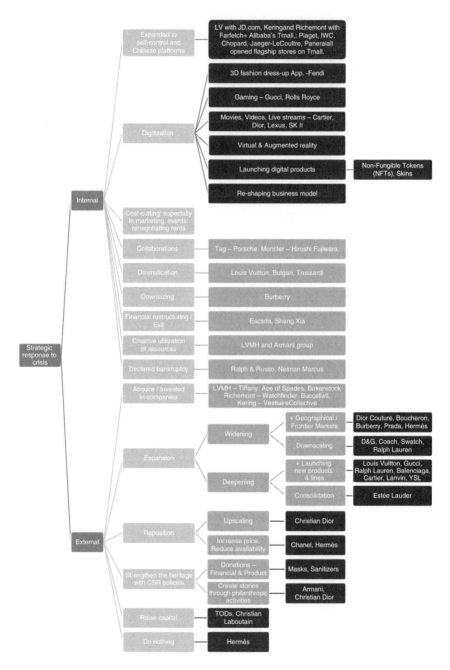

Figure 1.5   Luxury Brands and Their Crisis Management Strategies

Figure 1.5 summarizes the different strategic responses of luxury brands to the global financial crisis.

Chapter 2

Evolution of the Global Luxury Market

Luxury is the opposite of vulgarity. Luxury is the opposite of status. It is the ability to make a living by being oneself. It is the freedom to refuse to live by habit. Luxury is liberty. Luxury is elegance. True elegance is refusal.

—Coco Chanel

The term *Luxury goods* emerged due to the need of Wall Street analysts, who needed a way to describe companies such as LVMH, Richemont, and Gucci, which had recently become public. Previously, these companies were not really known as "luxury goods" companies, but rather for their specific areas of expertise and the global reputations they had garnered.

Luxury is freedom, and time. . .and being courageous. Because you have to be brave if you want to live better. And probably be connected with love, in a way. This word makes you feel really alive. It's not because you're in a relationship. It's another idea, it's the idea that you feel alive and love yourself, and you love that you are alive. So it's the same when you wake up and put a beautiful dress on. You feel love/alive.[1]

—Allesandro Michele, Creative Director, Gucci

Luxury is about exception and exclusivity, whether it comes to products, or services. A luxury product/service is unique, and not only because of its outstanding quality. It tells more than what it is. Beyond the usefulness or the wellness it brings, it tells a story, it reflects a style and a spirit that contribute to the dream. Luxury is about a product but also a brand, a universe.

—Eric Vallat, ex-Bonpoint

It is an association with a compelling and binding meaning in terms of emotional connectivity, personal harmony, spiritual connection or a connection to the world of the inherently beautiful, the greater the marginal value of the object to the seller.

—James Taylor, Harrison Group LLC

Luxury used to be "ordinary goods for exceptional people" but now can be defined as "exceptional goods for ordinary people." It had to do with an object, its use, five senses, it was an offering, attraction, a product, a niche and serendipity. Today it is about marketing push, process, synergy, volume and efficiency.

—Wilfried Guerrand, Hermès

Luxury is a state-of-mind. It is about a bridge between dream and daily routine, a way of appreciating one's time and life, a statement of being oneself.

—Franka Holtmann, Le Meurice, Paris, and Feng Gao, ex-Bottega Veneta, China

In the world of the *objet de luxe*, the notion of *value* holds a different meaning than that understood in common knowledge, where monetary value and authenticity are not synonymous.

---

[1]https://magazineantidote.com/english/alessandro-michele-exclusive-interview/.

*The value of luxury products is shaped by meaning content, not design;
even clumsy design can be valued, collected, and treasured.*
                          —James Taylor, Harrison Group, LLC

The Boston Consulting Group defines luxury goods as "items, products, and services that deliver higher levels of quality, taste, and aspiration than conventional ones."

Luxury is also about brands. Bernard Arnault's famous definition notes that "Our business is to create products that have a combination of quality and creativity that can create desire. . . .The brands which can create persistent desire can become star brands. . . .Star brands should be timeless, modern, fast-growing, and highly profitable. . . .There are fewer than 10 star brands in the luxury world, because it is very hard to balance all four characteristics at once—after all, fast growth is often at odds with high profitability—but that is what makes them stars. If you have a star brand, it is highly likely that you have mastered a paradox."

Marco Bizzari, CEO of Gucci explained, "Timeless does not mean being stuck in time. . . .One has to take risks, listen but have one's own vision."

Buyers in this segment are not only interested in the product but also in its associated values: class-consciousness, emotional and artistic appeal, unique design, and a cultured and refined taste. Yves Carcelle, former chief executive of Louis Vuitton, said "It's about coherence, reliability, quality, style, innovation, and authenticity."

Luxury products offer self-reflexive connections to a person's sense of self-esteem, competence, and personal value. They are said to be characterized by "inherent scarcity, sincerity, consistency, transitivity, emotional connectivity, mastery of excellence, service—elegance."

They are also defined as a break from the ordinary, presenting the consumer with additional value, comfort, style, and elegance. Luxury products are designed to ensure their consumers are perceived as defying the ordinary standards of beauty and popular fashion. They appear as a special movement of the wealthy and influential members of the society.

*Definition of Luxury is dialectic. Luxury is a break, a deviation from
what is ordinary and what is necessary. And it is the variations between
the ordinary and the necessary during different times, societies, and cultures that will lend themselves to major developments in luxury. Sacred*

in origin, secular when it becomes an instrument of worldly power (Louis XIV), reduced to a minimum for the emerging bourgeoisie (a comfort-based and necessity-based luxury), subject to market laws since the French revolution, a superfluous necessity of today. The dialectic is based on a double movement—on one hand, a human need to create a special moment, objects, practices, and behaviours discordant with the ordinary and necessary and on the other, a movement of integration for these gaps in the regular course of society. It is vital for human beings as they search for more, for better, for beautiful. . . . It is nothing other than humanity forever separated from a world governed by the order of our needs, into an ideal world, where one shall desire what is good for him or her. Nothing more, nothing less. Hence the moral dimension is always attached to luxury.

—Emmanuelle Sidem, Connex Consulting

Evolution

To understand the evolution of luxury over time, it is necessary to consider certain empirical factors, and to question whether such an industry can stand the test of time, and whether new brands can survive in this environment.

Has the luxury industry *itself* changed over time? At its core—regardless of the century—the term *luxus* (from Latin) signifies all that is exuberant, expensive, refined, and sumptuous. As stated above, the luxury industry seeks to sell a dream, an aspiration. It offers the possibility of raising one's status through the acquisition of certain elite and rare objects, governed by a sheer respect of aesthetics and faultless craftsmanship. A historical example of what luxury offers is that of the Roman baths. Access was select and limited. Only the elite could wear certain materials and participate in certain activities. The *Sumptuariae Leges* of Ancient Rome[2] encompassed a number of laws as a means of preventing inordinate expenses: in banquets, dresses, and the use of expensive Tyrian purple dye.[3] Individual garments were also regulated: ordinary male citizens were allowed to wear the *toga virilis* only upon reaching the age of

---

[2]Rebeiro, *Dress and Morality*, 22.
[3]Jacoby, "Silk in Western Byzantium before the Fourth Crusade."

political majority. In the early years of the Empire, men were forbidden to wear silk,[4] and details of clothing, such as the number of stripes on a tunic, were regulated according to social rank.

Despite the fact that such laws are no longer in operation today, the dichotomy of what is accessible, and to whom, remains present. The more monetarily inaccessible a good is, the more desirable it becomes. Early global trade can tell us a lot about how we came to use certain economic models for importing and exporting that play to a country's advantage. Consider trade between the Romans and the British. In Britain, internal commerce between the different Celtic tribes traded metals and pottery. The Romans and the Celts shipped pottery, glass, bronze and iron objects, and wine to Scotland. In return they received slaves, cattle, hides and furs, animals, and possibly wool. The Romans increased production of minerals, particularly lead, but also silver, gold, and tin. In every country, precious metals and gemstones and good cloth were considered *luxury goods*. Consider the Egyptians, in whose culture luxury items played a central role. Pharaohs were notoriously buried with an excessive amount of gold, jewelry, vases, etc., as a means to render the transition to the afterlife more pleasant. In the Renaissance (1400s) or Restoration periods, luxury meant still being able to afford jewelry, fine clothes, better transportation, better living conditions, and better food. It is by catering to this demand that companies such as Cartier, Louis Vuitton, and Hermès were able to experience such success.

Traditionally, Europe has always looked toward the East for gems, silk, and spices. Traders used the Silk Road—which expanded as a result of gifts given by the Chinese to Roman-Asian governments during the rise of the Roman Empire—as the main channel for commerce.[5]

Originally, the Chinese traded silk internally, within the empire. Caravans from the empire's interior would carry silk to the western edges of the region. Often small Central Asian tribes would attack these caravans, hoping to capture the traders' valuable commodities. As a result, the Han Dynasty extended its military defenses further into Central Asia from 135 to 90 B.C. in order to protect these caravans. Chan Ch'ien, the

---

[4]"Silk: History," *Columbia Encyclopedia*.
[5]"The Romans in Britain: Trade and Travel," http://h2g2.com/dna/h2g2/A3473967.

first known Chinese traveler to make contact with the Central Asian tribes, later came up with the idea to expand the silk trade to include these lesser tribes and thereby forge alliances with these Central Asian nomads. Because of this idea, the Silk Road was born.

Northwestern Indians who lived near the Ganges River played prominent roles as middlemen in the China-Mediterranean silk trade because as early as the third century A.D. they understood that silk was a lucrative product of the Chinese Empire. The trading relationship between the Chinese and the Indians grew stronger with increased Han expansion into Central Asia. The Chinese would trade their silk[6] with the Indians for precious stones and metals—such as jade, gold, and silver—and the Indians would trade the silk with the Roman Empire. Silk proved to be an expensive import for the Roman Empire, since its trade across Indian and Central Asia was heavily controlled by the Parthian Empire.

Despite playing a minor role in the Chinese economy, the silk trade did increase the number of foreign merchants present in China under the Han Dynasty, exposing both the Chinese and the foreign visitors to different cultures and religions.

In the luxury industry, the Silk Road is perhaps the birthplace of globalization as we know it today. The reason silk, gems, and other rare items were considered *luxuries* stemmed from their *unessential* nature. These were goods that were in no way indispensable to daily life (as are food, shelter, security). Yet, demand was strong and desire was high. This is the true essence of luxury.

But it did decline eventually and become specific to certain areas—such as the silk–fur trade with the Russians, north of the original Silk Road—as means of transportation were inconvenient. The era of the Song Dynasty—in the eleventh and twelfth centuries, when China became largely dependent on exporting its silk—saw the revival of the silk trade. In addition, trade to Central and Western Asia, as well as Europe, recovered for a period of time from 1276 to 1368 under the Yuan Dynasty, when the Mongols controlled China. As overland trade became increasingly dangerous, and overseas trade became more popular, trade along the Silk Road had declined by the end of the fourteenth century.

---

[6]Garthwaite, *The Persians*, 78.

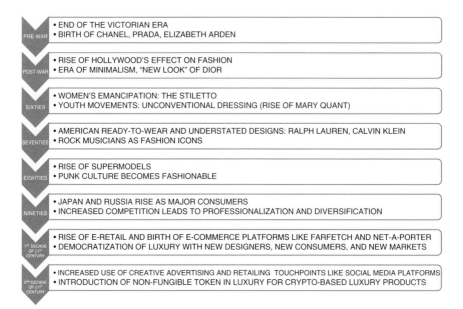

Figure 2.1 The Evolution of the Luxury Industry

China is an important factor in today's luxury economy. As a result of increasing globalization and the emergence of new markets, it is certainly a country to watch in the short-term. An early historical example, which allows us to discern certain trends and patterns over time, is that of Marco Polo. In the mid-thirteenth century, Marco Polo spent 17 years in China fulfilling a wide variety of tasks in Kublai Khan's administration. He was in effect a member of an occupying force, speaking Mongolian but not Chinese, so his understanding of the people was limited. But he traveled a great deal, often trading on his own as well as serving the emperor. Figure 2.1 gives a snapshot of the evolution of the luxury industry.

The twentieth century marks the rise of luxury brands as we know them today. Though these brands may have been established earlier, the 1900s saw them gain the distinct identity that they still possess. While the first half of the century generally saw fashion relegated to the background in favor of robust economic development, the second half saw the luxury economy grow into a major contributor to the modern-day economy. Throughout the course of this chapter, we intend to look at the major milestones in the evolution of luxury in the twentieth century.

Several luxury and prestige brands—such as Louis Vuitton, Burberry, and Chanel—were launched in the nineteenth and early twentieth centuries, when a strict social class system defined society, and royalty and aristocracy reigned supreme. During this period, designers like Christian Dior, Yves Saint Laurent, and Guccio Gucci designed clothes and leather goods exclusively for the noblemen and -women of society. Their work was an art form that took several weeks, and sometimes months, to produce; and this was all part of the "luxury and prestige" experience. During this period, it was the norm to literally dress in a single brand from head to toe.

In the present environment (the early 2020s), the story is different. The luxury market is no longer reserved for the elite; it has transcended boundaries. At the beginning of the century, luxury consumers were a small segment of the population who all looked the same. But this has changed in a number of ways. First, a class of wealthy people has emerged the world over. From the 1960s, a vast amount of wealth was accumulated by individuals due to economic, social, and technological breakthroughs. Second, there has emerged a sea of luxury brands, and this has affected the high entry barrier that the industry had guarded for centuries. It has also given luxury consumers more choice than ever before. Third, the rapid growth of digital information and communications technology has given consumers more variety in luxury product offerings, easier access to view the choices, and lower switching costs, especially on the Internet. This has empowered the consumers to become more individualistic, experimental, and bold enough to mix luxury and high-street fashion in one outfit: something that their mothers and grandmothers would have considered taboo.

The result of this change is the phenomenon of trading-up and -down. The new wealthy class, which is enjoying its ability to acquire luxury products, practices "trading-up." "Trading-down" is the practice of mixing the use of luxury items with fashion brands, popularly known as "the democratization of luxury." Therefore, it is no longer a surprise to find a wealthy celebrity wearing jeans from H&M, earrings from Chanel, shoes from Coach, a shirt from Zara, and a bag from Louis Vuitton.

In the early 2010s companies, including luxury businesses, began seeing China as a land of opportunities. The other way of looking at luxury, from a historical point of view, is to review the actual evolution of the brands and companies and evaluate if there is any difference in their success depending on their structure and business model. Traditionally, the luxury sector has been highly fragmented, characterized by a large number of family-owned and medium-sized enterprises. In the twenty-first century, however, it has become increasingly dominated by multi-brand luxury conglomerates. Some niche brands, such as Goyard, do survive as independent companies, but (in 2021) they are in some danger of being acquired. Acquisitions occur for a few different reasons. As in the case of LVMH, a company may be trying to gain market share and control as much of the industry as possible. On the other hand, Hermès is seeking vertical integration to be in control of its production and supply chains. Such conglomerates now dominate the industry: the day of the family-owned business is over, unless it is financed by a private, wealthy family such as Tiffany, Chanel, Armani, Ralph Lauren, or a few others.

Luxury has evolved over time: from family businesses to conglomerates, old luxury to new luxury, uber luxury to affordable luxury. Figure 2.2 shows the evolution of the luxury industry from family businesses into multibrand corporations. The connections and validations have to be made by royalty—whether it is as old as the Roman Period, when the emperor was given silks as gifts, or the modern era, when brands give celebrities gifts that they wear or use in public to legitimize the products. The main evolution has occurred in the way that luxury has been promoted during the years. We have discovered that desire or the dream factor of luxury has always been the same and will probably always remain the same. As long as consumers aspire to own things they cannot afford, and those things are rare, beautiful, or coveted, then the concept of luxury will remain the same.

The cycle continues—Europe will look East, either to benefit from acquiring new and exotic products such as silk and gemstones and ivory or, as is currently the case, they will consider expanding to the East

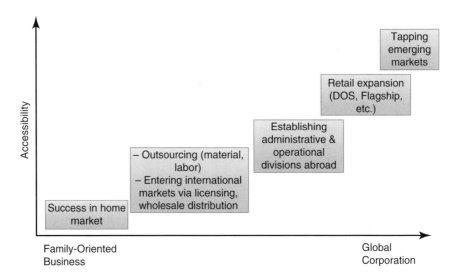

Figure 2.2   From Family Business to Multibrand Corporation

because that is where the growth is. Figure 2.3 depicts the circular path of luxury heritage. Globalization is an eternal subject, with maybe some changes of form through the centuries. As the saying goes, the more it changes, the more it remains the same.

How Has It Changed?

Plus ça change, plus c'est la même chose.
—Jean-Baptiste Alphonse Karr

Two decades ago, the luxury industry model was almost completely dominated by family businesses. However, the winds of change were felt in the 1990s, especially by one man—Bernard Arnault. The ensuing rivalry between Bernard, the owner of Dior Group, and Henry Racamier, husband of Mademoiselle Vuitton, owner of Louis Vuitton, created a historic structural shift within the industry, as each selfishly fought for market control through growth and acquisition. Until then, luxury had been about fashion. Within this struggle, Arnault came out the winner and went for consolidation to create the luxury empire of

Figure 2.3 The Circular Path of the Heritage of Luxury

today. He transformed fashion into a business. Buying and selling companies with intricate financial maneuvers, he conquered the luxury space by making Louis Vuitton Moët Hennessy (LVMH) the largest luxury conglomerate in the world. The interesting point to note about this conglomerate is that each brand was allowed to carry on its own culture and know-how and to be managed separately. However, if it was felt that the brand needed a push, Arnault stood right behind it. Furthermore, he created the famous notion of "star brands" that were timeless, modern, fast-growing, and highly profitable. He would find new brands, then mix and match a suitable designer and an apt management team for the brand. He would revamp production, control, storage, and distribution to offer a completely new and unique package to the customer. Hence, the development of the counterintuitive idea of "constrained freedom," wherein brands were allowed latitude; however, the latitude was limited to the lines that Arnault drew.

Some French companies stayed independent. Chanel, which was owned by the Wertheimer family, stayed fully independent. The Wertheimers have owned Chanel since 1954 and have never introduced it to the stock market. The house is showing longevity in its independence, which is rare in the sector. Not listed on the stock market, Maison Chanel continued to meticulously keep its financial data a top secret until 2018, when Chanel casually revealed that it is a US$10 bn company, while in the subsequent years reiterating that it was not for sale. Its aura of mystery is cultivated by the owners, Alain and Gérard Wertheimer, who drive the company firmly and discreetly. Hermès, owned by the families of Dumas, Puech, and Guerrand, was partially independent. The legendary leather-goods fashion house, established in 1837, remained family owned. In France, the Comité Colbert, founded in 1954 by Jean-Jacques Guerlain, consists today (2021) of 75 houses of French luxury that have different histories, cultures, sizes, and management. However, they share common governance rules and are willing to promote their values and know-how. The term "houses," as opposed to the luxury company members of the Comité Colbert, illustrates their respective stories, the transmission of their know-how from one generation to the next, which keeps their creation secrets. Indeed, most members of the familial business, and the family CEOs of the Comité Colbert, call each other "chef de Maison." In Italy, Altagamma (the Italian Association of Industries of Alta Gamma), founded in 1992, is an association whose purpose is to promote the work of several Italian companies on an international level and encourage their development. As of 2021, the Foundation Altagamma brings together 76 Italian companies operating in the fields of fashion, design, transport, jewelry, shoes, perfume, and hospitality.

Despite these tectonic shifts in the industry, the family business remained a paramount and dominating factor in Italian luxury enterprises until the 2010s. Slowly but steadily some famous brands were acquired by the three multibrand conglomerates—LVMH, Richemont, and Kering Group. LVMH, after acquiring more than 70 luxury brands, took possession of two of the largest Italian groups, Bulgari and Loro Piana, in 2011 and 2013, Belmond Group in 2018, and Tiffany in 2019. The Italian brands—Gucci, Brioni, Bottega Veneta, and others—were acquired by Kering. The financial crisis of 2008 spurred a desperate fight for survival, pushing the luxury industry further away from its historic structure as the key factors of success became access to financial resources instead of family, and the focus shifted from small artisan businesses to colossal conglomerates. During the COVID-19 pandemic it became clear that, as competition becomes more and more fierce, independent luxury brands will find it increasingly hard to thrive without financial and managerial support from a strong group.

Luxury Industry Trends

Luxury is a cyclical industry. Given the continuing deterioration of the macroeconomic backdrop and the cyclical nature of the luxury market, 2019 to 2020 was a very low year for luxury spending globally. It is expected that, after the health crisis, the industry will partially turn around in the latter part of 2021 and achieve 2019 levels in 2022–2023, when people will be able to travel again. Analysts believe that the rebound will be different in different markets. The rate of rebound will also vary according to sector. During this time consumption will be locally based. Those companies able to realign their priorities and restructure their value chain will be the winners.

If history can show the way, HENRYs (high-earning, not rich yet) surveyed during the last recession had returned within a year and were more positive about spending in the future. Despite global macroeconomic headwinds, worldwide sales of personal luxury goods grew an estimated 10% between 2012 and 2019.

After the pandemic, hard luxury players like watches and jewelers were expected to be particularly under pressure in this environment, as their underlying demand disadvantage was compounded by dependence on the wholesale and travel retail channels. Big-ticket-item purchases, such as mechanical watches, were likely to be delayed. Retailers, such as Barneys New York, Neiman Marcus, Lord & Taylor, John Varvatos, Brooks Bros, Diane von Furstenberg, TopShop, J Crew, Oasis,

Debenhams and True Religion, to name just a few, have either tipped over into bankruptcy or are on their way there.

There has been no hiding place at the high end. The notion that the luxury market high-end segment would be immune to the cycle appeared to be an investment myth: it was not supported by evidence and analysis. As of mid-2021, emerging markets, especially China, are seen to be the key for the industry's revival.[7]

Relative to the previous decade, growth slowed from 2013 and the personal luxury goods market increased by only 2%, to 217 billion. Market performance was penalized by euro fluctuations, despite real growth outpacing 2012. The growth rate was the same in 2014, at 223 billion. The US had played the role of growth engine during this period. Touristic spending started to drive the market. Chinese consumers represented the top and fastest-growing nationality for luxury, spending abroad more than three times what they spend locally, due to higher domestic prices caused by tax. The luxury market ballooned to more than €250 billion in 2015, representing 13% growth over 2014 at current exchange rates, while real growth (at constant exchange rates) eased to only 1–2%. In 2016, the market was essentially flat, at €249 billion. That represented a 1% contraction at current exchange rates and no change in market size from the €251 billion of 2015 (at constant exchange rates). Such consecutive modest growth, at constant exchange rates, confirmed a shift to a "new normal" of lower sales growth in the personal luxury goods market. Analysts suggested that Brexit, the election of Donald Trump in the US, and terrorism had all led to significant uncertainty and lower consumer confidence. In 2017, the market reached a record high of €262 billion, boosted by a revival of purchasing by Chinese customers both at home and abroad, as well as strong trends within other customer groups and in other regions. Chinese consumption bounced back, fueled by renewed consumer confidence and the rapid emergence of a new— and increasingly fashion-savvy—middle class. The American market (including both North and South America) struggled but managed to finish the year in positive territory. It remained a crucial market for luxury brands. The market reached a record high of €260 billion in 2018,

---

[7]Unity Marketing, *Luxury Report 2014*, April 2013. www.unitymarketingonline.com/catalog/product_detail.php?pid=72~subid=230/index.html.

representing 6% growth (2% at current exchange rates). Worldwide, the personal luxury goods market experienced growth across most regions, driven primarily by more robust local consumption. In contrast, purchases among tourists remained flat on average. In 2019, the market reached a record high of €285 billion,[8] representing 4% growth (7% at current exchange rates). The luxury market experienced sustained growth, although the US–China trade war, negotiations following Brexit, and political unrest such as the Yellow Vest Movement in France and Hong Kong's protests cast a shadow on the future growth of the industry.

Luxury Industry Trends & Challenges

One of the major trends the luxury goods industry has undergone is that of consolidation. Many of the major players in the industry have, since the 1980s, been transformed from small family-owned businesses into global powerhouses. This has resulted in a profound shift in the way in which many luxury companies are managed today. Such luxury conglomerates are driven by the bottom line and the companies who dominate are able to exploit synergies across brands and product categories.

The power of the conglomerates is underscored by the struggling small independent brands, the fashion doyennes of yesteryear, such as Pierre Balmain, who filed for bankruptcy, and Ungaro, which was sold in 2005. Nevertheless, consolidation has not always been successful, even for the large companies such as LVMH, whose earnings from Louis Vuitton are often eroded by losses from their less-than-successful brands.

In difficult times, investors should go back to fundamentals: megabrands. Scale rules in an industry where fixed costs have increasing importance. It is argued that "megabrands" will continue to dominate the luxury and fashion industry, enjoying faster top-line growth and superior profitability.

Scale pays, as megabrands can lead the advertising expenditure league while committing a smaller portion of their sales. Besides, scale allows superior downstream integration into retail. Various data confirm that there exists a direct relationship between sales per square meter and

---

[8]https://www.statista.com/study/61582/in-depth-luxury/#:~:text=The%20 global%20luxury%20goods%20market,to%20the%20COVID%2D19%20 pandemic.&text=Online%20sales%20of%20luxury%20goods,brick%2Dand%2Dmortar%20 share.

advertising expenditures. Direct retail operations are essential to luxury goods brands: luxury megabrands have an interest in "escalating the race" for direct retail operations, in order to further leverage their scale advantage. Escalating into larger, richer, more prominent, and ultimately more expensive, directly operated stores (DOS) allows megabrands to awe consumers even more and to extend the distance in consumers' minds between the megabrands and everything else. Downstream integration into profitable DOS allows megabrands to push the envelope on entry price points and to lead the way in globalization.

Recent trends show that luxury consumers are looking for brands that will help them to develop themselves through a unique and sensual experience throughout their customer journey. These consumers wish to own something authentic, with a heritage and with personalized style: luxury items that combine historical savoir-faire with modern designs, which would also be a means of self-expression for the new generation. For example, Bulgari was known for its classical chic design sensibilities, with jewelry pieces of voluminous precious stones for traditional clients and a modern, simpler, trendier line for younger clientele.

The main trend in consumption was a generational shift, with 85% of luxury growth in 2017 fueled by Generations Y and Z.[9] Generation Y (born between 1980 and 1994) are now well into their careers and are reaching their peak spending age. Generation Z (1995 to 2010), although much younger, are also appearing on the radar of the luxury market. Streetwear, which originated from skateboard subculture—the once underground skate culture and athleisure wear—is a trend which particularly reflects a broader "millennial state of mind." This aesthetic paradigm shift is pushing luxury brands to explore and redefine their supply and how they deliver it.[10] Louis Vuitton's collaboration with Supreme was an unprecedented success in the rejuvenation of LV's brand image. Almost all brands are expanding their sneaker collections, for example, as a result of the increasing desire and demand to forgo formal wear for a more "comfortable" wardrobe. T-shirts, down jackets

---

[9]Luxe Digital, https://luxe.digital/business/digital-luxury-trends/millennials-buy-sustainable-luxury/.

[10]Bain & Company, 10 January 2018, https://www.jobteaser.com/fr/companies/bain-and-company/newsfeed/other-19100-the-new-luxury-consumer-why-responding-to-the-millennial-mindset-will-be-key.

and sneakers were among the standout categories in 2017, growing by 25%, 15%, and 10%, respectively.[11] Fendi experimented with a WeChat-powered mini-game, Fendi Ways to Rome, to communicate brand culture to young consumers. Louis Vuitton, Gucci, Burberry, and Moschino also took the lead in VR and video games. Brands who are hesitant about staying relevant in the eyes of the new generations will soon be left out.

As Millennials and Gen Z consumers grew up in the digital age, building omni-channel experiences was becoming indispensable. E-Commerce sales still accounted for a small part of total sales, but they kept on increasing. L'Oreal reported in 2020 that they had achieved the same level of digitalization in three weeks during the pandemic and lockdown that they had achieved in the previous three years. Eighty percent of all luxury consumers go to brand websites to see, appreciate, observe, and decide on what they wish to buy. Luxury brands were experimenting with their websites in such a way as to communicate their appeal in more than one way. In response to this trend, the role of physical stores will likely need to change to better engage customers: evolving from brand temples into places that feel like home, where distinctive and immersive experiences host a genuine dialogue with customers. In the quest to foster loyalty in the younger generations, smart brands know that omni-channel experiences are key. Furthermore, corporate social responsibility (CSR) policies and practices need to be highlighted as they are becoming ever more urgent in response to the coronavirus. A study from Nielsen showed that 73% of Millennial respondents were willing to spend more on a product if it comes from a sustainable or socially conscious brand.[12] Yet, in contrast to the Great Recession of 2008–2009, the spread of coronavirus may have a deeper influence on consumers' psychology. We must look back to World War II or, to a lesser extent, 9/11 to find parallels.[13]

---

[11]LUXURY GOODS WORLDWIDE MARKET STUDY, FALL–WINTER 2018, Bain, https://www.bain.com/contentassets/8df501b9f8d6442eba00040246c6b4f9/bain_digest__luxury_goods_worldwide_market_study_fall_winter_2018.pdf.

[12]The Sustainability Imperative, Nielsen, December 2015, https://www.nielsen.com/us/en/insights/report/2015/the-sustainability-imperative-2/.

[13]*Forbes*, Mars 15, 2020, https://www.forbes.com/sites/pamdanziger/2020/03/15/what-the-aftermath-of-the-global-coronavirus-pandemic-will-mean-for-luxury-brands/#29f8b2f31e9f.

Not only are people's financial situations challenged, but so is their most basic need: health. In response to this, it is likely that consumers will turn to retaliatory spending in order to show the world that they are safe, and to rebuild and reinforce their identity: a positive outcome for the luxury industry. The values and identities of luxury brands will be more and more examined and cherished. People will be more willing to purchase luxury goods that represent what is good and right (in an ethical sense), turning to brands that engage in social responsibility, invest in gender equality, and that are mindful of the environment and of sustainability. If luxury brands do not take a long-term view, they will suffer from a lack of meaning once the pandemic lifts.

Stella McCartney is arguably the founder of the sustainable luxury movement. Established through a 50/50 joint venture with Kering, the House of Stella McCartney was founded as the first vegetarian luxury brand and embedded policies and practices of social responsibility into the foundation stone of the business. It has a "No fur, No leather, No skin policy," and strongly opposes animal testing. The brand promoted single-use material, virgin plastic and paper for packaging. Its charity efforts are equally central to its corporate mission. Over the years, Stella McCartney has partnered with not-for-profit organizations such as Canopy, Parley for the Oceans, and Wildlife Works. It also designed and operated stores and offices in an eco-friendly way by using greener energy, sustainable wood, and furniture bought at auction.

Consolidation is one of the most notable trends observed in the history of the luxury goods market. Since the 1980s, many of the major players in the industry have grown from small family-owned businesses into powerful multinationals, resulting in a radical shift in the way in which many luxury companies are managed today. These conglomerates are driven by the bottom line, and the companies that dominate are able to exploit synergies across brands and product categories. Nevertheless, consolidation has not always been successful, even for large companies such as LVMH, whose earnings from Louis Vuitton were often eroded by losses from the less-than-successful brands.

Economic difficulties facing the crisis: In the wake of September 11 and the Iraq war, the luxury goods industry faced one of the worst downturns for three decades, finally bouncing back in 2004 when many companies in the industry posted a 10–15% increase, and finally returning to the black. Since then, other major events, such as the sub-prime mortgage crisis, the Japanese tsunami, and the eurozone financial crisis have occurred, though the luxury market has been relatively untouched. Historically, the industry increased from 2010–2014, mainly due to the rapid growth of Chinese spending. After two sluggish years, the market then bounced back from 2017. The coronavirus halted the global economy in 2020.

Adding extra pressure to all luxury brands, the Covid-19 health crisis began to crush the industry in 2020. Many retailers in the US and the UK filed for bankruptcy. Market capitalization collapsed by almost 40% in the first trimester of 2020. The health crisis was expected to bring about a global revenue contraction of 20–40% in 2020 year-on-year. As I write in early 2021, the outlook for this year is not very good, either: only 1–4% growth is expected, compared to the 6% the industry had been observing.

The fall in the industry's global revenue can be explained first by the sudden cessation of a major part of the industry's key supply activities between February and April 2020, due to the lockdown situation faced by most countries. More specifically, most brands' factories and stores were forced to shut down, penalizing their sales processes in an industry particularly reliant on offline channels and travel retail. Thirty percent of luxury fashion companies declared that they would be in distress after more than two months of store closures.

A freeze in consumption: Aggravating the luxury supply-side crisis, the industry faced a real freeze in consumer spending. Afraid of a salary drop, or even of losing their job, consumers prioritized necessary goods. Even online sales declined—20% in Europe, 40% in the United States, and 25% in China. On the one hand, in Europe and the Western world, 75% of shoppers, asked in March, believed that their financial situation would be negatively affected by the Covid Pandemic. On the other hand, China recovered quickly, and other Asian countries followed. Furthermore, the pandemic has paused travel and travel-related shopping—which represented a considerable part of luxury brands' revenues—for an undefined period. As a result, many global luxury brands are expected to go bankrupt within the next 12 to 18 months if they don't rethink the way they produce and sell. It will very probably shake out the weakest brands, accelerate the decline of luxury brands that were already struggling, and embolden the strongest—which are more likely to adapt—increasing waves of consolidation around brands and M&A activities. Job losses are also likely to even further dampen consumer sentiment on buying luxury goods. In February 2020, the unemployment rate in China rose to 5.7%, a record high for the country. The consumer insecurity facing the new recessionary market has led to a rise of anti-consumerism. For example, in Europe and the US, more than 65% of consumers expect a decrease in their spending on apparel, and even 40% expect this decrease to be on the total household spending. Furthermore, 56% of them said that special promotions would be an important factor when shopping for clothes in 2020. The question is to know if luxury brands will be up to the challenge and ready to enter in a discount mindset, which is not the most compatible with promoting exceptional quality and rarity.

A forced digitalization: The pandemic has also accelerated digital escalation—digitalization reached levels that had not been expected until 2025—and reinforced the importance of digital channels, during lockdown and even after. During lockdown, 13% of European consumers browsed online e-tailers for the first time and continue to use them now. Besides, the digital escalation has pushed an appetite for in-season retail and seasonless designs, as well as a decline of wholesale. Digitalization also brought forth the use of new tools that increased operational agility in the supply chain and boosted productivity. New habits have already appeared during lockdown in the way people work in the industry, with 79% uptick in videoconferencing across the world and 58% increase in flexible working hours. The pandemic crisis has crushed luxury brands' previously planned strategies for 2020, leaving them exposed as they confront a disorienting future. Michael Burke, CEO of Louis Vuitton and Chairman of Tiffany, commented, "Who said this, was it Churchill? 'Planning is useless, but having a plan is indispensable.' I guess what that means is when the shit hits the fan you need to have a plan, but having a plan before the shit hits the fan is not that useful. It's really a statement to the importance of resilience and agility. That's what we really stressed in those six months. That's how we got through it in better shape than when we entered it. Vuitton is a better company today than six months ago."[14] But it has also opened the door to new opportunities in resetting the value chain and adapting to quickly changing consumers.

As of 2019, the luxury goods industry was estimated to be valued at around US$281 billion, which includes jewelry, watches, leather goods, wines and spirits, perfume, and apparel of the top 100 luxury companies.[15] In general, clothing and shoes accounted for the largest part of luxury sales, at approximately 30%, perfume and cosmetics for 22%, and the watches and jewelry sector for 21%, followed by leather goods at 20% and other (eyewear, textile accessories, etc.) at 7%.[16] It was estimated that, for FY2020–2021, the industry overall would have shrunk anywhere between 15 and 35%, depending on the sectors, but stock prices predict a sharp upheaval in the post-COVID scenario.

The growth markets of the future: The largest market for luxury goods is in Europe, which accounts for 33.7% of the world's expenditure, followed by Japan with 28.4%, and North America with 24.6%. Yet, the Asia Pacific region accounts for the largest sales of leather goods. Although these nations are strategically important, these markets are becoming increasingly mature.

Changing conditions in the world's two most populous nations, India and China, presented renewed growth opportunities for luxury brands. It was estimated that by 2025 these two nations will account for more than 50% of the world market. The increasing liberalization of the Chinese and Indian economies had resulted in an increase in average consumer purchasing power and the number of high-net-worth individuals. In fact, the average spending per consumer in China is on a par with Japanese spending. This had important implications for luxury brands, as the large population base could translate into a significant increase, not only in consumer numbers, but in revenues as well. This was the case for the Chinese market in particular. Aside from a hesitant

---

[14]https://www.businessoffashion.com/articles/luxury/louis-vuittons-michael-burke-on-hardwiring-accountability-in-a-state-of-flux.

[15]https://www.comitecolbert.com/app/uploads/2020/12/deloitte-global-luxury-goods-v4-2020.pdf.

[16]Statista, 2019, https://www.statista.com/statistics/245655/total-sales-of-the-luxury-goods-market-worldwide-by-product-category/.

recovery in Dubai, the Middle East was a subdued market, affected by lower consumer confidence and geopolitical uncertainties.[17]

Conclusion

In conclusion, there is no single definition of luxury: the definition resides in the mind of the luxury connoisseur; it is dynamic and ever-changing. What is luxury today for some may not be luxury for others and, over time, may even not be considered luxury anymore. For this reason, luxury goods have stood the test of time. The evolution of the luxury goods market has stood witness to the many fluctuations throughout history, from the Romans, Egyptians, Chinese, and Indians, to the Italians and the French through the formation of multibrand conglomerates. With globalization and the growth of emerging markets, the industry has veered East. Hong Kong, Shanghai, Singapore, Beijing, and Tokyo have the most sizeable concentrations of luxury and affordable luxury brands. This is a distinct trend that is here to stay. Consolidation of the luxury market is thus also here to stay. In addition, the rise of emerging market luxury brands will be a force to reckon with in the future. The luxury market is open to new definitions and new discoveries. The rise of affordable luxury brands, both from the West and the East, will open new possibilities and opportunities. New brands will emerge and new markets have emerged, making the industry more enigmatic than ever before.

---

[17]Bain & Company, February 05, 2020, https://www.bain.com/insights/eight-themes-that-are-rewriting-the-future-of-luxury-goods/.

Chapter 3

Who's Who of Luxury

T he top six players in the luxury industry—LVMH, Kering, Estée Lauder, Richemont, L'Oréal Lux and Chanel—account for 30% of the industry's turnover.

Luxury goods have traditionally been prevalent in France and Italy. Italy produces one third of the world's luxury goods, making it the largest luxury-goods-producing country. Italy is the birthplace of brands like Gucci, Armani, Bulgari, Moncler, Prada, Zegna, and Ferragamo.

Among the multibrand conglomerates, with revenues within or exceeding the US$10 billion bracket, are LVMH, Richemont, Kering, Swatch, Estée Lauder, Hermès, and L'Oréal and Luxottica.

Star monobrands—companies with revenues greater than US$1 billion—represent another subsection of the top-player category. Of these, Burberry, Tiffany, Armani, Ralph Lauren, Chanel, Lao Feng Xiang, and Dolce & Gabbana, are good examples among others. While many of these companies operate under a single brand name, they compete in a variety of product sectors. Table 3.1 shines light on the breakdown of mono- and multi-brands.

Table 3.1   Leaders in the Multibrand and Monobrand Luxury Sector

Multibrands	Monobrands
LVMH	Chanel
L'Oréal	Burberry
Richemont	Armani
Kering	Salvatore Ferragamo
Swatch	Ermenegildo Zegna
Hermès	Brunello Cucinelli
Prada	Chow Tai Fook
Capri Holdings	Goyard

The Consumers

In the last two decades, luxury goods were no longer exclusive to high-net-worth individuals. Worldwide today, 7.7 million people have the purchasing power to acquire goods from this category. Globally, women represent the largest segment of consumers of luxury goods, accounting for 80% of cosmetics and 70% of fashion. It is important here to note that the consumer profile is evolving. Men are also spending on luxury products that embody quality, service, prestige, grace, and elegance. Luxury brands give birth to a nonexistent prior need and seduce through the image it creates. Middle-class consumers are increasingly seeking quality designer clothes. For example, recent trends show luxury consumers are purchasing one Brioni suit for $3,000, instead of three ordinary suits at $1,000 each. These consumers are both quality- and price-conscious and weigh their options based on pleasure and aesthetics.

The last few years have witnessed a shift in purchasing behavior, from the traditional affluent target clientele to a broader and younger audience such as Gen Z and HENRYs. This phenomenon was driven by the conspicuous consumption movement influenced by celebrities' endorsements of luxury goods. This meant that younger consumers were accessing the luxury market by purchasing small-price-point items usually found in the "accessories" subdivision. Luxury goods companies saw these downward extensions as a positive externality, making their brands accessible to consumers who would not otherwise be able to afford luxury products. For example, Tiffany sold solid silver bangles and Louis Vuitton produced cheaper synthetic versions of its higher end leather and crocodile-skin bags. As of mid-2021, low-ticket items comprise approximately 55% of all luxury sales.

What Creates Demand in the Luxury Industry?

Luxury goods are particularly sensitive to the effects of economic cycles and world events since a large portion of the luxury goods industry was historically dependent on travelers. In 2003, the luxury goods industry was hit by three economic phenomena—the SARS epidemic, which impacted the Asia Pacific region; the Iraq war; and the strengthening of the euro versus the US dollar, which not only reduced consumers' purchasing power in Europe but also impacted companies' bottom lines, as revenues were in weaker currencies and costs were in the much stronger euro.

In 2006, the luxury industry was hit by war in Lebanon, and the bomb scare issued by the UK, which restricted the types and sizes of liquids that travelers could carry onboard a plane while traveling. Duty-free sales were estimated at $26 billion a year globally and $7 billion in the US liquor sector, and perfume makes up anywhere from 20% to 50% of sales. The travel retail channel was lucrative and most major luxury firms, including LVMH, L'Oréal, and Estée Lauder, produced fragrances and other beauty products that were exclusive to those shops.

Options to brace for this threat included stores delivering customers' items to the airline, which would stow them in the baggage hold and hand them over to passengers when they disembarked. Another option might be scanners capable of identifying dangerous liquids. In the wake of this sudden incident, Ed Brennan, ex–chief executive of DFS, LVMH's duty-free operation, commented, "I believe we will be able to restore the ability to sell those product categories to departing passengers in a safe way again. We have a strong partnership with airports around the world, and we will work together to find a solution."

Surprisingly, while a major economic downturn occurred between 2008 and 2011, the luxury industry remained strong. Luxury sales in Europe increased by 16%, with an increase in sales of Hugo Boss to €2.06 billion and record sales of €2.8 billion of Hermès in 2011. This showed that, in the face of the various economic cycles, the luxury industry remained resilient. In 2020, however, the industry collided with the negative impact of the COVID-19 pandemic. The lockdown of cities across the world froze the entire value chain. The personal luxury goods market contracted for the first time since 2009, declining by an average of 23% within a range of 10–35%, depending on the sector.

Why Demand Is Increasing in the Industry

As competition intensified in the luxury goods industry, more and more brands increased their average advertising expenditure in an effort to stimulate demand for their product.

Luxury goods companies attempting to garner consumer awareness have begun investing more heavily in retail store networks. Many luxury goods companies viewed flagship stores in key capital cities such as Milan, Tokyo, Hong Kong, New York, and Paris as vehicles for advertising their brands and conveying their brand images, thereby allocating a greater share of their capital to larger and larger flagship stores.

The increase in demand can partially be attributed to the growth of HENRYs (high earners not rich yet), along with the increase in the generation Z and Y populations across the globe. These consumers contribute significantly to the total luxury sales. Their increase, as a percentage of the population, increases the disposable income and thus increases demand. The power of these consumers was seen during the opening sales in China, in the year 2020 during the pandemic, where luxury brands like Gucci, Hermès, Cartier, and Louis Vuitton created record sales.

The Actors

Listed below are the profiles of eight of the top luxury brand companies.

LVMH—Louis Vuitton Möet Hennessy

LVMH, undeniably the world's largest luxury goods group, with revenues of about €44.7 billion in 2020 (down 17% due to the COVID-19 pandemic) and €53.7 billion in 2019 (up 15% with organic revenue growth of 10% from the previous year). It is often acknowledged as one of the most successful luxury goods groups in the world. LVMH boasts many of the industry's star brands, such as Louis Vuitton, Christian Dior, Moët & Chandon, and Sephora. Tiffany joined their stable of brands in 2021. LVMH's brands span across a variety of sectors, from fashion to leather goods, cosmetics, watches and jewelry, and wine and spirits.

The genesis of LVMH can be traced back as far as 1854, when Louis Vuitton started manufacturing luggage and trunks for the traveling aristocracy. The company was founded on January 1, 1923. Subsequent generations of the Vuitton family—most notably, Henry Racamier—transformed this business from a two-store operation into a billion-dollar giant by tapping into the lucrative Asian market.

This family business began its evolution into a luxury conglomerate when the CEO & President of Moët & Chandon, Alain Chevalier, fearing a stock-market takeover, formed a merger with Louis Vuitton in June 1987, resulting in LVMH. (The Moët and Hennessy brands had previously merged in 1971; this merger also inherited the rights to Parfums Christian Dior.) The parent company owned 98% of Vuitton shares but, more importantly, this union gave the four families 51% of the voting stock, thus staving off any takeover.

At this stage, Bernard Arnault had already obtained ownership of the failing Boussac empire in 1984, using $15 million of his own capital and $45 million from investors. Boussac owned the world-famous Christian Dior Haute Couture house, and in time Bernard Arnault returned Boussac to profitability through divestments and redundancies. He participated in the share capital of LVMH when he was approached by Henry Racamier to invest in LVMH as an ally against Alain Chevalier. The relationship between Louis Vuitton and Moët-Hennessey had quickly soured. Bernard Arnault, with the help of Guinness, initially purchased 24% of LVMH stock. It was Racamier's attempt to block Bernard Arnault from gaining control that pushed Arnault to purchase even more stock, and subsequently increase his shareholding to 37.5%. Shortly thereafter, he increased his shareholding to 43.5%, assuring his control of LVMH. This merger between Bernard Arnault and LVMH allowed Arnault to finally reunite Parfums Christian Dior with Dior couture.

Bernard Arnault and his family owned 47.2% of LVMH as of early 2021. As France's richest man, Bernard Arnault had an estimated personal fortune nearing $153 billion.[1]

Group Companies   LVMH specializes in the production and distribution of various consumer goods, including fashion and leather goods, wine and spirits, perfume and cosmetics, and watches and jewelry. The company's key products and services include the following, depicted in Table 3.2.

Organizational and Financial Structure   The Arnault family and Foreign Institutional investors owned 47.2% and 35.8% shares in the company respectively. The rest of the company shares were owned by French Institutional investors (11.6%), individuals (5%), and treasury stock (0.4%). In 2021, LVMH reported a consolidated revenue of €44.7 billion for the year 2020, down by 17% from the previous year.

Footprints/International Expansion   LVMH distributes its products through company-owned stores and licensed distributors across various regions worldwide, including Asia, Western Europe, and the United States. The group has established a strong presence in developed markets such as Europe, Japan, and the United States, and is rapidly expanding into the emerging economies of Asia, which provide a promising potential market. LVMH operated through more than 1,514 stores in Asia (excluding Japan), 1,175 in Europe (excluding France), 866 stores in the United States, 512 stores in France, 428 stores in Japan, and 508 stores in other countries. Asia (excluding Japan), the group's largest geographical market, in the year 2020 accounted for around 34.41% of the total revenue. A revenue growth of around 28.8% from this region partially offset the declining revenues from other mature markets, indicating that the geographical positioning to a certain extent enabled the company to weather the decline experienced in its major markets. Furthermore, in the year 2020, the group experienced an overall revenue decline of 16.8%, majorly due to the coronavirus pandemic. However,

---

[1] *Forbes*, as of 03/02/2021, https://www.forbes.com/profile/bernard-arnault/?sh=3f13d25066fa.

Asia (excluding Japan) remained the best-performing region, with the least decline of 5.09%.

Strategy LVMH pursued both an organic growth and a growth-by-acquisition strategy. LVMH focused most of its acquisition efforts on brands within the luxury segment. However, these brands span a range of diverse product segments.

The LVMH luxury goods group was organized into five different divisions: selective retailing, fashion and leather goods, perfume and cosmetics, wine and spirits, and watches and jewelry. However, LVMH also had interests in economic, financial, and investment publications, as well as other companies, such as the Jardin d'Acclimatation in Paris.

LVMH, in its acquisition choice, sought to purchase and restore heritage brands, transforming them into star brands that would evoke tradition, a certain savoir-faire, and uphold innovation and quality.

In order to achieve its organic growth objectives, LVMH focused on new product launches, expanding its retail network and increasing its expenditures on communications.

The LVMH group positioned itself as a socially responsible group. Since 2011, the group reports its initiatives and achievements through its social responsibility report. With programs like LIFE (LVMH initiatives for the environment), Sephora stands, and many more, social responsibility remained as part of the group's positioning strategy.

Growth, Mergers and Acquisitions After taking over as Chairman & CEO of LVMH, Bernard Arnault pursued growth by acquisition in order to build a portfolio of the world's most revered luxury brands.

The growth spree started through the acquisition of Céline and Givenchy couture, and eventually of Kenzo in 1993. Fashion and leather goods brands such as Donna Karan (DKNY—later on sold) and Kenzo were added to the stable, as well as watches and jewelry, with TAG Heuer, Zenith, Chaumet, and Fred in the mid-1990s.

In 1997 LVMH entered into selective retailing with a 61% ownership of DFS. This was further expanded to include Sephora cosmetics stores, France's leading cosmetic retailer, and Le Bon Marché, the Parisian department stores, and La Samaritaine.

Table 3.2 Brands under LVMH

Wine and Spirits	Fashion and Leather	Perfume and Cosmetics	Watches and Jewelry	Selective Retailing
Hennessy	Louis Vuitton	Parfums Christian Dior	TAG Heuer	DFS
Moët & Chandon	Fendi	Guerlain	Zenith	Sephora
Château Cheval Blanc	Céline	Parfums Givenchy	Chaumet	Le Bon Marché Rive Gauche
Château d'Yquem	Loewe	Makeup for Ever	Hublot	Starboard Cruise Services
Krug	Givenchy	Acqua di Parma	Fred	La Grande Epicerie de Paris
Dom Pérignon		BeneFit Cosmetics	Bulgari	
Belvedere	Kenzo	Kenzo Parfums	Tiffany & Co.	**Other Activities**
Mercier	Patou	Fresh		Belmond
Glenmorangie		Perfumes Loewe		Cheval Blanc
CLOS19	Berluti	Cha Ling		Connaissance des Arts
Ruinart	Marc Jacobs	Fenty Beauty by Rihanna		Jardin d'Acclimatation
Chandon California	Emilio Pucci	KVD Vegan Beauty		Cova
Chandon Argentina	Christian Dior	Maison Francis Kurkdjian		Investir
Chandon Australia	Fenty	Marc Jacobs Beauty		
Chandon Brazil Newton Vineyard	Loro Piana			
Cloudy Bay	Moynat			La Samaritaine
Cape Mentelle				Le Parisien
Woodinville	Rimowa			Les Echos
Cheval des Andes				Radio Classique

Terrazas des Los Andes
Bodega Numanthia
Clos Des Lambrays
Veuve Clicquot
Ardbeg
Chandon China
AOYUN
Chandon India
Volcan De Mi Tierra
Armand de Brignac

Royal Van Lent

From 1999 to 2000, LVMH spent an estimated US$1.1 billion on luxury-goods brands, from watches to edgy and trendy US cosmetic brands, such as Fresh and Benefit.

Not all acquisitions were successful. In January 1999, Bernard Arnault sought to gain a seat on the board of the famed Italian leather goods house, Gucci. Gucci countered this move by issuing additional shares, and then offered Pinault-Printemps-Redoute (PPR, now Kering Group) a 40% stake in Gucci for $2.9 billion. This forced Bernard Arnault to make a bid for 100% of Gucci for $4.9 billion. The takeover of Gucci sparked a bitter feud between François Pinault, then Chairman of PPR Group, and Bernard Arnault, Chairman of LVMH Group, resulting in litigation before the Dutch courts. The courts ultimately ruled in favor of Kering (ex-PPR) and in the year 2000 Bernard Arnault finally sold his Gucci stocks to François Pinault.

Over the course of 1999 to 2008, LVMH also undertook a series of divestments. In 2003, LVMH divested itself of some 50 unproductive brands (Michael Kors; Bliss Spas; and Philips, de Pury, and Luxembourg's auction house). And in 2005, LVMH sold Christian Lacroix, the fashion house that Bernard Arnault had helped to create in 1987.

History repeated itself in 2013, when Mr. Arnault attempted to take control of Hermés by gradually gaining hold of a 22.6% stake (valued at US$2 billion) of the company without making the stipulated declaration. It was called an "unfriendly attack" by Patrick Thomas, ex-CEO of Hermès. The dispute ended at this point with a symbolic USD 10 million amount fine on LVMH by the Financial Markets Authority. This action resulted in a very courageous and strong family reaction by the Hermès family, to block any possibility for LVMH to control the family maison by blocking more than 51% of the shares.

Nevertheless, this series of divestments did not dampen the company's growth-by-acquisition strategy. In 2004, LVMH purchased the whisky distillery Glenmorangie PLC for €300 million. In November 2011, LVMH acquired 100% of the shares of ArteCad, one of the leading Swiss manufacturers of watch dials. In October 2011, LVMH launched a public tender offer over all ordinary shares of Bulgari after which LVMH held 98.09% of the share capital of Bulgari. This helped LVMH increase its presence in the watch and jewelry segment. Also, in October 2011, the company and the Koh family, the founders and controlling shareholders of Heng Long International, signed an agreement to jointly own and control Heng Long International. The partnership with the Koh family strategically complemented LVMH in the procurement of high-quality crocodile skins. In 2013, LVMH acquired an 80% stake in Loro Piana, an Italian luxury textile and ready-to-wear company, and 52% in Nicholas Kirkwood, a British footwear company (which it later divested in 2020).

The period from 2015 to 2018 also saw ambitious moves by LVMH. In 2015, LVMH acquired a 41.7% stake in Repossi, a family-run Italian jewelry brand and upped its stake to 69% in 2019.

In 2016, LVMH acquired an 80% stake in Rimowa, a German luggage company. In 2018, it bought a majority stake in Jean Patou, a French couture label that it says it will revive by relaunching its ready-to-wear clothing collections. In 2019, LVMH officially launched a new label, Fenty, as part of a joint venture with musician Rihanna, who held a 49.99% stake in the new label, while LVMH owned the majority 50.01%. After two years, in early 2021, LVMH discontinued the partnership as the Fenty fashion brand had not taken off. The pandemic was cited as one of the reasons, though the brand was fully online and e-commerce-based, without any physical stores. Another reason, from Rihanna's side, was that her 110 million followers on social media were not used to buying expensive products, whereas LVMH focused on the higher end of the market, in line with the luxury ready-to-wear positioning of the Fenty fashion brand. However, the joint venture of Fenty Beauty with Sephora, through 40 shades of lipstick and more, continued, along with the investment from L. Catterton, the private equity arm of LVMH, for her lingerie brand known as SavageXFenty. LVMH entered into a "joint venture" with Stella McCartney, who ended its joint venture with rival conglomerate Kering. LVMH spent $3.2 billion in 2019 for luxury hospitality group Belmond, which owned or managed 46 hotels, trains and river cruise businesses. In 2021, LVMH bought a 50% stake in Armand de Brignac from the rapper Jay-Z.

After a bitter dispute LVMH finally acquired Tiffany & Co., a 182-year-old New York–based jewelry company, in early 2021 for $15.8 billion. Such strategic acquisitions helped the company to generate incremental revenues to contribute to future growth.

Key Success Factors   LVMH's success could be attributed to the way in which it managed brand independence and creativity. Bernard Arnault gave his designers free rein to invent, as seen in John Galliano's creations for Dior.

However, this costly creative process was counterbalanced by strong cost control measures in other areas, such as manufacturing, synergizing media and advertisement, renting retail space, logistics, sourcing and inventory control, and other back-end operations.

Another key success factor has been LVMH's stringent adherence to producing products of quality. It was able to maintain such strict quality controls as it manufactures most of its products, with some limited outsourcing. This strong control over the brand was also mirrored in LVMH's tight control over its supply chain and distribution network. In fact, Louis Vuitton was one of the few luxury goods companies that owned and operated 100% of its store networks.

The group kept innovation at the heart of its function. Constant innovation in the fields of product development, technology, distribution, and digital engagement were key to the brand's success. From fiber-optic color-changing Louis Vuitton bags and sneakers, launched by Virgil Abloh, to the personalized lipstick case and the first-ever digital radio for perfume enthusiasts, presented by Guerlain, the group's products and services embraced innovation.

Part of LVMH's success can be attributed to the group's ability to partner with the right creative talent and the right brand, like John Galliano with Dior before, Marc Jacobs with Louis Vuitton, Michael Kors, and later Phoebe Philo with Céline and others, all of which have been highly successful.

Outlook   LVMH's future will always be investment oriented. The group looks forward to continuing its growth and seizing new opportunities. A free cash flow of €12 billion enabled the company to invest in a substantial number of new acquisitions. The focus of the company was on innovation, expansion into new territories, and increasing their aggregate output. Also, the group remained committed to strengthening its cost control, investment selectivity, and digitalization of its houses.

Kering (Previously Known as PPR)[2]

Kering was founded in 1963 by François Pinault as a construction business trading in timber that later specialized in B2B and B2C retail, and subsequently entered the luxury goods market in 1999. In the 1990s, the group's B2C retail arm was comprised of mail-order fashion brands (Redcats), cultural products (Fnac), home furnishings and household appliances (Conforama), and a department store, Le Printemps. Kering marked a new stage in its development with the purchase of Gucci and Yves Saint Laurent in 1999, and thereafter built a multibrand luxury goods division. It continued to grow and develop its businesses through strong and highly reputed brands throughout the 2000s. Since 2005 the group has transformed itself from a diverse conglomerate into a cohesive, integrated group, progressively divesting its retail assets and reinforcing its luxury arm. In 2007 it seized a new growth opportunity with the purchase of a controlling stake in Puma, a world leader in sports and lifestyle, further establishing the group as a leader in apparel and accessories global brands. Following the demerger and flotation of FNAC and the disposal of Redcat's businesses, in 2013 the group would withdraw completely from the mass distribution sector. In March 2013, its name changed from PPR to Kering. While this phonetically sounded like "caring," it was also a play on the Brittany origins of the business. In Breton, "Ker" means "home" or "place to live," explained François-Henri Pinault. It demonstrated that the company protects, nurtures, and grows its brands while taking care of its businesses, its people, customers, and stakeholders—as well as the environment. In 2018, Kering started to gradually sell its stake in Puma in order to focus entirely on developing its luxury houses.

Group Companies   Diversified product and brand offerings helped the Retail division of the company cater to the various needs of its customer base. The Fnac retail chain offered cultural and technological products, including personal computers, photography, TV/video,

---

[2]On March 22, 2013, François-Henri Pinault announced that the group would change its name to "Kering." This new name was subject to approval at the Annual General Meeting on June 18, 2013.

software/games, office equipment, and telephony, and operated book and music stores. La Redoute retailed apparel, and Conforama sold home furnishings, appliances, and furniture. In addition, Kering's Sport & Lifestyle division offered athletic footwear, apparel, and accessories under the Puma, Volcom, Cobra, Electric, and Tretorn brand names; and the Luxury division still gathers the houses of Gucci, Bottega Veneta, Yves Saint Laurent, Alexander McQueen, Balenciaga, Brioni, Boucheron Pomellato, DoDo, Ulysse Nardin, Girard-Perregaux, Qeelin and Kering Eyewear.

Organizational and Financial Structure   As of late 2019, international institutional investors owned 44.7% of Kering's shares. Artémis group, the holding company, controlled by the Pinault family, owned 41.0%. The rest of the company was owned by French institutional investors (8.4%), private individual shareholders (4.8%), treasury shares (1.0%), and employee shareholders and executive corporate officers (0.1%).

During the fiscal year 2019, Kering generated €15.88 billion in revenue overall, 63% of which came from Gucci, 13% from Saint Laurent, 8% from Bottega Veneta, and the rest from other brands. Owing majorly to the coronavirus pandemic, the result in 2021 was €13.1 billion, a drop of 17.5%.

Footprints/International Expansion   Kering organized its luxury business into six geographical regions: Western Europe, Asia Pacific, North America (excluding Japan), Japan, and Other Countries (Eastern Europe, the Middle East, Africa). During the fiscal year 2019, Kering generated 34% of its revenue from Asia Pacific (excluding Japan), 32% from Western Europe, 19% from North America, 8% from Japan, and 7% from Other Countries. It had a total of 1,381 directly operated stores around the world.

Strategy   Kering has transformed itself to solely focus on the luxury sector, with a strategy primarily based on the organic growth of its current brands: to expand into new markets, reinforce their presence in mature markets, develop their distribution network and channels, and outpace their markets. Its strategy also includes integration and synergies, pooling resources in back-office functions. The group is also carrying out transversal projects to strengthen its houses, such as support their digital transformation and improve e-commerce activities.

Growth, Mergers and Acquisitions In 1999, the Gucci group purchased Yves Saint Laurent and Sergio Rossi. In 2001, Gucci Group bought Bottega Veneta and Balenciaga and signed partnership deals with Stella McCartney and Alexander McQueen. Between 2001 and 2004, PPR reinforced its capital participation in the Gucci Group. In 2003, PPR sold its company Pinault Bois et Matériaux to the British group Wolseley. After symbolizing the very first step of the group in the wood trade sector, and becoming a famous French retailer in wood material construction, import, and transformation, Pinault Bois was sold for €565 million. In 2004, PPR sold the electrical material manufacturer Rexel. After a public bid, Pinault-Printemps-Redoute increased its shares to 99.4% of Gucci Group's capital. In 2005, Pinault-Printemps-Redoute simplified its name to PPR. In 2007, it acquired a 27.1% controlling stake in Puma, followed by an increase in this stake to 62.1% on completion of a tender offer. The same year, Redcats USA acquired United Retail Group. In 2011, PPR announced acquisition of Brioni and Volcom, Inc. (Volcom and Electric brands). It also took a majority stake in Sowind Group, the owner of watchmakers Girard-Perregaux and JeanRichard. In December 2012, PPR bought a majority stake in Chinese jeweler Qeelin, which has four boutiques in Hong Kong and three in Europe, to enlarge its sales in the largest market for high-end goods. The acquisition price was undisclosed.[3] And it sold the Redcats USA business. In 2013, it acquired 51% of the luxury UK designer brand Christopher Kane. The same year, the group renamed itself to Kering. In the same year, Kering acquired a majority stake in Pomellato and brought Pomellato-owned Italian charm company DoDo under its umbrella. In 2014, Kering acquired the 171-year-old Swiss haute horlogerie brand Ulysse Nardin. That same year, the group shared its plan to take back control of its eyewear business value chain by creating Kering Eyewear.

[3] Roberts and Chan, 2012.

Previously, the eyewear business of its brands had been licensed to external partners. In 2015, Sergio Rossi was sold off. In the year 2017, Kering eyewear announced its partnership with Maison Cartier for the Cartier eyewear collection. In 2018, Kering announced plans to spin off the German sports brand Puma to its shareholders to concentrate on the development of its luxury business. It also sold the stake of Christopher Kane back to the namesake designer, a move following Kering's disposal of Stella McCartney's stake. In 2019, Kering confirmed that it had sold its US sports and lifestyle brand Volcom. By then, Kering had established itself as a pure luxury player.

Case Study: Gucci

Gucci, the world's third-largest multibrand luxury group, and the second most valuable luxury brand in the year 2020,[4] hails back to Florence, Italy, where in 1921 Guccio Gucci first opened a leather goods shop, creating products that sported a casual yet elegant style and catering to the wealthy.

Guccio's son, Aldo, became chairman of Gucci from 1953 to 1986. During the 1950s and 1960s, the company's intertwined "GG" logo became highly recognized in the accessories business, and later when Gucci expanded into fashion. Unfortunately, during the 1970s and 1980s Gucci's over-licensing negatively impacted on the company's image: the brand logo had been licensed to over 10,000 products.

Guccio Gucci had bequeathed a 50% share of the company to each of his sons, Rodolfo and Aldo. Upon the death of Rodolfo, his only son Maurizio Gucci inherited a half-share in the company. This marked the beginning of bitter family feuds between Maurizio and his Uncle Aldo, which also heralded a loss of direction for Gucci. This bickering culminated in Aldo being forced out from his position as chairman of the group

---

[4](Luxury & Premium 50 2020 | The Annual Brand Value Ranking | Brandirectory, 2021)

in 1986, ceding the position to Maurizio. Investcorp, a Bahrain investment bank, then entered the picture, purchasing the half shares of Aldo and his son, Vasco.

Maurizio, understanding that the company name had become devalued, attempted to restore the brand image by reducing the number of products, points of sale, and repurchasing licensing agreements retaining only perfumes, watches and sunglasses licenses. Unfortunately, Maurizio's zeal to restore Gucci to an up-market name, coupled with an economic downturn and poor production planning, resulted in Gucci being unable to make up for lost sales from discontinued products. Maurizio's excessive spending further exacerbated Gucci's woes, plunging the company into debt and potential bankruptcy.

This eventually culminated in Investcorp taking over Maurizio's share of Gucci in 1993 due to the violation of an agreement between Maurizio and Investcorp. Maurizio remained as consultant for Gucci until his untimely death in 1995 when Maurizio was murdered by a hit man, hired by his ex-wife Patrizia Reggiani.

In October 1995, Investcorp took Gucci public, eventually selling all of its shares in a secondary offering in March 1996 for over double the original asking price.

At this stage, Mr. Domenico De Sole, a native Roman and lawyer by profession, who had presided as president-CEO of Gucci since 1994, set about restoring the brand image by reorganizing distribution and investing heavily in promotion and merchandising. These efforts were spurred by the arrival of Tom Ford, an American designer, who infused the Gucci brand with a cocktail of racy advertising and sexy clothing. Although Gucci started out as an accessories company, its success hinged on its specific competency in fashion and on its reputation as the leading Italian luxury brand.

In 1999, PPR purchased a 40% stake in the Gucci group, resulting in the protracted LVMH/PPR battle for Gucci, with

(*continued*)

PPR eventually winning when the European Commission approved the PPR/Gucci deal. A 100% stake in Gucci was finally completed in 2003.

Sanofi Beauté, which owned the Yves Saint Laurent brands, was purchased from Artémis, Francois Pinault's private holding company, thus establishing a new luxury conglomerate.

Finally, in 2004, the winning duo of Gucci CEO Domenico de Sole and creative director Tom Ford departed Gucci after they failed to reach agreement over their contracts. This left many industry pundits questioning the future of Gucci. However, the brand continued to see success after Tom Ford left, with Frida Giannini becoming Creative Director of Gucci Women's ready-to-wear in 2005, and the sole creative director for the brand in 2006. The brand took a dip. Around the same time, Mr. Robert Polet, the ex-Unilever head of their ice-cream division, was named as the CEO of the Gucci Group following de Sole's departure. Patrizio de Marco was the President & CEO of Gucci from 2008 to 2014.

In 2011, a major restructuring took place, resulting in Polet leaving the company and François-Henri Pinault taking over management of the Gucci Group under his role as PPR CEO. He later renamed the group Kering.

In 2015, Marco Bizzarri, then CEO of Bottega Veneta, took over as CEO of Gucci. He appointed Alessandro Michele as creative director Alessandro introduced an eclectic reinterpretation of the house codes from the past in Gucci's design, while also dissolving the lines of gender divide in the name of self-expression. He also added a socially conscious stance to the brand by banning the use of fur in 2018, and steered the brand toward a stronger social media presence.[5] As a result, Gucci became a favorite among its clientele, especially the young. It grew at a stunning rate: 42.8% in 2017 and 34.9% in 2018, €9.6

[5]https://luxe.digital/business/digital-luxury-ranking/most-popular-luxury-brands/.

billion revenue in 2019. It was about to attain €10 billion revenue in 2020, before the pandemic. It became the second most valuable luxury brand in terms of brand value, just behind Porsche. The brand, under the leadership of Marco Bizzarri and creative direction of Alessandro Michele, embraced technological innovations through their seamless phygital strategy. Bizzarri said, "I was optimistic about technology because I saw the possibility of delegating the most boring tasks to technology and spending more time on doing the things that I like, like being creative."[6] Gucci implemented state-of-the-art technologies in its supply-chain management, sales analytics, merchandising, and voice assistance for store salespeople. All of these helped the brand stay ahead in the game of technology and its customer journey, through its app, interactive screens, augmented reality, Snapchat, and digital fashion weeks. In addition, under Bizzarri's leadership, in 2019 Gucci became fully carbon neutral within its own operations and across the supply chain, a unique achievement in the luxury industry that immediately set the tone for others. In another global first, the September 2019 fashion show was awarded ISO 20121 certification.

Analysis

Gucci's management team adopted a disruptive strategy, accomplished through diversification and communication. Gucci changed from carrying a single brand to branching out to become a multibrand group. This strategy allowed the positioning of the Gucci brand in the industry to differ depending on the number of brands and the number of business segments the group wants to compete in. This

(continued)

---

[6]https://www.fastcompany.com/90374520/how-a-century-old-luxury-brand-like-gucci-won-over-gen-z?utm_source=postup&utm_medium=email&utm_campaign=gucci&position=9&partner=newsletter&campaign_date=09082020.

strategy was also adopted by other conglomerates, such as Louis Vuitton and Prada. Some luxury companies, such as Armani, Ralph Lauren, and Versace, used a similar strategy of focusing on only one star brand and adding other business segments. This was the idea behind focus (monobrand) versus diversification (multibrand).

The strength of the brand itself was in its established, very strong brand image, interactivity, the ability to listen to customers of different ages, and international presence. With around 480 stores worldwide, Gucci has the most retail stores of all the luxury brands. Gucci worked with a select number of vendors and established an ability to control its distribution channels in this phenomenal growth phase. This has been a part of Gucci's defensive strategy in the value-chain to capture the value added instead of giving it to middlemen such as suppliers and retailers. In terms of customer focus, a digital marketing strategy that spoke to young generations is another of Gucci's strengths—millennials and Gen Z, groups that other luxury brands struggled to tap into.

Key Success Factors   Kering has a dominant position in the luxury market as one of the world's leading multibrand luxury goods companies. It has established its position by divesting sprawling businesses such as building materials, electronics, and sports products. It was then able to adjust to market changes with agility while producing strong organic growth of the luxury brands in its portfolio.

Its brands did exceptionally well in the 2010s. Gucci, Bottega Veneta, and Yves Saint Laurent brands are all star brands with high growth and profitability. Boucheron, Pomellato, Qeelin, and Ulysse Nardin offer complementary expertise in the jewelry and watches segment. Balenciaga, Alexander McQueen, and Brioni are cutting-edge couture brands with high potential for long-term growth. Furthermore, Gucci also distributed eyewear, fragrances and cosmetics, and home decor products. This vast range and the sharing of specific expertise among the various brands were the group's greatest assets. What is more, Kering has pursued wider global presence under the management of François-Henri Pinault. Thus, Kering established a strong presence in the luxury goods market, which allowed the company to take advantage of the scale and benefit resulting from the growth of the market.

The group allowed a great level of autonomy for the brands, as can be seen through diverging brand strategies. Gucci has continued to deepen its social media engagement through its aggressive and personalized multiple social media campaign, whereas Bottega Veneta has experimented differently by exiting most of the social media platforms. This diverse strategy and brand autonomy were key success factors in the group's overall success.

Future Outlook   The group has been transformed into a dedicated luxury business. In the future, Kering will pursue more sustainable growth and investment into digital initiatives for luxury business. Sustainability and digital transformation are at the heart of Kering's strategy.

Richemont

Richemont, controlled by the Rupert family, was the world's third-largest luxury-goods player, with an annual revenue of €14.24 billion and a free cash flow of €1 billion as of FY2020. Although the company had interests in leather goods, fashion, and pens, it predominantly owned jewelry and watch brands. Through its luxury goods subsidiary, the Vendôme luxury group, watch and jewelry sales accounted for 71% of Richemont's turnover.

Anton Rupert and his son Johann spun off Rembrandt's (a large South African tobacco and liquor giant) non–South African holdings, which included a 30% stake in Rothmans International. Rothmans had a controlling stake in Dunhill holdings (accessories and tobacco) as well as Cartier, which was acquired piecemeal through the 1970s and 1980s. The newly formed group was called the Compagnie Financière Richemont, which is based in Zug, Switzerland. Richemont went public in 1988. In order to avoid paying UK taxes, Richemont divided its assets into two publicly traded companies: Rothmans International (tobacco), which was subsequently sold to British Tobacco in 1999, and the Vendôme luxury group, which, since 1997, has been a wholly owned subsidiary of Richemont.

Organizational and Financial Structure   In order to grow its business, Richemont focused on allowing the companies to operate independently—marketing, development, distribution, and so forth were all handled separately by each brand. In terms of their distribution network, Richemont maintained a mix of directly operated stores and franchise operations.

Their operations were global in nature, with the largest market being in Asia Pacific. As of March 31, 2020, 35% of their sales were generated within Asia Pacific, and 30% in Europe.

Their organization was structured with central support services, regional support services, and the maisons. Its business activities divided into four operating divisions: (1) jewelry maisons with Cartier, Van Cleef & Arpels, and Buccellati; (2) specialist watchmakers with A. Lange & Söhne, Baume & Mercier, IWC, Jaeger-LeCoultre, Officine Panerai, Piaget, Roger DuBuis, and Vacheron Constantin; (3) online distributors with Watchfinder & Co. and YOOX NET-A-PORTER GROUP; and (4) other businesses with Alaïa, Chloé, Dunhill, Montblanc, Peter Millar, Purdey, and Serapian.

Additionally, their shareholder structure consisted of the Rupert family maintaining a key stake in the Richemont group, with other shares dispersed into the public sphere.

Footprints/International Expansion   Richemont, with a strong presence across the world, had operations in Europe, Asia Pacific, Japan, America and the Middle East. Asia, the company's largest market, generated 35% revenues in FY20. Europe contributed 30% of the revenue, the United States 20%, Japan 8%, and the Middle East 7%.

The focus on high growth markets was evident from increased investment in mainland China with the expansion of its retail network to 323 stores. During the same period, the jeweler Cartier had 37 stores in China while developing its digital strategy with its app and third-generation social media to reach out to younger generation. Moreover, the company's strategy in China was to continue to develop its distribution network and offer its customers a high-quality shopping experience

in keeping with the values of the maisons. Over the years, it has conducted rigorous inventory buyback from distributors in order to have
stricter control on brand images. Richemont has positioned itself to take
advantage of Chinese active e-commerce culture. Its joint venture with
Alibaba, China's leading technology company, went live in September
2019, presenting 130 brands on the Tmall site. Given its longstanding
experience in luxury goods, and its omni channel presence in China,
Richemont is well-placed to take advantage of the growing Chinese
luxury market.

Strategy   To manage some of the world's leading hard-luxury goods
companies was not an easy task, especially during the pandemic. All
of these companies, or "maisons," were kept independent. The growth
strategy of the Richemont group focused on creating innovative
products and marketing them appropriately. Richemont continued
investing in digital ventures with online platforms like Net-a-porter and
Farfetch. The group has also focused on four areas of sustainable strategy:
Environment, Communities, People, and Sourcing.

Growth, Mergers and Acquisitions   In recent history, Richemont
did not have major watch-related mergers and acquisitions. It mainly
used M&A to increase its production capabilities. Aside from Dunhill and
Cartier, Richemont's stable of luxury brands included 80% ownership
of Van Cleef and Arpels, Piaget, and Vacheron Constantin. In 2000,
Richemont acquired Jaeger le Coultre, IWC, and Lange & Söhne for
$1.8 billion against the bid by LVMH, enabling Richemont to gain a
large stake in the high-end luxury watch market. In 2010, Richemont
acquired the majority of the shares of Net-a-Porter.com, and merged
it with YOOX Group in 2015. Following the merger, Richemont
held 50% of the share capital of the YOOX Net-A-Porter (YNAP)
Group, while its voting rights were limited to 25%. In 2018, Richemont
acquired YNAP Group and Watchfinder & Co., a leading pre owned
premium watch specialist. In 2019, Richemont acquired Buccellati, an
Italian jewelry maison which was previously owned by Shangdon Rui,
a Chinese conglomerate with primary interests in goldmines. By 2019,
specialist watches increased to 21% of the group sales while the jewelry
segment represented 51% of total sales. Online distributors represented

15%. Richemont and Alibaba announced an investment of $300 million each in Farfetch, and $250 million each for a 25% stake in the joint venture that will include Farfetch's marketplace operations in China. An overview of Richemont's M&A history is listed in Table 3.3.

Table 3.3   Richemont's Mergers and Acquisitions

Company	Description	Acquisition Date
Cartier	Jewelry and watches	1970s and 1980s
Piaget	Watches	1988
Alfred Dunhill	Menswear and accessories	1988
Montblanc	Writing instruments	Held through Dunhill
Chloe	Womenswear, jewelry, fragrances, and accessories	Held through Dunhill
Baume & Mercier	Watches	1988
Philip Morris	Tobacco	1989
Purdey	Firearms	1994
NetHold pay television group	TV	1995
Vacheron Constantin	Watches	1996
Canal+	TV	1997
Officine Panerai	Watches	1997
Lancel	Leather goods	1997, sold in 2018
Exit from pay-television and electronic media investments		1999
Van Cleef & Arpels	Jewelry and watches	1999 (60%) 2001 (20%) 2003 (20%)
IWC	Watches	2000
Jaeger le Coultre	Watches	2000
A. Lange & Söhne	Watches	2000 (90%) 2003 (10%)
Minerva	Watch producer	2006
Greubel Forsey	Watch manufacturer	2006
Alaïa	Fashion	2007
Roger Dubuis	Watch components	2007 (Component manufacturing operations) 2008 (60%)
Donzé-Baume	Watch case manufacturer	2007
Non-luxury business demerged to Reinet Investments S.C.A.		2008
NET-A-PORTER.COM	Online distributor	2010

(Continued)

Table 3.3 (Continued)

Company	Description	Acquisition Date
Varin-Lampar & Varin	Exterior components for watches Gold & precious metal	2012
Peter Millar LLC	Luxury apparel	2012
Serapian	Leather goods and accessories	2017
Watchfinder & Co.	Online watch finder	2018
Yoox Net-a-Porter Group	Online distributor	2018
Buccellati	Jewelry	2019
AZ Factory	Fashion (with Alber Elbaz)	2019

Key Success Factors The key success factor for Richemont was actually the amalgamation of companies in its portfolio. The brands were some of the most prestigious brands in the hard-luxury sector and were known for their exclusivity and status. For example, Van Cleef & Arpels had been the first jewelry house on Place Vendôme and was known to be one of the most exclusive brands within the industry of high-end jewelry.

Beyond the brand portfolio, Richemont's geographic reach contributed to its success. Asia was the prime growth market for the luxury industry during the last decade; Richemont's presence in pan-Asia was an asset. This was evident based on the financial results of Richemont within Asia Pacific. Further to underscore simply their presence in the market, Richemont's focus on developing its distribution network was a huge asset. This ensured consistency within the retail experience for all consumers.

The group chairman, Mr. Rupert, had in the past advocated for a unified online platform to sell luxury goods and continued to collaborate with different groups to utilize the expertise. Maison Cartier's partnership with Kering, as well as Montblanc's, are examples of efficient collaboration.

Future Outlook Richemont targeted the Asia–Pacific market, which could compensate for slow growth in European markets. But the group was unsure about the growth prospects in the Asia–Pacific as a result of the slow growth of wholesale goods. It was expected that the strong demands in the Chinese and Middle-East markets might offset the weakness in the Japan and United States markets. Richemont's digital strategy and operation with Alibaba may help capture the online growth of the Chinese market.

Swatch

Swatch, the world's largest watchmaking firm, was formed from the merger of ASUAG (which was founded in 1931 and which owned many watch making companies such as Rado and Longines) and SSIH (which was forged from the merger of Tissot and Omega in 1930). Its revenues before the pandemic were around €8 billion, with a growth of 5–7% in 2017 and 2018, and a decline of 4% in 2019.[7]

By the 1970s, the Swiss watch making industry was suffering due to the onslaught of cheap Japanese imports. Ironically, many of the popular Japanese watches employed quartz technology, which, although discovered by the Swiss, had largely been ignored by the industry.

As these Swiss watch making companies faced bankruptcy, Nicolas Hayek was recruited as a consultant to make recommendations on the future of the Swiss watch making industry. Mr. Hayek suggested that SSIH and ASUAG merge and that they produce a low-cost watch that could be sold globally at a set price to compete at the lower end of the market, in which Swiss watch manufacturers had a 0% market share at the time.

As a result, in 1983 the two companies merged to form SMH (Société Suisse de Microélectronique & d'Horlogerie), with its headquarters located in Biel, Switzerland. Later that year the Swatch watch was launched to become an international success and icon.

Nicolas Hayek later purchased a 51% controlling stake in SMH and he became CEO in 1985. SMH changed its name to the Swatch Group in 1998.

In 2002, Nicolas Hayek Sr. resigned as CEO with the post now being occupied by his son, Nicolas Hayek Jr.

Group Companies   The Swatch watch company is composed of several divisions, including watches and jewelry (which accounted for

---

[7]https://www.macrotrends.net/stocks/charts/SWGAY/swatch-group-ag/revenue.

96.6% of Swatch's sales for the year 2019), production, electronic systems, corporate (legal entities that manage real estate, IP, quality control, R&D and other group services for the Swatch group), landmarks (Brand museums, exhibition centers, etc.) and distribution (two multibrand retailers, namely Tourbillon and Hour Passion). Under the watches and jewelry division, Swatch owned the following brands: Breguet, Harry Winston, Blancpain, Glashütte Original, Jaquet Droz, Léon Hatot, Omega, Longines, Rado, Union Glashütte, Tissot, CK watch & jewelry, Balmain, Certina, Mido, Hamilton, Swatch, and Flik Flak (see Table 3.4). Under the famous production subsidiary ETA, Swatch Group also owns Endura, a private label and licensing division.

There were a number of production companies under the Swatch Group. The company also followed forward integration with the establishment of direct distribution and/or retail channels. Its own retail channels included monobrand stores and a network of multibrand prestige watch and jewelry boutiques. Thus, the company held an outstanding industrial position with a high degree of verticalization (forward and backward) in the sector of watch movements and components production as well as in the electronic systems sector.

Swatch, as a group, controlled 25% of the world's watch market and was a dominant player in the Luxury Swiss watch market, controlling 30%, followed by Rolex with 22%, and Richemont with 20%.

Organizational and Financial Structure Swatch Group has two reporting segments, namely Watches & Jewelry, and Electronic Systems. The company's watches and jewelry business segment included

Table 3.4 Luxury Watches

Private Label	Mass	Mid	Prestige	Luxury
Endura	Flik Flak	Calvin Klein	Longines	Breguet
	Swatch	Certina	Rado	Blancpain
		Hamilton	Union Glashütte	Harry Winston
		Mido		Glashütte
		Pierre Balmain		Jaquet-Droz
		Tissot		Léon Hatot
				Omega

design, production, and commercialization of watches and jewelry. The electronic systems segment engaged in the design, production, and commercialization of electronic components and sports timing activities.

In 2019, Greater China accounted for 35.9% of Swatch's net sales; other Asian countries accounted for 25.5%. Switzerland represented 9%, Other Europe 19% and Total America another 9%. The rest came from Oceania and Africa.

Footprints/International Expansion The company has its operations in Europe, America, the Middle East, Australia, South East Asia, Africa, and a few other regions. Swatch Group has subsidiaries in many countries, including: Switzerland, Austria, Belgium, Denmark, Finland, Germany, Greece, Australia, China, Hong Kong, the United States, India, Brazil, Canada, Mexico, Panama, the United Arab Emirates, and South Africa. Its production centers are located principally in France, Italy, Germany, Malaysia, Switzerland, Thailand, and China. The group operates more than 160 affiliated companies in over 30 countries around the globe. The countries in which Swatch Group has no subsidiaries, it operates through local distributors. The company distributes its products through a global distribution network or its own retail channels (monobrand stores and a network of multibrand prestige watch and jewelry boutiques). Its prestige and luxury brands are represented at its Tourbillon, Hour Passion multibrand, and monobrand boutiques located in the world's most prestigious shopping districts.[8] Tourbillon is a multi-brand retail network that operates in Europe and the US and locates in high-end shopping sites. Hour Passion operates in Europe, the US, and South East Asia and locates in airports and outlets.

Strategy

- **Growth strategy:** Historically, Swatch achieved a large portion of its growth through acquisition. In fact, all brands in the Swatch group have been acquired, with the exception of Swatch itself, which was built from the bottom up—a complete greenfield venture. This series of acquisitions enabled Swatch to further entrench its position in all watch segments.

---

[8]Swatchgroup.com., www.swatchgroup.com/en/brands_and_companies/distribution.

While Swatch's sales growth was boosted by increased demand in the luxury watch segment, Swatch has been quoted as saying that, while its focus will continue to remain on organic growth, further expansion via acquisition has not been discounted.

- **Integration:** As a luxury goods company, Swatch's distinguishing feature is its highly integrated structure, which encompasses components suppliers, manufacturing, and retail.

A key part of Swatch's strategy is to integrate backward by purchasing key suppliers of watch components. The purpose of integration is to control quality and costs in all watch segments. Swatch currently owns 160 production facilities in Switzerland, Italy, France, Germany, the United States, the Virgin Islands, Thailand, Malaysia, and China.

While Swatch has some overseas production facilities the bulk of Swatch's manufacturing remains in Switzerland, unlike many other manufacturers who have shifted their entire production to low-cost countries. The strategic rationale behind this decision was to leverage the renown of Swiss-made watches.

- **Technology:** However, backward integration is not the only strategy that Swatch has pursued to reduce costs. New product techniques and technology—such as radical innovation in product design, automation, and assembly—also contributed to Swatch's competitiveness in the marketplace. Swatch also directed its efforts toward increasing efficiency in its supply chain, particularly between its component suppliers and watch manufacturers.

- **Product:** The Swatch Group offers watches at every price point, from the very top of the range to children's watches, a strategy that maximizes market penetration. At the luxury end, the group owns some of the best brands of grand complication watches and also aspires to be more competitive at jewelry and jewelry watch segments, evident in the acquisition of Harry Winston.

- **Distribution strategy:** Swatch's distribution strategy had always been to have one profitable, growing brand in each watch segment. While the mass watch segment was important for Swatch the luxury watch segment with Omega was reputed to provide some 44% of Swatch's margin.

Swatch's distribution strategy had always been marked by forward integration into fully owned stores, particularly in major capital cities such as Paris's Place Vendôme, New York's Times Square, and Tokyo's Ginza district. In addition, Swatch had diversified into new product groups such as its Dress Your Body line of jewelry.

Furthermore, the Swatch Group was one of the first luxury groups to enter into emerging markets. Swatch, which was present in India for some time, planned to open eight new Omega boutiques in India in non-metropolitan cities through multibrand stores in these markets.

- **Communication:** Swatch's communication strategies hinged upon sponsorship of events such as the Swatch Alternative Fashion week, targeted toward young consumers. Table 3.4 gives an overview of different watch brands owned by the premier luxury groups.

Growth, Mergers and Acquisitions   The company in 2009 renewed its agreement with the International Olympic Committee (IOC) for a long-term partnership in the areas of timing, scoring, and venue results services for the Olympic Games. It also foresaw the provision of similar services for the Paralympics games. This renewal of the contract emphasized the long standing successful relationship with the IOC.

Strategic Acquisitions   The company in 2009 acquired the remaining 90% of its Swiss Precision Watches (Pty) Ltd, a watch distribution company located in Johannesburg, South Africa. Swiss Precision Watches was formed in 2003, with the Moss Family, for the distribution of watches produced by the group. It was subsequently renamed The Swatch Group (South Africa) (Pty) Ltd. This acquisition helped in controlling a network of nine Swatch franchise stores that were operated by the distribution company. In March 2013, Swatch acquired the Canadian-owned watch and jewelry brand Harry Winston for US$1 billion.[9] The acquisition helped Swatch compete against Richemont in the high-end jewelry market, as well as for watches decorated with precious stones, after their previous collaboration with Tiffany & Co. fell into legal dispute in 2011. Since then, Swatch has focused on its brands' organic growth.

Key Success Factors   Swatch's key strength was definitely in its manufacturing prowess and vertical integration; these were the factors

---

[9]DeMarco, "Swatch Group."

that enabled Swatch to launch a high-quality mass product and produce it in a high-cost country like Switzerland. The highly vertically integrated model of Swatch enabled it to maintain its strategic independence in the marketplace and better control over its brands.

This success has also been emphasized by the Swatch Group's strong brand portfolio with high-profile brands such as Omega. Each brand, from a marketing perspective, operated independently of each other while, from a manufacturing perspective, coherence among the divisions is high. Finally, Swatch's presence in all areas of the market, spanning from mass to luxury, enabled it to achieve a critical mass that increased its competitiveness in the marketplace.

Future Outlook   The performance of 2019 was positive in all regions, excluding Hong Kong. HK's political unrest caused a negative effect on the group. So did the weakening of the US dollar and the euro versus the Swiss franc.

For the year 2020, the group suffered significant losses due to the coronavirus pandemic. With CHF 5,595 million, net sales were down 28.7% at a constant exchange rate and 32.1% at 2021 rates. The group recorded a net loss of CHF −53 million (compared to the net income of CHF 748 million for the previous year).

The group remained optimistic about their recovery from the losses and a special highlight for the group will be the Olympic Summer Games, which had earlier been canceled due to the pandemic, in Tokyo, where Omega can uniquely showcase itself in Japan, one of the largest luxury markets in the world.

L'Oréal

L'Oréal, the world's largest cosmetics and fragrances manufacturer, was founded in 1909 by the French Chemist Eugene Schueller who, in 1907, developed innovative hair dyes. In fact, since the company's inception, innovation in product technology has been the guiding principle at L'Oréal.

L'Oréal's activities were divided into three major areas: cosmetics, dermatology, and other. The cosmetics division, which accounts for 98% of L'Oréal's turnover, was divided into the professional, consumer, luxury, and active cosmetics product divisions.

The professional division offered specific hair care products for use by professional hairdressers; therefore, distribution of these products is limited to professional salons and outlets. The consumer division encompasses all of the products that are sold in the mass-market channels and it accounts for approximately 40% of L'Oréal's cosmetics turnover. The active cosmetics division markets dermatological and cosmetic brands to pharmacy and Beauté outlets. Although a predominant portion of L'Oréal's cosmetics business is not luxury, L'Oréal's luxury business accounts for approximately 40% of its turnover, making the L'Oréal Luxury division a dominant player in the luxury perfumes and cosmetics industry.

By 2019, the company was generating 32% of its sales in Asia Pacific.

Group Companies   L'Oreal's global brand recognition, product quality, and marketing experience enabled it to create one of the strongest consumer brand franchises in the world. The company marketed its products under 46 international, diverse, and complementary brands.

Some of the well-known brands of L'Oreal included L'Oreal Paris, Lancome, Vichy and L'Oréal Professionnel, Body Shop, Garnier, Maybelline, Giorgio Armani Parfums, Yves Saint Laurent, Kerastase, Vichy and Redken (see Table 3.5).

Organizational and Financial Structure   L'Oréal, a publicly listed company, marked by a very concentrated shareholding structure with the Bettencourt family, France's richest family, (33.27%) and Nestlé (23.27%) collectively owned 56.54% of the stock.

The company registered revenue of €29.87 billion in 2019, with its best year for sales growth since 2007. The company's operating profit also increased to €5.547 billion, with the biggest growth in luxe of 17.6%.

Footprints/International Expansion   A strong global presence helped the company mitigate the various risks associated with overdependence on a particular region. L'Oréal was one of the largest cosmetics companies, with a presence in 150 countries and over 23 international brands with more than 674 patents. The company generated 27% of its total revenues from the Western European region, 25% from North America, and 47% in New Markets (comprising Asia Pacific, Eastern Europe, Latin America,

Table 3.5   L'Oréal's Portfolio of Brands

Professional Products	Consumer Products	L'Oréal Luxe	Active Cosmetics
L'Oréal Professionnel	L'Oréal Paris	Lancome	La Roche Posay
Kerastase	MG	Yves Saint Laurent	Vichy
Redken	Garnier	Giorgio Armani	SkinCeuticals
Matrix	Maybelline	Biotherm	Roger & Gallet
Pureology	ABB	Kiehl's	Sanoflore
Shu Uemura Art of Hair	Essie	Ralph Lauren Fragrance	Cerave
Mizani	NYX	Shu Uemura	
Décléor	Niely	Cacharel	
Cartia		Helena Rubinstein	
Biolage		Clarisonic	
Seed Phytonutrients		Maison Martin Margiela	
		Victor & Rolf	
		Yue Sai	
		Diesel	
		Urban Decay	
		Guy Laroche Paris	
		Paloma Picasso	
		Atelier Cologne	
		House 99	
		It Cosmetics	
		Proenza Schouler	

Africa, and the Middle East). A wide geographical presence decreased the business risk of the company. This also facilitated smooth expansion of the company, as wider reach in terms of geography would mean reaping more benefits, improving profit margins, and attaining economies of scale and recognition on a worldwide basis.

Strategy

- **Growth strategy:** L'Oréal's evolution focused on a mix of both organic and inorganic growth strategy.

  L'Oréal achieved its organic growth by making adjustments swiftly in line with industry trends. Its growth in 2019 was at +8.0% like-for-like, which was contributed mostly by the biggest brands, such as

L'Oréal Paris, Maybelline, and Lancome, despite the increasingly lower entry barrier in the dynamic beauty market. According to Lubomira Rochet, chief digital officer in L'Oréal, these big brands' territories were not overrun as a result of the adoption of new marketing codes, such as shorter formats, new platforms, touchpoints, and services.[10] Social media, e-commerce, data, and artificial intelligence are among the top priorities of L'Oréal, as seen in the acquisition of Modiface in 2018, an AR company that can help facilitate consumer preferences.

The L'Oréal group's acquisition strategy is Buy-and-Grow, according to ex-CEO Jean Paul Agon.[11] This meant that L'Oréal buys a brand at an early stage. Once bought, L'Oréal strives to build the brand into a globally successful player. Kiehl's was an ideal proof of concept. L'Oréal bought Kiehl's in 2000 and began a campaign to put the brand on the world map. Within a decade, Kiehl's has grown into a global brand.

With a mission of beauty-for-all, L'Oréal kept looking for promising brands in all beauty segments and in all markets for growth. In recent times, L'Oréal acquired Niely Cosmeticos, a leading hair coloration and hair care company in Brazil. L'Oréal acquired Atelier Cologne, a niche fragrance brand, in order to extend its lux perfume brand portfolio, as it is one of the fast-growing segments.

Much of L'Oréal's continuous strong sales result can be attributed to its growth strategy of focusing on emerging markets in previous years. The importance of emerging markets to L'Oréal's business is underscored by an increasingly mature cosmetics and fragrance market in Western Europe. Asia Pacific markets have now contributed number-one sales. L'Oréal is currently scouting for potential brands to acquire in India, as it is one of the top three or four most strategic countries in the world.[12]

- **Diversification strategy:** L'Oréal's overall strategy was to focus solely on cosmetic and beauty products, preferring instead to direct its diversification efforts at retail channels. L'Oréal is unique in that

---

[10]https://www.marketingweek.com/loreal-is-embracing-new-marketing-codes/.

[11]https://capitalmind.com/why-loreal-remains-1-in-beauty/.

[12]https://economictimes.indiatimes.com/industry/cons-products/fashion-/-cosmetics-/-jewellery/loral-looking-to-acquire-beauty-brands-startups-in-india-jean-paul-agon-chairman/articleshow/72215721.cms?from=mdr.

it is present across mass, luxury, niche, and direct market channels. To date, L'Oréal was one of the few cosmetics and perfume groups to be successful in multiple distribution channels. As of 2013, L'Oréal also integrated into its own retail outlets with the opening of Kiehl's, Lancôme, and Biotherm boutiques. Other boutiques in the L'Oréal stable include shop-in-shops in London's Heathrow, New York's JFK, and Montreal's Trudeau airports.

- **Product strategy:** A cornerstone of L'Oréal's strategy is to continually produce products that are at the cutting edge of technology. As a result, L'Oréal invests heavily in research and development by allocating 3% of its annual turnover to R&D, one of the highest benchmarks in the cosmetics and perfume industry.

Not surprisingly, L'Oréal's innovativeness pushed it to enter new product categories, such as men's products. In 2018 David Beckham founded House 99 in partnership with L'Oréal, to provide diverse solutions for all hair and skin types. It unveiled Perso, the world's first AI-powered device for skincare and cosmetics in January 2020 and aimed to launch it commercially in 2021. L'Oréal continually focused on strong product launches to drive sales, particularly in the Luxury fragrance segment, such as Armani Privé, and Le Vestiaire des Parfums by Yves Saint Laurent.

Growth, Mergers and Acquisitions   In 2009, L'Oréal USA acquired Idaho Barber and Beauté Supply (IBB), a distributor of professional products to hair salons in the United States. The company had acquired a 50% stake in the Club des Créateurs de Beauté, and YSL Beauté, a luxury products company. It also acquired CollaGenex in the United States and expanded its operations into the area of dermatology. Further, in 2009, the company acquired three distributors in the United States, namely Idaho, Maly's Midwest, and Marshall Salon Services. These three distributors cover up to 80% of the United States under the Salon Centric brand. In April 2010, the company's subsidiary, L'Oréal USA, announced the acquisition of Essie Cosmetics, the nail color authority in the United States, sold mainly in American salons and spas. This acquisition enabled the company to increase its share in the nail color and care market. In November 2012, L'Oréal announced its purchase of the cosmetics brand

Urban Decay, known for its young, edgy, and fashion-forward luxury image. With these acquisitions, the company increased opportunities to gain leadership positions in the global luxury cosmetics market. In 2013, L'Oréal acquired the health and beauty business Interconsumer Products Limited (ICP) in Kenya. This acquisition furthered L'Oréal's strategy of expanding in the African and Asian markets. In 2014, L'Oréal acquired a major Chinese beauty brand, Magic Holdings, hoping to extend its consumer product line in China. It purchased two brands from Shiseido, namely Carita and Decléor. It also acquired NYX cosmetics and Carol's Daughter. In 2015, it acquired Niely Cosmetico Group in Brazil. In 2016, it acquired IT Cosmetics, Atelier Cologne and Saint-Gervais Mont Blanc. In 2017, L'Oréal announced plans to purchase skincare brands CeraVe, AcneFree, and Ambi. In 2018, L'Oréal announced a brand-new beauty and fragrance partnership with Valentino. L'Oréal also announced that it had acquired Modiface, an augmented reality and artificial intelligence entity, in line with its digital acceleration strategy. L'Oréal also purchased all of La Roche-Posay's parent company, Societe des thermes de la Roche-Posay.

Key Success Factors   L'Oréal has enjoyed annual growth in pretax profits for the last 20 years, with the final 10 years witnessing double-digit sales growth. A key factor behind this success was the synergies that L'Oréal had been able to exploit among the brands and the various channels.

First, through its wide stable of brands L'Oréal was able to leverage R&D technology between brands, which other competitors in the mass and luxury channels cannot do. That is, L'Oréal first used its innovation technology in its luxury products, eventually rolling them out to mass products. This strategy enabled L'Oréal to both maximize sales and minimize cannibalization of its high-end brands from its mass brands.

Second, L'Oréal's broad channel strategy insulated it from economic downturns in its various channels: in particular if, for economic reasons, consumers shifted from purchasing in the luxury segment to the mass segment, or vice versa.

Another important driving force behind L'Oréal's success has been the strength of top management, coupled with a unique and driven corporate culture.

With an innovative recruitment policy, L'Oréal's management hired young university graduates and offered them a lifelong career and training at L'Oréal. New employees benefit from tools to help them better understand the corporate culture and allow them to contribute to it. New employee orientation, known as FIT, has been strengthened through the inclusion of events focused on corporate culture and strategic vision. Each new employee is encouraged to download the latest FIT culture app. This digital coach helps employees appropriate key values through challenges, personal stories, and videos. In addition to this daily guidance, employees can also benefit from MOOCs and corporate culture learning games.[13] The group has committed to ensuring that 100% of employees will benefit from at least one training session annually by 2020.[14]

At L'Oréal a strong corporate culture has fostered competitiveness among the different brands and encouraged an internal drive to succeed.

The management style that this corporate culture engenders can be likened to that of coaching: responsibility was delegated to managers although top management is involved in all major brand decisions. This management model served to mitigate the risk of a potential brand failure if a wrong decision is made. Multiculturalism played an important part in maintaining global–local balance.[15] Decentralized marketing is essential for L'Oréal to have its finger on the pulse and skin in the game in an ever-changing beauty market.[16]

Finally, L'Oréal enjoyed a premier position in the cosmetics and fragrance industry as it was not a technologically led organization, but rather marketing and technology carry an equal weight within the organization, conferring both marketing and technological prowess on L'Oréal.

Future Outlook   The company's growth has been driven by innovations in emerging markets. Along with the consumer division, the focus of the group is on the professional (salon) and luxury segments.

---

[13]https://www.loreal-finance.com/en/annual-report-2017/human-relations/corporate-culture.

[14]https://www.loreal.com/developing/putting-employees-at-the-centre-of-our-commitments/prioritising-learning-and-development?Type=Group.

[15]https://hbr.org/2013/06/loreal-masters-multiculturalism.

[16]https://www.marketingweek.com/loreal-is-embracing-new-marketing-codes/.

L'Oréal appointed Nicolas Hieronimus, an ESSEC alumnus and a 30-year veteran at L'Oréal, as CEO in 2020.

Hermès

Hermès International SA was founded in 1837 by Thierry Hermès. The business began in saddle making and its origins can still be seen today in the Hermès trademark—a horse-drawn carriage.

Over time the business evolved into designing luggage, wallets, and most notably handbags. Today, Hermès International SA designs, produces, and markets leather goods (luggage, handbags, and belts), silk goods (ties, scarves, and accessories), perfume, clothing, watches, shoes, tableware (china and crystal), accessories (jewelry, gloves, and hats), art of living products, and cosmetics.

Hermès is one of the few luxury goods houses that remains predominantly in the hands of family members. It was Emile-Maurice, Thierry's son, who began Hermès' evolution into an international luxury house; he was the first to incorporate zippers into products. Succession then passed to son-in-law Robert Dumas, who brought Hermès to notoriety in the 1950s with the "Kelly" bag, named after actress Grace Kelly, which remains Hermès' iconic product.

Interestingly enough, Hermès does not see itself as a luxury brand but rather as a brand that designs quality products made by skilled artisans.

Organizational and Financial Structure   Hermès became a public company in 1993, yet the family retained the majority of the equity. The shareholder breakup was H51 SAS with 54.2%, the Hermès family with 12.55%, Nicolas Puech with 4.91%, the Arnault family with 1.87%, and the rest lies with the Capital research & management group, Hermès International société en commandite par actions, Morgan Stanley Asia Ltd., Norges investment management bank, The Vanguard Group Inc., and Fondation Nicolas Puech.

Footprints/International Expansion   Geographically diverse operations helped the company mitigate the various risks associated with over-dependence on a particular market. The company was engaged in the design, manufacturing, marketing, and retailing of luxury goods. The company had a strong market position in Europe, the Americas, and Asia Pacific. In 2019, the group generated a consolidated revenue of €6.9 billion, of which 32% revenue came from Europe (13% from France and 19% from the rest of Europe); 18% from the Americas; 49% from Asia Pacific (13% from Japan and 36% from the rest of Asia Pacific); and 1% from others.

Strategy   There had been a conscious effort on the part of Hermès to differentiate itself from its rivals and this has never been more evident than in the strategies that Hermès pursued that were in contrast to its competitors.

First, Hermès targeted a more elite and exclusive clientele, as opposed to the aspirational ones of its competitors, maintaining the highest level of quality and innovation.

Second, while Hermès has continually invested in expanding its store network like a plethora of other luxury goods houses, Hermès did not follow the industry trend of building "luxury cathedrals"; instead, it directed most of its efforts toward renovating its current network of stores and controlling its growth. Such a strategy is possible given the strong family ownership structure. A strong focus on product innovation has been a competitive advantage for the company. Hermès for over 180 years has been creating and inventing a wide range of products. The company started designing new and innovative products in 1837 and launched with extreme care. Correspondingly, with only about 300 stores and a website, Hermès continues to adopt a limited distribution strategy to preserve its exclusivity.

Third, unlike its competitors, Hermès' main focus has been on achieving organic growth and, to a much lesser extent, growth by acquisition. Hermès' acquisitions were made in a bid to both preserve luxury craftsmanship and enhance Hermès' own expertise. In fact, many of these companies, like the silversmith Puiforcat, are small niche brands.

Growth, Mergers and Acquisitions   Hermès' growth strategy had been dependent on its ability to open and operate new stores and the availability of suitable store locations on acceptable terms. The company's products are available worldwide through a network of around 300 exclusive stores, of which 165 are branches.

Beyond store expansion, Hermès has also invested in brand extension, rolling out a home collection in Paris. As of 2013, 20 boutiques were dedicated to presenting a home interior range of products, which included new furniture creations. In addition to its tableware and art-of-living collections, Hermès also developed a complete range for the home, including upholstery fabrics and wallpaper. This line was created in partnership with an established brand in the sector: the Italian fabric specialist Dedar. In 2020, it launched its first range of lipstick, Rouge Hermès, as a prelude of its extension into cosmetics.

Key Success Factors   Undoubtedly, the cornerstone to Hermès' success is its strong brand franchise, which is fostered by the company's meticulous attention to impeccable craftsmanship: its harnesses and saddlebags, and its unquenchable spirit of innovation. Hermès changes every six months a third of its 50,000 store keeping units (SKUs). Thus, a strong focus on innovation has strengthened the company's product offerings and brand image. The company's new product development capabilities helped it to broaden its product portfolio and expand its market share.

Future Outlook   Hermès group looks forward to expanding its network all over the world, and especially its production capacities in France and the rest of Europe. The focus of the group is also on innovation, to give it a strategic advantage in the luxury goods market. Hermès, which already sells perfume and made its first foray into cosmetics with lipstick, will roll out other products in its cosmetics segment, probably even skincare.

Estée Lauder

Founded in the year 1946 by Estée and Joseph Lauder, The Estée Lauder Companies Inc. is an American-origin multinational manufacturer and promoter of prestige skincare, cosmetics, fragrances, and hair care products. The group is headquartered in New York, USA. With over 25 prestige brands operating in over 150 countries and territories, and generating total net sales of US$14.29 billion in 2020, the group is recognized as one of the world's leading manufacturers and marketers in its segments.

Some of the well-known brand names include Estée Lauder, Clinique, Origins, M·A·C, Bobbi Brown, La Mer, Aveda, Jo Malone London, Too Faced, and Dr. Jart+. The group was controlled by the Lauder family since its foundation, having, as of August 2020, shares of Class A Common stock and Class B Common Stock with 86% of the outstanding voting power of the common stock.

Organizational and Financial Structure   As the privately held company grew, Estée Lauder and her husband involved their sons in their decision-making about the company. Leonard Lauder took over as chief executive officer in 1982 and had nearly quadrupled annual sales by 1995.

In part as an estate planning measure and a method for some Lauder family members to cash out portions of their company stakes, The Estée Lauder Companies Inc. went public in November 1995, raising more than $450 million through the IPO. Secondary offerings over the following few years lowered the Lauder family's stake in the company to about 65% of common stock and 93% of the voting stock.

Footprints/International Expansion   Estée Lauder Companies began its international expansion 15 years after its creation. In 1960, the company signed its first international contract with the famous Harrods Department Store in London, UK. Because of its visibility in Europe, it served as a springboard to other European markets. Within a few short years they opened outlets in Central America, Denmark, Hong Kong, Italy, Spain, Sweden, Belgium, New Zealand, and Switzerland. In the 1970s, Clinique was introduced overseas and Estée Lauder began to explore new opportunities in the Soviet Union. During the 1980s, the company made considerable progress in reaching markets which were still out of reach for many American companies. The group operates in over 150 countries and territories with over 1,500 freestanding stores and over 1,700 e-commerce and m-commerce sites in 50+ countries and territories.

Strategy   Part of Estée Lauder's legacy lies in the products and brands she created while the other part is reflected in the culture, values, quality, style and unsurpassed service that has made The Estée Lauder Companies a global leader in prestige beauty. Estée Lauder had a personal impact on everyone she met and was determined that no matter how much the company grew, its continued success would rely on the company's commitment of "Bringing the Best to Everyone We Touch." Since their early beginnings, Estée Lauder companies had a holistic approach to business. The same philosophy continued to guide their efforts in preserving natural resources and caring for communities.

Over the years, Estée Lauder's brands and employees adopted their own unique approach and causes, such as the M.A.C. AIDS Fund, Aveda's sustainable packaging, and the employee volunteer programs in local communities. The company-wide success included offsetting, with renewable credits, 100% of the energy use in their Global Operations facilities, significant advances in reducing packaging waste, and a continuing commitment to local and global philanthropic initiatives.

Growth, Mergers and Acquisitions   In the mid-1990s Estée Lauder began a new trend toward external expansion by acquiring new companies, obtaining licensing agreements, and entering into joint ventures to produce new products. Following this trend, in 1995 Estée Lauder acquired a majority interest (51%) in the Canadian cosmetic company M.A.C. Two years later, it increased its majority ownership position to 70%. Similarly, in October 1995, Estée Lauder purchased another popular skin care and color cosmetic company, Bobbi Brown Essentials, which had a distinct customer profile from that of M.A.C. Both companies went on to enjoy considerable success. In 1994, Estée Lauder obtained a licensing agreement with the American fashion designer Tommy Hilfiger to market Tommy perfume. In 1995, the group acquired La Mer, a leading global luxury skin care brand. The group also acquired prestigious fragrance brands such as La Labo, Editions de Parfums Frederic Malle, and By Kilian.

Under exclusive global license arrangements with Tommy Hilfiger, Donna Karan New York, DKNY, Michael Kors, and Ermenegildo Zegna, the group managed a diversified designer fragrance portfolio.

Future Outlook   The Estée Lauder Companies Inc., with its strategy of acquiring leading brands and obtaining exclusive global license arrangements, remains the undisputed leader in its market. The group keeps a positive outlook toward the market and expected growth.

Chanel

Chanel, a privately held company, is fully owned by the Wertheimer family. Although revenues were not officially disclosed it was estimated that worldwide sales of Chanel were to the tune of around €12 billion in 2019.

Chanel began as a Parisian hat shop in 1910. Gabrielle "Coco" Chanel was renowned for her revolutionary innovative style. She freed women from the fettered, corseted clothing of the times by designing free-flowing trousers, cardigans, and the famous *little black dress* in 1926. In 1924, Chanel was the first designer to launch a fragrance bearing her name: Chanel No. 5.

In 1924, Chanel, Pierre, and Paul Wertheimer worked together to create Parfum Chanel, in which Chanel herself possessed 10% of the capital and profits. In 1954 the Wertheimer family finally purchased Chanel.

In 1983, several years after Coco Chanel's death, the fashion house was revived by the entry of Karl Lagerfeld, who was artful in his ability to rework iconic Chanel products, such as the "Chanel" blazer, to keep them modern and relevant.

Strategy   Chanel's approach to the luxury goods industry has been very consistent and it could be argued that this is the result of the very stable family-owned ownership structure.

Chanel owns over 100 boutiques worldwide where a single jacket may retail for as much as $5,000. However, like many other luxury houses, Chanel has expanded its product lines, in a limited way, into less expensive accessories and bags, making them more accessible to a wider and younger consumer base. In fact, this strategy has been credited with the brand's success in Asian markets, particularly in Japan.

Chanel partnered with online brand Farfetch to create the store of the future by embedding smart AR mirrors in store dressing rooms. The functionality of the high-tech mirror detects clothing items as they're brought into the room and responds by displaying the runway look.

Key Success Factors   Product quality remains one of the main strengths of Chanel. Craftsmanship has always been the core value of the brand and it is perceived to be one of the best luxury brands. Some of its products, like Chanel No. 5, have achieved an iconic status and have been able to connect with consumers across different generations because of their timeless appeal. Since establishment in 1910, its unique brand DNA and heritage around Coco Chanel have held Chanel in its place as one of the most famous luxury companies in the world. Its traditional quality and location at the Place de Vendôme reaffirmed this image.

By associating Chanel with Coco, who gave the company the rights to use her name as well as her style and image, customers perceived Chanel as "luxury." Coco Chanel, as a core personality of Chanel, was indeed the DNA of brand Chanel and the company's greatest strength. The French chic style she presented and the "little black dress" she designed made her immortal. Because of her legendary lifestyle and the fact that she has remained celebrated as an icon for generations shows the strong personality she had and the significance of her image to the brand. The brand understands very well her influence and has launched a series of books and films around her stories. The mix of immortality and ladylikeness of Coco gives Chanel an exotic touch of deluxe which maintains a consistency and relevance to current market needs.

- **Brand signatures—Camelia and Double C logo and celebrity endorsements:** The brand has a rich heritage. Even some of its products have a long history. Chanel has been able to develop a couple of strong brand signatures that give it instant recognition among consumers.

   The change of image in the 1980s by Karl Lagerfeld turned out to be another great success. His uncanny ability to interpret Coco Chanel's work and translate it into the present made him an icon for Chanel and brought the label to the 18–25 age group. Through his designs, the luxury brand achieved a high level of exposure among its target customer audience into the twenty-first century.

   In addition, Chanel's strength lay in its endorsements by celebrities such as Kate Moss, who was the main personality for Coco Mademoiselle from 2001 until 2005 and was succeeded by Keira Knightley in 2007. Knightley adhered to the brand's unique mix of boyish and ladylike charm. Chanel's policy of celebrity endorsement can be traced back to early 1952, when Marilyn Monroe said "I only wear Chanel No. 5 to bed."

- **Successful social media efforts to build visibility among young generations:** Chanel is credited with the most successful marketing efforts to reach out to consumers on social media. It is the leading brand on all platforms, with more than 70 million followers globally. In 2019, it boasted 34.9 million followers on Instagram, 13.23 million on Twitter, and 21.96 million on Facebook. Its contents are of great quality and centered on video. The buzz on social media that Chanel is able to create contributes to its worldwide fame as one of the most wanted brands. However, Chanel is conservative about e-commerce. As Bruno Pavlovsky, Chanel's President of Fashion, said, "We are quite active on a day-to-day basis on all digital social networks, but that's for communication, to inspire our customers. The objective is to attract them to the boutiques, where we are able to offer them the best service and expertise. That's the objective of the brand."

- **Limited productions:** Their limited productions helped to establish a super-premium luxury aura for the brand: waiting lists for a product became the accepted norm. In fact, for certain products it was normal to have a brand waiting list, and then another waiting list to get onto the brand waiting list.

  Having a waiting list and not being able to meet the entire demand, definitely affected its turnover. In certain cases, consumers who were no longer willing to wait moved on to other brands. In a way, one of Chanel's strengths was at the same time one of its weaknesses.

- **Strong competition in the Chinese markets:** Chanel did not have first-mover advantage in China, though it was extremely successful in Europe, the United States, Asia, and Japan. Some other brands, such as Burberry, made an early entry and were able to entrench themselves quite strongly in the market. Moreover, initially China's was a men's and gift-dominated market, as far as the luxury sector was concerned: so, the major brands that did well had strong men's lines (Armani, Dunhill, and others). This highly competitive fashion market presented a dangerous factor for the couture house.

Chinese buyers, as they have become more educated, no longer see luxury consumption as a one-time purchase. They are rapidly making luxury consumption a lifestyle choice. They are also increasingly becoming committed to high-end niche products. Though Chanel was a late entrant, it has become a favorite luxury brand, according to reports in 2013. It was the third-most-sought-after luxury brand, after Audi and BMW and ahead of Louis Vuitton, Prada, Dior, Burberry, Giorgio Armani, and Versace.[17]

Future Outlook   In the case of Chanel, as observed, the double-C logo strategy worked well in China. Together with their bling strategy, Chanel has extended to cover three divisions: fashion, cosmetics & skin care, and jewelry & watches. It was ranked the second most valuable luxury brand of 2019. Interestingly, four of the top five luxury brands are publicly traded, while Chanel did not have to worry about the pressures of the stock market or external/internal stakeholders. It started to share its financial results with the public in 2018. However, it has also sworn to remain independent, although it has acquired several upstream suppliers in recent years. With the death of the long-celebrated Karl Lagerfeld, who spearheaded the brand from 1983, Chanel has entered the era of Virginie Viard. In the future, Chanel will continue to invest in preserving its artisan traditions and bring the brand full circle to what was originally envisioned by Gabrielle Coco Chanel.

Conclusion

It would seem that the luxury industry has become increasingly consolidated, with many converging strategies (see Table 3.6 for a summary). But the quest to solve the industry's paradox remains: How does a luxury brand retain its exclusivity and desirability while appealing to the expanding middle class?

---

[17] *World Luxury Index China 2013*, Digital Luxury Group.

Table 3.6 Brand Comparisons of Some Major Labels

	LVMH	Kering (PPR)	Richemont	Swatch	L'Oreal	Hermès	Estee Lauder	Chanel
Marketing Model								
Marketing Strategy / Target Consumers	Aspirational	Aspirational	Elite	Mass to super-premium	Mass and elite	Elite	Mass and Elite	Aspirational Elite –Fashion
Channel Strategy / Store Network Structure	Rapid expansion	Cautious	Slow	Rapid expansion	Rapid expansion mixed	Slow expansion	Rapid with Digital media	Slow Expansion
Store Structure	100% store network	Retail, wholesale, and franchise	Boutiques, franchise, third party	Fully owned stores		100% own store network	Own, JV, Licenses	Retail & Wholesale
Communication Channel Strategy	Luxury only	Luxury only	Luxury only	All channels	All channels	Luxury only	All, focused on CSR & sustainability	All Channels
	Sponsorship of events that reflect travel heritage	Sponsorship reflecting new luxury	Events, celebrity placements	Sponsorship of events	Sponsorship of Aggressive events	Events that reflect equestrian heritage	Celebrity endorsements	Sponsorship reflecting old luxury
Product Strategy / Level of Accessibility	Entry-level products	Entry-level products	High-jewelry to entry-level	Fashionable, collectible watches	Mass and premium, R&D	Entry-level products	Entry-level sub-brand	Entry-level products
Licensing Origins	Minimal Accessories	Fragrances Accessories	Yes	None	None Cosmetics	None Accessories	None Cosmetics	Eyewear Hats
Organizational Model / Integration	Forward integration into selective retailing	Mixed	Independent maisons	Full vertical	Forward integration into retail	Backward and forward integration	Digital synchronization	Full Vertical

(Continued)

Table 3.6 (Continued)

	LVMH	Kering (PPR)	Richemont	Swatch	L'Oreal	Hermès	Estee Lauder	Chanel
Synergies	Excellent	Good	Not evident	Excellent, pure watch player	Good	Medium	Good	Low
Growth Strategy	Organic and acquisition	Organic and acquisition	Organic & inorganic	Organic	Mostly organic	Mostly organic	Organic and inorganic	Organic
Emerging Markets	Fast, pioneer	Slow expansion	Moderate	Fast, pioneer India	Strong expansion	Cautious	Aggressive	Expansion Russia, India
Heritage Strongest Markets	Asia	Europe	Europe followed by China	Airport	Europe	Europe	China	Europe & Middle East
Iconic Product	LV Monogram	Gucci Loafers	High-jewelry	Irony, paparazzi	Cosmetics	Kelly bag	Cosmetics	Blazer, Quilted handbag
Founded in	1854	1923	1988	1931	1909	1946	1856	1910

Chapter 4

Branding

In consumer electronics, aviation, and the automobile industry, technology is and always has been the principal vector of evolution. The first video recorder illustrates this phenomenon well: upon its release, the choice of standard was vital—Sony's Betamax, Philips's VCR, or JVC's VHS? VHS won out in the end. The Airbus A380 is an aircraft capable of carrying 600 passengers and in recent history Concorde could fly to New York in three hours and 45 minutes. In these cases, technology seems to be what has altered the relationship with customers (DVD, BlackBerry, and the smartphone, for example).

Until recently, in the luxury industry the role of technology appears to be quantifiably small in comparison to its role in other industries. Most luxury goods are hand-made, with the exception of watches and jewelry where precision tools are required to produce complex designs and movements. Fragrances, materials, shapes, tastes, colors, decoration, and architecture are what have been, and will continue to be, the driving forces behind new trends and changes.

In industrial companies—aviation, transportation, energy—engineers are the drivers, while in luxury creators are the ones who lead, bring along the company, and seduce the clientele.

In reality, one world is dominated by reason and logic, whereas in the other, emotion and intuition outweigh pure reason. Finally, it is important to note that the supply side does not merely cater to preferences on the demand side; creativity and innovation don't respond to market analysis. This approach is always a gamble, but it is also what produces the unforeseen dream that consumers didn't know they wanted.

Market Saturation

In the context of market analysis, *saturation* implies that a good has a finite number of times it can or will be purchased by a single household. In consumer electronics, for example, a household that already owns two televisions and two refrigerators is unlikely to buy one more television or one more refrigerator. This principle is easily applicable to other classical consumer goods, such as cars.

Unlike the aforementioned industries, luxury does not experience saturation in the same way. Due to the non-essentiality of luxury goods (A handbag is still a handbag. One does not *need* an LV bag in order to carry personal belongings around. A woman will never have too many pairs of shoes, can always try out a new perfume, and will always be tempted by a new dress, pair of gloves, belt, or gem), saturation is close to zero. Two factors explain this phenomenon. Firstly, marketing strategies are not determined as a result of classical market analysis. Secondly, due to the limitless possibility of acquiring luxury goods, it is unclear how analysts can establish the interval within which the luxury product market is contained.

It is a world without limits, borders, or measurement.

As a result, sales in the luxury sector depend on creation, innovation, and a capacity for seduction. This is why we see enormous successes and incredible failures. The perfumes expert, Guerlain, can create a perfume like Champs Élysées, which completely missed the mark. Tom Ford, a celebrated designer, never managed to fit in well at YSL, but revived Gucci overnight.

The purveyors of famous names are all astonished when failure strikes and sometimes are just as surprised at their unpredictable successes! The marketing of luxury products is an improbable and uncertain endeavor.

The shape of a bottle can be tested, the contents subjected to trials, jewelry can be shown to female consumers, and men can be questioned about the colors and shapes they want and expect in a tie. Each has its own idea, its own "marketing." It is limitless. Each individual's preferences can be customized; such is the scope of desire.

Luxury marketing is something of an exercise in futility for market analysists, who tend to introduce more uncertainty about the possible ways to understand this market and its trends.

In reality, success in fashion has never been prepared, analyzed, or predicted by a study. Neither the Kelly bag, the Birkin bag by Hermès, the classic bag by Chanel, nor the trunk by Louis Vuitton were born from market analysis. In a similar vein, never did Yves Saint Laurent, Jean-Paul Gaultier, Karl Lagerfeld, or Alessandro Michele read any market studies on women consumers to create a collection and show.

In luxury, marketing is counterintuitive. Marketing generally helps a company gain better understanding of consumers' preferences and expectations. Yet in luxury, anticipating, suggesting, and persuading the consumer is at the core of the problem. It is a diametrically opposed approach that emphasizes breaking with the past and relying on intuition rather than logic.

Surprise and *chaos* can be understood as the *maîtres-mots* when it comes to approaches in the marketing of luxury. In luxury, one of the most important dualities to harmonize is that of the creative process and that of corporate management. Together, these teams' mission is to know what is working and why, and to imagine and reinvent trends that consumers have yet to discover appeal to them. Being able to anticipate consumer preferences through a certain analysis and comprehension of their behavior is what produces the winning ticket of a season. However, these teams also have a duty to respect and honor the traditions of their brands. Thus, part of their mission statement is to masterfully marry the old and the new: not only by embodying heritage, but also by embracing modernity and everything that it stands for.

In luxury, marketing is about inspiring desire or need in a potential consumer. It is about showing potential consumers how they can equip themselves with rare and valuable "tools" that allow them to create and exhibit what makes them a unique individual. For this reason, marketing in luxury is strongly affiliated with knowledge pertaining to other domains: technology, art history, contemporary cultural movements, as well as nascent innovations on an international scale.

Before an aircraft, a landscape, and especially when encountering beauty in the streets, we breathe deeply and admire. In a museum we discover a shape or a color; marketing is then a matter of taking information from here and there to create a fabric, an armchair, a dress, a bag, a bottle, a luxury object.

While luxury marketing is peculiar, it does exist. It is a kind of marketing that emerges from a global approach, day and night, everywhere on the planet, at home, while in the company of others, in an effort to identify and discover some detail, or to make a connection to another detail elsewhere in another realm, and to then innovate by assembling them.

Could carbon fiber, a material for aviation, be used to make an attaché case? Hermès thought so. Could rubber (from trees) and metal (from under the earth) fuse together to make a watch? The Big Bang. Hublot thought so.

And what if, one day, leather was no longer the only material to be used to make suitcases, bags, belts, and watch straps?

Luxury marketing also means thinking about materials, possible substitutions, and incisive innovations.

It cannot be said that marketing does not exist in luxury, but it is very specific, the polar opposite of what is commonly understood as "marketing." First, the new product is created through design and innovation. Sometimes it may fail as there has been no prior market research to check whether the product will succeed. But when it is successful the customer follows. So, marketing is not part of the product's creation. Marketing only comes in after the product has been developed. Marketing's role is then to create desire in the customer: by designing pleasant in-shop environments and presenting the new product well; by creating stories around the product's development and communicating by advertisement and films, both physically and digitally.

Luxury Marketing: Highly Creative and Selective

We must always try to be a little bit against the current.

As the Chinese proverb goes—only a dead fish sails in the direction of flow.

We do not do marketing. . . . We are in a group that creates. The creation of our innovations is what creates the market and not vice versa. . . . We create, invent, and from there, as our inventions are quite successful, the market adheres. . . . The success of our group is based on the combination of creativity and organization.

—Bernard Arnault

Branding is one of the many paradoxes in luxury, and modern-day principles of marketing, as it relies on an amalgam of approaches rather than classical methodology. The focus is primarily on brand management, less on mere advertising. Though the modern discipline of brand management is officially accredited to Procter & Gamble, and to a memo written in 1931 by Neil McElroy, luxury brands had been practicing the art of branding long before McElroy was born, and even before P&G was founded. For instance, nearly a century ago Gabrielle "Coco" Chanel redefined the whole nature of categories: the tweed suit, the little black dress, the cashmere cardigan, No. 5 perfume, costume jewelry, and the notion of the "total look," among others. In passing, Coco Chanel commented: "Fashion passes, style remains." Such was her power in branding Chanel with her own name that after a hundred years all of these inventions are part of the fashion legend. Luxury brand management is thus a place where tradition and creativity coincide, a place where ancient founders, artisans, and models meet and make mad magic together. It is a place where impoverished artisans make a brand with their products that endures for generations. Thus, on the one hand, luxury brands represent the origin of brand management; on the other, building a brand questions the fundamentals of marketing principles.

Managers who have worked in the luxury industry with multiple brands agree with the above notion. For example, Ashish Sensharma, former CEO of Wolford and previously COO of Vilebrequin, luxury

swimwear, commented: "I'm not a follower of the classic marketing techniques used by FMCG (fast-moving consumer goods) companies—my
reasoning? They lack the emotion to convey the 'soul.' In luxury, the real
sense of marketing is about creating and conveying the passion we have
in creating the product—it is a real story, which the user can see and
feel. There is no one better than the luxury brands to convey a story,
provide a dream, and sell aspirations."

Emmanuelle Sidem, senior partner and founder of Connex Consulting in Paris, also agreed with the paradox of marketing and the universe
of luxury branding. She commented: "Marketing is luxury's childhood
disease. Like all childhood diseases, the best way to prevent it is vaccination. The vaccine strain is based on the cultivation of the maison's
identity, its history, its values. . . ."

The concept of marketing is a misnomer in the luxury industry.
The Eight *P*s—product, price, place, promotion, people, process, physical evidence, and productivity—of marketing do not work in the same
way as they do in other industries. Simply put: classic marketing strategy
suggests that unique and differentiated brand positioning allows a brand
to win market share over its competitors via strategies that are valuable,
rare, and difficult to imitate, thereby ensuring sustainable competitive
advantages for a brand. Though the principles remain the same, for every
principle there is a contrasting notion in the luxury industry.

- **Brand:** The consumer in the luxury industry is more conscious of
  the brand. The story of the brand is vital for the aspiration it creates.
  It is never about the functional qualities of a product. For example,
  if someone wants a Ferrari, a Maserati or BMW or Mercedes will
  not fulfill his needs. Even at a similar price point, no other brand
  can compete with their "needs." The "need" for a Ferrari has nothing to do with utility (fuel efficiency, seating capacity, design, etc.).
  A Ferrari is a Ferrari because the brand transposes the essence of the
  product, its heritage and history, into one's desire to own it.
- **Positioning:** Brand positioning is about finding ways to mark out
  a brand in relation to its competitors, and plant itself into the consumer's mind. Consumers use comparative methods to select a product, based on functional and emotional perceptions that the brand
  has managed to instill in their minds. For example, in manufacturing

industries, engineers innovate and invent the product while marketing managers pilot the positioning of the brand. Coco Chanel's comment that "luxury is a necessity that begins where necessity ends,"
was in fact a positioning strategy she used in the luxury industry.
While designers are solely responsible for imagining and producing
the goods, marketing teams hold the reins of media presence. Purchasing decisions are thus "superlative" and not "comparative," having little to do with "needs" or "utility." Luxury consumers choose
the brand that best reflects who *they are* and how *they want to be
perceived* by society. Each luxury brand offers a unique character and/
or identity for which there is no substitute. Comparing two luxury
brands is much like comparing the work of two painters or two
musicians. Who is a better painter: Monet or Manet? Which com-
poser is greater: Mozart or Beethoven? It also doesn't make sense to
ask which bag is better, the one from Hermès, Chanel, Bottega Veneta, or Vuitton? Comparison here has no value, given that consumer
behavior and preferences are purely subjective in nature.

- **Product:** Marketing managers identify consumer needs and trends.
  Once these needs are identified the company designs and markets
  a product with features that then become standardized and mass-
  produced. Mass production renders economies of scale, reducing
  unit cost. Profit being a function of cost and price, by keeping
  differentiation and service constant, greater profitability can be
  achieved through the lowering of costs. Yet, in luxury the opposite
  principle is at play: luxury brands are never mass-produced. Given
  that craftsmanship (being handmade, and being uniquely personalized to an individual's taste and preferences) is a central factor of
  production, and that this process characteristically renders lower
  quantities of output, the production model becomes about the
  creation of the designer, their skills and personality, and less about
  the results of market analysis. Consumers are advised and taught
  about the characteristics, unique history, and merits of the brand,
  thereby increasing the value (authority) and worth (desirability) of
  the brand in their eyes.
- **Place:** In marketing strategy, place is about *where* and *how* goods
  are sold. It is about distribution strategy, and how to get the product
  into as many people's hands as possible. The underlying premise is

that goods have to be readily available. Exclusivity and inaccessibility being the essence of luxury goods, consumer behavior is very specific to the industry in question. In almost any other industry, consumers will not go out of their way to purchase a good or service. In the luxury industry, however, products represent a journey toward excellence, toward an experience, or even toward a form of initiation into a cult. The principle of rarity is what creates the demand frustration. The greater the inaccessibility, the greater the desire. The place for distribution has to be carefully selected: ideally in directly managed stores where brand message can be controlled and properly communicated. Moreover, when it comes to client loyalty, place is crucial.

- **Price:** Pricing strategy in consumer brand management is about launching a product at a low price and trading up. When the segment becomes competitive, brand managers often use price incentives to maintain and/or increase demand. Contrary to conventional wisdom, when the estimated price is higher than the actual price, it creates a higher perceived value. Moreover—and in contrast to the traditional understanding of pricing as a function of demand— luxury pricing is supply-based. In luxury, first the product is created, then the pricing is set. The more a good is perceived as "luxury" by the consumer, the higher the price it can fetch. In a standard market model, when the price falls, demand rises. In luxury, this relationship is reversed. This means that over time, rising prices lead to higher demand, all the while maintaining product exclusivity. For example, in the wine and champagne industry, selling great quantities is the norm. But the luxury segment has reversed this principle by selling fewer products at a higher price, thereby increasing margins while maintaining exclusivity. Growth and profits thus migrate from top line products. For a very similar reason, as the LV monogram became accessible and overexposed, LV stopped selling the €800 monogram handbags, instead concentrating on the Capuccine line of €4,000 bags. The all-too-accessible €800 handbags were actually damaging their business and the brand's image.

- **Promotion:** Conventional wisdom suggests that advertising is done for brands using a mix of rational and emotional messages that entice clients to consider it. In luxury, the dream is what sells. There is no need for rationality to justify a purchase. Conventionally, even with premium brands, people buy emotionally and justify rationally. In the world of luxury, products must be original and/or have a unique character. This uniqueness may bring unique flaws, which can also bring increased desirability. For example, mechanical luxury watches are known to be less accurate at keeping time than quartz watches. A Ferrari uses "hot" technology, rather than the meticulous "cold" technology characteristic of German automobiles.

While exposure is never the priority, the content is. Only high-quality advertisements will be found in a highly selective communication channel, all consistent with the brand's image. Every brand generates its own story, which is told through different channels. No brand can imitate the marketing of another: what works for Chanel will not work for Louis Vuitton, and vice versa. Promotion in luxury is linked to a deep understanding of the DNA of the brand, and it is essential to stay faithful to the brand's assets. Each luxury brand has its own DNA, and success cannot be duplicated. Graphically, a luxury brand advertisement promotion almost always uses suggestive imagery with a minimum number of words, if any at all. Ford's management of the Jaguar and Land Rover brands is an example of applying the classical principles of marketing to luxury products. Both brands ended up being sold at a loss to Tata Motors of India, which is turning around the image of these brands.

- **Process:** It is traditionally understood that following process routines is the way to create success. The process in the luxury world is, however, uncertain. For example, no one could predict that Chanel No. 5 would be so successful when thousands of perfume launches are failures. Its success is thus both creative and selective. The process may be known, but what will be successful is unknown. Night and day, the designer strives to create a product that fits the brand. He travels, visits museums, talks to people in the street but also reads, refers to journals, analyzes, asks questions, reflects, and may finally discover a detail that changes everything. A color may trigger his imagination, or he may be struck by an idea, he may take the risk to go far beyond present-day routines and processes, never looking at other brands, break the rules and give birth to a product. This is the marketing process. This is the genesis of luxury.

- **Physical evidence:** It is necessary in the luxury world to understand art, food, architecture, and everything that is living. Creators who launch the products, all the "métiers of luxury," have to be as close as possible to the contemporary "mood." They visit New York and Tokyo, they are on the go all the time, in the midst of current happenings. They have to sense one or two years in advance what new colors and shapes will attract consumers. They have to marry two divergent concepts during their creation. They have to create the physical evidence, which is not only driven in some way by a mix of rational factors (price, price elasticity, brand positioning), but mainly by irrational factors (surprise, emotion, innovation). The logic is different. It is dominated by forces, which are in the field of "offers" and not in the ground of "demands." In the field of appliances, one knows the level of equipment a certain kind of household will buy, one knows that one cannot sell more than one or two TVs or refrigerators to a couple. In luxury, who can say how many pairs of shoes a brand can sell to a customer!

- **Productivity:** Marketing in luxury is not driven by market analysis of potential customers. In luxury, traditional marketing studies can only give an indication, as it is practically impossible to assess the market reaction of a new product. A new dress, a new bag, or a new pair of glasses—it is almost impossible to predict if it will be a failure or a success. Classical marketing tools may not be the answer. The luxury world in this case has no frontier and no limit. No explanation can be put forward to explain consumer behavior.

The one distinctive feature of luxury marketing is that it is highly creative and discrete. When Moncler decides to show its ski jackets with snow and ski chair-lifts, and men and women wearing ski boots in the middle of Paris, the brand is going back to its roots and marketing its products, not as skiwear, but as luxury goods.

With the increase in marketing communication, it is challenging to draw a clear line between marketing campaigns of big FMCG brands and those of luxury brands. In effect they can draw inspiration from each other. For example, Coca-Cola's success with printing popular first names on its labels was picked up by Moët & Chandon, who offered customers the opportunity to write a personalized message on their

Impérial champagne bottles. This idea of customization is very success-ful, a creative way of saying "Congratulations!," "Happy anniversary!," or simply "Thank you." To go one step further, customers can also ask for hand-customized bottles, which can be decorated in genuine gold or silver Swarovski crystals, according to their preferences and budgets.

Productivity in marketing in the luxury industry essentially boils down to an *advanced understanding of the future*. It is an understanding that emanates from the passion of people working in this industry. Can someone teach this? Can it be replicated productively? It is more like the job of an astrologer or a fortuneteller who is looking into a crystal ball. This type of marketing can be tough—no technique can help. What then is the key? The answer is in finding the right talent. And talent is rare. Luxury brands are primarily dependent on the unique talent that can be found in the minds of creators, and in their abilities. When the creators succeed productivity soars.

- **People:** Brands need people who are experts in marketing. In the luxury world, designers are in fact marketers. Consider the birth of the first Dior perfume, right after the creation of the couture house: it was an original idea of Christian Dior to complement a dress with a final touch. "I created a perfume to wrap every woman in glorious femininity, as though each of my dresses was emerging from the bot-tle, one by one," said Dior for Miss Dior. Before him no designer had considered linking perfume and couture; now, almost every fashion brand has its own perfume, from the haute couture houses to fast-fashion brands like Zara. Another example is the late Karl Lagerfeld, who rejuvenated Chanel No. 5 and made it the ultimate dream of almost all women, of all ages, all over the world. When he decided to turn the Grand Palais into a huge "Chanel Shopping Center" for its 2014 "Défilé" runway show, in the middle of a busy food mar-ket, reinventing the packaging of Chanel, it was the only thing that people were talking about during fashion week, like it or not. It was followed by an ephemeral supermarket, a department store in the Grand Palais in 2015; a circle of games as the backdrop, with surprise celebrities and 3D-designed silhouettes for his fall/haute couture winter collection in 2016; Coco's salon in 2017; space and rockets in 2018; a classic French garden with a fountain, sandy paths, and rose-threaded pergolas in 2019. His successor, Virgine Viard, staged the "circular library like the library of Frederick II of Prussia in his Rococo palace in Sanssouci that Karl Lagerfeld adored" in 2020, followed by a "more bohemian style—more a wedding or a family celebration in a village. . .the mother and the aunt, [and] the 15-year-old girl dressing up for the first time" in 2021. The creative director is by all means the chief marketing manager, and one of the best that one can find in the market. As the chief marketing manager, the designer must satisfy the "nomad" of today and of the future.

The Nomad

With the COVID pandemic, travel has almost come to a halt. The world was more nomadic prior to the pandemic. The number of travelers, tourists, and businesspeople was increasing and it was no coincidence that the Airbus A380 had been launched. As Jacques Attali wrote in his book Lignes d'horizon, "There is no safe haven, the nomad individual will work without stopping because natural separations between night and day, and of time itself, have been abandoned. . . . For the first time in history, the nomad will have no fixed address. Our sense of ties will gradually fade to a memory. There will be nowhere left to hide."

After the pandemic, will 2,000-seat airplanes be slicing across the skyline, or will there be many more private jets, with a handful of people? There will be hyper loop and gigantic ships for space travel to deal with the movement of nomads. Nomads come from all over the place. Pre-pandemic, demanding customers traveled the world, seeking riches and beauty and purchasing extraordinary clothes, flashy one-off pieces that made them feel and look good. They bought apartments, villas, on beaches across the world. They felt at home in several places.

In 2014, more Chinese people visited France than Japanese. It was predicted that in 2020, there would be 200 million Chinese people traveling around the world, and seven hundred million tourists visiting Europe. But alas! The pandemic crisis changed all that. Who and what will seduce them to come again when the COVID pandemic is under control and most of the world has been vaccinated? How can we stimulate the appetites of nomads who think only of themselves, want spas, body treatments, nature and seclusion, but are also attracted to design and receiving perfect service?

How do we communicate with these nomads?

How can we sell to the nomads of the future? What should we sell them?

Anything is possible. All sorts of stores can be envisaged for nomads, all sorts of products.

The nomads travel with electronic tablets, mobiles at their fingertips, browse, choose, purchase. They might enter a megastore or a small boutique, they go everywhere, to places where a luxury goods store would never have dreamed of setting up business. Nomads are constantly on the move, pursued by information. They never stop working and stay connected.

What if we designed flying stores? A mobile sales unit? Stores in trains dedicated to luxury; temporary stores, like kiosks set up where people don't expect them. It's up to us to discover new ways of becoming irresistible!

Everything revolves around the nomad's mobility. We don't know when or how the nomad develops an appetite and luxury houses need to place their wares somewhere in their chain of desire.

Should we produce small sensual objects sold in unexpected places? Or should we invent transformable objects? For rich, demanding people, who have no home and no fixed address, luxury goods should offer pleasure and serenity—be personalized and more egotistical than ever.

Nomads travel. They visit China, Japan, Hawaii, the West Coast of the United States, and then the East Coast and on to Europe. Where do they stop over? Where will they buy? How will they get back to base? Where is their base?

Nomads buy instinctively, have things delivered, and want everything right now. They often live in several places and feed on cult images and objects. There are no longer any settlers. The world is full of people who move and buy on the go.

(continued)

Some goods are to be displayed or complement goods that are worn. Luxury items help distinguish people and make them unique individuals in a homogenized, trivialized, sterilized world.

Luxury goods for nomads will be light, foldable, mobile, seductive, shown, eternal. The quality must be perfect.

Innovation can be found everywhere, in fabrics, in touch, scent, and the aura of these goods. To persuade, creativity is a constant element, and competition is cutthroat.

How can you seduce a nomad who sees everything, compares, hears everything that is going on, and gathers information at the speed of light?

It's a mad dash to catch their attention, but the key will always be in the same longstanding values.

The nomad is a human being, sensitive to beauty, elegance, and softness.

Nomads might like dark chocolate or praline—they know what they like and they have an appetite for it. They are in a way quite simple.

In this world—where everything goes too fast, in which everything gets diluted, lost, where everything is public, everything is publicized—nomads are attracted to safe-haven products, natural products, signed products, tailor-made products . . . made just for them. The silence of the static luxury object is a welcome contrast to the cruelty of unlimited speed.

Nomads need somewhere to hide and to feel protected.

The crowds of nomads imbue personalized goods with a certain extravagant quality. The fortunate paradox is that a nomadic lifestyle is compatible with all sorts of creativity that bring more comfort, more beauty.

Nomads define luxury as the ultimate refinement to calm the anguish of traveling too fast. Fortunately, there is sure to be a contrast between the speed of travel, how random and fleeting it is, and the solidity of the purchase of a luxury good that the nomad will keep as a reminder of a flying visit. Eternity and the ephemeral go hand-in-hand: the object offsets the nomad's regret at having gone too fast, at not having taken the time to experience a sunset, or exchange a look of mutual understanding.

You can find refuge in the luxury of tomorrow.

Nomadism is an unprecedented path to luxury. It sets up in the middle of a large, unavoidable movement toward an emotional lifestyle—in the right place, at the right time, and in the best way. Capitals for nomads are major cities: Peking, Tokyo, Shanghai, Los Angeles, New York, Paris, London, Milan, and Berlin. From these places the nomad will move on to other "peripheral" places that might be more suited to real, serene, reassuring luxury.

Nomads are attracted to monuments, museums, places of culture and relaxation, care and well-being; luxury goods houses should be set up near attraction points such as these.

Emotion, desire, beauty, care, and culture are the natural companions of nomads—and of luxury.

The Nine *P*s of Luxury Brand Marketing for the Nomad of Tomorrow

Performance: When luxury goods were born due to the creativity, attention to detail, and craftsmanship of artisans, the goods sold themselves. They were bought by families, friends, and friends-of-friends. The creators did not chase their customers, or push their goods to be sold, by using different tools of modern-day marketing. The creators drew their customers by their constant pursuit of excellent product quality. For example, the Patek Philippe "generation" campaign harped on the fact that Patek Philippe watches were passed on to the third generation in a family. That is why Patek came out with the storyline "You never actually own a Patek Philippe. You merely take care of it for the next generation." Performance also means durability. Hermès defines it as "that which can be repaired." Thus, the concept of performance is associated with the timelessness of the product. Though a young woman may wear a Tiffany ring from her grandmother's wedding, she and her peers have their own tastes and preferences, they buy their own jewelry, and yet the products of earlier years are of such quality that they can be passed down from generation to generation. It is the excellent quality and their performance that makes luxury products desirable and timeless.

Provenance: Luxury brands have their own universe. The legend usually begins with an influential founder, a creative genius. For example, Chanel was much admired not only for the neat hand-sewn stitches on its famous tweed jacket, but also for the unique character of Coco Chanel. Coco Chanel, with her distinctive signature style, gave the brand life which still inspires women from all over the world today. Rolex was created by Hans Wilsdorf and it will remain in the foundation created by Hans. Provenance doesn't always have to be a particular person: it can also be an iconic emblem, a history of a family, or everything that built the mystique of the brand. The combination makes up a story of a brand that with time becomes an integral part of the brand's story and personality. For example, those who buy Rolls-Royces are definitely not only paying for outstanding performance, but for the prestige of the name, which has been associated with royalty for over 100 years.

Paucity: Luxury is, by its nature, nonessential, desirable, and exclusive. Luxury goods have to be earned. Luxury has to be inaccessible. The fact that it is accessible only to elites increases its desirability. Although luxury goods are no longer confined to only a small group of people, they are still relatively scarce compared to FMCG. This scarcity is certainly decided by the excellent performance of the products, the unique provenance of the brand, but also by marketing strategies, such as pricing, geographic differentiation of product offering, collaboration, and limited editions. For example, not all Hermès products are available in all of its stores. The stores have to order the products that they want to sell. So, at any point in time no Hermès store will have all of the collection. Paris stores will have about 35% of the collection. So, at any point in time Hermès expresses the creativity of its brand through its very large collection. Each store will have a different assortment of products, which causes some products to be inaccessible and exclusive, by design, not by planning. This also means that the regular Hermès customer who travels will always discover some products that are new.

Persona: The persona of a luxury brand is characterized by the sum of its parts, which depict a brand's identity. It is the personality, the character of a brand, conveyed by visual advertising, consumer touchpoints, in stores and online as well, and by the events of brand communication. It is the ensemble of the brand's essence, the material and emotional values, the distinct and consistent brand image and all the codes that make the brand unique and identifiable. It is the fundamental key in the brand's visual advertising, to establish a clear, charming, distinctive persona which consumers can easily recognize and relate to and emotionally engage with even as it changes and continuously evolves. For example, companies use the persona of a brand (sometimes that of its creator) to encourage consumers to trade up to more expensive lines when their disposable income increases. Armani is a good example: while Giorgio Armani Privé serves up haute couture fashion, it also offers lines such as Giorgio Armani, Armani CoUezioni, Emporio Armani, Armani Jeans, AIX Armani Exchange, Armani Junior, and Armani Casa, which portray the Armani persona while targeting different sets of consumers.

Personage: Brands use public figures, celebrities, and notable personalities from different walks of life to promote the brand. Brands use advertising to sell dreams, not to sell a product per se. The advertisements are not for direct responses but to promote the dreams to many more people than the ones who can actually afford to buy. Promoting the brand with endorsements from public figures and celebrities, from movie stars to musicians, from political or royal figures to sportsmen, and from designers to bloggers, is becoming more and more common. Endorsements from public figures continue to garner attention and credibility, though those same public figures can also be associated with non-luxury brands, and sometimes even competing brands. Yet it can be a double-edged sword for companies to use celebrity endorsement as a means to increase the awareness of the brand. Using celebrity endorsement to increase the reach of a brand also in some way means that the brand needs some of the star's status to enhance its own status. It is in one way admitting that the brand cannot make an impact on its own. On the other hand, in emerging markets, with millions of potential new consumers, this is one of the ways to increase a brand's awareness in countries where the history and the heritage of the brand are unknown. They have both to select the most influential figures without blurring the brand image with others, but also to find the most suitable endorser, who is consistent with the brand's ethos, aesthetics, and values. For example, the endorsement of Shah Rukh Khan, the number one movie star of Bollywood, worked favorably for Tag Heuer to build its image in India, North Africa, and the Middle East.

Phygital: The COVID-19 pandemic has accelerated the adoption of e-commerce purchases and most of the consumers enjoy the convenience and comfort of online shopping, fast deliveries, and cost-free return labels. On the other hand, the personal in-store experience allows consumers to try on different items, personally feel the fabric, and evaluate if the products suit their individual style and appearance. Friendly chats with a sales associate or the surprising discovery of a lovely unexpected item on the next clothing rack are crucial factors which are still able to amaze customers. In this case, intuitively, phygital simply means the fusion of physical and digital experiences that relates to the concept of using technology that enables the connection of the digital world with the physical world. With this, the primary and overall purpose is to provide consumers with an interactive, unique, and sensory pleasing experience. This smart marriage between the offline and online environments considers an essential fact, post-pandemic: phygital is a blended customer experience where digital applications relate to the physical world and actual space of the customer's journey. Most often, phygital experiences are immersive, interactive real-time experiences that offer immediate transactions and/or engagement. It is this creation of a blended customer experience where both the physical and the digital coexist in the same journey. Often, this is through immersive in-person activities that also offer the immediate opportunity to make a purchase. Phygital experiences require methodical collaboration between all vendors, engineers, content strategists, designers, and retail experts, and should aim to elevate the human experience through digital innovation. This digitalization can also be brought about by the introduction of different technologies such as beacons, NFC, geolocation, Wi-Fi. . . . This can also be realized by equipping salespeople with tablets so they can give consumers better advice, installing touchscreens so customers can access information on the store's e-commerce website, or by setting up RFID checkouts that offer a real-time saving. The cashier moves the product over the RFID mat or tray; the tag is detected by the system and automatically added to the receipt. Phygital is governed by immediacy, immersion, and interaction. The first two "I's," immediacy and immersion, come from the digital realm, while the final "I," interaction, comes from the physical realm. Nespresso was the pioneer in the implementation of this "phygitalization" strategy. The brand was one of the first to reengage with the consumer experience by creating different customer journeys according to their profiles (quick buys, product experts, etc.) and over the last ten years has become a benchmark for excellence in the creation of the customer experience. The famous coffee capsule producer communicates in the style of a luxury brand even though they offer a mass-market product. Luxury brands are still grappling with this phygital paradox. Louis Vuitton's chatbot on Facebook messenger allows customers a more "sophisticated, personalised, visual and conversational online shopping experience for each client." In order to do so, it was necessary to implement Natural Language Processing (NLP) into chatbots, which allowed for a conversation between the customer and the brand in a natural way. During the pandemic quarantine, Louis Vuitton offered a home-based experience to its clients by launching a series of virtual exhibitions (a visit to the Louis Vuitton Foundation) and cultural agenda to entertain them. In 2020, Gucci made an essential but clear decision about the future of its fashion shows by representing a new digital narrative through a 12-hour live stream for the reveal of the Spring/Summer 2021 *Epilogue* collection in Milan. With 35.2 million views, the digital fashion show hit record numbers and is the brand's most viewed online event ever. Furthermore, it created the Gucci Equilibrium, a new online portal and Instagram site to highlight and engage consumers on the brand's Corporate Social Responsibility activities, labeling them Gucci's "ongoing commitment to generate positive change for people and the planet." It created "Gucci Live," a new video service for physically distant clients who are connected with sales personnel in-store, recreating a phygital trip to the Gucci shop. The staff can show the requested items to the camera and provide factual product information during the live video chat. The Gucci App will enable customers everything from virtual try-on (available for watches, sneakers, lipstick, eyewear, hats, and décor) to a comfortable live stream platform for runway features, over the playful exploration of the brand's aesthetics with the vintage style Game "Arcade" as well as a podcast, providing rich storytelling and candid conversation based on Gucci's philosophy. In its new New York store in Soho, Gucci has lined the walls with state-of-the-art interactive screens and installed a connected DIY space where customers can design the personalization of their products. Also, in each of their points of sale, it is possible to use dematerialized payment via Apple Pay, for example.

Position: The physical store (especially the flagship stores) is not just a shopping space akin to a website. It is a sacred place. Luxury brands use the codes, symbols, rituals of the sacred to create an in-store sacred experience—almost mystical, religious. It is like a temple. This includes the architecture but also interactions with the salespeople, the layout of the products. A store can go beyond the utilitarian meaning of the space to go into the symbolic and incarnate the heart and savoir-faire of the brand; the store helps cultivate myths, the myth of the brand and the myth of luxury as a whole. The store provides *insight* into the personality and soul of the company. The stores help build the image of the brand and its legitimacy through storytelling. For this reason, the competition for retail space (which will be further discussed in the chapter on Omnichannel) is fierce as availability of store spaces for luxury brands is limited. Only the super-brands in the luxury business tend to successfully negotiate acquisition of real estate for their stores in the most sought-after places in the world: the Champs-Élysées in Paris, Madison Avenue in New York, Hong Kong International airport, the first-class cabins on the Emirates Airlines, from thousand-square-meter flagship stores to ground-floor entrances in the world's biggest malls. As a rule, it should be understood that position ranking is one of the most important parameters. Not only is it important in terms of retail store location, but also in terms of venue choice for events, placement for media coverage, and online inventory when it comes to digital strategy. Premium positioning implies high exposure, maximum traffic, and prestige. On average, retail spaces amount to about 35% of costs in the luxury industry; the high rent may be coupled with questionable profitability. For example, retail space on the Champs-Élysées, a tree-lined avenue with broad sidewalks that extends two kilometers from the Arc de Triomphe to the Place de la Concorde in Paris, can boast 300,000 window shoppers per day and commands up to 14,000 euros per square meter per year. Champs-Élysées was ranked as the fourth most expensive retail street in the world by Cushman & Wakefield, after Causeway Bay in Hong Kong, Upper Fifth Avenue in New York, and New Bond Street in London. Sightseers can be seen taking photos of the Louis Vuitton flagship store, and there is often a line of people waiting outside to browse the French fashion house's monogrammed bags and *prêt à porter* collections.

Publicity: Publicity plays an indispensable role in branding as one of the most important ways to influence public opinion, right after visual advertising. Publicity is also a very sophisticated tool to increase the visibility of the brand, to forge a relationship with the customer, and to reinforce the creative side of the brand. Publicity is a way to keep the aspiration high, such that the creator can communicate his or her vision in the long term. Thus, publicity is not only limited to the launch of a new product, but it can also be a reward for VIP clients, or linked with other cultural or social events. It is one of the most powerful ways to generate buzz and draw attention to the brands, especially in fashion, where every year the fashion weeks are the most important festivals for buyers, bloggers, and reporters, and the film festivals are the most important events for celebrities. Again, the competition is intense as influential brands can often get a free buzz when celebrities wear their goods, whereas smaller brands need to compete to sponsor the outfits of a star. For example, in the summer of 2014, Van Cleef & Arpels showed its collection of high jewelry with the fairytale theme "Peau d'Ane," which means "Donkey Skin," at Château de Chambord in the Loire valley. The French fairytale describes a princess who disguises herself with a donkey skin but in the end finds happiness with her Prince Charming. The French jewelry house created artistic images with gemstones that gave a twenty-first-century interpretation of their own art, expressed through exceptional stones and workmanship. It was like going back in history to discover the art, poetry, literature, and architecture of the early sixteenth century and of its place in nature. The event was complete with parakeets and owls clinging to the shoulders of masked courtiers parading on a terrace with fruit, flowers, and food; wine; and waiting staff dressed in Renaissance costumes like sweet princesses in silken dresses lit by jewels. There was a model of an enchanted forest, with a diamond barn hidden in emerald foliage; the chateau was recreated in diamonds circling a 39-carat Brazilian emerald. It was a rare event that had a combination of imagination and elegance far removed from the luxury world, which is more and more focused on celebrity, showmanship, and brand promotion. With no visible logos, the event transported guests to an enchanted world, while at the same time showcasing five centuries of the finest French traditions and, with a sweet simplicity, focusing on craftsmanship and skill.[1]

Pricing: Pricing is a delicate issue in the luxury business. Unlike FMCG, the demand for luxury goods is relatively inelastic. However, the information age and the growth story in emerging markets have brought democratization to the luxury industry. Consumers of today, compared to yesteryear, have far more knowledge of luxury brands. Consumers now are more price-sensitive and tend to pick the best buy. They have become more value-conscious. How to set the price is really an important paradox in the luxury business. The pricing strategy has to ensure that the price won't be so low that it dilutes the brand's image but also not so high as to lose the desired number of potential customers. For example, in the luxury business it is almost universally understood that the price always reflects the cost, but in some cases that may not be so at all. It can be wholly dependent on the aspiration of the customers. An interesting question to ponder might be how to decide on the price of the first growth of Chateaux Margaux. If Dom Pérignon is a vibrant, living, perpetually renewed brand that evokes Dom Pierre Pérignon, the spiritual father of champagne, and is only produced when the grapes are exactly right, in that case what is the price of a vintage Dom Pérignon?

Figure 4.1 depicts the differences between the *P*s of marketing in general brands versus luxury brands.

---

[1]Menkes, 2014.

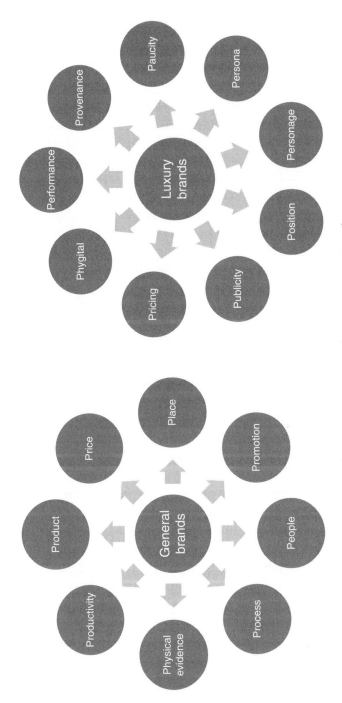

Figure 4.1   General Brands versus Luxury Brands

Cobranding: Does It Enhance Branding or Selling?

In the luxury world each brand is unique and has its own story to tell. A brand has its own image and personality. A brand can hardly imitate and/or copy the success of another brand. People have tried to replicate Harley Davidson—its free and rebellious lifestyle—but were unsuccessful. However, as lifestyles of the rich and famous converge, collaborations between brands are more commonplace. It seems as though it is possible to create some synergy between brands, either in branding impact or in sales performance. The questions remain for cobranding: who, what, and how? Whom does the brand choose to collaborate with? What objectives do brands have in mind for those collaborations? How has cobranding worked for both of the brands?

Some collaborations enhance the functional aspect to produce a superior product whereas others might enhance an image in a symbolic way. One of the most memorable functional cobranding examples is the Bugatti Veyron FBG Hermès supercar, created in 2008 through a brand partnership between supercar manufacturer Bugatti and luxury fashion house Hermès. This cobranding combined iconic Hermès styling with Bugatti's world-class engineering to create an extraordinary product. More recently, Bugatti and Jacob & Co.—a Swiss luxury watchmaker—released the Bugatti Chiron Tourbillion watche, which resembles a miniature, working mechanical model of the Twin Turbo Furious W16 engine and Epic X Chrono.

Examples of symbolic cobranding abound in the luxury industry. Symbolic cobranding enhances the brand image of one partner while it gives access to new markets and clientele for the other. Some iconic examples over the years have been with Adidas X Stella McCartney; Missioni X Target; Absolut Vodka X Swarovski; Givenchy X Nike; LV X Supreme; Rimova X Dior, and others.

Some collaborations are not directly linked to sales; the choice is more about lifestyle. For example, Martini developed a brand with Dolce & Gabbana, two brands that blend Italian tradition and modernity. The Bar Martini was the result.

Some collaborations result from personal relationships, or are simply unique. For example, Hermès did a collaboration with Yamaha at the time that one of the family members was the boss of Yamaha in France. The idea grew from a special order made to measure upholstery that

Hermès had been producing since the 1930s for planes, cars, and yachts. The collaboration was more of an exception, it seemed, as it was a limited series.

Some cobranding occurs at a more equal level to copromote the brands for the specific clientele of each brand. For example, BMW and Louis Vuitton collaborated on state-of-the-art luggage with green signature colors to complement the i8 sports car. This collaboration between premium automobile manufacturers and luxury brands is not something new. In the nineteenth century, when cars had become a status symbol for the rich, Louis Vuitton, which was the largest travel goods store, created durable luggage pieces that fit in with the automobiles of the time and made a bold statement while perched on the roof. The collaboration between BMW and LV reinforces the shared values of creativity, technological innovation, and style. It synergizes perfectly with the pure expression of the art of travel.

Some collaborations have clear business goals—to boost sales as well as brand awareness and brand perception, as is the case, for example, with fast fashion and designers. Today, these are the most common. Examples would be H&M's collaborations with Karl Lagerfeld, Stella McCartney, Viktor & Rolf, Roberto Cavalli, Comme des Garçons, Matthew Williamson, Balmain, Jimmy Choo, Marni, Versace, Maison Margiela, Alexander Wang, and Lanvin. These collaborations have won H&M enormous attention, reestablishing it as one of the leaders in the world of fast fashion. Their collaborations won back many lost fashion fans and also regained the favor of the fashion press and bloggers. The Vuitton X Supreme collaboration stirred new interest in 2017 after Vuitton sent a summons to Supreme in 2000 for misappropriating their monogram on its skateboards. The American streetwear brand had to withdraw its collection from sale. Seventeen years later Supreme is a globally renowned streetwear brand, a statutory symbol of cool, hip-hop, and rarity, and worshipped like a cult. They created an entire line, much more than the usual capsule collection for collaborations. Following in the footsteps of the masterful collaboration between LV and Supreme, after its acquisition by LVMH, Rimova frantically established agreements with Supreme, Anti Social Club, Off-White, Bape, 032C, United Arrows of Japan, Nasaseasons, Solebox, Fendi, and others. Consequently, Rimova upped its ante over the span of three years.

It seems from the above discussion that collaborations achieve different objectives for the partners. For brands each cobranding project is a one-time affair. For the luxury brand collaborations of this nature cannot be too frequent. With such collaborations, the brands can harness the power of the mass market through this mode. But the brands need to maintain their rarity, their paucity. Larger fast fashion brands like H&M differentiated themselves against intense competition by trading-up by working with respected designers and luxury brands. It may be that the benefits of cobranding are differentiation in a crowded market and the attention these collaborations draw. Furthermore, luxury brands get exposed for a very brief period of time in 5,000 H&M stores worldwide, a boost to their awareness drive.

Brand Extensions Brand extension is the art of using a brand's image and proficiency in one area and stretching it to another area or an entirely new range of products. This use of an existing brand in a new product or service category is a central growth driver for luxury brands. It is essential for their business models, since most of them offer a wide range of products, most often including fashion apparel, accessories, cosmetics, luggage, jewelry, watches, and sometimes cell phones, ski helmets, furniture, and bicycles. Had brands not been extending themselves, Hermès would still be making only saddles and Burberry would still be specialising in trench coats. On the other hand, there are two paradoxes within the framework of brand extensions in the luxury business. First, extensions imply some movement away from the original product, which has such a well-established history. So, the new product has to be an innovation or product extension—or related in some way to the history of the brand. In the luxury business it is risky, though, to move too far away from the history of the brand. Second, brand extension implies expansion and more products, which is contrary to scarcity. One can argue that the brand's exclusivity will be maintained within the product category by increasing its uniqueness or, alternatively, by appealing more to the mass market.

Luxury brands have extended their segments with relative ease due to their trading-down capacity. Brands such as Louis Vuitton, Gucci, and Chanel have expanded beyond their core business and offer a wide range of products, including fashion apparel, accessories, bags, watches, or jewelry. Some manufacturers of luxury products—for brands such as Armani, Bulgari, Versace, and LVMH Group through its Cheval Blanc—offer hotels and services under their brand. Although Armani began as a brand in the fashion industry, its offerings and sub-brands range from books, flowers, furniture, and chocolates to restaurants, bars, and spas. Through cobranding, other brands—such as Prada, D&G, Armani, Hugo Boss—have even offered mobile telephones. Dior's mobile phone venture was not successful. With these types of extension, luxury brands need to differentiate from their non-luxury counterparts. If not, their aspirational value will no longer be preserved. As discussed before, the trade-off between accessibility and exclusivity thus becomes a fundamental strategic challenge, which is particularly relevant in the context of brand extensions and growth strategies.

Other than growth strategies, brands agree to extensions in order to evolve from a luxury brand to a lifestyle brand. It is also a way to gain a bigger share of the pie. However, not all such extensions are received positively by consumers. French couturier Pierre Cardin, who passed away in 2020 at the age of 98, was the master of extensions. For instance, in 1980, Cardin lent his name to pens, lighters, cigarettes, baseball caps, shoes, lingerie, blouses, wallets, belts, perfume, foods, industrial design, real estate, entertainment, frying pans, alarm clocks, cassette tapes, chocolates, more recently Android tablets, and even flowers. Ultimately, he sold some 800 licenses in more than 140 countries on five continents. By the mid-1980s, he had a network of licensees paying him royalties of 5–12%, a stream of income that earned him the unofficial title "the Napoleon of licensors." "I was born an artiste," he told *The New York Times* in 1987, "but I am a businessman." This didn't bother him. "I wash with my own soap," he once boasted, "I wear my own perfume, go to bed with my own sheets, have my own food products. I live on me." He even had his initials, PC, etched into rolls of toilet paper, and was the inspiration for a phallus-like perfume flask.[2] Clearly, this led to brand dilution and heavy losses, but Cardin was not concerned. It was because of him that, decades later, Armani could dream of chocolates, Gucci of sunglasses, and Bulgari of its hotels.

---

[2] https://www.businessoffashion.com/news/news-analysis/pierre-cardin-dies-at-98.

Given that so many brand extension initiatives fail, it is imperative to ensure that some basic conditions are met. First and foremost, the brand must benefit from a heavy premium. The brand should be considered one of the leaders in its area of expertise. The more revered the brand, the more it can extend. On the other hand, if the extension does not work out, brand dilution is much higher in the case of a super-premium brand than of a premium brand. One has to think of brand building and not brand milking. Second, the core of the brand should be protected. In other words, brand extension is risky if the extension moves too far from the brand's DNA. Adjacency and coherence are preconditions for successful brand extension; which is to say, the extension must be in line with the values personified by the basic brand. For instance, Cartier's expansion into high jewelry was in line with its basic portfolio of luxury watches and rings. Their customers needed little mental effort to correlate watches with jewelry. This close adjacency was therefore a profitable venture for Cartier. An example of a failed venture is when Hermès launched a lighter about 30 years ago. It was made by ST Dupont with some leather art created by Hermès. It did not workout. The quality was not there because the leather could easily be torn off. Maybe the creation was not strong enough, or maybe the coherence of style and quality was missing. It was basically a Dupont lighter with some leather. This was repeated when Hermès collaborated with Apple Watch. Discussion boards asked the same question(s): Is Apple watch Hermès worth it? It was the Apple design with a bit of leather as the strap.

Brand extensions can be envisaged in a variety of ways. For example, Ansoff's grid, a two-by-two matrix, gives an idea of how extensions can be implemented (Table 4.1).

Table 4.1 Ansoff's Matrix for Growth

	Current Product (Exploitation)	**New Product (Exploration)**
Current Market	Market penetration (Manage)	Product development (Incremental)
New Market	Market development (Capsule)	Diversification (Boldest)

When the product and the market remain the same it is necessary to penetrate the market. For example, Berluti extended from leather shoes to menswear and, to penetrate the market, opened four stores in Paris. Within the matrix, Berluti not only sought to sell more shoes but also wanted to produce more new products through brand extensions in menswear. They tried to increase their sales by increasing the frequency of purchases. Similarly, Dior and LV extended into high jewelry after 2005. Now they are trying to tap the markets of the 2020s with more product development. Gucci, Bottega Veneta, Ralph Lauren, and Prada have all extended their lines from clothes to jewelry, handbags, shoes, sunglasses, and others. For Bottega Veneta, though accessories remain the core proposition, the brand has re-contextualized its signature "intrecciato" (basket-woven) leather goods, situating those bags in a wardrobe complete with shoes, ready-to-wear, and jewelry. "With Daniel's arrival, we moved from a single product to a silhouette, and an attitude," commented Bartolomeo Rongone. "The financial results are a consequence of that vision." Daniel Lee's breakout item in incremental innovation has been "the Pouch," a clutch in pillowy cinched leather sans a solitary strap from which to dangle it. Lee's designs have been sufficiently eye-catching to carry a show, but when taken product-by-product feature no shortage of eminently wearable, saleable items. His vision: sleek yet tactile, minimal but warm, with novelty products that nonetheless maintain a strong connection to the house's existing codes, giving Bottega the jumpstart it needed. "His vision is not only bold, it's immediate and pure." Bottega Veneta returned to growth, as reported in 2020, with sales rising 2.2% to nearly €1.2 billion, excluding currency shifts.[3]

Hermès is the only brand that has still not extended to sunglasses. But it has extended to cosmetics and fragrances. The luxury brands that entered new markets in Asia with their current product are still in the market development phase in some countries, while creating awareness about their products in the minds of regional customers. For example, geographic expansion of Armani in the Middle East and Asia has led it to extend into nightclubs, cafés, and restaurants. Hermès' extension as Sang Xia in China is an example of diversification with a new product idea suited to the Chinese market.

---

[3]https://www.businessoffashion.com/articles/luxury/bottega-veneta-ceo-bartolomeo-rongone-interview-kering-daniel-lee.

In the luxury world, both vertical and horizontal brand extensions are common within the stronger brands. However, with the slowdown of the global market, many brands have returned to increasing the desirability and turnover of existing stores. Product extension has gone far beyond the original frontier: Vuitton has stepped into high jewelry to enhance its luxury image, Armani has gone into house deco to express its lifestyle image, Guerlain has opened its own restaurant right under its flagship store on the Champs-Élysées, and developed teas representing its perfumes. Hermès has added a stationery corner in its store on the Rive Gauche. The frontier between each métier has blurred, with new products for highly demanding customers, most of whom are difficult to satisfy. Product diversification has become a key in brand extension.

Storytelling: Culture, Event, and Communication

During the 1960s, the world of communication changed and post-production marketing came into action. Marketing communicated the brand's presence: its personality and DNA. Luxury brands became the combination of a great offering with fantastic communication. The offers from luxury brands were limited series, craftsmanship, and strong artistic vision—and a product that doesn't exactly fulfill a market or a need. And therefore, the market was created. It was visually recognizable and expressed a journey, an environment, a universe that was coherent with the brand. The offer was an iconic product with fantastic quality.

With time, markets expanded and the luxury industry globalized their brand stories, which needed to be communicated to a diverse clientele across nations. From here on the story of the brand was at the heart of brand-building exercises, making a brand into a globally renowned luxury brand. It was about the unique history, the heritage, and the cultural roots of the brand, which could not be replicated by another brand.

The dilemma for brands was to decide which stories to communicate and which not. Should they express their uniqueness or their differences? Comparing products within a luxury brand category has very little meaning, as we have discussed before. The story that essentially can be communicated is based on cultural roots: the codes are different and this difference has to be understood through semiotics. What needed to be communicated was what differentiated a Berluti pair of shoes from Louis Vuitton's or Christian Dior's. Or the difference between Tom Ford's sunglasses and Moncler's. Here the consumer point of view was necessary, but the brand needed to educate and guide the consumer. For example, Chanel can be identified by its well-preserved code of using tweed or the symbol of the camellia flower: the "offering" had its codes and those codes were not changeable. Krug champagne's brand portrays the dream of a man who wants to give the best to his clients every year, rather than wait for a good year. This was the story that the brand needed to communicate as it was the reason for Krug's existence. On the other hand, Chanel is involved in multiple foundations, especially involving children, but they don't communicate this. In fact, very few even know about it.

The storytelling is also about cultural heritage. Chanel is a master-storyteller in this regard. The interesting part of this discourse is the balance between reinvention of the thoughts of Gabrielle Chanel and the interpretations of Karl Lagerfeld. It's always about playing these two facets: knowing how to balance them, where to expose them, who to expose to what, and not to communicate in a way that suggests any conflict between the two images. An interesting story concerns Chanel No. 5. The perfume placed Chanel so that No. 5, while hugely successful, was perceived as being only for mature women. Chanel wanted to attract a younger audience. The management decided to shift the way women had always thought about it: instead of talking about "My No. 5," they decided to focus on seduction, because women want to be seductive, and to actually have a man who would talk about Chanel No. 5. The idea in itself was very powerful, but the way it was executed, with Brad Pitt as the celebrity spokesman, boomeranged. This broke too many rules in one go and directly affected sales of No. 5. They had to backtrack and that's why they revived the myth of Marilyn Monroe, to go back to the roots of the perfume.

When Chanel launched the face cream, Le Weekend, they had a story to tell. Due to the complex world of beauty and the variety of cultural heritages of women from different countries, a simple story that could be understood by women universally was needed. Chanel created a differentiating and creative viewpoint on what beauty and skin care, and in particular facial skin care, are about. Thus, they developed a range of facial skin care for the day called Le matin and for the night called Le soir. Le matin would make the skin more radiant for the day and ready for makeup. Le soir is more for nourishing the skin and calming during the night. The creams feel different, smell different, and have different ingredient profiles. Chanel's innovation was to say, in effect, "Six days a week it's good to have a morning–night routine, but once a week, give your face a special treatment." The weekend (not in the literal sense) is one day of the week, whichever day one wants, for something that deeply cleanses and replenishes the skin; hence, Le Weekend. Chanel developed a completely new routine, which was basically the equivalent of what Clinique had done in 1968, when it launched its three-step series. The story needed to be told this way because this is what women sought.

To promote the aforementioned stories of luxury brands events requires an important outlet. A shop is a very good place to talk about a story, as a one-to-one relationship occurs in a controlled environment. Fabulous single-brand stores are apparently one effective way to display the history, emotion, and the dream factor of the brand. However, it is costly and difficult to open stores all over the world. Luxury brands tend to leverage on art and cultural elements to express the aesthetic and time-less value of their products. The short film Odysée of Cartier was a huge hit on YouTube, the exposition Miss Dior has seen unprecedented success in each stop in big cities over the world, and the biography of Coco Chanel has inspired countless women. Examples of events abound. Some of them are Louis Vuitton with VIP Maison openings, events at Johnny Walker house in Shanghai, events at the Martel pop-up cognac bar in Hong Kong International Airport, events at the Hennessy shop at Heath-row, and Burberry's events at Kean. The events were essentially taking away the very marketing aspect of the luxury house while injecting interaction or a creative angle to the business of reaching their elite customers. It was a way to rebalance the commercial aspect with a more cultural dimension. It also explains why so many houses have collaborations with artists, art galleries, and art events. Notable are Gucci Film Foundation, The Fonda-tion Cartier for contemporary art, Le Cerc by Pernod Ricard in Asia, and others. In 2014, Fondation Louis Vuitton provided a permanent center for charities, centered around the promotion of contemporary arts both in France and internationally. Designed by Canadian-American archi-tect Frank Gehry to resemble a cloud of glass, the building resembles 12 curving sails made up of 3,600 glass panels in the Jardin d'Acclimatation, Paris. These types of collaboration are very tax efficient.

An example of an event that is widely communicated is the Biennale des Antiquaires in Jewelry in Paris. The Biennale collections, presented at the Biennale des Antiquaires in Paris, was a resounding demonstration of Cartier's ability to celebrate its creative flair and storytelling while mastering the highest and finest craftsmanship.

Similarly, with a theatrical, multimedia event and an immersive new flagship, Burberry underscored the importance of storytelling in its China market.

"I think [storytelling] is important globally, but in China it stops things from being [mere] products and starts to give it life. Everything has a story—your clothes, buildings, videos, music. I think it is important people go along with this journey, otherwise it becomes a faceless product," said Burberry's ex-CEO Christopher Bailey[4] following a multimedia, Broadway-like show—billed as an "immersive, theatrical journey through the Burberry world of music, heritage, product, and innovation"—that the British megabrand staged in Shanghai at one of the city's shipyards. He continued:

> It's all about touching people emotionally. Tonight language doesn't matter—no matter where you are from, when you do something properly, people respond to that. It always surprises me how many people discover Burberry through our music projects for example. It's important to keep innovating with your product and keep telling different stories with it. History and heritage are important to have as a foundation, but you have to build on top of that to keep it moving forward. Technology helps us do that. . . . It's about fashion, music, dance, technology, and innovation. . . . It's about inspiring people and making them have an experience, tonight and every day.

The Digital Paradox

The digital channel has long been a question mark for the luxury industry. It can be accessed by one and all at leisure, can be reached by the masses.

---

[4]"Christopher Bailey," business of fashion.com, www.businessoffashion.com/christopher-bailey.

This access gives wide scope for commoditization of the luxury goods industry. Information access from mass advertising in print media sought to achieve recognition of a brand by the 1 percent of the population who could actually afford the products. There was an inherent preselection with glossy magazines and elite newspapers, the journals where the luxury industry advertised. The remaining 99% of the campaign was to create awareness. But, with the growth of digital-savvy consumers, the digital channel can no longer be ignored—it transcends barriers. The growing popularity and dispersion of digitalization, in particular social media, is an attractive opportunity for luxury brands. But they have been slow to adopt and execute digital strategies.

The slow pace of digital adoption is inherent in the paradox between digitalization and luxury. First, luxury brands are built on tradition over time, whereas digital communication is a recent phenomenon. Second, luxury brand communication is usually constant and harps substantially on the brand's identity and DNA, whereas digital communication is dynamic and ever-changing. Third, luxury brands are typically reserved for the elite, whereas the Internet is extremely democratic, especially with respect to social media. And finally, luxury brands exert firm control of all aspects of their communication, unlike social media and the Internet, which are flexible and, particularly in the case of social media, largely dependent on user engagement and contribution.

Though the paradox exists, the current geo-economic shift from the USA–Europe–Japan triad to the emerging economies of China, Brazil, Russia, India, South Africa, and other nations has witnessed the rise of dominant luxury consumers from these regions. The consumption habits of this clientele are new and also expected to evolve over time. The arrival of new wealth centers that are redefining the profile of the luxury consumer offers opportunities. It also brings new challenges, chiefly catering to a dynamic nomadic class that carries its own value systems while traveling and shopping. The emerging middle class is increasingly Internet savvy. Its denizens are mobile; they use tablets and smartphones to search and research their interests before they actually buy. This behavior has led to far-reaching implications for the distribution of luxury goods.

Given their age, location, and the era in which these consumers grew up, it is perhaps not surprising that this generation of luxury clientele is incredibly tech-savvy. According to a recent study the average global penetration rate for smartphone usage is roughly 15%. However, in countries like South Korea, where smartphone saturation is highest (67% of the 50 million residents have smartphones), or in Brazil, where social media has been adopted by luxury consumers on an order of magnitude that dwarfs rates in first-world countries, it is no surprise that brands have started to leverage this obvious opportunity. Among other emerging markets, clearly the Chinese rank as the world's largest Internet population and continue to adopt and adapt to new technology at a staggering rate, with over 720 million users online by the end of 2013. China's most popular microblogging site, Sina Weibo—long considered the biggest name in the Chinese Twitterverse with a reported 500 million registered users—has new competition in the latest iteration in micro-blogging, WeChat (Weixin), which is expected to overtake Weibo in the near future. With such a reach in such a vast geographic spread, it is difficult to locate high-net-worth individuals. It is like searching for a needle in a haystack!

After initial hesitation, even luxury companies from Italy and France—considered to be laggards in terms of web adoption—have come to embrace the opportunity to engage hundreds of millions of potential new customers via smartphones and tablets. Digital is not as easy as it seems. If done badly, without a concerted strategy, the internet's democratizing effect can have adverse effects that erode the aura of exclusivity which the brand has preserved for generations. Soul-searching is needed to find the right communication strategy and social media platforms that will appeal to prospective consumers. The digital strategy needs to be authentic, experiential, and relevant to mobile consumers. Burberry, Gucci, and Ralph Lauren are the three frontrunners in this strategy. Their digital campaigns are discrete yet effective. Burberry's digitalization is part of their brand's culture and is communicated from the inside out. Gucci is ahead in e-commerce. Ralph Lauren is always the first to market with the most innovative ideas. Louis Vuitton is quickly catching up, with a proactive and consistent digital strategy, focusing their communication on the art of travel.

As the Internet—and the mobile Internet in particular—is the fastest growing channel of retailing, there will be a tectonic shift from brick-and-mortar retail to online retail, which the luxury purveyors cannot totally escape from. As sales of smartphones and computer tablets have surged globally, it's a different way to shop. The younger generation is more at ease with screens than with people. It is low-touch luxury and its footprint is having a major impact on the way people shop.

The Phygital Dilemma: The world is constantly changing and so is the luxury industry. It started with e-commerce challenges at the beginning of the decade. The most recent disruption, caused by the ongoing global pandemic, has forced the luxury industry to quickly adapt and push their digital implementation efforts to the next level. The fast creation and establishment of a seamless integration between offline and online channels are inevitable in order to be successful in today's luxury industry, in which most brands face more than ever the difficulty of managing the luxury paradox: being timeless, legitimate, and exclusive on the one hand as well as being modern, democratic, and innovative on the other hand. This balancing act, which represents a successfully connecting bridge between the two sides of the paradox, is here to stay in order to reach young, fashionable, and affluent consumers around the globe, who consequently can generate sales and strongly drive business growth and profitability in the highly competitive global environment.

On the one hand, digital technology is a means to attract a wider consumer base. On the other hand, there is the risk of cannibalizing brick-and-mortar sales, encouraging discount activity, and fueling online counterfeits. It was estimated that 80% of brands sold online using the Hermès label were fakes, for example.

Luxury branding may not be enough to capture new generations of consumers anymore. Millennials and Gen Z want more than just the product: they want to encounter the product and experience it, both inside the store and outside, in the digital world. Thus, movies, streaming real-time fashion shows, mini-We Chat engagements, interactive screens, apps, mirrors, augmented reality, games, snapchat moments, storytelling podcasts, AI-enabled chatbots, social retail, and scannable QR codes are being embraced by brands as never before. Brands use modern art, screens, and anything that raises the aspirational level to get customers into the shop. Buying a product is about taking part even virtually in this glamour. But one has to balance the bricks (the physical stores) with the clicks (the online experience).

Luxury revenues are about 5% of the world's sales of products. Whether luxury companies should want to tap into the 95% is questionable. But it is imperative to create awareness of these new groups of multicultural, multimarket consumers. Studies have revealed that about 94% of ultra-affluent consumers find out about products through digital technology and online information. Luxury merchants need to stay relevant and close to their customers, say by offering apps for mobile phones, a capacity that has become an imperative rather than an option.

For example, Burberry represents a heritage brand which started implementing digital solutions early on, but their recent phygital boutique—an interactive and immersive shop, the so-called "social retail" store in Shenzhen China—has transformed shopping and showcases their pioneering spirit in the area of phygital innovation. Ricardo Tisci, Burberry's CCO, sees customers' behavior on social media as a magic key for the design of future retail outlets: "Our social retail concept is just the next step in giving our community a truly personal, luxury experience. What I find so exciting is the ability [for our customers] to experience the Burberry world both physically and digitally." Burberry's reopened its London flagship store. It brought to life the company's digital experience, allowing customers to connect to the boutique through numerous interactive devices. This connectivity helped to create an individual, customized experience. During the opening of the store, products were seen floating around the place, attached to golden helium-filled balloons. Full-length screens were turned into mirrors. Some items had chips attached that, when placed near a screen, initiated a presentation giving information about the product, including catwalk footage. There were no tills, just good-looking staff wandering about with iPads. This being London, and Burberry being famous for its trench coats, from time to time there was even a "digital rain shower."

The growth of mobile shopping through clicks means that luxury brands are working harder to get people into their brick-and-mortar stores. In addition to opening new flagship stores across cities, Louis Vuitton, Hugo Boss, and Gucci have also launched mobile sites. Similarly, some brands have quickly realized the importance of the digital space and have become leaders in digital media across the world: notably, Ralph Lauren, Tory Burch, Estée Lauder, and Coach, as well as large brands such as Gucci, Louis Vuitton, Cartier—and, to a lesser extent, Celine, Dior, and Chanel.

Discussion

The COVID-19 pandemic has proved that digitalization is now a necessity. It provides more engagement by first creating an open space for people to express and exchange their personal information, and then pushing the story toward the consumer. In the luxury universe, the desire to know and to talk about luxury brands and products is strong. With social media, consumers have now unprecedented access to information about the brands and products, and have almost full freedom to express their feelings and comments on them. It caters to a large audience instantaneously. No one has to queue for hours to see the latest collection of Louis Vuitton or Chanel. Consumers can check their favorite brands on their computers, tablets, or mobile phones—anywhere, anytime that they want to. They can go back to check and recheck before they make a decision. A girl from the most remote country can have access to the Fashion Week catwalk through online video, just like any front-row celebrity. Targeting can be reasonably accurate to increase the number of potential customers with the demographic data that is available on the different social media platforms and with the interest of searches and visits. Likeminded consumers can be identified and reached with the same needs and interests through billions of small network circles. It is time-independent, unlike other channels such as print media.

Conclusion

The world of luxury branding comprises multiple paradoxes. It is a place where tradition and creativity find common ground. Where ancient founders, recent artistic directors, savvy managers, and models meet and make magic together.

The key is building a dream. What makes the dream is the connection between brand and consumer. Consumers are ready to pay a premium because they love the brand and the experience. And when people love the brand, that is magic. If you try to do it fast, though, you destroy the dream: there is no fast track to luxury.

Building a brand takes time, resources and patience. Stakeholders are impatient; they want results every quarter—focusing both on growth and profitability.
This is how impoverished artisans, through sheer innovation and attention to quality, rise to become emperors of incredible fortunes.

Adam Smith spoke about the four necessities of production as land, labor, capital, and entrepreneurship. Karl Marx spoke about Labor as the most important factor. Capitalism spoke about squeezing Labor for maximizing output. Luxury respects craftsmanship and thus can justify the price of the product.

When one understands that comprehension of history is what helps in the quest for self-knowledge, then one's reason for existence and one's values, which are timeless, have to be in line with the vision of the founder. There is always a tension between the past and the future. It is this tension, this contrast, that allows luxury products to continually innovate while respecting their roots. But the tension is absolutely necessary: the day it ceases, and a brand is no longer inspired by its roots, the brand starts on a free-fall.

Luxury needs to feed on people's experiences, their stories, made elsewhere, so it can understand the world better, expand a brand's vision, and innovate. Luxury is not an exclusive 'members only' club with a bouncer at the door; there is no need to have been born into this world to have access to it.

Some brands will never sell in great volume, but this is a desirable characteristic. As soon as one wants to include one product in the totality of the brand, it takes time, money, work, people, image, and resources. If one does not succeed, it is better to stop than to continue doing things that are not in line with the brand and can therefore damage its image. To manage *coherence* is the most difficult thing in the world, because everything that hurts the image hurts the business. Without coherence the brand loses its *raison-d'etre*.

The more desirable the brand becomes, the more it sells, but the more it sells, the less desirable it becomes!

Figure 4.2 summarizes the discussion of some of the differences in luxury brands' branding principles.

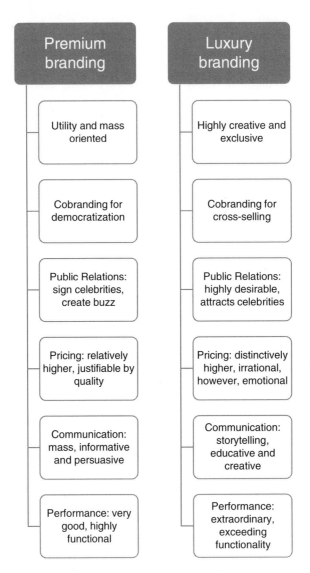

Figure 4.2   Differences in Branding Principles of Luxury Brands and Premium Brands

Chapter 5

Brand Identity, Ethos, Clients

*T*he young child walks with halting, hesitant steps as the grandfather walks slowly beside him, watching and encouraging.

Both are out for a stroll in a park adjacent to the Avenue des Champs-Élysées, just a few steps away from the luxury meccas of Avenue Montaigne and Rue du Faubourg-Saint-Honoré.

On Sundays in this park, there is a puppet show, the last Guignol, and the grandfather and grandson find seats on a front-row bench.

Guignol hits the thief on the head and the child bursts out laughing as the grandfather smiles. What is he thinking? He certainly is not thinking about luxury, which means nothing to him in this precious moment when he is simply enjoying life, this warm intimacy between two beings who are enjoying each other's company without the encumbrance of wondering why. Guignol has finished. The grandfather and grandchild wander toward the merry-go-round.

Then the child speaks. He has seen and understood. His view is pure, simple, and direct.

He doesn't like the person in front of him, a "poorly dressed" woman.

He dislikes the color of the horse, an old faded gray, an ugly color!

This, too, is luxury, the observation of a child who reacts spontaneously without forethought, without constraint, the look of a child who guides the creator as closely as possible to simplicity, reality, a truth often in disguise.

The grandfather knows this perfectly well: The child's view is the key to luxury.

Brand Identity

Brand identity is about the *raison d'être* of a product: how it is perceived by consumers and by competitors, what it stands for, what makes it unique, the promise it offers, and the value it holds for its customers. A brand's identity embodies its history, savoir-faire, and mystique. It is the sum of constitutive parts that make us recognize it as special and original. For luxury brands, the core of their identity is strongly correlated with the consumer's perception of the brand as having value and a timeless essence. This core is not easily alterable and does not change regularly. These intrinsic values are what make a brand unique, valuable, rare, and difficult to imitate. They also have cultural representations, not only because of their roots, but also because of their historical customers, their likes and dislikes, the archetype of aspiration, and how they perceive the brand when they have used it for a certain amount of time. For example, in the words of Jean Paul Gaultier, "The nirvana of Hermès is Hermès! I like to twist their centuries-old codes a little and put in some Gaultier. For my first collection, I designed a leather corset with clasps reminiscent of the Kelly bag."

Through the ages, brands have been built with strong cultural connotations. This is because culture integrates an accumulation of shared meanings, rituals, norms, and traditions among the members of society. In this way, luxury brands determine the overall desire a consumer feels toward different activities, narratives, products, and archetypes or aspirations. A luxury brand's identity is closely linked to the narratives that derive from a context and a subject. While the narratives of context can be linked to time, place, lifestyle, founder, or group, the narratives of subject are linked to character archetypes, know-how, or material used as craft or component. For example, Burberry has been related to the trench coat used in England, Rolex is associated with sports, perseverance, and time, Hermès evokes saddles and leather interiors, and Louis Vuitton brings to mind connotations of luggage and travel.

I love playing with classic things to make them new. The Vuitton monogram is an icon, over a hundred years old, but it's still something you can play with and make new.
—Marc Jacobs, former chief designer of Louis Vuitton

In this case, Louis Vuitton is a symbol of wealth, freedom, and travel. Travel implies a journey taken by a traveler who seeks to discover herself, others, and the world, to learn about the meaning of life. Louis Vuitton represents a rich French heritage, wealth, success, craftsmanship, quality, travel, timelessness, precision, and innovation. In all these descriptions, what stands out is the "art of travel."

Brands have been defined in many ways. Pirate ships raised flags on their masts with a threatening and terrifying symbol of death. Their victims fled or surrendered. In recent times, brands are built collectively: messages are sent through social media, advertisements—digital and physical—public relations events, news articles, product designs, and customer experiences. So, how is a luxury brand different from other iconic brands?

Most luxury brands have been built over time with either a person, a product, a symbol, an organization, or a mix of one or more of these factors as the frame of reference. This is because the elements and patterns are what allow us to differentiate the identity via image clarity and enrichment. For example, a person might be Coco Chanel, Ralph Lauren, or Yves Saint Laurent. A product could suggest associations such as product scope, product-related attributes, quality, value, a link to a country or region—Swiss watches or perfume from France, or a place like Avenue Montaigne or Rive Gauche in Paris. A symbol could be the double-C logo of Chanel. An iconic product resembling the brand could be the travel trunk of LV, 2.55 leather bag of Cartier, the Kelly bag of Hermès, the little black dress from Chanel, or the saddle bag, the bar suit from Dior, the Burberry trench, the Gucci loafers or Bamboo bags, and so much more. As an organization, it focuses on the culture and style of top management within the organization rather than on the specific attributes of the product, as is evident in the cosmetics industry, for example, L'Oréal and Estée Lauder.

Building and growing a luxury brand depends on managing some key paradoxes. The first paradox is to manage the *timelessness* and *modernity* of a brand. The second paradox is the trade-off between *exclusivity* and *accessibility*. The third paradox is to increase *brand awareness, brand mystery*, and *brand likeness*, then manage them all together. The fourth paradox is to balance between *aesthetics* and *economic value*. The fifth is to maintain the *brand's identity from its historic roots while identifying the social, cultural, political, and economic trends of new and emerging markets*. The sixth paradox is to manage coherence and singularity between all the touch-points, be it digital or physical—the phygital paradox. The following quote depicts some key aspects of the paradoxes:

> *I'm not a fashion person. I'm anti-fashion. I don't like to be part of the world. It's too transient. I have never been influenced by it. I'm interested in longevity, timelessness, style—not fashion.*
> **—Ralph Lauren, founder of Ralph Lauren**

Many authors have tried to classify and present brand identity with different frameworks in order to explain the meaning that the brand depicts and how they manage these paradoxes. For example, Jean-Noel Kapferer developed a six-sided prism to demonstrate the six aspects of brand identity: *physique* (physical appearance), *personality* (inner source), *culture* (the roots of the brand and how they are communicated), *relationship* (between the brand and its consumers), *reflection* (how the brand is perceived by its consumers), and *self-image* (how consumers feel wearing/owning the brand). These six sides are grouped with pictures of sender, receiver, externalization, and internalization.[1] Here the term *competitors* takes a back seat as the luxury brand focuses on telling its story, be it anecdotal (from real life), as for Coco Chanel and René Lacoste, or fictional (invented from scratch), as for Ralph Lauren. These stories

---

[1] Kapferer and Bastien, 2012

create identity and consumer relationships. Figure 5.1 depicts Chanel's brand identity prism.

As depicted in its brand identity, Chanel embodies the strong woman who has climbed the social ladder. This was Gabrielle Chanel's story. Her modest origins, and the fact that she reached the pinnacle of society at a time when most women did not have a prestigious career, is part of the brand's identity. To express this core identity, Chanel's retail locations worldwide have majestic staircases, usually in white, symbolizing their founder's upward social mobility. Chanel also freed women from their corsets. Her idea was to dress women who favored convenience, comfort, and style. Doing so, she started a revolution by completely changing the code of women's dressing. The historical context of World War I may have favored this revolution, as well as Gabrielle Chanel's personality. In these post–World War conditions, women were working and needed to feel comfortable in what they wore. To this day, Chanel's style remains chic but convenient. The eternal classic of the Chanel suit is an example of elegance and comfort. Another important symbol of Chanel's Pantheon is the use of black and white. In terms of symbols, black is a symbol of masculinity, whereas white represents femininity. Gabrielle Chanel was a pioneer, by mixing masculine and feminine qualities, since the entire twentieth century was about mixing up and playing with feminine and

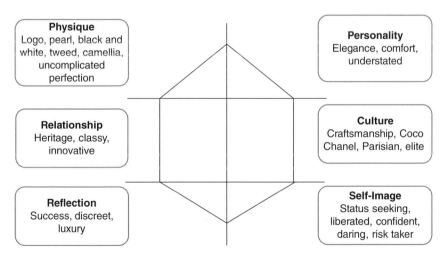

Figure 5.1 Chanel's Brand Identity Prism

masculine characteristics and stereotypes, in fashion and in social behavior in general. Again, returning to her roots, Gabrielle Chanel personified a mix of traits traditionally attributed to men and women—her strength and will to attain a higher rank in society, and her general attitude as an independent and self-confident woman. Many pictures portray her sitting on a staircase. Chanel clients are usually women who identify with these symbols of strength and success. They are in charge. They are successful and powerful, or that is what they aspire to. This is in line with the image of Chanel women as seen in advertisement campaigns. The Chanel woman always looks like she knows who she is and she gets what she wants. The symbol behind this representation is the queen. She is a powerful woman who seems confident, unafraid, free, respected, a risk-taker who is adventurous, successful, intellectually innovative, and elitist. Her posture shows strength and confidence. That is who Coco Chanel was, or wanted to be seen as, and this is the identity Chanel's clients share. The key challenge for luxury brands like Chanel is therefore to maintain this identity, one which was created decades before. Together with maintaining identity brands have to be relevant, desirable, and inspirational in today's socio cultural climate. A brand also has to be exclusive, while at the same time accessible, in order to achieve sales growth. Achieving growth in traditional markets, while expanding into new markets, entails exporting the brand's DNA across cultures, recruiting new clients while maintaining the traditional aesthetics and thereby creating economic value. Figure 5.2 portrays the brand–customer–employee (BCE) triangle.

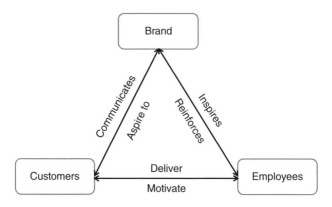

Figure 5.2   Brand–Customer–Employee (BCE) Triangle

While managing the above paradoxes, another key word that represents core identity is that of brand *nirvana*. Regarding American brands, Ralph Lauren's values—for example—include longevity, style, East Coast culture, the Bostonian dream, American heritage, the American dream, and timelessness. Amid them, the brand nirvana, or core proposition, of Ralph Lauren is the "Bostonian dream." In the same spirit, brand characteristics of Coach include young, fun-loving, stylish, independent, cute and colorful, interactive, open, public, responsive, and trendy. The brand nirvana for Coach is "Let me be free" and "New York dream," which is based on the value of "fun" and "cool." The brand identity of Coach strongly transmits their heritage: they are different because the brand originates from Madison Avenue in Manhattan, New York. What matters to them is the fact that they are distinguished by their uniqueness and coolness. In the same spirit, for Stanley Marcus, founder of Neiman Marcus, which filed for bankruptcy during the pandemic, there was a right customer for every piece of merchandise, and it was the retailer's prerogative to bring the two together and prevent a mismatch. The brand values that Neiman Marcus aspired to are distinguished service, right service, professionalism, expertise, chicness, high taste, customer satisfaction, insatiable curiosity, and passion. The brand nirvana of Neiman Marcus was "the right service." Thus, the real offer of Neiman Marcus was to help the customer make the right choice.

Luxury brands also play with the paradox of alternative images, such as masculinity–femininity. Within this framework of diverse brand identity the luxury product prides itself on being unique, the expression of a creative identity, of the intrinsic passion of a creator.

> *The image is born of itself, not of surveys showing where there might be a niche or a business opportunity, but in the very spontaneous identity of the creator, their background and their idiosyncrasies.*[2]

For example, both Chanel and Armani seek to be masculine and feminine at the same time. Coco Chanel freed women from their corsets, a symbol of confinement and restriction, by offering new, spirited designs. She was innovative and intellectual, but simultaneously she argued that a girl should be both classy and fabulous. She did not speak

---

[2] Kapferer and Bastien, 2009.

of masculinity. Armani, on the other hand, has the personality of a professional who is sophisticated, rich, free, classy, athletic, and successful. Moreover, the brand Armani, like Giorgio Armani himself, embodies a person who is successful in his or her life and pursues personal desires, such as dreams, adventure, and love. Armani projects the image of a smart professional who knows what he or she wants in life.

Marketing professionals calculate a brand's value by isolating the net additional cash flows created by the brand. These additional cash flows are the result of customers' willingness to buy from one brand over another, even when the other brand is cheaper. The hallmark of competitive theory is the premise that the beliefs and bonds created over time in consumers' minds, through marketing, are the key differentiator. So, customer equity is in fact financial equity. Brands have financial value because they have created intangible assets in the minds and hearts of their employees, customers, distributors, subscribers, and opinion leaders. These assets are brand awareness, beliefs of exclusivity and superiority of some valued benefit, and emotional bonding. This links back to the brand identity, referred to as the brand DNA circle, depicted in Figure 5.3.

Ethos

Now that we have a better understanding of the nature and function of brand identity, in this section we will cover what distinguishes luxury goods from other product categories. Luxury goods do not cater to primary needs. This means that they are "non-essential." Production and distribution therefore heavily depend on a company's capacity to create desire for luxury goods by instilling a dream around the product that appeals to the consumer. Creation of "the dream" is strongly linked to the manner in which the brand DNA is marketed and communicated, so as to put forth a unique and unforgettable brand identity. When the market was local, in France or in Italy, this was easy, but with the globalization of markets today, the dream has to cross borders and cultures. Different cultures dream differently, though, and their aspirations vary. Storytelling has, as a result, been a key enabler for the dream factor. A brand's story is built on its ethos, which is in fact the myth, the history of the brand.

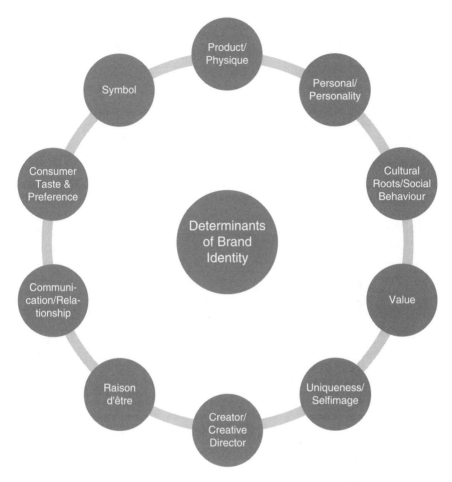

Figure 5.3   Brand DNA Circle

A classic example of this is the tagline of DeBeers, which stated way back in 1947 that "A diamond is forever. How else could two months' salary last forever?" It persists after 70 years. It was written by copywriter Mary Frances Gerety at Philadelphia agency N.W. Ayer, which made it one of the best campaigns of the twentieth century. The advertisement invented the modern concept of the engagement ring and the diamond's relationship with love and marriage. Another example of storytelling is that of the intimate history of Marilyn Monroe and the perfume Chanel No. 5. Chanel enticed consumers with a two-and-a-half-minute video featuring photographs of Marilyn Monroe as she appeared in *Life* magazine and *Modern Screen* magazine in the early 1950s, and her famous quote about wearing only Chanel No. 5 to bed. J'Adore, the perfume from Dior, tells the story of its creation in the short film *Le Parfum*. It emphasizes the story that the perfume was created from flowers around the world, combining the scents of Damask rose, Arabian jasmine, and Indian tuberose, while the glass bottles are blown in Murano, Italy.

A brand's ethos can also be communicated by the story of its origins, its founder, and the identity of the brand over time. When the founder creates a brand with his or her name, their character, understanding, beliefs, aesthetics, interests, and their attitudes form the ethos of the brand. For example, Louis Vuitton still insists that its ethos is represented by rolling luggage, crafted in leather and bearing the trademark LV motif, although the brand has developed many extensions, such as adventure products, fashion, accessories, and others. The ethos, though still true to the core, communicates differently with different meanings to its potentially different individual owners. For some, like the Indian bride, it may represent a very high-value gift that she receives on her wedding; to the Japanese, it may mean a well-made, functional, convenient travel accessory; and, to still others, it may appear to be an overpriced and unnecessary suitcase.[3]

When the founder is still alive, as in the case of Ralph Lauren or Giorgio Armani, brands reflect the ethos of their founders and owners. But as brands evolve, or are bought by conglomerates—as happened to Givenchy, Guerlain, Chaumet, Dior, Van Cleef & Arpel, among others—this may no longer be the case. The ethos remains the same as it reflects the brand's core identity, but new creative directors may introduce some new ideals. They can modify the brand's legitimate territory, as with Gucci before and after the years of Tom Ford and Domenico De Sole.

Let's now discuss the ethos of Yves Saint Laurent (YSL). YSL is historically known as one of the greatest French fashion houses. Yves Saint Laurent and his partner, Pierre Bergé, founded his eponymous brand in 1962. Saint Laurent revolutionized the fashion industry with such iconic creations as "Le Smoking," the safari jacket, and the beatnik look. In 1966, he democratized the industry by creating his first ready-to-wear

---

[3]Berthon et al., "Aesthetics and Ephemerality," 2009.

line, Rive Gauche. Throughout the 1970s and 1980s, the famed fashion house enjoyed success. Historically, YSL was known as a haute couture and ready-to-wear brand. Yves Saint Laurent enjoyed the company of women and was often surrounded by female artists. He was inspired by muses such as Loulou de la Falaise, an aristocrat model and designer; Betty Catroux, a socialite and daughter of a diplomat; and Catherine Deneuve, the iconic French actress. This was not a coincidence. The Saint Laurent woman was seductive and possessed an artistic sense. She was unconventional and challenged the rules. This is what the Saint-Germain Rive Gauche spirit was about. On the seduction side, the woman was sophisticated and fascinating. She played games, pretending to be innocent. Saint Laurent had created a tuxedo for women and some other feminine interpretations of masculine pieces like the blazer or the safari jacket. The archetype of this woman was the mistress, Parisian chic and unconventional.

However, in the 1990s the brand was sold to the pharmaceutical company, Sanofi, and later to the Gucci Group. While Saint Laurent continued to design for the haute couture house, Tom Ford took over the design responsibilities for Rive Gauche, where he infused the brand with his own personal "porno chic" aesthetic, ultimately making the brand unrecognizable to YSL loyalists. By 2002, Saint Laurent's personal problems overshadowed his ability to design and his haute couture house was eventually closed, leaving only Rive Gauche in the hands of Gucci Group. In 2004, Tom Ford left Gucci Group and his protégé at YSL, Stefano Pilati, took over as designer of the Rive Gauche collection. It started by announcing in 2010 the opening of a new three-story flagship store on Avenue Montaigne, located in the Golden Triangle of Paris, next door to the world-famous Christian Dior flagship store. Since Ford's departure, the brand has focused on returning to the roots of the brand and for many years did not engage in retail expansion.

The brand has also extended further into higher margin products, including leather goods, accessories, and cosmetics. Although YSL has strayed from its roots in ready-to-wear, the brand has made investments into product categories that drive profits while maintaining the brand's identity. Under Pilati the brand has returned to its roots, its ethos as a trendsetter and tastemaker, and has produced some popular items, such as the Muse handbag and the Tribute shoe, which could be compared to historical YSL icons such as "Le Smoking" and the safari jacket.

In 2011, Yves Saint Laurent Couture decided to change its brand name from the iconic Yves Saint Laurent, that everyone in the industry called YSL, to Saint Laurent Paris. This decision was made by Hedi Slimane when he was appointed as the creative director in 2012. The new name was supposed to restore "the house to its truth, purity, and essence as well as to take it into a new era." It was true that Yves Saint Laurent had not been profitable for years, since Pierre Bergé and Yves Saint Laurent sold the brand. Some may have wondered if the brand ethos needed rejuvenation. Instantaneously, criticism and anger were generated by the decision and it seemed that the designer had touched a sore spot, something sacred to fashion-house lovers. It soon became clear that the name Yves Saint Laurent is part of the brand's ethos. This was no surprise to anyone familiar with the brand, who knew how much the brand was the expression of its founder's personality. The reaction of certain loyal clients was so violent that they created a logo expressing their hatred of the new name. A name which was no longer visible; it had probably been erased by the brand. In 2016, Hedi Slimane (currently at Celine) left Saint Laurent. His successor, Belgian national Anthony Vaccarello, was appointed as creative director. Francesca Bellettini, President and CEO of Yves Saint Laurent, declared: ". . . Anthony Vaccarello's modern, pure aesthetic is the perfect fit for the maison. He impeccably balances elements of provocative femininity and sharp masculinity in his silhouettes. He is the natural choice to express the essence of Yves Saint Laurent. I am enthusiastic about embarking on a new era with Anthony Vaccarello, and together bringing the maison further success."[4] François-Henri Pinault, chairman and CEO of Kering, added: " . . . (at 36), I am very proud to welcome such a vivid and young force among today's creative fashion talents to Yves Saint Laurent. . . ." It is interesting to note that the name was changed back to YSL. This vignette demonstrates how valuable a brand name (and its ethos) is to its loyal clients.

The example of YSL shows that a brand's ethos is powerful as the tool that allows potential customers to project themselves into the

---

[4]https://www.kering.com/en/news/yves-saint-laurent-appoints-anthony-vaccarello-as-creative-director.

universe that is a label's legacy. That universe is nothing other than all the ingredients that make up the identity. The intricate weaving of identity threads, such as the founders, the creator, the era when the brand was born, its place of origin, its *savoir faire* and expertise, its original customers—is what they sell. It is not the product alone, but the brand's ethos. In summary, ethos is not intrinsically visible to the consumer. It is not a color, texture, shape, or size. It cannot be experienced through the five senses. Thus, for clients, especially new clients from new markets, today luxury brands need to redefine and communicate their aesthetic, using visible elements, so that consumers can recognize and feel the ethos.

The financial results of Kering in 2020[5] revealed that YSL's turnover had risen to €2.05 bn, from €500 mn in 2013. That growth had been achieved while almost doubling operating margins, from 13.8% in 2013 to 27% in 2019. It became the second star brand for Kering, after Gucci, which was €9.63 bn in 2020, just before the pandemic.

Clients

The previous section covered the importance of brand identity and the ethos of luxury brands. This section explores how these factors relate to the consumer. Once a brand has established its existence, potential clients can identify themselves with the brand and ultimately become loyal consumers.

Luxury consumption is not a rational decision. Here emotion takes precedence over reason: a brand's personality and essence create allure and entice consumers to abandon rationality and succumb to their desires. Yet, in a time when brands must manage the contradiction between maintaining exclusivity and growing their businesses through accessibility, the question of how a brand can lure its clientele takes precedence.

The published literature has come up with several typologies of consumers of the luxury industry, based on categorization. Categorization here is about the "haves/rich" and "have nots/poor" in one continuum and "status seekers/public" and "non-status seekers/private" in the other continuum. Figure 5.4 provides a snapshot of the different types of consumer.

---

[5]https://www.ft.com/content/7d7c7f3e-4cc4-11ea-95a0-43d18ec715f5.

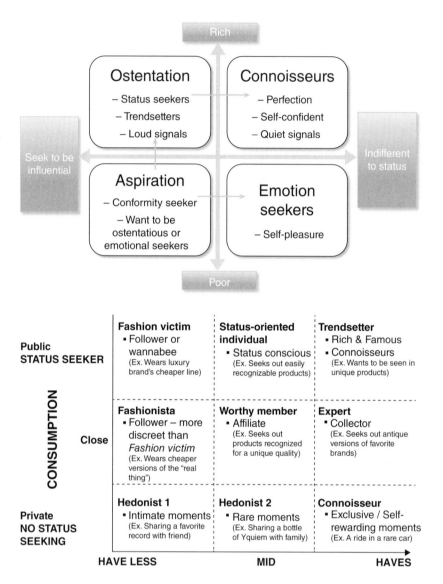

Figure 5.4   Different Types of Consumer

The nature of the consumer: Keeping in mind the involvement of consumers in luxury purchases and their motives for purchase, researchers have tried to classify different segments as haves/have-lesses and status-seeking. For example, *luxury hedonists* are not status seekers; they are usually young people who are successful and thus optimistic about life. They are pleasure seekers and like to live king-size, combining travel with active social lives. They like to be up-to-date on the latest trends and love to spend on themselves in a guilt-free way. They use luxury brands as a way to express themselves to the world, as they have varied interests. They are fond of brands such as Marc Jacobs, D&G, Michael Kors, and others. The next group can be classified as *the traditional ones*—the loyalists, the fashionistas, and the worthy members— who are mature, mostly male, and are of an older age group (for example, Japanese consumers). These are the *aspirational consumers* who like spending on themselves. Their purchases are driven by the need for quality and timelessness in their lives. They don't constantly monitor the media for information on luxury items. They find out about luxury brands and trends more through word of mouth. The *luxury experts, the connoisseurs,* are the richest and the most educated (for example, French and Italian consumers). Highly creative and discerning, this segment is characterized by their openness. They are open to new people, new cultures, and new ideas. For them, luxury has to be discreet in nature, not flamboyant. Paying close attention to products, they value superior quality and exquisite craftsmanship. They are not driven to purchase luxury products as a status symbol. They prefer natural products, such as organic. They tend to purchase brands such as Hermès, Chanel, and Bentley. The next segments are the *ostentatious, status-oriented individuals* who are also trendsetters (for example, Chinese consumers). They are relatively financially constrained, they save to spend, thus sometimes finding it hard to meet all their luxury cravings. They wish to travel abroad and shop. Highly fashionable, women and men in this segment are very sensitive about the brands and the logos that they display. Consumers in this segment are health conscious and spend a lot of time grooming themselves. They prefer brands such as Armani, Gucci, Prada, BMW, and so on.

The luxury consumer may be classified on the basis of characteristics such as (1) tastes and preferences and (2) nature of wealth.

1. **Tastes and preferences:** Consumers may be divided into categories such as the traditional luxury consumer (the elitists, the connoisseurs, who believe in established brands such as Hermès or Rolex) and the democrats or the "new luxury consumers" who would have no qualms in accepting new brands if they were more satisfactory. These consumers know exactly what they want and are unwilling to settle for anything less in the name of tradition. They feel luxury should be available to all and thus they spearhead the democratization of luxury.

2. **Nature of wealth:** Being rich is not the primary source of consumption of luxury goods. Time is the key factor. Here, time is not to be understood as a unit of measure, but rather that of the longevity of wealth. For example, those who became wealthy in the twentieth century (professional actors, sports personalities, and entrepreneurs) have different consumption patterns from those who have newly acquired wealth through hardship. In the same light, those who have inherited wealth have different consumption patterns from salary-earning executives and other working professionals.

These different types of customer have evolved over the past few years. For example, a consumer may no longer be a brand loyalist, wearing products from the same brand from head to toe. She may have become more discerning when selecting the products she wears. There has also been a convergence in terms of dressing. Women of different ages can today dress similarly. The old have ways of looking younger and, irrespective of their age, everyone has started looking very similar. The following characteristics paint a portrait of today's luxury consumers:

- **Sharp:** well-traveled, familiar with different cultures, and intellectually sound. They are more aware of the minute differences between products. They are well-informed about product characteristics. They understand the difference between genuine branding exercises and marketing gimmicks and question the price premium that brands charge, refusing to pay a price that products don't seem to be worth. For instance, LVMH has been trying hard to sell its Dior and Tag Heuer watches in India. Most customers who bought watches abroad felt models were not launched in time and were more expensive in India. Thus, LVMH and other luxury brands, despite not breaking in India even after a decade, are pushing hard to cater to the potentially huge Indian market, which is sharp about comparing prices worldwide.

- **Influential:** In the early days of luxury, the quantity of consumers outweighed luxury brands. This led to brands having leverage over the consumer. Given that competition among luxury brands has intensified, power has now shifted to the consumer. Switching costs have also decreased, as each brand has undergone extensions. Consumers have greater options between products, brands, payment methods, and channels of purchase.

- **Unique:** Today's consumers know themselves and know what they want. Each woman is her own fashion designer. She uses her own mind and doesn't blindly follow what brands throw at her. She is bold enough to mix Chanel with Gucci and streetwear with luxury. She understands that people who don't know her gauge her from her clothes. So, she ensures that her purchases suit her personality.

- **Demanding:** They want perfect quality, impeccable service, and superior craftsmanship. They are not willing to settle for anything less than the best. They crave customization and expect foresight from fashion brands, that the brands will understand their fashion needs before they spell them out. They want creativity and authenticity from a brand. Their demanding nature can be illustrated by the rising market for custom-made luxury products, wherein each item is hand-picked by the consumer. Companies like Tiffany's and Rolex are catering to this clientele with custom-made watches.

- **Attention span:** The need to be trendy propels consumers to replace clothes, shoes, and accessories frequently. Brands also launch new products regularly, which encourages consumers to replace their wardrobes accordingly.

- **Ethical / Sustainable:** They want brands that are socially conscious. They are not willing to wear shoes that are made by children in a developing country. They do not want to wear clothing that has been made in an environmentally unfriendly fashion. They like to associate themselves with brands that invest in social causes. They also like it when brands share their values with them. For instance, a female consumer of this segment would purchase Viva Glam lipstick to support the fight against AIDS in addition to enjoying a fashionable lipstick.

Discussion

Having segmented luxury consumers on the basis of their involvement and preferences, we must not forget that luxury spending also has a cultural element. Culture has an effect both in terms of the kinds of consumer (the demand side) and the kinds of brand produced by the country (the supply side). Each country stands for a certain ethos: French tradition, German practicality, Italian style, Japanese passion—all are well-established traits. On the basis of the nature of the people in a nation, luxury products evolve in the same way. When people buy a certain luxury brand, they also buy the culture that the brand belongs to. Consumers buying Hermès buy a little bit of France and those buying Burberry a little bit of Britain, while those buying Ralph Lauren buy the American dream. For example, in the automobile industry, cars such as Ferrari, Lamborghini, Maserati, have cutting-edge design and the most modern technology. It is no coincidence that all these cars are Italian. Cars such as Porsche, BMW, and Mercedes epitomize quality, efficiency, and comfort. These are all German brands. Jaguar (now owned by Tata Motors, a part of the Indian conglomerate of TATA Group), Bentley, and Rolls Royce all speak of British traditions and lifestyles.

It is a fact that consumers from different cultures have their own specific modes of behavior. Though the brands might sell the same product, the buying behavior differs from culture to culture, be it the brands they purchase or the way they use luxury items. For instance, one can try to recognize the nationality of a person from the way they wear their jewelry. French women have an understated style as they are always worried about looking vulgar or out of place. Italians look for motion, and like decorative pieces that flow. German women buy their jewelry from their own salaries. Thus, when they wear jewels, there is an aura of pride. They sport solid pieces of bold jewelry with ease. Indians are famous for consuming gold as jewelry, not only during weddings but in their daily lives. In the perfume segment, the way perfumes sell in

France is entirely different from the way they sell in Japan and now in China. This is probably due to the fact that the Japanese have a greater focus on natural scents. Perfume is considered unhealthy for babies in Japan, propelling new mothers to eschew fragrances. Only very under-stated perfumes do well in Japan. Strong perfumes sell heavily in other parts of the world, especially the Middle East and North America. The new evolving market for perfume is China. With the rise of female con-sciousness in recent years, perfume has become a tool for independent Chinese women wanting to express and pamper themselves. At the same time, Chinese male consumers have also been leaning toward perfume to showcase their taste and sophistication.[6] In conclusion, though the product might be the same, the way it sells in different parts of the world might be different. This has bearing on the pricing.

Pricing of Luxury Goods

Economics suggests that as prices increase the demand curve slopes downwards. The quantity demanded decreases. In contrast to traditional demand-based marketing, luxury is supply-based: the product comes first. Depending on the style and quality of the product, one sets the price based on market perception and the amount of time, resources, and related costs it took to produce the product. The more it is perceived by the client to be a luxury, the higher the price it can fetch. Thus, luxury economics is counterintuitive. Luxury goods are known to experience the Veblen effect, wherein rising prices fuel demand for the product.

A recent study, undertaken by a group of researchers, revealed that the four main factors that influence the price of luxury goods are: cost of the goods sold, perceived customer value, predecessor prices, and com-petitor prices. It also revealed that more than half of the price-setting decisions among luxury brands are informed by the cost of manufac-ture and the product's previous prices. Twenty percent are set because of competitor price levels and just a third are given a level according to their perceived consumer value. In this study, managers at luxury goods companies believe that in the consumer's eye, price ranks fourth in order

---

[6]https://jingdaily.com/bvlgari-allegra-perfume-china-jackson-yee/.

of importance after brand/image, quality, and design. The study in some way illustrates the rationale of pricing issues in the luxury world.

In a counterintuitive sense, perceived customer value is the main reason consumers tend to pay a relatively higher price for a luxury item compared to the functional utility that they derive from it. The symbolic or aesthetic utility to the price ratio is considerably higher for luxury goods than the utility value of the good. It means that consumers derive status satisfaction, or are able to express their own style through luxury consumption, which is worth more than the price they paid.

Apart from the above mentioned conditions, what makes the pricing of luxury brands exceptional is the secrecy, the heritage, and the image associated with them. Very few luxury brands would openly proclaim the price of a luxury item that they are selling, though they closely follow their competitor's pricing as a benchmark. For example, when Bottega Veneta makes bags using the softest and most supple leather imaginable, the buyer doesn't care about the price the company quotes for this ultra-luxury product. The price, from the point of view of the customer, is not as relevant as the situational utility he or she derives from it.

Having said that, price should not be completely ignored. Veblen effects are real, but only up to a certain price point, when price elasticity may come into play. Price elasticity of demand is defined as the responsiveness of the quantity demanded to change in price. This could mean the quantity demanded could rise, fall, or remain unaffected by a rise in price. The elasticity coefficient could be negative, positive, or zero (Figure 5.5). When the elasticity is negative, companies launch new products or extend their product lines to boost demand and thereby

Figure 5.5   Brands and Price Elasticity

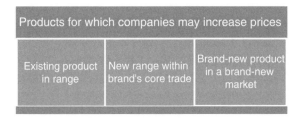

Figure 5.6   Types of Product That Have Price Increases

growth. At zero elasticity, price has no effect on demand. At positive elasticity, companies are better off to increase the price over time, which implies that with a rise in price, demand has also risen (Figure 5.6).

Traditional companies try to achieve economies of scale and cut down costs and hence choose prices to propel demand. Such companies also want to increase the number of consumers within their ambit by competing on price. Luxury companies, on the other hand, try to push prices up over time. They want to increase the number of "wealthy" consumers within their ambit.

In the past couple of years luxury brands have elevated their prices by about 10% at least once, and usually twice a year. This is becoming a trend, and with this trend the luxury brands no longer seek to justify their price increases to the extent that they did before. Increasing the price of an existing product without justifying why may not be acceptable to traditional customers. The Veblen effect does not apply in this case. Clarifying to the client the reason for the increase is always a good idea. For instance, established luxury brands always clarify to their consumers if exchange rates are eating into their profit margin, or that they had to raise prices due to the closure of stores during the pandemic. In 2021, LV, Dior, Chanel, and others raised prices.

When launching a new range, the aim of the company is to "trade up," and not vulgarize the product. The motive is to increase the aspirational appeal associated with the brand. It is not to misuse the status symbol associated with it. Thus, it is a common phenomenon to launch a new range of products at a higher price point than the previous range. Also, consumers believe that the new range is more evolved than the previous one, and thus must cost more for the company to produce. In this way the company is able to justify the higher prices.

For instance, both Bulgari and Tiffany & Co. hiked prices to clearly communicate their luxury position by using a larger proportion of gold and diamonds in their products. The story remained the same. This trading-up in prices was correctly accompanied by a trading-up in preciousness.

When launching a new product in an absolutely unexplored market, it makes sense for the luxury brand to fix the price at the lower end and slowly increase it. This is done in order to increase the trial rate of the product, given that it is a completely unexplored market.

Having discussed elasticity and related aspects of pricing, we now move on to how companies manage pricing. There are two distinct ways in which companies price their products: supply-driven pricing and demand-driven pricing.

Supply-Driven Pricing

In this case, the company sets the price of a commodity as it deems fit. Consumers indicate only whether they want to pay this price or not. As fixing the price now demarcates the brand's price territory, the company's responsibility is to ensure that the price evolves correctly with the offer. Also, the company must ensure that it is able to set the global price of the product carefully, to minimize arbitrage and have a healthy profit margin.

The company may set global prices in two ways.

The first is a "cost-plus" strategy. Here, the differential between the prices of two countries is linked to the transport cost, customs, exchange rate fluctuations, and local distribution costs. Thus, each country has a different price, but the profit margin of the company is stabilized.

The second way to tackle this is by setting a high common global price. In this case, travel and distribution costs are considered to be too small to majorly affect the margin of the company. A common price closes all possibilities of price arbitrage.

Demand-Driven Pricing

In the earlier days of luxury, there used to be client-driven pricing. Giving one-time discounts and offers to win customers may be justified in this kind of pricing. Here the concept of yield management comes into play, wherein a one-off lowering of prices may be considered rational in order to spur a series of future purchases. A few things must be kept in mind by the brands: lower prices should not be at the cost of lower service quality; this will scar the brand name. Also, former customers should not feel cheated for having bought the product at a higher price, only to see others get the same product at a lower price. Demand-driven pricing means that the company should try to capture the entire consumer surplus (through differential pricing, capture the entire amount that the consumer is willing to pay). However, this should not be done at throwaway prices as a rule, as that will diminish brand goodwill. Figure 5.7 describes the logic of price premium.

Figure 5.7   Logic of Price Premium

Conclusion

In branding a product, there are a few important aspects to remember. Firstly, it must have great quality. People tend to forget the price, but not the quality. Secondly, there must be creativity; this ensures staying ahead of the game and further innovation. During innovation, every new improvement of the product is reinterpreted by the designer so that the product remains true to the DNA of the brand. It is almost impossible to please everyone. To be a successful brand, the designer is almost always not going to please someone.

Building a brand identity takes time. Nothing ever happens quickly in luxury. To build credibility, legitimacy, and authenticity takes a lifetime. The time invested in building the identity, clarifying the ethos, and being true to the clients is what is often missed by many. It is something that is not taken into account when one calculates sales using different pricing models. To make a brand well known is an art in and of itself. It is not a science. The meaning of the brand, and what it stands for, needs to be clarified both internally and externally. The codes need to be defined: the brand needs to know who it is, what it represents, and why it exists. One can buy an accessory and it is accessible. One can buy a little something and one belongs to a certain group. When a luxury product is extremely exclusive, people forget it. It needs to be present, in the right way with the right dimension, but to be present is not the function of price. People need to think that they potentially have access to the product and dream about it. This is why the world is changing and not everyone can be satisfied with the same dream. People dream differently. It takes a lot of time and courage to make people dream and yet do the right thing. Once people start dreaming, there is nothing to hide. This is when the codes become timeless and yet modern with a clear style. It takes ages before people really feel it. People associated with a brand feel it because it is seen all the time, but for onlookers to feel it, it takes much more time.

That is why the use of story is perhaps the best way to convey a brand's identity and ethos to its clients. This is perhaps what people want most: the stories of today, the anecdotes, stories of people who are connected and who share experiences. People don't forget. If one speaks about a brand and associates it with an important experience from one's life, people will remember it much better than if one merely explains the product to them. At the end of the day, the most important thing is that people enjoy it.

Part II

LUXURY MANAGEMENT
AND MARKETS

Chapter 6

Family-Run Houses, Corporatization, and New Entrants

Forty years ago, the luxury industry was completely dominated by family-run businesses in France. These families knew each other, and their habits followed the same protocols. They would spend summers together in Monte Carlo and winters in Zermatt. They worked at Place Vendôme, Rue du Faubourg-Saint-Honoré, or Avenue Montaigne.

It was the natural order of things. French luxury families were known and well-established. And their customers were confident in them.

The House of Chaumet jewelers and watchmakers was the first family to rock the boat. Luxury was turned on its head. What was it that began this change? Cavalry? Shady dealings? In the 1980s, the Chaumet brothers started down a path without knowing its course or where their journey would end. Confidence collapsed. Customers preferred to say nothing, abandoning their treasures to fraud and bankruptcy, so as not to risk a scandal and to be able to return to anonymity. But it weighed heavily upon them. The family jewels had slipped into an unpredictable torrent. Grandmother's diamond had been sold twice, with the emerald going along for the ride. In short, there was no public scandal, but the discreet and felt-lined world of luxury took a major hit.

The world of luxury had been shaken, and the field had already been more broadly undermined.

The nephews, cousins, brothers, and sisters of luxury company families had had enough of seeing their parents or their uncle living high on the hog while they, as second-in-line, were left behind, since the rule was very simple: no dividends!

When income was limited all around, they made do, but as their hunger grew with the profits, the "bosses" had acquired a taste for privilege and benefits. Luxury was for them—and no one else—in the family.

True, some room was made for a cousin here or a brother there who was growing a little too impatient, but they were paid "triflings."

And then came the avalanche. Businesses revived and strengthened and families that previously were merely comfortable became truly wealthy. And families then began to fall apart.

Some sold off quickly under pressure from some shrewd gluttons who could see the luxury wave coming, while a few others resisted, and still others died in despair.

In 20 years, every family in the luxury business disappeared from the scene: Boucheron, Guerlain, Chaumet, Lanvin, Fred, Kenzo, Givenchy, Gucci, Cartier, Arpels, Krug, Hennessy . . . Puiforcat, Canovas, Souleaïdo, Patou, and Vuitton—all sold.

The Taittingers sold Baccarat, le Crillon, le Martinez, Annick Goutal perfumes, Concorde hotels . . . the Bouilhets sold Christofle off very quickly to their cousin Borletti, who quickly resold it to the Chalhoubs . . . even Alexandre de Lur Saluces lost Château d'Yquem. The family that owned Cheval Blanc sold it to the Arnault Group.

Fortunately, there remained Pierre Frey, Hermès, Rothschild, Laurent-Perrier (the Nonancourts), Taillevent (the Gardiniers), Chanel (the Wertheimers), Rémy Cointreau (the Hériard Dubreuils), Michel

Guérard, Delisle, Roederer (the Rouzauds), Piper Heidseick, Weston, Bonpoint (the Descours), Chopard (the Scheufeles from Germany), Patek Philippe (the Sterns from Switzerland) and many others, of course, who are still luxury families.

In this highly disrupted landscape, a few major entities were formed: LVMH, Kering, Richemont, L'Oréal . . . and they picked up the pieces.

Many, however, died. Who remembers the wonderful Roger Faré, the most famous glovemaker of his time? Who remembers the incredible Draeger, the unrivaled printer? What remains of the images of Gelot, Jansen, Rouard, Paul Portes, Bianchini-Férier, Barroux, Leleu, Richard de Bas, Bagués, Jean Dessès, Jean Prud'homme . . . all famous in their day and today unknown!

The families remaining today are tightening their ranks, but there are so few of them in France, Italy, and the United States that they are regarded as survivors of the earthquake of planet luxury.

Will they hold up?

Over the past quarter-century, luxury sectors in Italy and France have faced transformations due to the evolution of the external environment and evolution of the family businesses in Europe. Family played an important role in the luxury goods industry as the industry historically began as small-scale family-owned companies, especially prior to World War II, when bonds of kinship were often more important than legal and regulatory institutions.

Before the 1990s, the luxury industry, particularly high fashion, consisted mostly of small privately owned companies, often run by the founder or their descendants. Many were poorly managed by conventional standards and suffered from the aftereffects of the cultural and social chaos of the 1960s, which had left the luxury business in a delicate situation. The 1980s brought new opportunities for the industry, including favorable demographics, a new socioeconomic climate, and breakthrough cultural trends. Through the constant growth in affluence, the collapse of traditional family structures, and lifestyle diversification, luxury became an extremely heterogeneous and individual phenomenon in the second half of the twentieth century.

With the advent of the twenty-first century and considerable changes, first in the development of the luxury goods industry and then in the economic world, many of these luxury companies have transformed themselves from closely held, small-scale family companies into larger-scale, family-controlled companies with various product categories, and/or into publicly listed companies run by a professional manager, or acquired into a brand portfolio under an international conglomerate group. It is fair to say that the industry has experienced a significant shift from a system of centralized family-based creative power to that of a more decentralized and delegated professionally managed structure.

At this point, the role of family in the luxury goods industry transformed from the founders and/or designers of the brand to the brand's identity and personality. A sort of *death of the author*. Progressively morphing from small-scale individual family-run companies to an international, multibillion-dollar industry, the family names of the men and women responsible for this transformation have become more familiar as brands than as individuals. Yet, as the modern industry has struggled to reconcile its artisanal heritage with today's public offering, it was the personal, family connection that bridged the gap.

In order to understand the clearly observable trends within this industry, we must now consider the different models that can better render integration strategies and the adopted practices that more effectively deliver results.

What Is a Family-Run Business?

Family-run businesses are the oldest and most common type of organization throughout history and across the world. They represent more than 70% of all companies in certain countries.

A family-run business is one where more than half of all shares belong to the members of one family. It can also be defined as a business that has passed from one generation to another, which includes family members from different related family units and may be across multiple generations.

In the luxury industry, family-run businesses once came in all sizes—from SMEs to big conglomerates that operated in various subsectors and countries (Figure 6.1).

But the majority of family businesses have had a very short life span; 95% of these businesses didn't survive after their third generation

Figure 6.1   Brands of Different Sizes

of owners. Extant literature suggests that successions were not well-prepared to integrate into the management and that there was a lack of the good governance structures needed to survive long-term.

Development Cycle of a Family Business

It has generally been observed that the corporate governance structures of family-run businesses vary with the stage of development and the family's ownership percentage. The initial structure of an organization, in cases when the founder of the company was running the business, will be different when the next generation takes over, which will be different again from that of a business wholly owned by the family. The evolution happens in three phases. First is the initial phase: all dimensions are decided by one family, by groups of families, or by the sole founder. Second is the growth phase: over time the company grows and transfers ownership to succeeding generations. Third is the maturity phase: the firm reaches maturity by renewing and recycling strategies and rejuvenating practices.

Characteristics of Family-Run Businesses

In the previous sections we saw that time is a crucial factor in the evolution of the family-run business, and that they face particular and unique challenges during these different phases. Family houses (businesses) are expected to uphold their *long-term focus and commitment*. In the luxury sector, strong commitment to the brand and delivering quality and service are a must. This is because the family name and legacy are borne by the products. The family name is, after all, one of the main reasons for the pride. It seems that families have a different long-term business focus from shareholders: they don't get caught up on quarterly targets. Instead, they make what they consider to be the decisions for the brand, the benefit of which might be realized only far into the future. Family houses also entail a type of *loyalty and commitment* from their employees, especially in the luxury sector. It has been observed that such businesses may experience lower turnover. They are considered to be more humane in the workplace; employees are most often treated as part of the extended family. There is a level of care and concern that is specific to the culture of this type of business approach. The turnover, however, might be higher among upper-level positions as there could be a "glass ceiling" for non-family members. Professional managers may only ever be able to reach a certain level at the top; there always remains a chance that the topmost spot will be occupied by a family member. For this reason, it may be difficult to attract highly professional talent. But it can also be argued that, though professional managers may feel intimidated, they will work closely with the owner of the company. Another perception might be that the final control rests with a family member who may strangle creativity and discourage diversity of opinions. But it has been observed that, when objectives are clarified, the luxury industry has witnessed great leadership from family members and also from professional managers. Chapter 7 further explores the people working for the luxury industry. Figure 6.2 provides a snapshot that suggests why luxury family houses were able to outshine the conglomerates up until the 1980s.

The luxury industry abounds with examples that explain why family firms failed to successfully maintain their business from generation to generation. Here are some reasons that may explain this phenomenon. With globalization and the rise of emerging markets the owner may have lacked *viability in the business* and could not *finance the growth options*. The owner either wanted to *exit* or died of old age; succession planning does not always work, perhaps due to *infighting* among siblings, cashing-in by family members, or the sheer *reluctance* of offspring to join the firm. Finally, the off-chance of the appointment of *incapable members* of the family destroyed the company's value. *Succession planning* has always been a key concern. Family members who are not at the helm want out or are

Commitment	• As there exists a connection with the business: emotional value attached to personal financial stake
Bureaucracy	• Bureaucracy levels in such a firm are lesser, thus leading to fewer complications
Stronger corporate culture	• This leads to a lower employee turnover
Alignment of interests	• Managerial and shareholder interests are aligned, thus leading to better management
Perpetuity of know-how	• Transmission of oral knowledge and competencies from one generation to the next
Trust and pride	• Pride associated with the family name • Trust within the family

Figure 6.2   Reasons Luxury Family Houses Lasted Until the 1980s

not comfortable discussing topics such as aging, death, and their financial affairs. Perhaps this is why, at a global aggregate level (more than 70%), family-owned businesses do not survive the transition from founder to second generation. Figure 6.3 provides a snapshot that suggests why luxury family houses were taken over by the conglomerates after the 1980s.

Luxury brands have historically been suppliers to royal families and other special clients.

> *A well-known artisan ("supplier to His Majesty") or a famous company (Saint-Gobain, makers of mirrors) were linked in a unique fashion to a trade, sometimes even to a single product (the Gobelin tapestries). This structure lasted until the Belle Époque, when Hermès was a saddler, Vuitton was a luggage and trunk-maker, Christofle a goldsmith, but began to experience profound change after the First World War. The big luxury houses began to manufacture or to put their name to things that they had not originally known how to make.*[1]

---

[1]"Kapferer and Bastien, 2012.

Figure 6.3 Reasons Luxury Family Houses Were Taken Over by Conglomerates After the 1980s

Overall, luxury family-owned businesses had a strong historical background that was deeply related to the culture in the region. The business ran for over half a century and became integrated into the heritage of the country. People were proud of their names.

The Evolution of the French Fashion Houses

In fashion, particularly high fashion, the evolution of the luxury industry is difficult to grasp. Departments of haute couture have always been true artisanal workshops. They have usually been completely separate from the rest of the business, both economically and geographically. Yet, without haute couture there would have only been, for the most part, a division of perfume and a division of ready-to-wear; at least until the 1990s. Haute couture has been both the origin and the facilitator for major developments in the luxury goods sectors. The financial investors who had bought the major luxury brands were less and less willing to finance the designers. The financial investors were not ready to accept the risk of failure linked to each collection. Since the late nineteenth century, a few key players, such as Guerlain (perfume) and Worth (haute couture), provoked a revolution in the French luxury goods sector and helped to change the interests of traditional consumers. A new definition of luxury thus emerged; the "arts of fashion" started to bloom. From then on, people started to display their wealth with new status symbols; the automobile, or via new identification factors such as perfume or clothes ("la mode"), are some such examples. After World War I, new names emerged: Chanel, Poiret, and Schiaparelli became symbols of the *art de vivre à la française* because they gave an industrial dimension to their creations.

The situation became bleak with the recession of 1929. However, a few companies such as Chanel managed to expand despite the economic downturn. Post–World War II, designers themselves became financiers, and that's when the luxury industry began to boom. By 1947, some designers—among them the couturier Lucien Lelong and perfumer Jacques Guerlain—founded the Comité Colbert. The foundation of the committee illustrated the changes triggered by the industrialization of the sector. Over the course of the next 50 years, more and more brands emerged, but the number of companies owning the brands decreased since several *groupes de luxe* appeared. Until the early 1970s, entrepreneurs in the sector changed from being creative designers and artists to establishing themselves as "industrials of luxury." This new concept sought to characterize the challenge of finding a balance between maintaining everything that luxury stands for (tradition, know-how, precious materials, scarcity, craftsmanship, authenticity, legitimacy, credibility, and others) and economic requirements ("industrial scale" production, focus on costs, economies of scale, etc.).

Fashion was the main beneficiary of economic growth during the 1930s. It marked the beginning of a new era, with various young designers following the example of successful companies like Chanel by founding their own fashion houses, often with the support of major entrepreneurs. The most famous examples are Christian Dior in 1947, Pierre Balmain in 1945, Hubert de Givenchy in 1953, Guy Laroche in 1957, and Andre Courreges in 1964. The large number of fashion houses (France had 106 haute couture houses in the late 1940s), the quality of the work, and the unwavering support of the international media were factors that contributed to the outstanding reputation of Parisian fashion. Moreover, after the economic crisis of the 1930s, and the scarcity of resources in the 1940s, demand for beautiful objects picked up significantly, which allowed for the success of prêt-à-porter and perfumes. The perfume sector was the first in the luxury industry to adopt mass production and to widen its distribution network to perfumeries and, later, also to airport shops. This led also to a certain trivialization and a greater accessibility of luxury products. The economic crisis of the early 1970s was a difficult period for luxury goods manufacturers: some houses that were already facing difficulties didn't manage to overcome them, especially in the light of the evolution of society, the emergence of new ways of life, and an increasing internationalization up to the end of the 1960s.

The economic situation of the luxury goods sector was very unstable throughout the 1970s and 1980s: many believed that luxury was synonymous with continuous growth and record dividends proved increasingly difficult. Several businessmen (Bernard Tapie, Alain Chevalier, and Henry Racamier) started to invest in the sector to create new groups. However, their attempts failed, often due to the high costs of development. In 1989, the merger of Louis Vuitton with Moét Hennessy—the first luxury conglomerate—gave birth to a new version of the industry. This event changed the luxury world and ushered in a movement of corporatization, acquisition, and expansion of family businesses within the fold of a conglomerate. At the end of the 1990s, Francois Pinault founded a similar group that became the main competitor of LVMH. During the same time Hermès started to diversify its operations. The group Vendôme (owned by the Richemont family), with its prestigious brands (Van Cleef & Arpels, Cartier, Piaget, Chloé, Lancel, Montblanc, and others), emerged as another major foreign competitor of the French luxury houses. By the end of 2002, 12 out of 77 members of the Comité Colbert belonged to LVMH. Over half of the members of this Comité belonged to luxury conglomerates. Witnessing the changes, in 1989 the president of the Comité Colbert defined the luxury goods industry as being "characterized by six factors: international perspective of the management, high-quality products, a strong and coherent image (often with a connotation of the *art de vivre*), accessibility for the grand public in terms of the prices, creativity and innovativeness and a perfectly chosen, controlled, and managed distribution."

The Evolution of Italian Brands

Italy has a notably long history of successful entrepreneurship across many sectors. In addition to fashion, art, literature, and music, Italians became known over the centuries for a wide range of excellent products—olive oil from Tuscany, cheese from Reggio Emilia, and vinegar from Modena, to name just a few. Entrepreneurs and their family enterprises have stood at the center of the Italian economy, which has greatly influenced Italians' view of business. Italian middle-sized companies have some similar characteristics across different sectors and industries. These common features show clearly how history has shaped this dynamic section of the Italian economy. Family-run businesses tend to focus on long-term goals and viability rather than short-term gains, because owners wish to pass their companies down to future generations. Yet a number of factors can hamper their economic growth and prevent them from focusing on innovation, anticipating market trends and producing high-quality goods. Many suffer from a lack of strategic vision among the founders, family members' inability to communicate effectively, excessive control by the entrepreneur, and conflicting opinions among family members on which direction the business should take.

The origins of a large part of the Italian Mittelstand can be found in many industrial districts scattered all over the country. They were entrepreneurs who started with small and medium-sized enterprises that concentrated mainly on textiles, clothing, furniture, and footwear businesses. These small entrepreneurs, who successfully coordinated the resources that were locally available to them and, if necessary, expanded by creating extensive distribution networks, are the genesis of many of today's medium-sized companies. A relevant example is the case of Della Valle group (internationally known through brands like Tod's), which emerged from the Marches shoemaking district. More or less the same conditions of entrepreneurial family-based organizations have fostered, during the 1960s and 1970s, the consolidation of the Benetton group, and later the creation of Diesel. These examples highlight the importance of the relationship between these mid-size corporations and their surroundings, especially that of local production systems as industrial districts.

Since the opening of the formerly highly regulated markets (during the Cold War era) and the proliferation of Asian-made products, as well as the introduction of the euro, Italian companies have been forced to change their strategies to catch up with their international competitors. Organizational changes were needed to adapt to the changing environment. The family organizations voted almost unanimously to integrate vertically so that they could control the complete value chain. The emerging organizational form favored a family controlling a large number of internationally scattered, independent productive units (frequently run through joint ventures with local entrepreneurs). The birth of these "pocket multinationals" was a consequence of a rational strategy aimed at the minimization of administrative and coordination costs. With this change to small to medium-sized corporations came a transformation of the entrepreneurial role. The transition from small workshop to structured enterprise generally was carried out by the second, and sometimes third, generation of the founder's family. Usually, the "younger generations" had a higher educational level than their predecessors, who had often received little formal schooling but compensated with intense commitment and attachment to their companies. The enlargement of the firm's boundaries, and the adoption of a relatively complex organizational structure, brought about a transformation of the decision-making process, which seemed to be much more participative than in the past, involving co-opted managers or professionals. The family, however, remained as in the past the main decision-making structure and influenced succession strategies. Familism[2] was, however, still a dominating feature, especially when succession strategies are considered.

After the terrorist attacks of September 11, 2001, Italian family businesses went through a difficult phase. Luxury family goods companies depended on tourists, particularly Asians, visiting Europe. However, the fallout from the dot-com boom, the events of 9/11, SARS in Asia, and the war in Iraq dented consumer confidence and decreased international travel, which came to a virtual stop with the health crisis of COVID-19 from 2020.

---

[2] Defined as the identification between the family and the enterprise and the consequent adaptation of the company's goals and strategies to the family's benefit.

By contrast, the financial and economic crisis in 2008 affected Italian luxury goods companies only slightly; those few companies that were present in different international markets recovered quickly from the downturn. Post-2008, Italian companies struggled with competitors in France. French firms dominated the luxury-goods industry, with 36% of the global market share.

From 2009–2020, the luxury industry witnessed an acquisition spree of Italy's family-run businesses. Many Italian family businesses—such as Bulgari, Brioni, Loro Piana, and others—were acquired by French conglomerates. But there still remained some robust independent family houses, such as Ermenegildo Zegna, Ferragamo, Luxottica, Moncler, Prada, Armani, Dolce & Gabbana, Tod's, and others. The main challenge for these family firms was to keep growing profitably to compete effectively. The growth needed to happen in terms of turnover and geographical expansion, especially in the Asia Pacific region, an area where the new generation of luxury customers was fast rising. They had to think of succession planning and the next strategy. They were all managed differently within complex organizational structures that had their own strengths and weaknesses and were perhaps impossible to generalize. Their key strength was in fact in the diversity of these management structures. Figure 6.4 depicts the key engines of growth for luxury houses.

The larger challenge in Italy was for the smaller family-owned companies with sales of US$20 million to US$40 million, trying to break into the US$200 million range. This type of expansion was traditionally done by relying on markets in the United States, Europe, and some mature Asian markets, such as Japan, through forging close links with department stores, distributors, and high-net-worth buyers. Entering markets in countries in the growing regions, such as the frontier markets of Asia-Pacific, Russia, and Latin America, was more complicated because they often lacked the consumer retail infrastructure. Additionally, the demand for Italian goods started to move away from ready-to-wear to leather goods to accessories. Some examples of family businesses are illustrated in the next section.

Prada　Prada was started in 1913 by Mario Prada. It began as a luxury store based in Galleria Vittorio Emmanuelle II in Milan, Italy. It started selling leather goods: handbags, trunks, and small leather accessories, as well as beauty cases and other articles of value. By 1919, the company's reputation had grown and it was known for its fine craftsmanship and exclusive design. It was appointed as official supplier to the Italian royal family.

After World War II, Mario Prada lost interest in his business, and the company continued without much happening. In 1958, Luisa Bianchi, Mario Prada's daughter, took over running the business. The company continued for another 20 years with little-to-no real success to talk about. Things started to turn around for the company when Luisa's daughter, Miuccia Bianchi Prada, took over the business in 1978.

In 1979, Miuccia partnered with Patrizio Bertelli, a leather goods manufacturer from Tuscany. Their business relationship evolved into a romantic one and they married in 1987. Together they built up Prada into a leather goods and accessories company. In 1993, they opened Miu Miu, a new brand that was an extension of Prada, which focused on women's fashion and accessories. Miuccia was the creative brain behind Prada and Patrizio headed the business side of the company. Patrizio built the company from a value of $25 million in 1991 to $750 million in 1997. Patrizio took advantage of the war for Gucci, taking place in the late 1990s, and sold Prada's 10% share in Gucci to LVMH for $140 million in 1999. Within six months of having sold the Gucci shares, Patrizio went about expanding the Prada group. He bought a stake in three different companies: Helmut Lang, Jill Sander, and Church and Co., thus creating a fully privately owned luxury group. Patrizio's overspending meant that by the 2000s the company had a growing debt, estimated at about $1.7 billion by November 2001, about the same as that year's revenues. To make matters worse, the CEO and the designer of Jill Sander both quit.

After this event, Prada started to prepare for its initial IPO. However, because of the terrorist attacks of September 11, 2001, this had to be put off. The group had to shed Jill Sander and Helmut Lang. Both companies were sold off and the group soldiered on. The company continued to grow, and later even acquired Car Shoe. It was finally listed on the Hong Kong stock exchange, after an IPO in June 2011, raising $2.14 billion. It was a much-needed financial injection for a company that, by this time, had acquired large debts. Despite the IPO, Prada was still managed as a family business: a majority of its shares were still family-held.

Its growth was slow, and it wasn't until Patrizio partnered with Miuccia that the company started to grow from a small family business that was draining family funds to one of the big players of today's luxury industry. It was strong enough not to fall into the category of a small family business in the luxury industry that either dwindled into nonexistence or was bought out by one of the large conglomerates. It continued to grow by focusing on acquisitions and strengthening the Prada brand; thus, Patrizio and Miuccia managed to build a leader in the luxury industry. What was key in the whole equation was the aggressive acquisition but also the focus on the cornerstone brand. The IPO in Hong Kong brought a much-needed capital injection into the group to help it continue to expand. The group was made up of Prada, Miu Miu, Car Shoe, Church's, and Pasticceria Marchesi, a Milanese pastry shop acquired in 2014. In 2019, just before the pandemic, the Prada brand was valued at approximately $4.8 billion. In 2020, Prada named the Belgian designer, Raf Simons, ex-Dior creative director, as their co-creative director. Prada reported a revenue of €3 billion in 2020. Since the onset of the pandemic, it reported an average drop of 40% but a strong rebound in China in 2021.

Salvatore Ferragamo   In the world of designer shoes, the brand Salvatore Ferragamo is a star. Mr. Salvatore Ferragamo became famous when he moved to Hollywood in the 1920s and made bespoke shoes for film stars. In 1923 he took over the Hollywood Boot Shop in California and was known as the "Shoemaker to the Stars." In 1927, he returned to Florence, the center of the Renaissance, and in 1936 bought the historical Palazzo Spini-Feroni and opened the first Ferragamo store. The company flourished after World War II, expanding its workforce to 700 craftsmen producing 350 pairs of handmade shoes a day. Salvatore Ferragamo died in 1960 at the age of 62. After his death, his wife Wanda, and later their six children (Fiamma, Giovanna, Fulvia, Ferruccio, Massimo, and Leonardo), ran the Ferragamo company and made his name live on as an international company.

The Ferragamo family was among the first to go to the Asian market. In 1986, it opened its first store in Hong Kong, an early expansion into the Oriental market. In 1998, Ferragamo licensed its eyewear line to Luxottica. In 2001, Ferragamo created and launched its first perfume.

In 2007, it licensed its watch line to Timex. And the year 2011 saw the launch of its first jewelry collection, in collaboration with Mr. Gianni Bulgari, grandson of the founder of Bulgari, and a renowned jewelry designer himself. The same year, the company was quoted for the first time on the Stock Exchange market in Italy, after its failed attempt in 2006. Now, the Ferragamo family has built a luxury fashion empire, released books, opened a museum, and branched out into hotels and restaurants. The opening of the Salvatore Ferragamo Museum in 1995, in the Spini Feroni Palace, the historic headquarters of the brand, is dedicated to the founder's history and his celebrated shoes, and is nowadays referred to alongside mentions of famous museums such as the Louvre of Paris and the Victoria and Albert of London.

Over the years, the brand had always been run by family members until 2006, when Michele Norsa was appointed CEO. Michele Norsa was the first CEO appointed from outside the Ferragamo family. He had over 35 years of experience as CEO of Italian family firms, in diverse sectors such as fashion (Benetton), publishing (Rizzoli), and luxury (Valentino). Norsa orchestrated the successful IPO for Ferragamo. He had done the same for Valentino before. Norsa used 22% of the company to open 25 stores, of which 10 were in China, thereby doubling its number of stores to 66. He also refurbished the flagship stores in world capitals, such as London and New York. In 2014, Ferragamo expanded its operations from luxury shoes, to bags, eyewear, silk accessories, watches, jewelry, perfume, and a ready-to-wear clothing line.

Along with Norsa, Massimiliano Giornetti, from the family, was named the chief creative director (CDD). Since the appointment of the creative director and chief executive, the brand has made a significant effort to expand its business globally. Michele Norsa left the company in 2016 and became Vice Chairman of a rival company Missoni. In 2018, Paul Andrew was appointed as the brand's creative director and Micaela Le Divelec Lemmi CEO.

Following in the footsteps of expansion, travel retail, and shops in major Asian airports, particularly in China and for Chinese customers, it achieved €1,377 million turnover in 2019. Best known for its luxury footwear, the brand's portfolio had grown over the years to include ready-to-wear clothing, silk scarves, accessories, and jewelry. Following the pandemic crisis, which wrecked the travel retail industry in 2020, Michele Norsa was reappointed as Executive Deputy Chairman to weather the COVID-19 storm, which saw a 30% decline in its revenue in 2020. Ferruccio Ferragamo, with the family holding company Ferragamo Rinanziaria, remained as Chairman while delegating his executive powers to Norsa. In mid-2021, Marco Gobbetti, CEO of Burberry was appointed to be the new CEO of Ferragamo from 2022.

Armani   Giorgio Armani is another tangible example of a brand that has a strong founder as its asset who plays an important role in the development of the firm and the strong existence of the brand. Giorgio Armani is a designer and businessman who created the Armani empire. It is one of the conspicuous icons of Italian luxury brands. He is a details-driven person who has an unwavering desire to create the world of Armani, offering a timeless Italian lifestyle for consumers. The embrace of the business's product line started with fashion and moved on to cosmetics and home products. Armani's vitality and ideas for his business built the company as one of the most influential players in the industry.

Armani launched about 15 product line extensions, including outlets. It started from couture and expanded to a sports line, accessories, cosmetics, home products, and ultimately extending to a hotel resort range. Armani started with men's suits and, from that point, has always been keen to keep a balance between men's and womenswear every time it launched a new line. Also, Armani was a pioneer of making luxury affordable before the concept of masstige existed in the luxury marketing arena. Clearly, this was a major success for Armani, which expanded its customer profiles in terms of gender, age, and social class. The licensing business is a huge success factor for those firms run by entrepreneurs to stretch their product lines worldwide. Though there was no choice besides licensing in the beginning, due to the lack of financial support, it was a wise choice to implement this strategy since Armani has been successful with licensing business throughout its history. Armani did well to find the right partner and distributors while strictly controlling its brand, partly by guaranteeing its "Made in Italy" promise by hiring Italian manufacturers. The licensing business started from apparel to hotel resorts. For instance, L'Oréal is their partner in the perfume business and Armani had an agreement with Fossil for watch manufacturing and

Luxottica for eyewear. Just before the pandemic, in 2020, Armani's revenue was around €2.1 billion.

Dolce & Gabbana   Founded in 1985, Dolce & Gabbana is one of the leading international firms in the fashion world. The founders, Domenico Dolce and Stefano Gabbana, had always been the creative and stylistic inspiration of the brand. Together they originated growth strategies that were based on balanced development while focusing on the core business. Over the years, the creation of collections was integrated by many of the brand's activities, such as publications, cultural, and social events. They were done at the Metropol space in Milan, the blogazine Swide.com, the Martini Bar, the Gold restaurant, and others.

In 1989, Dolce & Gabbana opened their first store in Japan under partnership with Kashiyama Co. They started to export to the United States, where they founded their own showroom in 1990. In 1992 the brand launched its first in-house perfume, the same year that they presented their first men's collection. Their perfumes were successful and won awards from the Perfume Academy. In 2001, they launched their children's wear collection. In 2006, the company started a new journey in accessories and leather goods for men and women. The company also stepped into cosmetics, with Scarlett Johansson as the face of their advertising campaign. The first fine jewelry line came in late 2011 with 80 pieces, including bracelets, necklaces, and later on, watches. The duo was originally inspired by an eclectic, bohemian style. Their animal prints took inspiration from Italy's movie industry and were referred to as "haute hippydom," which always followed a story, especially from the roots of Sicily and Sicilian culture.

Dolce & Gabbana have always found themselves thinking out of the box in their campaigns. Their campaigns have had several controversies, with governments banning their advertisements over the years. For example, their 2007 advertisement, which featured models brandishing knives, was banned in Britain; a man holding a woman to the ground by her wrists, as other men looked on, was banned in Spain the same year, and created renewed debate in 2015. In 2012, Dolce & Gabbana banned Hong Kong residents from taking pictures of their window displays, which created anti–mainland Chinese sentiment. Again in 2015, the duo was in the eye of a storm in Italy when they opposed gay adoption. In 2018, Dolce & Gabbana advertised a series of videos on Instagram, Facebook and Twitter in preparation for the catwalk in Expo Shanghai. It featured a Chinese model with narrow eyes dressed up in the brand's garments and accessories. She was clumsily attempting to use chopsticks to eat Italian food. It led to a media outcry. In all the above cases the duo has apologized publicly.

Due to underperformance and the blurring of the brand's image, the company decided to erase the sub-brand D&G and integrate it into the main Dolce & Gabbana brand. In the same year, Mr. Dolce and Mr. Gabbana made their debut in couture with the collection Alta Moda, after 26 years of designing ready-to-wear. Their first-ever haute couture line made history at the San Domenica Palace Hotel in Taormina, Sicily. With 73 looks full of Dolce & Gabbana signature style, the Alta Moda collection was, according to Mr. Gabbana, the co-founder and designer of the brand, "not because of us, but the customers. They really do not want to see their dresses in a magazine." His partner, the other founder and designer of the brand, Mr. Dolce commented that, "This is our style. It is not a trend. . ... Here, we are completely free. So for me this is not work but pleasure." Just before the pandemic, in 2020, Dolce & Gabbana's revenue was around €900 million.

Zegna

A great family makes a great company, a great company makes a great family. . ... Let's look out for each other. Let's get through this together.
—Ermenegildo Zegna, CEO, grandson of the founder and third generation of the Zegna family

Zegna is a world leader in menswear. They hold this position by maintaining utmost quality in their fabrics at each step in the value chain, be it from selection of the finest raw materials to development of innovative customer relations. Gildo's grandfather built a series of business-related infrastructures for his fellow citizens: he constructed roads to schools and always took a sincere interest in the welfare of the workforce in his wool mills. And his sense of social responsibility—his commitment to people—endures as a basic principle for the Zegna family. The company has assimilated and enlarged upon Ermenegildo Zegna's environmental awareness. The group is presently involved in a number of major conservation projects, an expression of the good corporate citizenship that has distinguished the company throughout its history. Inspired by their grandfather's legacy, the new generation of Zegnas are carrying on his work—weaving the future on the loom of the past. Zegna reported an annual revenue of €1 billion just before the pandemic.

Tod's   Tod's S.p.A. engages in the production and sale of shoes and leather goods under the Tod's, Hogan, Fay, and Roger Vivier brand names. It offers shoe collections for women, men, and children under the Hogan brand. The company also offers a range of casual wear, including seasonal men's, women's, and junior's collections under the FAY brand. It sells its products globally. The company is based in Sant'Elpidio a Mare, Italy. It is presided over by businessman Diego Della Valle. Dorino Della Valle started the shoemaking business out of a basement in the late 1920s. Diego Della Valle, Dorino's elder son, expanded the workshop and turned it into a factory that started manufacturing shoes for American department stores in the 1970s. Diego brought in innovative marketing strategies in the early 1980s, kept the handmade manufacturing process, and went on to create brands of lifestyle named Tod's, Hogan, and Fay. Roger Vivier, maker of high luxury shoes was acquired in the mid-1990s and developed during the beginning of this millennium. In 2003, Italian designer Bruno Frisoni was hired as Roger Vivier's Creative Director. The Della Valle family, which owns a majority of the luxury maker, also has stakes in RCS Media Group, the football team Fiorentina, and other companies. All members of the family were born in the middle Italian region of Marche, and many of them continue to reside there. Tod's now has 404 stores over the world, including DOS and franchised stores. It is present in 41 countries. Tod's Group reported an annual revenue of €916 million just before the pandemic, with a decline of 44% during the pandemic. It was reported that Dela Valle may want to sale his company to LVMH group, which increased its stake to 10% in 2021.

Versace   Gianni Versace S.r.l, is an Italian fashion label founded by Gianni Versace in 1978. The first Versace boutique was opened in Milan's Via della Spiga in 1978 (though the Versace family are from Reggio Calabria) and its popularity was immediate. Today, Versace is one of the world's leading international fashion houses. Versace designs, markets, and distributes luxury clothing, accessories, fragrances, makeup, and home furnishings under the various brands of the Versace Group. Gianni Versace was killed by Andrew Cunanan on July 15, 1997. His sister Donatella Versace, formerly vice president, then stepped in as creative director of Versace, and his elder brother Santo Versace became CEO. Donatella's daughter Allegra Versace has owned 50% of the company since 2004, a wish expressed by Gianni in his last will. Versace's Style Department employs a group of designers and stylists who work in teams. Each team is specifically dedicated to each fashion line or label. These teams operate under the close supervision and guidance of Donatella Versace. There are several lines that make up Versace. They are Versace, Atelier Versace, Versace Fine Jewelry, Versace Home, Versace Children, Versace Jeans Couture, Versace Fragrances, Versace Watches and Versace Eyewear. In addition to clothing and accessories, Versace also operates a hotel, the Palazzo Versace.

The Versace label, named Versace Couture, includes high-end, often handmade apparel, jewelry, watches, fragrances, cosmetics, handbags, shoes, and home furnishings. Traditionally, the couture is presented on the runway during Milan's fashion week, but this has not been strictly the case in recent years. Couture dresses in this line may cost about $10,000 and suits cost approximately $5,000. Donatella Versace directly heads this line and designs a vast number of the items. The Versace label named Versace Collection is the second high-end line of the group and is designed for younger, more fashionable people. The logo is discreet and consists of the outline of a V surrounded by the classic Greek frieze, or is signed with the word "collection" written smaller in black at the bottom line of the name Versace in outlined letters or in white. The Versace Sport line ended in 2008 due to extensive counterfeiting of this line, damaging the Versace group image. Versace Jeans Couture, a casual clothing line, focuses on informal clothing and high-end denim and classic Versace print shirts. It is readily available and comparably affordable but has been discontinued in the United States for the most part. This line is distributed through 56 boutiques and flagship stores, and 1,800 multi-brand points of sale, including Internet-based shops. Versace Sport encompassed active wear and accessories. The name was often printed on T-shirts.

Versace planned an IPO in 2006 but it was not realized. In 2011 the group returned to profit. In 2014 it sold a 20% stake to Blackstone for €210 million, to fund expansion before taking another chance at an IPO. In September 2018 Versace announced that 100% of all Blackstone and Versace family shares had been sold to the Group Michael Kors Limited. In January 2019, Gianni Versace S.r.l. joined Capri Holdings Limited, forming a new global fashion luxury group together with Michael Kors and Jimmy Choo. Versace reported a revenue of €843 million in 2020 while Capri Group warned of losses up to 70% due to the pandemic.

Family-Run Business During a Crisis

Even with the dominance of such French luxury conglomerates as LVMH and Kering, some family-run businesses have managed not only to survive but also to retain their place as strong competitors. Although family-run firms grow and flourish for many different reasons, analysis of such businesses globally reveals that the most critical factor to their success is the families' coordinated and sustained long-term strategy for growing and controlling their businesses. This strategy can take many forms, but usually involves an exercise of patience in terms of the investment of capital, the retention of companies through tough times, long-term development of talent, a focus on core businesses, the maintenance of strong and enduring values, and the emphasis of long-term performance over quarterly gains.

As we have seen, family-run luxury businesses survived crises relatively better than their larger competitors. Experts argue that this is mainly due to the fact that, in periods of economic difficulty, the long-term vision of family entrepreneurs is a true competitive advantage.

Moreover, businesses run by a team, or by family members, tend to be more resilient and more likely to succeed than any other kind of company since they have one indisputable defining quality: family values (vs only company culture). Since family-run businesses have their name and reputation associated with their products and/or services, they strive to increase the quality of their products and services and to maintain a good relationship with their partners. Several studies have shown that family-owned companies do indeed outperform their non-family counterparts when it comes to sales, profits, and other measures of growth.

During the crisis, and long before, there was debate that the formation of the LVMH Group in 1989 would lead to the extinction of family-run businesses in the luxury goods sector. The competition became international and more and more volatile. The arguments put forward were based on lines of diversification and synergy. Without attaining synergy, individual family-owned brands could eventually lose market share and hence margins. It was touted that the nature of retail in the luxury industry required a consolidated approach and a strong supply chain to support them. Thus, a portfolio of several brands would hold a better position to face the challenge of not only accessing the share of the wallet but also synergies in real estate, supply chain, accessing resources, and more.

Family-Run Businesses of the Future: Corporatization

Family-run businesses will continue to play a greater and greater role in the world economy as we move forward into the next century. Data suggests that over 50% of the leaders of family businesses in the United States think their businesses will be owned and managed by two or more of their children. Two brands that require discussion in this regard are those of Jimmy Choo and Brunello Cucinelli.

Jimmy Choo

Jimmy Choo, one of the new entrants into the luxury goods industry, was founded in 1996 by Tamara Mellon and the London-based couture shoemaker, Jimmy Choo. Jimmy Choo was already known around London for his made-to-measure shoes; he was well known within certain social circles in London for his craftsmanship and had a solid customer base of celebrities and royalty. Tamara Mellon brought the finances and Choo brought his name to the partnership. However, in-fighting broke out between Ms. Mellon and Mr. Choo. The latter struggled to make the transition from a couture shoemaker to a ready-to-wear shoe designer and was upset when his niece Sandra Choi took over as the company's creative director. By 2001, Ms. Mellon and Mr. Choo were ready to split.

In 2001, Choo's 51% of the company was bought by Equinox Luxury Holdings, the fashion arm of Phoenix Equity Partners, a private equity fund, for approximately $10.6 million. Mr. Robert Bensoussan, one of the shareholders of Equinox and a former executive of LVMH, became CEO of Jimmy Choo. Tamara Mellon held on to her 49% stake in the company, and Sandra Choi became the creative director of the brand.

In 2004, Equinox sold its stake in Jimmy Choo to Hicks Muse Tate & Furst for £101 million. Mr. Bensoussan remained as CEO and the Mellon family's stake in the company remained the same. The company continued to grow at an extraordinary rate between 2004 and 2007; the number of stores went from 23 to 60. Hicks Muse Tate & Furst became Lion Capital LLP. Partnering with private equity firms was paying off for Jimmy Choo. Financing was not an issue and it had a strong enough financial base at all times to aid its expansion.

In 2007, Lion Capital LLP was ready to sell its share of Jimmy Choo. TowerBrook Capital Partners, an international private equity fund, bought the 51% stake in Jimmy Choo for £185 million. In three years, Lion Capital had made £85 million by buying and selling Jimmy Choo. The luxury goods company continued to grow and began to diversify its product offering; they introduced handbags and small leather accessories into the collection. Shortly after the sale to TowerBrook Capital Partners L.P., Mr. Bensoussan, CEO of Jimmy Choo, left and was replaced by Mr. Josh Schulman. Tamar Mellon still owned 41% of the company and remained as the company's president even after Mr. Bensoussan left.

In 2010, TowerBrook Capital Partners announced they were looking to sell their stake in the shoe and accessories company. The company's revenues had more than doubled since TowerBrook purchased Jimmy Choo in 2007. In May 2011, both Tower Brook Capital Partners LP and Tamara Mellon sold their stake in Jimmy Choo for a value of GBP 500 million to Labelux, a luxury goods company from Germany. Labelux was Jimmy Choo's first non–private equity owner since Mr. Choo sold his stake in the company in 2001. Although Ms. Mellon had sold her stake in the company, she remained as Chief Creative Officer, while Mr. Schulman also remained as CEO and Ms. Sandra Choi as the creative director of the company. The management of the company looked as if it would not change. However, in November 2011 Ms. Mellon announced that she would be leaving the company and Mr. Schulman would be leaving as well in a reorganization of the company. In 2012, the company hired ex-LVMH executive Pierre Denis as its CEO.

As a new entrant in the luxury business, Jimmy Choo managed to survive outside of a luxury group, thanks to financing from its multiple private equity stakeholders. It was co-founded by Ms. Mellon and its eponymous designer Jimmy Choo but quickly evolved into a listed company. The company was never structured as a family business. Apart from Ms. Mellon, co-founder and the biggest stake owner of the company, it always relied on a business manager. The aim of the company has always been to make solid returns on the investments of its private equity owners. The company was able to grow and develop as quickly as it did because of the fresh capital investment that came each time the ownership of the company changed hands. The constant change in ownership did not affect the company's performance because one thing always remained the same: Tamara Mellon, the face of the company. The constant injection of capital meant that the company could invest in retail and expand without worrying about how it was going to raise the capital to further develop. To date, Jimmy Choo has had four leveraged buyouts.

In 2011, Labelux GmBH, the German luxury goods company acquired Jimmy Choo for a reported £500 million ($811 million) from TowerBrook Capital Partners. In 2014, about 25% of the company was sold in a London IPO at $2.24, giving it a market capitalization of about $870 million. Jimmy Choo became the first luxury footwear brand to go public. The company was listed on the London Stock Exchange until it was acquired at $1.2 billion in July 2017 by Michael Kors Holdings, now Capri Holdings. Sandra Choi remained as Creative Director throughout. In 2020, the annual revenue of Jimmy Choo was reported to be $555 million, a drop of about 10% on the preceding year.

Brunello Cucinelli

Brunello Cucinelli is an Italian company in the fashion industry that produces high-end cashmere clothing and accessories. The company controls the whole value chain from design to manufacturing to distribution. Combining its Italian heritage, outstanding quality, and artisan craftsmanship with great creativity, Brunello Cucinelli has built up a strong brand identity and positioned itself in the absolute luxury segment of the market. The company was founded in 1978 when cashmere was only produced in a natural color, but Brunello Cucinelli, the founder of this company, thought that colorful cashmere could be a breakthrough; therefore, he established the first cashmere knitwear company in Ellera di Corciano in the province of Perugia. The product range was expanded through the multibrand wholesale distribution strategy. First of all, the company purchased stakes in Rivamonti, a producer specializing in design and producing wool knitwear in the mid-1980s. Following this, the company acquired Gunex and expanded its product line to women's skirts and trousers. At the same time, the company established its US branch, which was responsible for the import and sale of cashmere knits in the US market. In 1994, Brunello Cucinelli started its men's collection and opened its first boutique in Porto Cervo. Starting in 2005, the company opened directly operated stores (DOS) in Milan, Paris, New York, and Miami, and franchising shops, such as ones in London, Tokyo, Moscow, Saint Petersburg, Sylt, Cortina, and Saint Tropez. Those stores are opened on the main streets of major cities in Italy and abroad and in some exclusive resort locations.

Cashmere is a very rare fiber and is the main raw material of Brunello Cucinelli's products. To secure the highest quality cashmere, the company cooperates with the most prestigious cashmere spinners in Italy and has signed long-term contracts to provide the highest quality yarn. A clause in each contract suggests that the contract would be renewed every three years in order to ensure the unhindered supply of stable quality and softness of cashmere.

All Brunello Cucinelli's products are made in Italy, relying on the internalization of intellectual and manual skills. The strong commitment to high quality and focus on every detail at each stage of manufacturing led the company to manage the whole process of production, from raw material to the finished products. As a result, Brunello Cucinelli employs the top craftsmen in the field, those who maintain high quality and produce creative products. They could ensure this control over the value chain due to their new prototype research and long-term commitment in their production process.

The Brunello Cucinelli Group markets its products through several different channels, which include retail distribution channel, wholesale monobrand channel, and wholesale multibrand channel. As of December 31, 2019, the retail channel consisted of 77 DOS. Apart from DOS, it also includes 29 sales points managed under the Group's responsibility and with direct employees located inside the department stores. The direct managed sales points are located in Japan, Canada, China, and Europe. In 2019, Brunello Cucinelli achieved €608 million total turnover, of which the retail distribution channel contributed 55.8%. The wholesale multibrand channel consists of independent multibrand stores and dedicated spaces within department stores (shop-in-shops). It contributed to 38.8% of the turnover. The wholesale monobrand channel consists of 30 monobrand stores operated under commercial distribution agreements. It accounted for the remaining 5.4% of the turnover.[3]

Brunello Cucinelli adopts a strictly selective strategy in distribution. The company chooses knowledgeable distributors who not only appreciate the true value of the brand but also reinforce its image in the local markets. By doing this, the company preserves the exclusiveness of Brunello Cucinelli. The 59 stores of Brunello Cucinelli over the world in the prestige luxury locations could ensure the transfer of the brand identity, and ideas of culture and lifestyle. In the multibrand sales channels and particularly in luxury department stores, Brunello Cucinelli products are often presented in dedicated places: "soft-corner" (discreet) corners and shops within shops.

In order to not only have financial stability but to also raise its visibility and attract talent for international expansion, Brunello Cucinelli listed itself on the Milan stock exchange in 2012. Unlike other luxury brands, such as Prada, which went to the Hong Kong stock exchange, Brunello Cucinelli listed in Milan because its founder, Mr. Cucinelli, had confidence in his home country and was proud of being Italian. After the IPO, the majority of shareholders are still members of the Cucinelli family. Although Brunello Cucinelli could not take advantage of the Asia market, Mr. Cucinelli has an optimistic vision of future global

---

[3]Brunello Cucinelli Annual Report, 2019.
http://investor.brunellocucinelli.com/yep-content/media/CUCINELLI_CONSOLI-DATO_ENG_2019_web2.pdf.

development since brand visibility and financial support have increased due to this listing.

After years of regular growth, the company has had to deal with the health and economic crisis that has affected the whole world caused by Covid-19, which had a strong negative impact on the results of 2020. The company's turnover, indeed, has suffered a decrease of 29.6% compared to the same period of last year. This result has been strongly affected by the closure of a significant number of boutiques in the world following the lockdown measures to halt the spread of the coronavirus.

In order to recover from the aftermath of the health crisis, the anti-crisis strategy adopted by Brunello Cucinelli consisted of four different steps. First, to continue increasing the planned investments in the areas of retail and technology. Second, the company will continue to focus its attention on *humanistic capitalism*, the importance of human relationships and contact, which have always been the pillars of the brand's culture. It meant an equilibrium between *profit* and *giving*. In his vision, these values will be crucial for the industry's resumption, and companies should start investing in them, integrating them into their corporate culture, and teaching them to their employees.

Therefore, probably not in line with the visions of many of his competitors, Brunello Cucinelli believes that the key skills required from current and future employees to face the uncertain post-pandemic future will undoubtedly be interpersonal skills: empathy, communication, emotional intelligence, a creative mindset, a predisposition to *listen* and with *graceful technology*. An initiative during the pandemic outbreak was the "Project in Support of Mankind," according to which the company gifted the unsold stock (worth €30M), in line with the company's sustainable vision. CEO Brunello Cucinelli commented, it "raises the dignity of mankind and pays tribute to all those who have taken part in the manufacturing of these garments. . .. Let's look to 2020 positively, aware that it will still be a year to look at and read carefully. But it will not affect our 2019–2022 project and the 2019–2028 ten-year plan, where we expect to double our turnover and achieve healthy, balanced and sustainable profits." Annual turnover was reported at around €608 million in 2020, with an expected drop of 10% due to the pandemic crisis.

Changes During the Transition from a Family-Run Business Model to That of a Corporation

The sustainability of the conglomerate business model has been questioned since it was born. The formation, growth, and success of LVMH opened up opportunities for ailing family businesses to be acquired and run within a conglomerate. It revolutionized the luxury industry's mode of function. As a series of acquisitions were orchestrated and the acquisitions integrated, family businesses and designer brands—such as Givenchy, Cristallerie de Saint Louis, Céline, and Kenzo—were saved from going bankrupt. Anecdotes of turnaround were fascinating as brand after brand was turned around and its heritage protected. The turnaround occurred by rejuvenating the brands, launching new products, undergoing expansion, and leveraging existent synergies within the group. With the success of the growth-through-acquisition model, the formation of similar conglomerates such as Richemont and Kering was triggered, and another wave of new acquisitions of some of the most renowned brands in fashion, jewelry, cosmetics, and other sectors began. It started to become clear that the size of these groups contributed in a relevant manner to the growth, diversification, synergies, opportunities, and better vertical integration that were all necessary for the success of the brands involved. It was difficult for smaller brands to transition to become part of the larger group. Though freedom was maintained for each brand to operate independently, strict financial rigor made them responsive to the market. The products that they created needed to have a market and the market needed to have consumers aspiring to those products.

Not all the brands were acquired. Some smaller business houses and designer labels remained faithful to their original market position as family-owned brands and focused on serving niche segments, specializing in their core business while highlighting the importance of craftsmanship and creativity. They were small in number. They were strong enough to resist the offers of acquisition from the luxury conglomerates. Some of them prospered while remaining independent. Among them were names such as Hermès, Chanel, Tiffany, and the Italian brands. They had extremely robust balance sheets and enjoyed unprecedented

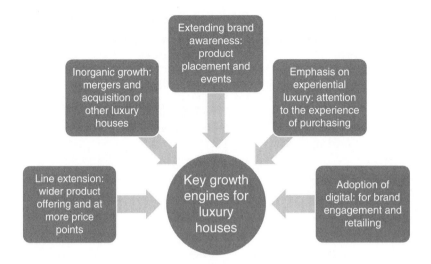

Figure 6.4   Key Engines of Growth for Luxury Houses

brand recognition. Hermès, for example, was consistently ranked very high in value within all luxury companies, proving to be a vivid competitor regardless of its apparently old but most efficient business model. Figure 6.4 shows the different engines that drove the growth of luxury houses.

It remained a challenge during this transition to compete with the brands of conglomerates and fund for sustainable growth. Most of these family businesses had to go public in order to provide the appropriate amount of financing required for the global expansion. The 1990s were famous for the number of IPOs of fashion houses, including those of Ralph Lauren, Tod's, and Hermès. In 2021, the return of IPOs and M&A had been forecast. The advantage was still in favor of IPOs as the family still kept the controlling interest. It meant that the pressure from shareholders was much less than that in conglomerates, while M&A meant that family houses might be acquired by a conglomerate, a private equity company, or might themselves build a conglomerate. For example, VF Corporation, owner of Timberland, Vans, and North Face, acquired Supreme, the streetwear brand for $2.1 billion. Moncler acquired menswear brand Stone Island for $1.4 billion. LVMH acquired Tiffany for $15.8 billion, and mythesersa.com had a successful IPO. Poshmark and

Table 6.1   Competitive Advantages of a Conglomerate and a Family House

Competitive Advantage of a Conglomerate	Competitive Advantage of a Family House
Strategic imperative:	Strategic imperative:
Global positioning of different brands	Common shared values defined by family (not shareholders)
Access to strategic resources	Strong commitment
Economies of scale and scope	Loyalty
Synergy	Stability
International expansion	Expansion as a consequence of business
Organization imperative:	strategy
Management quality	Emphasis on long-term creation of value
Organizational design	rather than quarterly gains
Shared research and development	Organization imperative:
Integration into selective retailing	Flexible and prudent decision making
Operational imperative:	Homogeneity in internal culture
Merchandizing know-how	Long-term development of talent
Product line extension	Operational imperative:
Inventory management	Partnership with suppliers
Sourcing and supply-chain integration	Financial imperative:
Financial imperative:	Not answerable to shareholders for every quarter
Financial discipline	Decision can be consensus based
Synergy in marketing budget	Not in a hurry
High bargaining power— advertisement and retain space	

ThreadUp are planning theirs. The competitive advantages during the transition were more or less similar for both the conglomerate and the family house, as Table 6.1 shows.

Succession Planning

With the transition from family houses to corporations, another key issue was succession planning. The stars of yesteryear were talented, creative, and charismatic, and they created an empire with their own names. What happens when they retire? Be it a family house or a conglomerate, the luxury businesses are still run by individuals who are immensely passionate about their business.

According to the literature on family businesses, seven out of 10 family-owned businesses fail to make the transition to management by the second generation and just one in 10 makes it to the third generation. Simply put, the statistics are against the successful continuation of family businesses over multiple generations. Based on the previous discussion, most luxury brands were founded in the nineteenth century or later as small-scale family businesses. A large number of these establishments are now being managed by members of the second or third generation. Figure 6.5 depicts corporatization of the luxury family business.

Armani is a case in point—a very specific one, though. But the luxury industry is in fact full of these personalities who were and are larger than life. The brand of Giorgio Armani has been very well grounded; it is tied to its founders but may not be able to stand alone for long once Mr. Armani retires. What will happen to the Armani brand after Armani? Will it continue to be as strong or will the empire slowly deteriorate? And what if the founder himself is better known than the company brand? Giorgio Armani has clearly built a worldwide business but it is very much dependent on his own involvement. What happens when he moves on? The question then becomes: How will the next generation of entrepreneurs preserve the brand's identity and keep it profitable?

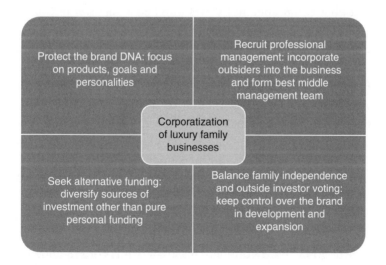

Figure 6.5   Corporatization of a Family Business

Entrepreneurs and New Entrants into Existing Markets

The rising trend has been billion-dollar businesses created by designers with their own names. They are the new entrants. We discuss two such new entrants who have developed their brands—Tom Ford by himself and Marc Jacobs with help from LVMH Group.

Tom Ford

Thomas Carlyle "Tom" Ford is an American fashion designer and film director. He joined Gucci in 1990 as the brand's chief designer for its women's ready-to-wear line. At that time, Gucci had a very blurry brand image—"No one would dream of wearing Gucci," said Dawn Mello, the company's creative director at the time. The brand was struggling to re-establish its status in women's fashion. In 1992, Ford took over Richard Lambertson's position as the design director, leading the brand's ready-to-wear, fragrance, image, advertising, and visual merchandizing. In 1994, Ford was promoted to creative director. In 1995, he worked with French stylist Carine Roitfeld and photographer Mario Testino to create a series of new, modern advertisement campaigns. Between 1995 and 1996, sales of Gucci increased by 90%. In early 1999, luxury product conglomerate LVMH initiated a takeover bid on Gucci. Tom Ford and Domenico de Sole, CEO at that time, were not comfortable with the management style of Bernard Arnault. Ford and De Sole approached PPR group (later Kering). François Pinault, the group's founder, agreed to purchase 37 million shares in Gucci, equivalent to a 40% stake. Arnault's share was diluted to 20%. At the same time, Tom Ford was the largest individual shareholder in Gucci. During Ford's 10 years as Creative Director at Gucci and Gucci Group, sales increased from $230 million in 1994 to almost $3 billion in 2003, making Gucci one of the largest and most profitable luxury brands in the world. When Ford left in 2004, Gucci Group was valued at $10 billion. He was also behind the Gucci Group's decision to buy Yves Saint Laurent and was named in 2000 the creative director of that brand as well.

In April 2005, Ford founded his own Tom Ford brand. Having already built his fame as a designer at Gucci, his new fashion lines for men became a big success. Domenico De Sole joined in the start-up and became chairman of the company. In that same year, Ford partnered with Marcolin Group to produce and distribute optical frames and sunglasses. At the same time, he cooperated with Estée Lauder to create and produce the Tom Ford Beauty brand, and he posed for his own named fragrance advertisement campaign. With the fame of Tom Ford as a celebrity-like public figure, the eyewear and beauty products with his name became huge successes, which funded the launch of his first luxury menswear collection. The strategy was to focus on superior fashion design and luxury products, attention to detail, and made-in-Italy roots, while the production and distribution under the Tom Ford label were licensed to Ermenegildo Zegna in February 2006. In April 2007, Tom Ford opened its first flagship store in New York at 845 Madison Avenue, for luxury men's ready-to-wear and made-to-measure clothing, footwear, and accessories. Later in autumn 2010, he presented his much-anticipated womenswear collection. The first unisex store opened after the womenswear launch in Beverly Hills, California. Globally, there were 49 directly owned freestanding stores and 77 shop-in-shops in 2017. Total retail sales of the Tom Ford brand—including eyewear, fragrance, cosmetics, ready-to-wear, men's and women's accessories—is estimated to have hit $2 billion. The brand is diversifying in terms of geographical reach and demographic. It has also revealed an ambition to increase its presence in the skin care category.

Marc Jacobs

The talented fashion designer, Marc Jacobs, was born in New York City on April 9, 1963. After graduating from the High School of Art and Design in 1981 he entered Parsons School of Design. As a design student at Parsons, Jacobs met Robert Duffy, an executive with Ruben Thomas, Inc. when he showed his senior collection. After seeing Jacob's collection, Robert inquired about having Jacobs develop a ready-to-wear collection for Ruben Thomas, Inc., under the sketchbook label.

This conversation started a partnership, called Jacobs Duffy Designs, Inc. The main concepts of this partnership were love for fashion and commitment to quality. In 1986, Jacobs designed his first collection bearing the Marc Jacobs label, with the support of Kashiyama USA, Inc.

The following year, Jacobs was awarded the Council of Fashion Designers of America Perry Ellis Award for New Fashion Talent. In 1989 Jacobs and Duffy joined Perry Ellis and were named vice president of women's design and president respectively. While at Perry Ellis, Jacobs created a designer collection and was in charge of the various women's licensees as well. In 1992, the CFDA once again gave Jacobs a distinct honor: Womenswear Designer of the Year. In the fall of 1993, Jacobs Duffy Designs, Inc. launched its licensing and design company: Marc Jacobs International Company, LP, and in 1994, the company licensed to Look, Inc., and Mitsubishi Corporation for distribution of the Marc Jacobs designer collection in Japan. Soon after, Marc Jacobs International Company, LP, entrusted Iris S.R.L., the Italian shoe producer, with the production of all Marc Jacobs shoe collections. Then in 1995, Jacobs launched his first collection of men's ready-to-wear.

In 1997, Jacobs was struggling to keep his namesake brand business. Bernard Arnault approached him with an irresistible offer: Jacobs would relaunch the famous but stodgy Louis Vuitton label in return for LVMH underwriting Jacobs's design company. Therefore, Jacobs, and his partner Duffy, joined Louis Vuitton as artistic director and studio director, respectively. During his tenure, Jacobs worked on many of the French luxury house's lines, including handbags, men's and women's ready-to-wear, shoes, and small leather goods. Jacobs's designs helped boost sales of the Louis Vuitton brand to the tune of €3.8 billion, which accounted for 60% of LVMH's operating profit. At the same time, sales of the Marc Jacobs brand increased to about $75 million through a 50% investment from LVMH. The company launched its first handbag collection in the fall of 2000 and a second Marc Jacobs store was opened on San Francisco's historic Maiden Lane in August 2000. The first freestanding men's collection store opened on Bleecker Street in New York City in September 2000, marking the beginning of what would become a street of shops. In the same year, a licensed agreement was signed with L.S.A S.p.A., an Italian company based outside of Milan, to produce men's and women's ties and scarves. The secondary line, Marc by Marc Jacobs, was launched in the Spring/Summer 2001 Runway show. The Marc by Marc Jacobs collection included shoes, handbags, and other signature accessories. A licensed agreement with Calza Turificio Rossimoda S.p.A. was signed in 2001 to produce all women and men's Marc by Marc

Jacobs's shoes. In September 2001, the company launched its first fragrance. The scent, called Marc Jacobs Perfume, was inspired by gardenias in water. The launch took place on Pier 54 on the Hudson River and was staged as a benefit to a dozen downtown New York City charities. In 2003, the USA fragrance division of the Marc Jacobs brand was sold to Coty Inc. All fragrances were developed and produced by the company's fragrance partner, Lancaster Group US, LLC, the prestige division of Coty Inc. The company's eyewear collection is produced by Italian luxury eyewear partner, Safilo S.p.A.

In 2004, the company had a distribution agreement with Imaginex Holdings, Ltd. (a division of the groups whose companies include Lane Crawford and Joyce Boutiques) for distribution in the territory of Hong Kong and mainland China. It was also the beginning of a partnership that included the opening of its first flagship store in Shanghai in August 2004, as well as stores in Beijing and Chengdu. The first US multi-brand store opened in July 2004 on Boston's Newbury Street. March 2005 marked the opening of two stores in Los Angeles: a collection store at 8400 Melrose Place and a Marc by Marc Jacobs store located at 8410 Melrose Avenue. In the same year, Marc Jacobs launched its first watch line and a collection store in Paris, in partnership with Fossil. Later that month the company opened a collection store at the Bal Harbor Shops in Bal Harbor, Florida. In January 2008, a Marc by Marc Jacobs boutique opened in Chicago's Bucktown and several limited-edition fragrances were launched. The fall brought openings in Paris, London, Madrid, Istanbul, and Athens—all with their first Marc by Marc Jacobs locations. The year 2009 saw the start of a new venture, with Sumitomo Corp., that represented a new beginning for the Marc Jacobs business in Japan.

The Marc by Marc Jacobs line, which accounted for as much as 80% of the brand's retail revenue, suffered in 2015 with an effort to bring the brand under one label. Stores under this line were closed. The brand has been struggling ever since, with its sales flat or declining. Personnel changes have also rattled the brand. Co-founder and president Robert Duffy departed in 2015. CEO Sebastian Suhl was replaced by former Kenzo CEO Eric Marechalle in 2017. In February 2018, Marechalle appointed Baja East designer John Targon to lead the direction of a new lower-priced Marc Jacobs collection, with Targon installing a new team of designers from scratch. After a mere two months, Targon left the company, indicating the brand's effort to reintroduce itself back to square one. In October 2018, the brand closed its last remaining London store. In 2019, Marc Jacobs launched a new affordable label "The Marc Jacobs." Later in April, Coty and Marc Jacobs announced the renewal of their long-term fragrance license partnership. The brand is being sustained mainly by the Coty licensing deal and outlet sales, according to Glossy.[4]

Trends and Discussion

With the downturn in the economy, political unrest such as the Hong Kong protests, the US–China trade war, and the surprising coronavirus pandemic, globalization may be posing a challenge to family-owned SMEs, which account for up to 90% of Italian companies and around 60% of French. The threat arises from the lack of financial power that the family-owned luxury goods firms require for weathering crises and for international expansion to compete against international conglomerates and to attract buyers to their products. Post the crisis era there may be more frequent acquisitions. The conglomerates may become stronger as they have cash in hand to buy out struggling brands. On the other hand, many economists are optimistic that Italian and French firms can capitalize on their sense of beauty and style through effective branding of their trademark craftsmanship.

With the discussion of growth and profitable growth across geographies, it seems reasonable to conclude that globalization has placed new demands on even the most established brands and that could cause old strategies of attracting high-net-worth customers to fail. It may not be only the pull phenomenon of attracting the customer to one's stores in their home country but may also be the effect of the push phenomenon of reaching out to those high-net-worth customers in distant mature and emerging markets who do not have a passport or do not travel as much as their Western counterparts. Following on those lines of discussion,

---

[4]Glossy, 2019,
https://www.glossy.co/evolution-of-luxury/it-cut-itself-off-at-the-legs-what-happened-to-marc-jacobs.

Asians, especially the Chinese, are now the biggest consumers of luxury goods. So, the key question would be to ask how family businesses can travel across borders and, if so, to which destinations?

Historically, there have been three strategies to leverage brands globally. These three strategies were the key growth engines for the luxury houses. First, the growth engine was inorganic, thereby acquiring family-owned luxury brands, a strategy that was followed by LVMH, Kering, and Richemont. Second were line extensions, which involved offering consumers different designs at tiered price points. Examples would be Armani's wide range of clothing lines and luxury goods, Hugo Boss's red-and-black line, and others focusing on different customer segments. Third was extending brand awareness through product placements, gala events, advertisements, and other methods. The general trend for family houses was thus a choice that was dependent on the amount of resources one could deploy.

Despite the growing popularity of the conglomerate model, there is no optimal route to growing a family-run luxury goods business, managing its succession, or growing a particular brand within it. The optimal strategy will always depend on the company and its products, goals, and personalities. Yet there are some general guidelines in this context. Investors like to see that families can incorporate outsiders into the existing business model and believe that family firms need good middle management. They also advise businesses to protect the brand DNA and find the best professional management possible. Ownership remains one of the key issues of internationalization and expansion of family businesses. For example, Etro, a growing family-owned fashion and textiles house from Milan, has shown that family businesses in the luxury sector can internationalize without giving up their independence. Over the past years, Etro has been growing slowly, but in a structured way, while also managing the transition from the vision of its original founder to that of the next generation. Its ample internal capital and collaborative family members have allowed Etro to retain its independence.

Nevertheless, this may not always be the case: the majority of family companies that historically financed their businesses through personal resources now realize that they need to seek alternative funding to compete globally and penetrate new markets, and that this might entail giving up ownership (or part) of the family business.

From analysis of the luxury business houses, its road toward corporatization, to the birth of conglomerates, it is clear that its evolution has led to vertical integration. The challenge faced by most luxury brands, especially the family houses, is how to finance their expansion, control their production, protect the value chain, and promote core values while minimizing counterfeiting. The story of Louis Vuitton focused on their ability to vertically integrate and scale up. It was imperative in developing the company and growing it further. For its successful growth story, diversification of the product offering, vertical integration, and control of the supply chain have been key success factors. The conglomerates owned a large part of their manufacturing and retail outlets. They could synergize, share existing resources, take advantage of cumulative sourcing and advertising, create supply-chain efficiencies, and foster economies of scale. With their portfolio of brands, they also had high bargaining power in retail outlets, luxury malls, and luxury streets. New entrants, on the other hand, had to adapt faster, especially when they did not have the backing of large groups or exterior financiers. For example, Jimmy Choo, due to its solid financing base, was able to grow at a double-digit rate. We have also seen that a weakness that haunts the family business is the issue of succession planning, as seen in the case of Armani.

With time, the number of smaller players, with a turnover in the range of €20–50 million, has shrunk over time. To raise financial resources for expansion has been the most important challenge for the smaller houses. For example, in the case of Prada, Hermès, and a number of others, going public did not mean that the family lost control. It meant that, though they remained majority shareholders, families needed to answer to shareholders who care about quarterly returns. Those who have succeeded on their own have involved the help of professional managers.

There have been a number of new entrants over the years in the industry but very few are alone and unassociated with any group or conglomerate. Conglomerates owned and nurtured a large number of the new entrants as we see in the case of Kering group with Alexander McQueen and Stella McCartney. Having the financial backing of a group meant that professionals had been at the helm from the outset and that they have had strong financial bases to enable them to compete in an extremely competitive industry. The added advantage was that they were able to lean on the larger brands from the group to negotiate retail space and advertising space and share part of the supply chain. This gave them an advantage in controlling their costs while leveraging their competencies of the group. For any new entrant the opportunities availed to them would be few and far between. The question that still remains unanswered, and will only become clear in time, is if there is room in the luxury industry today for small independent players, and if there is, how they can survive in a competitive market and remain completely privately owned.

On the other hand, the paradox of maintaining heritage and increasing the bottom line is a common struggle in this industry. The activities of the conglomerates show that size alone cannot overcome this paradox. While conglomerates have been creative in exploiting synergies across brands, they have not always been successful. Some brands garner the profit—the so-called star brands—while others in the portfolio continue to be loss-making. Today's loss-making brand in the portfolio may be the star brand of the future. While portfolio theory accepts ebbs and flows in profit generation, it is more often the case that for most conglomerates one or two brands represent the majority of the profit. Further, the less successful brands often erode the profits of the other portfolio brands. Figure 6.6 summarizes the paradoxical challenges of the luxury family houses.

To summarize, three key organizational trends in the luxury industry, which affected family businesses and led to corporatization and creation of conglomerates and spurred new entrants, were: globalization, increasing diversity of consumers, and flexibility in adaptation. They embraced

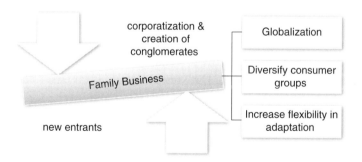

Figure 6.6   Paradoxical Challenges Faced by the Luxury Family Houses

new cultures while remaining true to their values and heritage, which in fact gives them their competitive advantage.

Conclusion

It is evident that, if there weren't successfully built family-owned luxury businesses, luxury conglomerates would have never been able to shape themselves into what we see today. They rely on the heritage and tradition brought in by these family-owned companies, which give them the legitimacy to play in the luxury field. Conglomerates do make sense in the luxury-goods sector, which requires large marketing budgets to drive sales and increase product visibility, but the heritage of each brand is what fundamentally allows them to exist. From this perspective, it can be said that the family businesses are in fact stronger than the conglomerates, given that they build the base for further development. Even if conglomerates seem to be a route with no return, there always has to be room for the family-owned businesses to shine as this is really the part of the luxury industry that best creates the myth and the mystery of true craftsmanship behind unique products.

With increased competition in the luxury market, a critical issue for family houses as well as entrepreneurs is how to leverage the substantial growth and preserve the brand's autonomy. The biggest luxury conglomerate could be a panacea for the family-owned business. However, to some extent, being just one in a luxury conglomerate portfolio could have the dependent brand facing a disaster or being a neglected orphan under the umbrella of a multibrand conglomerate. Therefore, to be or not to be a part of the multibrand companies is a question that needs a rethink. Sometimes, it may be the only way to survival. Financing through the capital market could be the white knight for them. The critical issue would be how to balance long-term development and short-term sales growth under the pressure of stockholders. The question remains: Is the growth of a luxury brand sustainable in the long term?

Chapter 7

Management Styles in the Luxury Industry

Managerial people in the luxury industry are often referred to as homoluxus. They are applauded in all social circles, with their names or the names of the companies they lead flying everywhere, from magazines at the corner newsstand to the most luxurious streets in megacities. Their images are everywhere, seen in fine clothes and surrounded by stars. They are thrilled to speak about their brands. They love journalists, even if they deny it—they say that they hate to talk about themselves but they keep telling everybody their opinions. How can such people be afraid of anything?

The homoluxus are confident, thinking that they grasp the true knowledge of what is good or bad for their brands. They claim to love teamwork but very often we observe a "one-man show," or at the least, they impose their views with authority. They are convinced that they are able to reach the sky even if the reality turns out to be a different picture.

They are everywhere but actually nowhere; they travel constantly while pretending to be on the ground all the time. There is no way for them to admit mistakes, why should they? Mistakes are always caused by others—the crisis, the creators, the shareholders—never by themselves. They don't really care about contradictions or opposition, even if they claim to—the homoluxus are living in a paradox: a small figure bearing a huge name, a modest attitude accompanied by an immense ego. They will never mess things up, they think to themselves.

However, there are some better than that. The best homoluxus are always asking themselves what to do next: whether to go further, and with whom. They are like Mao Tse-tung on the Long March, running with comrades, afraid of missing targets, choosing wrong locations, setting wrong prices, and appointing wrong creators. They are wary of the "ephemera" of luxury brands, whose collapse sometimes comes so quick. Neither are they overly concerned with quarterly gains and losses, but rather with product quality and long-term goals. They weather the pressure with Zen-like focus. Such managers are rare to find.

As discussed in Chapter 3, most of the industry's iconic brands were established more than 100 years ago and were originally owned and run by families. In France, these companies were called "maisons," or houses. From the 1980s onward, Bernard Arnault (LVMH), Francois Pinault (Kering), and Johann Rupert (Richemont), later on houses such as Prada, Tod's Group, and much later on other conglomerates such as the US bases Tapestry Inc. (Coach, Kate Spade, Stuart Weitzman), Capri Holdings (Michael Kors, Versace, Jimmy Choo), and Qatar-based Mayhoola Group (Balmain, Valentino, Pal Zileri) began to apply the strategies of large, multinational corporations to the luxury industry. By acquiring many of the traditional family-owned and -run brands, the three major luxury groups—LVMH, Kering, and Richemont—were founded, thereby recreating an industry that had been not only fragmented but run by the head of each maison.

Formerly accessible to only a small group of elite consumers, the luxury industry was democratized during the late twentieth century as brands became more accessible. Many companies began introducing brand extensions, such as eyewear and perfumes, into the luxury landscape, thus attracting larger (and younger) audiences. Another development during 2000–2021 was the expansion of most luxury brands into emerging markets. The main focus was on Asia, and more specifically China. According to Bain & Company, Chinese customers accounted for 90% of the constant growth of the market in 2020, reaching 35% of the value of luxury goods.[1] Online channels continued to gain shares as the digital-savvy generation Z have become steady luxury buyers.

Luxury was built on the foundation of certain principles that can neither be ignored nor compromised. It was a culture and a philosophy that required understanding before the adoption of business practices, because its intricacies and output were essentially different from other types of goods. Its path dependency pointed to the culture, heritage, and style that need to be understood in order to practice it with flair and spontaneity.

Path Dependency and Its Influence on Management Styles

The creator: One concocts extraordinary olive oil that the creator presents in beautiful, elegant bottles. The creator intends to sell them in luxury delis and he will no doubt succeed. The creator has the energy, the taste, the talent, and the patience that it takes.

Another loves jewelry, makes one-off pieces with stones that she finds from who knows where. Another mixes colors, matches fabrics, and makes necklaces of unusual shapes.

One creator was a designer but his former luxury house laid him off after closing its doors. He opened a little boutique, but it didn't work; he wasn't a good manager. He is a creator, not a businessman.

Then there's the one who makes sandals and the other one who makes dresses. They are all in luxury's waiting room. They struggle.

Creators often are susceptible to illusions. Mistakenly, the world thought that luxury designers could do anything they liked! A creator's freedom had to be based on rules and knowledge; otherwise, nothing good could come of it.

That said, the golden rule in real luxury was to make sure that creators had few managerial responsibilities, and were given free rein. The

---

[1]Bain & Company, 2019 https://www.bain.com/about/media-center/press-releases/2019/fall-luxury-report/.

truth was that luxury could only work if the products were unexpected and unplanned.

If design became standardized, luxury would not be able to distinguish itself from mass-produced goods. There would be no chance of surprising the customers and making a sale. Producing articles that bear no artistic inspiration and creativity would doom the luxury market to failure.

Creation, by definition, went beyond a system or habits. The organization of a luxury house had to allow for this. Of course, creators could be unbearable megalomaniacs, demanding and obnoxious. But it is in their very nature. The rest of us just have to accept that.

Luxury also could not exist without artists. Creators drove luxury and so sometimes reason must give way to imagination, reality must give way to the irrational, and truth succumbs to dreams! That's what luxury is all about. At least, that's how it should be.

What is the common thread running between Gabrielle Chanel, Hubert de Givenchy, Yves Saint Laurent, and Christian Dior? Are these the names of designers or brands? This is one of those rare questions where one can never truly be wrong. These were designers who gave their names to their brands. In the earlier days of luxury, the designer stood for the brand. Each brand displayed the eccentricities, the enigma, and the individuality of the designer it stood for. What remains important to date was that the designer gave identity to the brand, making the designer and the brand inseparable. Thus, we were in a regime where the "Creator was the Controller." But can the creators actually run a global business or manage the value chain of the business? What will happen after they leave the brand? And when they leave, most importantly, who would be able to sell their brand?

The store manager: *Martha must be about 50, but that's not important. The important thing is the energy that she has.*

She is striking. She's elegant, tall with long flowing hair. Her energetic walk conveys her vivacity and immediately gives a good impression that seduces the visitor.

Martha is a great saleswoman. She knows it and she is proud of it.

Her lightly tanned skin and the scattering of freckles on her face give her a mysterious, animal-like quality that conveys her taste for freedom. It is obvious that Martha is an independent woman.

This morning she is wearing a full-skirted blue dress designed by Jean Paul Gaultier for Hermès. Her beauty is impeccable—not aggressive, but serene. It is the way she looks at you that makes her beautiful—as well as her clothes, her height, and the color of her skin.

Martha is dignified. That is obvious.

She is not one to be scorned or humiliated. She is prepared for everything, from tough negotiations to difficult questions and unexpected arguments.

Martha is good at selling because she loves it.

She likes the challenge of the job and the products. She takes her share of responsibility for the brand. She sells only what she knows.

Martha was a sales assistant, promoted to be a supervisor, now a manager of the whole store. She now manages a large team of very different people, who are difficult to lead. They are so different that it is surprising she can actually manage to impose her point of view.

Yet she sees everything. When the customer enters the store and speaks to a sales assistant, Martha, from a distance, observes the gestures—the salesperson who suggests, the customer who touches, weighs, examines, and replaces the precious object delicately, or clumsily.

Martha is vigilant as she has a full overview of the store. Her attention is like radar. Nothing escapes her. She always chooses the right vantage point from which to observe all goings-on in the store. Quickly, she makes her way toward the men's department where she can hear that an irritated customer, impatient to obtain an answer to his question, is on the verge of leaving. Martha sees that the person serving him is too slow, that another pair of sales assistants is whispering in the corner (not about work, she imagines). They are giggling like two schoolgirls and this is neither the time nor the place. The shoes are brought to the customer, but in the wrong size. Martha anticipated this and hurries over to smooth matters over with the gentleman and makes sure another lady who has been waiting patiently is served a coffee.

Martha is a fairy. Her magic wand gives her store a tone, a rhythm, and a style that would not be there without her.

She chooses the flowers, tidies up, refolds a shirt, moves a tie that has been put in the wrong place, murmurs instructions, gives advice, picks up a stray piece of paper, sees a customer to the door, says "good morning" and "thank you," and generally plays hostess and boss, nurse and psychologist. A sales assistant is in tears because a customer told her she was "too poor to buy a bag like this for yourself!"

The cruelty of the remark caught the girl off-guard and she crumbled. Martha explains, reassures, and the saleswoman goes back "on stage" once the injury has been bandaged over.

Martha directs a "company of actors," as she calls them. The sales floor is their stage and their role is to "bring happiness." Martha leaves her worries at home—her mother's paralysis, her father's Alzheimer's, the stress of her son's "A" levels, and her daughter's exams.

Martha had decided that when on duty she has to put her anguish to one side and be a dream-maker. She pilots her store from the top deck and keeps it shipshape with the regal air of a mighty admiral directing a battle.

Martha takes her role as leader very seriously. She enjoys motivating her team, seducing her clients, and practicing her art.

For Martha is, in essence, an actress. She is a woman of few words, and what she does say, she always says calmly. For the rest, her stature and the way she holds herself are all the eloquence she needs. She is a store manager.

As explained in Chapter 2, three decades ago, the luxury industry model was almost completely dominated by family-run businesses. However, the rivalry between Bernard Arnault, Henri Racamier (LV), and Michel Chevalier (MH), and their newly founded conglomerate LVMH, created a historic structural shift within the industry as each aimed for market control through growth and acquisition. As a consequence, the industry started consolidating and family houses that could not survive were absorbed within the multibrand conglomerate except for a select group of French and Italian companies such as Hermès, Chanel (Wertheimer Family), Armani, and Tod's, to name a few. This tectonic shift from the family business model to corporatization pushed the luxury industry away from its historic style of management as the key factors of success became more financial management and shareholder value oriented instead of family business oriented. The focus shifted to the colossal conglomerate instead of the small, artisan business, which became "inadequate" for a global business strategy.

To understand the management styles found in the luxury industry we need to understand the role managers play—and the typology of management styles.

By definition, the role of a manager was to plan, organize, lead, and control. Since managers perform multiple roles in an organization during the strategy-making process, their method to realize the aforementioned

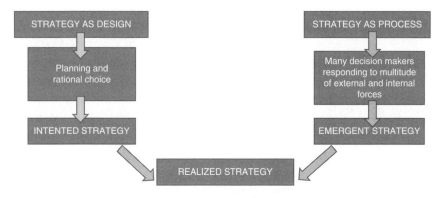

Figure 7.1 Strategy-Making—Design or Process?

role depended on their style of management. Figure 7.1 depicts strategy making as a design and as a process.

Under the same circumstances the roles of leaders are different. They are there to define the future and vision of the company, inspire, motivate their employees, energize and innovate the organization. More often than not the sector strategy-making process during the evolutionary period was more based on the style of the top management.

Literature over the past 70 years puts forth that management styles that incorporate both the contents of decision making and the process of decision making are aligned to goal setting, strategy formulations, and strategy implementation. Management style is also profoundly influenced by the distinctive sociocultural environment and climate in which an organization operates. The distinctive way in which managers perform the various functions in an organization decide their management styles. The core management style is reflected within the values and norms of organizational climate and culture. Three factors are usually analyzed: (1) degree of control in decision making,[2] on a scale from autocratic to democratic; (2) degree of production- or task-oriented and people- or relationship-focused;[3] and (3) social orientation—human capital linked with knowledge and customer orientation. Such a core management

---

[2] Robert Tannenbaum and Warren Schmidt developed the Leadership Continuum Theory in 1958.
[3] Blake and Mouton, 1972.

style may have variations that include *conservative style, entrepreneurial style, professional style, bureaucratic style, organic style, authoritarian style, participative style, intuitive style, familiar style, altruistic style, innovative style,* and so forth. Given the choices, an unlimited number of management styles can be visualized. For the sake of simplicity, we will focus on four primary management styles: (1) autocratic, (2) democratic, (3) participative, and (4) laissez faire, all in the context of the luxury industry.

Managing Paradoxes

As discussed in Chapter 4, the luxury industry is riddled with paradox. Managing people in this industry is also a paradox.

The Ambidextrous Luxury Manager

Gods, goddesses, and demons in ancient mythology had multiple heads and eyes to balance diverse needs. Brahma, the Hindu god, who is also the creator, had four heads to look in all directions and master the four Vedas, the ancient religious text of the Hindus. Similarly, Janus, the Roman god, had two sets of eyes—one pair focusing on what lay behind, the other on what lay ahead.

Combining the right and the left brain: The left brain uses logic, facts, and science. It is pragmatic and forms strategies. The right brain is creative, imaginative, perceptive, risk-taking, and oriented toward the big picture. Managers in the luxury industry are required to understand the unique properties of the luxury experience, manage highly creative people, apply tough management disciplines, and be sensitive to the cultural nuances involved in running a global business.

Speed versus time: The manager has to grapple with timelessness and modernity, which translates to profitability in modern times. For example, Hermès and Chanel might be of the opinion that they are not looking at short-term profits, yet during every quarter they have to keep an eye on the revenues, which in turn will determine their growth and investment plan. The focus on profitability extends across the portfolio to highly prestigious, loss-making brands. Above that, the introduction of IFRS and cross-border transactions forces greater transparency in financial reporting by large groups. The speed of growth and the time required for such profitable growth has a direct bearing on the talent management of the companies. On the one hand, they have to nurture talent that understands and communicates the story of the brand, the product characteristics, timelessness, quality, and service experience of the luxury business; while, on the other hand, they have to cater to the speed of marketing, sales, and after-sales in international markets.

Everywhere or nowhere: The luxury manager has to understand French and Italian *savoir faire* while selling products in Shenzhen, Sao Paulo, Singapore, or San Francisco. Dispatching expatriates to manage stores is one realistic option although the expatriates more often than not do not speak the local language. The expatriate manager on his or her "colonizing" mission of distant markets is probably well equipped but finds himself or herself short of understanding the local nuances. It could lead to failure. Research from Martens & Heads! shows that not more than 15% of the actual operating CEOs are from the local markets. Maxine Martens, CEO of Martens & Heads! rightly questions, "How many French or Italian luxury firms that do 30% of their business in Asia have 30% of their top management from Asia?"[4] Some propose that, with globalization and corporatization, the luxury industry should also follow the path of the global corporation. They should also hire more locals in distant markets and bring more emerging-market professionals to the HQ.

Internal versus external: Should the ambidextrous manager be recruited/hired internally or externally? Research shows that there is a trend to hire executive people from outside the luxury industry because they have more experience dealing with crises and global expansion in distant markets. There are highly capable leaders in other sectors whose experience managing brands and whose international mindset could be invaluable to luxury businesses needing to operate more effectively in a globalized marketplace. The next question is how to identify those leaders who can bring new skills and a fresh outlook, adapt to the idiosyncrasies of the sector, empathize with the product and the consumer, manage the creative process, get the best out of existing talent, handle operational complexity, shorten the production cycle, and yet remain flexible and agile enough to respond to and run with innovative ideas.

---

[4]Luxury Society, 2010.

Leaving it up to employees to take the initiative and gain education and experience on their own, however, is a gradual process that has prompted many eager companies to look for an alternative quick fix by pursuing talent outside the luxury industry. Gucci's Robert Polet was president of the ice cream and frozen foods division of Unilever before joining Gucci in 2004. LVMH has recruited several non-industry or outsiders as leaders, including Toni Belloni and Chris de Lapuente, formerly from Procter & Gamble, and Laurent Boillot, formerly of Unilever. Liberty Global plc hired Geoffroy de La Bourdonnaye, who was with Disney for many years before joining LMVH, while Dr. Bruno E. Sälzer worked at Beiersdorf and Schwarzkopf before becoming CEO of Hugo Boss. Stanislas de Quercize, Cartier and Van Cleef & Arpels, started his career at Procter & Gamble.

But the big three (LVMH, Richemont, and Kering), although open to external high-potential recruits, are undoubtedly more comfortable trying to nurture employees who are already within the organization or at least within the industry, and are now investing in their talent resources to nurture leaders for tomorrow.

Big or small: The big three, with time, have transformed themselves into multicultural, multibrand conglomerates. While it is difficult to generalize, managers coming into the industry from outside tend to be more effective when joining larger businesses than smaller ones. Culturally, and in other ways, it is easier for larger companies to assimilate outsiders, but that is not to say that smaller companies could not benefit greatly from an infusion of leadership talent with experience of different sectors and global markets. The challenge is to find leaders who possess a high level of sensitivity and who recognize the importance of preserving the inherent value of a brand.

International versus local: The industry is in a state of flux and is undecided. There is little consensus, even from an academic point of view, on how to modernize the luxury industry. The post-COVID scenario has changed this dilemma for good. Those who defend exclusivity and brand coherence are equally passionate about adapting to, and meeting the needs of, distant markets. Some state that local distribution will be the key to success, and that new ways of doing business (such as going digital and e-commerce) are critical, while still arguing against employing mass-market tactics for fear of diluting that sense of exclusivity and even opulence that is the very hallmark of luxury. Thus, where can one find this manager, the leader who is best equipped to handle the seemingly contradictory elements of developing new markets, opening up new distribution channels, adapting to diverse cultural expectations, and preserving exclusivity and brand coherence, while operating within a far tougher, more competitive commercial environment?

Manage talent in the digital era or stick to the traditional: The competencies required for the digital and the traditional luxury world are not the same. To be ambidextrous in this area is a key challenge. One side is pure technology while the other is the art of creating desire. Burberry and Raph Lauren for a decade embraced the digital world with ease while many were still struggling. For example, Burberry was often recognized and is still recognized as a digital luxury leader. This was the work of then-CEO Angela Ahrendts and chief creative officer Christopher Bailey. The firm has intertwined creativity, technology, and management in a way that has helped generate consumer interest in Burberry's products via its digital projects. Through their Art of the Trench crowdsourcing site, a three-dimensional Livestream show, and, most recently, an interactive digital ad campaign, Ahrendts and Bailey have facilitated collaboration across several functional departments, making everyone work together in the name of digital innovation. Another recent example, in 2021, was the creation of AZ Factory by Albar Elbaz (with A of Albar and Z of Elbaz), sponsored by Richemont Group. Here fashion is conceptualized both as digital and physical to reach a middle ground.

The ambidextrous luxury manager needs to have a portfolio of skill-sets that will make him or her comfortable in this industry. Figure 7.2 explains the ambidextrous nature of style in the decision-making process.

As in all industries, one size does not fit all. As the luxury industry has witnessed a sea-change in the internal and external environments during the past 30 years, the styles of top management have evolved over that time. The specificities pertaining to these changes had profound implications on the styles of management and governance of these companies.

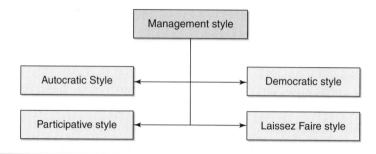

Management Style	Pros	Cons		
Autocratic	Instruction is forceful Facilitates fast decision No unexpected side track due to lack of communication among staff New policies/changes can be implemented swiftly	Staff feel demotivated as they are not consulted Do not favor innovative ideas from staff as they will not be considered anyway Lack of discussion has a negative impact on team work Wait for instruction thus causing delays No initiative from team members		
Democratic	Encourages group decision Everyone can voice their opinion Opinion from staff considered important and value adding Reduce implementation conflicts	Decision made may not be the best for the company Time consuming Conflict among support and non-support group Staff may not have enough knowledge about the decision		
Participative	Boosts staff morale Idea generation Networking among team Friendly Reduce implementation conflicts	Time consuming Staff feel offended if their ideas are not implemented Sometimes consultation may look artificial and not genuine if idea is not implemented		
Laissez Faire	Maximum delegation Manger can devote more time to strategy formulation Learning and knowledge-creating atmosphere Seen as empowering staff May create synergies between different subsidiaries	Less control Trust might be hampered Overall goal might not be achieved Time consuming in some emergent situations		

Figure 7.2   Differences in Management Styles

Familial Autonomy

"Family ownership is very specific to French luxury," once commented Elisabeth Ponsolle, General Secretary of Comité Colbert. The Comité Colbert, founded in 1954 by Jean-Jacques Guerlain with 14 houses, consists today of 84 French luxury houses, each with a different history, culture, size, and management. However, they share common governance rules and are willing to copromote their values and know-how. The term "houses," as opposed to the luxury company members of the Comité Colbert, illustrates their respective stories and the transmission of their know-how from one generation to another, which retains the secrets of their creations. Indeed, most of the members of familial business, and the family CEOs of the Comité Colbert, call each other *chef de maison* and not chairman or CEO. Thus, the span of control and decision making, by definition, was with the *chef de maison* who rendered complete autonomy to the brand. For example, the House of Lanvin was founded by Jeanne Lanvin in 1889. Bernard Lanvin, the grandnephew of the founder of the couture house, always refused to give up control of the couture, ready-to-wear, and fragrance businesses. Lanvin was acquired by Fosun International, one of the largest private Chinese conglomerates, that had Club Med and Caruso in their portfolio. Similarly, Pierre Frey founded his manufacturing house in 1935, and to date it is 100% family-owned, with Patrick Frey as head of the house since 1978. Patrick Frey has managed to keep control and expand internationally.

Broadly speaking there are three types of luxury company. The first is the luxury house that was built by several successive family generations. These are still run by the descendants of the founders, such as Estée Lauder and Hermès. The second type is the house acquired by rich families from their founders, at the very beginning, that still remain with those acquiring families—Chanel (with the Wertheimer family) and Guerlain (owned by LVMH Group). The third category is of conglomerates that have built a portfolio of luxury brands within their own structures and focused on specific luxury sectors—Lanvin (owned by Fosun International), Versace and Jimmy Choo (owned by Capri Holdings). In general, it was observed that family companies were more often profitable than listed financial groups, and survive well, at least while the family had the ability and will to manage the house. One reason might

be the style and principle of management, their long-term orientation, the family cared more about their employees, the relationship with
their employees and their customers, and the value and the image of the
name (which as previously discussed was most often their own name).
Moreover, since they were not listed companies, they were not bound
to reveal their financial figures or development strategies. This freedom
resulted in minimal distraction in implementing their consistent strategy
while maintaining control over the brand. This in turn allowed them to
emphasize and focus on long-term positioning rather than short-term
quarter-wise profit motivation.

Resisting Financial and Stakeholder Pressure

Some families managed to maintain their independence, such as the
Hermès Family, the Wertheimer family (Chanel), the Frey family (Pierre
Frey), and the Tribouillard family (Leonard Fashion), and many others
in France. In Italy, it was Armani, Tod's group and some others. Each
of these families had created profitable business models that encircled
powerful and independent brands, with minor debt and fixed expenses.
For instance, LV, Gucci, and Hermès had been very successful, with valu-
ations of $47 billion, $23 billion, and $22 billion in 2021. All three of
them with limited distribution, exclusivity, and controlled marketing—
for many of its product categories had regularly registered double-digit
growth rates year-on-year. Axel Dumas, Executive Chairman of Hermès,
had commented: "This sound growth reflects the House's creative drive,
outstanding know-how, and the relevance of its craftsmanship model
which helps strengthen local integration."

Louis Vuitton and Hermès products were available worldwide
through a network of 460 and 310 exclusive stores, with an annual
expansion of around three stores. Hermès watches, perfumes, and
tableware are also sold through networks of specialized stores and
in airport duty-free stores while LV had no specialized stores in the
airport duty-free.

Hermès, along with Prada, was one of the most profitable companies
in the world of luxury. It was also why Hermès did not need anyone to
support its capital structure. Due to unprecedented success of Hermès,
both at home and in international markets, it had long been the target of

the LVMH Group. The Group for years purchased bonds and stocks on the financial market. Analysts suggest that the aggressive entry of LVMH into the capital structure of Hermès brought nothing positive to Hermès, other than trouble. Still, LVMH increased its stake in Hermès to more than 20%. This was the reason the family members created a controlling family holding for more than 50% of the share capital within the group to fend off any attempted hostile takeover. During this incident, Patrick Thomas, the first nonfamily CEO, had commented that "Hermès is not managed only on financial principles. It is managed on the principle of the artefact in the best possible finish with the finest raw materials, with creativity as strong as possible that make people come into our stores and the strong assertion of the Hermès style." He continued to state that "all these features have nothing to do with a group that is much younger, and which is essentially a financial strategy group. And if you give economic control to financiers, they will kill the economy because they want short-term results. Finance should be a means to develop the economy but not the objective of the economy." The message was well understood. Axel Dumas and Bernard Arnault agreed to a peace agreement in September 2014. According to the agreement, LVMH kept only 8.5% of Hermès shares and the Hermès family controlled directly about 70% of the share capital. This was a victory for Hermès to stay independent and also a fantastic deal for LVMH, which in the process made a profit of over 3 billion euro.

Similarly, other families had succeeded and managed to stand up for their independence. Each of these families had created profitable business models that encircled powerful and independent brands, with negligible debt and fixed expenses, which allowed them to be independent and in full control.

Leonard, a French house created in 1958 by Daniel Tribouillard, had a geographical expansion strategy, and thus it was more famous in Japan than in France. The simplistic design of an "orchid on silk," which has been the signature symbol of his brand since the 1970s (when the first shop was opened in Paris), is famous there. It all began in 1958, when Daniel Tribouillard developed his idea into reality and made the brand name famous for its fully fashioned printed pullovers. He was soon known as "the man behind the flowers." He remains the proprietor of the company and refuses to sell to a big group. In Asia, printed patterns are still highly fashionable, and the public is in awe of Leonard's creations. From design to canvas to garment, the Leonard creation process stands out as unique in the world of Parisian couture. Despite past achievements, the future lies in the preservation of identity. It remains one of the last French family businesses in the ready-to-wear sector. Strong bonds between the French house and Japan have grown during the hundreds of trips made by Daniel Tribouillard and Nathalie, his daughter, to Asia. Today, 80% of the sales of Leonard are generated abroad, of which 60% are in Asia. In addition, many licenses have been granted in Japan. It is evident that the brand is turning its strategy toward Asia; however, it remains rooted in France.

Conglomerate: The Strategic Mix of Independence

However, during the process of globalization in the last decade, family-owned luxury houses found it more and more difficult to fund the necessary expansion and communication for their brands. This is where the large multibrand conglomerates had considerable synergistic advantage.

Three conglomerates—Paris-based LVMH, Kering, and Switzerland's Richemont—have quadrupled their combined share of the global luxury market over the past decade. In 2021, they posted a total of $72 billion in sales.

As discussed earlier these groups were considered to be multibrand or multiproduct players. They operated on a large scale with turnover figures usually over €10 billion. These groups, such as LVMH, Kering, Richemont, and Swatch Group, have reached a high level of diversification compared to their smaller competitors.

Examples of Styles

Houses from different countries can generally be said to have their own approach in management styles.

The French

France is luxury.

Louis Vuitton, Chanel, Hermès, Saint Laurent, Cartier, Christian Dior, Baccarat . . . these, together with others, are recognized brand names, all of which are French.

The French are on parade. High fashion is like a flag waving in the wind, announcing perfume, clothing, wine and spirits, hotels, accessories, shoes, bags, and so forth. Television before, and now live streaming, relay the message, images enchant, and French luxury is present.

A number of brand names come to mind as representing top luxury—Chloé, Sonia Rykiel, Lanvin, Longchamp, Agnès B., Leonard, Bernardaud, Bonpoint, Givenchy—constituting a French armada. The Americans counterattack with Tiffany, Ralph Lauren, Donna Karen, and Calvin Klein, while the English do their part with Dunhill, Burberry, and Paul Smith. Even the Germans won't be left out of the luxury market, taking up the rear with Escada, Hugo Boss, Jil Sander, and others.

The Belgians innovate with Martin Margiela, Dries Van Noten, and Ann Demeulemeester in the lead.

With so much at stake, the entire world wants a piece of the luxury pie.

But France still leads, with 50% of the world market.

The jewelry market has been the subject of a bitter fight. Entering into the fray are Cartier, Tiffany, Harry Winston, Van Cleef, Bulgari, Boucheron, Fred, Chopard, Stern, and others. Here again, the French have a top-rank position.

In watches, France, thanks to LVMH, is regaining strength against the Swiss, who dominate with Rolex, Oméga, Jaeger-LeCoultre, Baume et Mercier, Breitling, Patek Philippe, Audemars Piguet, Breguet, Vacheron Constantin, Girard-Perregaux, and Blancpain, among others.

France is in the lead in the luxury market. It is due to star brands such as Louis Vuitton, Hermès, Hennessy, Cartier, Moët et Chandon, Chanel, Christian Dior, Rémy Martin, and Lacoste, who together dominate the luxury business world in terms of sales. Their ranks are joined by the major French hotels and conquistadors of cuisine, such as Alain Ducasse and others.

It's wise to benefit from, invest in, act, and take shelter behind the red, white, and blue umbrella that naturally promotes the international development of French luxury companies.

LVMH: Bernard Arnault   Bernard Arnault says he is deeply involved in the creative process, far more than his peers. He believes that in the creative and highly seasonal fashion business, the ability to match effective CEOs with temperamental designers can make the difference between a star and a failure. He believes that "to have the right DNA in a team is very rare. It's almost like a miracle." Deemed the "Billionaire Matchmaker," in the past 40 years, he has formed close creative bonds with designers and managers. He was always at the helm of decision making during final key appointments. His vision of the luxury and fashion industry as he states it is: "This link to creativity, it's not far from art, and I like it very much. You must like to be with designers and creators. You have to like an image. That's also a key to success. And at the same time, you must be able to organize a business worldwide."

The key to success can also be the ability to build a "dream team" with a strong collaboration between the CEO and the creative director. In this case, the manager has to create a nonconventional style of management. He needs to give autonomy to the creative director and be able to deal with paradox, contradictions, and uncertainty.

> *Artists must be completely unfettered by financial and commercial concerns to do their best work. You don't "manage" John Galliano, just as no one could have "managed" Leonardo da Vinci or Frank Lloyd Wright.*
> **—Bernard Arnault**

In almost all its acquisitions, LVMH maintained the creative talent as an independent pool without attempting to generate synergies across product lines or brands. Lately, though, the sourcing has slowly been centralized to gain synergies and cost savings with a centralized purchasing mechanism.

Arnault's secret was to "remain deeply involved in the creative process, far more than his peers . . . convinced that the ability to match effective executives with temperamental designers can make the difference between a star and a failure in the luxury goods business." The article quotes Arnault as saying that "if you think and act like a typical manager around creative people—with rules, policies, data on consumer preferences and so forth—you will quickly kill their talents."

From the above discussion it can be summarized that Bernard Arnault did not believe in managerial limit setting. In 2000, Galliano sent models down the haute couture runways wearing dresses made of newspaper. To block the plan would have crushed the designer's spirit. When Dior manufactured the dresses in news-type printed fabric, they sold out immediately. It was a huge success for Dior.

Therefore, one can deduce that the management style of a CEO of a luxury company has to be significantly different from any other industry. They must both work within the business environment and the artistic world, where the typical personalities encountered are polar opposites of each other.

From the interviews with Bernard Arnault, it was always suggestive that that innovation was the primary factor of importance for growth and profitability. "Our whole business is based on giving our artists and designers complete freedom to invent without limits." This suggested that human resources and management were critical as the company tried to build a work environment that promoted creativity as well as adherence to strict business discipline. However, it was the vast range of disparate and diverse brands that caused the problem for coherence.

Another concern was the ruthless pursuit toward the bottom line. LVMH believed in running businesses profitably. Managers were supported as long as they made money over the stipulated minimum. "You have the freedom as long as you exceed your targets. Once you do not . . . there is no freedom anymore." For example, LVMH in 1988 acquired the French brand Celine, which was founded in 1945 by Celine Vipiana. But for years it did not do much with it. In 2008, Arnault found Phoebe Philo, who was the former creative director of Chloe. He instantly believed Philo to be the perfect match for Celine. He gave his full support and freedom, as always, to the new Chief Creative Officer. In the following two years she erased all the old collections, closed the non-performing stores, refurbished the main stores, and moved the headquarters to London, on the request of Philo. With substantial investments and losses for two years, Phoebe Philo proved her talents and rejuvenated the house, which has now become one of the most profitable and desirable brands in the luxury world. Phoebe Philo had in all senses of the word *reinvented* Celine by interpreting the brand in her own way. It may be safely assumed that during her 10-year tenure with Celine, the top-line increased about 20 times to close to euro 1 billion.[5] Following Phoebe's footsteps, Heidi Slimane joined as the creative director of Celine in 2018. At that time, Bernard Arnault, in a matter-of-fact way, stated: "The objective with him [Slimane] is to reach at least €2 billion to €3 billion, and perhaps more, within five years." The expectation was not something out-of-the-blue. During Heidi Slimane's four-year tenure at Saint Laurent, sales had rose from €400m to more than €1 billion, leapfrogging Bottega Veneta to become the second-largest fashion brand in the stable of LVMH's rival Kering.

However, industry insiders cite that all was not well with a financial man like Bernard Arnault at the helm. His management style has been described as providing "constrained freedom." The emphasis was on profit and if any division or company did not deliver, it would promptly be warned, management changed or sold off. This approach contrasted with the traditional and creative view of haute couture, which patiently allowed losses on different sets of collections, and waited for the market to accept its designs over a period of time. Having said that, for the previous 30 years LVMH had always beaten analysts' estimates over 120 quarters.

LVMH's leadership had been sustained by new product launches, store openings, and increased investment in communications, but it is now well documented that the key to its success rested with Bernard Arnault himself and his personal view of what makes an appropriate management style in this industry. Before the pandemic of 2020, in 2019 LVMH achieved a further double-digit increase in revenue and profit from recurring operations, a record level. Arnault attributed the success to "the desirability of LVMH brands; the creativity and quality of the products, the unique experience offered to customers, and the talent and the commitment of our teams are the Group's strengths." In the future, he was dedicated to "combining a long-term vision with a sense of responsibility in all the corporate actions, notably in its commitment for the preservation of the environment, sustainability and inclusion."

---

[5]https://www.ft.com/content/e8a5bd80-d2d5-11e8-9a3c-5d5eac8f1ab4.

Hermès: Jean-Louis Dumas

Be natural, say what you want to.

—Jean-Louis Dumas

He helped a lot of people to bloom.

—Pascale Mussard (niece of Jean-Louis Dumas)

Jean-Louis Dumas within Hermès was an icon in his own right in the luxury world. Some considered him a legend. He assumed the leadership of Hermès in 1978, at a low point in the company's fortunes. In his nearly 30 years as the company's chief executive, he transformed it into one of the world's most successful luxury brands. Dumas was both a business-oriented CEO and an artistic director. He was a very atypical leader, who cultivated his garden with creative talents and exceptional know-how. He was a visionary, guided by the love of people, of beauty, of travel and culture. He made Hermès much more than a "luxury" brand. In fact, Jean-Louis never used the word *luxury*. He created a "maison" of talent, excellence, craftsmanship, and creativity, and he achieved a goal that he didn't even have: he made Hermès the most luxurious brand in the world—some people say that it may be the "only one left."

> *We've got to remain true to ourselves, but we've got to change constantly. And it's that tension which is at the heart of Hermès. You have to make a reaction. You have to surprise. You have to astonish yourself. Be always on a wire, a thread.*
>
> **—Jean-Louis Dumas**

With a free, sometimes audacious hand, he shook things up, by hiring exciting new designers, extending the company's lines, and creating iconic products such as the Birkin bag, inspired by the actress and singer Jane Birkin, and expanding internationally and taking the business into new markets such as China. He also invested in companies like the glassware maker Saint-Louis, the tableware company Puiforcat, and the fashion house of Jean Paul Gaultier. In 2003, Dumas again surprised the industry, this time[6] by hiring Jean Paul Gaultier as creative director.

---

[6]After he had hired Martin Margiela.

I would love to work on it. It's a house that allows for great creative freedom with no limits.

—Jean Paul Gaultier

Jean-Louis Dumas's style was different from the rest. Frederic Mitterrand, the French Minister of Culture described him as follows: "Jean-Louis Dumas was an extraordinary man whose charisma was entirely devoted to creation and excellence. His name, his person, and his humor, remain inseparable from the famous maison—Hermès. Man of taste and culture, passionate for drawing, he knew how to treat the designers with the kindness and respect they deserved. He did not hesitate to make bold decisions, as when he invited Jean Paul Gaultier to reinvent ready-to-wear at Hermès. He devoted his whole life to serving this great house and French creation, which he has succeeded in renewing the codes and traditions with an endless imagination and vision."

At Hermès, the management style was clear. No member of the family got a position unless he or she deserved it. If an outsider was better qualified, he or she would get the job. When Jean-Louis Dumas promoted his niece Pascale Mussard into advertising and public relations, she was at first surprised as she was shy and wasn't sure she would fit the job. He told her, "Be natural, say what you want to." He believed in her. "He helped a lot of people to bloom," she said.

During Jean-Louis Dumas's time, Hermès's core business strategy was to produce products that were of unrivalled quality using traditional craftsmanship and the finest quality natural materials such as leather and silk. The house had built its success over time with an excellence and authenticity of expertise in craftsmanship and prided itself on core values of elegance, timelessness, and quality creations. Hermès's strategy was to continually expand and innovate its product range while at the same time staying true to its roots and continuing to produce timeless creations. Some legendary models have never gone out of style and are still produced today, such as the iconic Kelly Bag and silk scarves.

A key management style was to maintain extremely high levels of in-house production and treat people extremely well. Hermès produced more than two-thirds of its products in-house with manufacturing operations that encompass more than 30 production units spread across France and one each in Great Britain, Italy, Switzerland, and the United

States. To keep up with demand the group further expanded production capacity over the years. During the COVID-19 period, Hermès had announced that it will open its twenty-first leather goods factory in France. The twentieth was opened in Normandy while the last one would be opened in the Auvergne region of France by 2023, creating 250 new jobs.

Another key management style was to retain tight control over outsourced production, carrying out targeted audits to ascertain that the suppliers' operations meet the group's expectations. In some cases, the company bought into carefully selected companies to ensure the stability of these relationships. Hermès maintained its long-term strategy of maintaining control over its know-how and distribution network. The group continued to invest in projects to expand production capacity in its different sectors. As an "outside" successor of Jean-Louis Dumas, Patrick Thomas followed Dumas' style and succeeded extremely well in pushing sales and profitability to a level that had never been achieved before. Pierre-Alexis Dumas, the son of Jean-Louis; Guillaume de Seynes, another nephew of Jean-Louis; and Henri-Louis Bauer, a cousin, took over as the new management team in 2014, under the leadership of Axel Dumas as the CEO of Hermès.

Hermès's business style had a dual focus of accentuating the house's unique position as the ultimate in quality and craftsmanship while at the same time focusing on business growth. Their core business strategy was to have "full control of the value chain, own stores, no licenses, no delocalization of production, worship of the product, products partly handmade, importance of creation, capitalization on heritage and history."[7]

The family "dream team" was fully dedicated to pursue this strategy in the future.

The Swiss

The Swiss are known for their watches. The Swatch Group Ltd., hailing from Switzerland, is the number-one manufacturer of finished watches in the world. The Group not only manufactured finished watches but also was in the business of producing jewelry, watch movements, and

---

[7]Kapferer and Tabatoni, 2010, 17.

watch components. The journey of Swatch Group started in 1983 when the first Swatch watches were released. The following years had seen the recovery of the Swiss watchmaking industry as a whole, and the establishment of The Swatch Group as a strong, diversified industrial holding, a leader in the watch business that was based out of Switzerland. The watch industry was Switzerland's third largest exporter after the machine and chemical industries. Switzerland harbored the retail operations of most of the world's most sought-after brands, often found concentrated on Zurich's Bahnhofstrasse and Geneva's "luxury mile," the rue du Rhône.

Baselworld was the place to be. It started in 1917, when a handful of Swiss watchmakers collaborated to organize an exhibition to show the world the delicate craft of watchmaking and promote the value of "Made in Switzerland." The heavyweight independents were Rolex, Patek Philippe, Audemars Piguet. The rest were part of multibrand conglomerates, such as TAG Heuer of LVMH Group, watch brands such as IWC, Jaeger-LeCoultre, Officine Panerai, Vacheron Constantin of the Richemont Group and the Breguet, Harry Winston, Blancpain, and Omega, among others of the Swatch Group. However, the Baselworld faced uncertainty, especially after the pandemic. Due to coronavirus, the 2020 fair was first postponed to early 2021 and then officially canceled. There was no news on whether Baselworld will return after 2021, but the management team was looking at options. According to Michel Loris-Melikoff, managing director of Baselworld, together with the exhibitors and visitors, they were working intensively on clarifying and discussing the requirements and options for new platforms, new concepts to re-define the Baselworld of yesteryear.

Richemont: Johann Rupert

> *Richemont has weathered the economic crisis to date and is in a strong financial position. There will still be plenty of challenges ahead but we are confident that Richemont's Maisons will surmount them.*
>
> **—Johann Rupert, CEO**

Rupert described his management style as "hands off" and depicts how he often adopted a disguise to check up on some of the group's boutiques. He was quoted as saying "I don't need to worry about operational issues. I know I can trust my colleagues to do that. I'm no longer involved in supply-chain management, the IT infrastructure or even, come to that, the financial disciplines. We have the people to do all that. Don't postpone until tomorrow what you can delegate today."

Admittedly, it was more of a holding of a group of individual companies. "Years ago, I determined that we would vertically integrate to the fullest extent. Although that was not the most popular, or financially lucrative, choice, I made sure every brand had its own manufacturing and structure. Each could be autonomous." It was interesting that this approach worked so well in this case, while LVMH has been known to experience problems trying to follow this model. Perhaps the answer lay in the fact that the Richemont brand range was much smaller and much more interrelated. In addition, despite the autonomy, synergies still existed behind the scenes. Rupert introduced structural changes early on, so that each of his brands, known as *maisons*, could enjoy independence over their products, strategies, and communications. The model had been replicated by rivals, notably LVMH, but remained conspicuously distant from more autocratic styles of competitors, such as Swatch Group and other groups that focus on a founding father, for example, Georgio Armani.

Brand control in Richemont rested in the hands of the strategic product and communications committee, which was "the ultimate brand guardian. We have a very collegiate style, and people with immense experience, going back years. We are Richemont's institutional memory."

Rupert, a man of frankness, which seemed typical of his affable style, had earned respect around the world as a great business figure, who hinted at a certain personal distance from luxury goods and the social circles that surround the industry. "In an industry characterized by high-profile leaders, Johann Rupert stands out as an exception. Unlike Bernard Arnault, chairman and chief executive of LVMH, or the father-and-son teams at Kering and Swatch Group, the Richemont boss remains content—even determined—to remain out of sight. Richemont holds no news conferences and Mr. Rupert gives few interviews."

The group keeps to the background in favor of its brands. "I even discourage my colleagues from getting into the papers too often. I'm against this trend of turning businessmen into cult figures," he says. Rupert's vision was clear: "All we're trying to do is keep the products and the message consistent. If we do that right, the numbers will come out right, too."

Rolex: Hans Wilsdorf   Rolex was a private foundation and had benefited from remarkable stability since its beginning. It had an unparalleled consistency of purpose of its founder. It had three CEOs in the first century of its history. The private nature of the foundation had enabled the company to control and innovate. Each of its leaders had in turn made bold moves, embraced progress, and broken with tradition when necessary, to ensure the success of the company. Rolex never lost its focus. It has only three values linked to its DNA: timeless, sports and adventure, and reliability. It created "a crown for every achievement—extreme athletes, racing pilots, deep sea divers." Its strategy revolved around those three concepts. It had no brand extensions. It had only watches and only five models—Daytona, Submariner, Sea Dweller, Yacht-Master, Milgauss (with date-just, day-date, or date).

Hans Wilsdorf, the founder, started the company in 1905 and envisioned the wristwatch in an era of pocket watches. He was fascinated with watches and obsessed with creating movements small enough to be worn on the wrist, at a time when men's fashion favored large-face pocket watches. With a visionary spirit, he detected that a reliable and accurate wristwatch could change the overall market.

After Hans Wilsdorf, Rolex engaged in almost half a century of leadership under the Heiniger family. André Heiniger became managing director in 1962, two years after Wilsdorf died. He was a true commercial strategist, moved by inspiration and enthusiasm, always keeping his profile low. Like Hans Wilsdorf, he had a strong sense of anticipation and was continuously pursuing perfection. André Heiniger was one of the greatest visionaries of contemporary watchmaking. One important decision, for instance, was to remain faithful to the mechanical watch. He also gave rise to partnerships with sports events and personalities of world renown. Upon André Heiniger's leadership, philanthropy efforts were developed and the Rolex Award for Enterprise was created, with the purpose to honor and support pioneering individuals whose projects have brought major benefits to their communities and beyond. Under

André Heiniger's leadership, Rolex experienced years of expansion. He brought the company to the next level, defined its marketing vision, and contributed to increasing the brand's recognition, paving the way for the next chapter in the history of the company.

In 1992, Patrick Heiniger, his son, succeeded him. He focused on strengthening the brand worldwide and, most important, he was responsible for the fundamental strategic choice of vertical integration of Rolex's production facility. Full control of the value chain guaranteed control over the manufacture of the essential components of the brand's watches, thus ensuring its autonomy. He was responsible for increasing quality and productivity within the company. Patrick Heiniger left the company in 2008 but remained as an advisor. He was succeeded by Bruno Meier. This was the first time the company had not been run by either Wilsdorf or a member of the Heiniger family.

In 2011, Bruno Meier was replaced by Riccardo Marini, who was previously the head of Rolex Italia. In 2015, Riccardo Marini was appointed to the board. Jean-Frédéric Dufour succeeded as new CEO. He was recognized as the man who had turned Zenith around. Well aware of the challenges arising from globalization, he steered a careful course between the legacy of the past and the demands of a constantly changing world to allow Rolex to build on its success. Under his leadership, Rolex continued to optimize its industrial and commercial structure to heighten its passion for innovation, perfection, and achievement.

The Italians

Despite arriving in the world of ready-to-wear after the French, the Italians had the strongest worldwide sales in this segment. The advantages they have over the French are those of novelty, diversity, and reach. A point to be noted about the Italian brands was that they mostly started out with accessories: the beginning of great designers was in Gucci handbags, Fendi fur, and Prada shoes. However, they slowly increased their reach to include ready-to-wear collections, which became an instant hit with the ladies. Despite never having promoted *Haute Couture* (which is a very French concept), these Italian brands were never afraid to hit Paris Fashion week with their latest collections.

The Milan fashion show. You have to be there.

Along with the French, the Italians were the kings of the world of luxury. They are everywhere in fashion—clothing, wines, and hotels—everywhere you go! Italy has numerous luxury brand names: Armani, Prada, Furla, Gucci, Bulgari, Versace, Moncler, Ferragamo . . . but the country that comes to mind throughout the world, when luxury is mentioned, is France.

Armani has built a luxury empire, encompassing everything from sunglasses to haute couture and luxury hotels. Armani even makes television sets, fountain pens, jewelry and all sorts of accessories that look like a disorganized ensemble "à la Cardin," in true Italian style, packed with charm, and as always, rather successful too. On planet luxury, Armani pops up at every street corner, in one disguise or another, under his own trade name or that of one spinoff or another: Emporio, Armani Casa, Marni, Armani Collezioni, Armani hotels . . .. So, what will be the next Armani venture? And what does the future hold for the Armani group?

Now that Gianfranco Ferré is dead, Valentino is standing aloof. Versace has been through tragic rough patches, but the family still knows the ropes . . . though Donetella decided to join Capri Holdings.

Tod's is the one that has beaten them all to the post, its founding president Diego della Valle being a darling of the media. Tod's is a planetary success story, an Italian symbol of luxury and creativity positioned in the best places, a conquering and innovative spirit.

Luxottica, the discreet maker of Rayban sunglasses, also makes eyewear for Chanel, Versace, Prada, Bulgari, Tiffany, Dolce & Gabbana, Paul Smith, Ferragamo, and others. With over 60,000 employees, it produces over 40 million pairs of eyeglasses on three continents. And the world's No. 1 eyewear maker is the Del Vecchio, another Italian luxury family business, with sales of over €7 billion. It merged with Essilor of France to form EssilorLuxotticain 2018.[8]

The list of the Italian luxury players goes on forever, featuring Armani, Moncler, Prada, Gucci, Dolce & Gabbana, Pucci, Versace, Zanotti, Valentino, Furla, Fendi, Bulgari, Ferragamo, Cavalli, and Rossi, not to mention Ferrari and all the others.

---

[8]Essilor Luxottica thus became the leading groups in the design, production and marketing of ophthalmic lenses, optical equipment and prescription glasses and sunglasses with more than 20 premium brands including Ray-Ban, Oakley, Michael Kors, LensCrafters, and more. The company has €16 billion in revenues and €50 billion capitalization as of 2021.

Italy is the kingdom of design and Torino is the capital. The Italians often group their export operations with those of the rest of the family, but will they find a way to join up like the French to create large groups in order to brace themselves against the competition of tomorrow, or will they wither away when their founding fathers die?

The French believe that the Italians view LVMH or Kering with envy and are forced to admit that they have never been able to create one almighty, all-encompassing luxury conglomerate. The timing would be perfect now that so many questions arise about the future of family-run businesses left to their own devices through lack of planning for their succession. Will Armani, Ferragamo, Prada, among others, find a solution for the future or will they crumble under the pressure of family quarrels and poor succession planning?

Where succession is concerned, Italian luxury is still in the ice age compared with its French counterpart, having failed to plan ahead. As a result, some superb talents have already passed over to the French side, led by LVMH or Kering, such as Gucci or Pucci, and others may follow suit! Will the Italians know how to preserve their luxury houses or will French luxury become Franco-Italian? This may turn out to be the best option, because the great Italian brand names will no doubt prefer to fly the French colors if they survive. We can all live with that. In the end, Europe is here to stay at the helm of world luxury for many years to come, and within Europe, the Franco-Italian pair is way ahead of its time.

Armani: Giorgio Armani

> *When people stop to ask me for an autograph, what I hear most often is, Mr. Armani, you make beautiful things, but I like you so much as a person. You are so nice, so real. That's my reward. Being famous very often means sacrificing your privacy and that of others. I have never compromised. I learned to get where I am by work, I learned slowly. I wasn't certain of succeeding. I am trying to optimize my ability, which still seems very acute to me, to manage this empire as if I were immortal—for now, I should add.*
>
> **—Giorgio Armani**

Giorgio Armani sees himself as a talented designer, an idol, someone famous, a celebrity. He is the type of leader who likes to have control of every detail. He created his company from scratch, building it up into a successful empire with a lot of hard work and a hands-on attitude. It is all about him, and he manages his empire as if he were immortal. He oversees every aspect of the business and makes all the decisions. Giorgio Armani was a pioneer in terms of making luxury affordable a long time before the concept of "masstige" came up in the marketing arena. As early as 1979, he launched Armani Collezioni, first in the United States, then a year later in the rest of the world as a diffusion line. But even more innovative was his vision in 1981 to create the world of Emporio Armani, a brand that he decided to create as valuable and strong as Giorgio Armani but more affordable and also more creative and fashionable with one concept in mind: to make fashion affordable for the masses. This was still quite revolutionary at the time for a brand that remained luxury positioned, as Emporio Armani distribution was and still is restricted to free-standing stores and shops in prestigious department stores. One of the key ingredients to success was the passion, professionalism, and consistency brought by Giorgio Armani and his team of designers in the development of all the collections from Giorgio Armani to Emporio Amani, from Armani Collezioni to Armani Jeans. Mr. Armani has always controlled every detail of every collection. For him, whether the product was Giorgio Armani or Armani Jeans, a suit or a pair of jeans, did not make a difference: he wanted to check and control every product with the same attention before giving his final approval. This level of control has been essential in maintaining the consistency of the brand identity with so many brands created, so many product extensions, and so many partners involved.

> *There is no doubt that there are difficult years for the fashion and luxury market. Nevertheless, the good results achieved by the Armani Group, joining Yoox-Net-a-Porter for our e-commerce business consistently bear witness once again to the strength of our brand and confirm the solidity of our successful business model. We continue to believe in our vision, our goals, and our strategic choices, and this belief encourages us to maintain a long-term view in any initiative we undertake.*
>
> **—Giorgio Armani**

Gucci: A Sequence of Dream Teams   Domenico de Sole and Tom Ford formed a very famous dream team—the "Dom-Tom" power duo. They conceived the turnaround of Gucci from a suffering leather goods company into one of the world's hottest luxury goods companies.

One important aspect of this dream team was that they had mutual respect and total trust in each other. Domenico de Sole recognized that Tom was a creative genius and gave him freedom to work in his field, while Tom recognized Dom's management skills and abilities as the company's CEO. "Our [Tom Ford and Domenico de Sole's] mutual respect for each other and total trust in each other's abilities has been key to our success," stated Tom Ford.

After Domenico de Sole and Tom Ford's teamwork, Gucci was in the hands of another good team—Patrizio Di Marco and Frida Giannini. "I don't have to tell Frida to do anything other than to be herself. She's made beautiful products from the beginning." said Patrizio Di Marco. Di Marco was also very successful in turning around Bottega Veneta, giving full creative freedom to Thomas Meier, a former employee of Hermès. The team left Gucci in 2015. During their management, profitability of the Gucci brand reached very high levels, making Gucci one of the best performing brands in the luxury industry.

Succeeding them was Marco Bizzarri as new CEO. He joined Kering Group in 2005, and was CEO of Stella McCartney and Bottega Veneta. He appointed Alessandro Michele as Creative Director and made another dream team. With Alessandro Michele's quirky and less rigidly gendered style, Gucci attracted a new batch of young customers. During 2016–2021, the brand grew on the frenzy of Alesandro's creation and able management of Marco, riding the wave of success and reaching almost 10 billion euro just before the pandemic of 2020.

Prada: Patrizio Bertelli and Miuccia Prada Prada, the Italian family-owned brand, had long been known for its intense management by its owners, Patrizio Bertelli and Miuccia Prada. The Bertelli–Prada partnership was the heart of a firm that had thrived for the past quarter century as a distinctly family-run enterprise. Bertelli, Prada, and her siblings own close to 95% of the company. Bertelli and Prada served as chief executive officer and chairman, respectively. Bertelli brought the same intensity to the business side of the brand as she did to the creative. Past and present executives describe them as an indefatigable and charismatic boss with an intimate knowledge of the company, from the stitching of shoe seams to the color of the walls in Prada boutiques. He has the last word on everything from hiring to how many precious skins to order for a line of handbags. When a top manager leaves—and several have after clashing with the boss—Bertelli often takes over the position in an interim capacity. Executives are loath to make decisions without his approval, and few dare to contradict him. "It's the law of the jungle," says Gian Giacomo Ferraris, chief executive of Versace, who worked at the Prada group earlier this decade. "He expects a lot from himself, and therefore from others. Either you play at his level, or he writes you off." One example could prove Bertelli's autocracy and bad temper. When he was overseeing the decor of a new Miu Miu store in Manhattan in 1997, he did not like a mirror and smashed it simply because he thought the mirror made people look fat. Bertelli loves his autocratic style and his total control over the creative designers. He believes in the crucial points that the creative and commercial needs of the brand have to be on equal footing for the company to be a true success. Thus, designers have to make consensus between their creative thinking and the demands imposed on them by the managers. Clashes between the creative and business sides have led to legendary bust-ups, and resulted in the German designer Jil Sander's acrimonious exit from her eponymous firm when Prada bought it in 1999.

As the decision maker of the company, the Bertelli-Prada duo is so important to the business that when the company was preparing a stock market listing, banking advisers laid out as a "risk factor" for investors any eventuality that the two might decide not to work together anymore. According to the brand's COO Sebastian Suhl, "They are not managers, they are owners and entrepreneurs, and they are the brand!" In 2020, Raf Simons was appointed as co-creative director at Prada.

Coach: Lew Frankfort and Reed Krakoff

Before [Lew Frankfort] acted, he began to formulate a plan. He likes to have a vision and a sense of where he's going. That way he can communicate his expectations to his staff and others.
                    —Marilyn Much, journalist at Investor

Lew Frankfort has been with Coach since 1979. He is currently the CEO. He brought Coach from a $19 million company to a $3.6 billion international group. What vision did he have for the brand?

I realized that we were plateauing. I recognized that I needed first to transform myself from believing that Coach could continue to be successful as a house of American leather goods, to believing that it [. . .could] evolve into a modern American lifestyle accessories brand. At the same time I knew I had to persuade consumers to embrace the changes at Coach.

—Lew Frankfort

He decided to recruit Reed Krakoff as president and creative director of Coach, who introduced accessories and new products to the stores monthly instead of semiannually, and he increased the profitability of the company by supplying in Asia.

They're [Lew Frankfort and Reed Krakoff] an excellent balance for each other, which is critical. One is strong operationally; one is a strong creative force. It's rare to find that combination.

—David Lamer, analyst with Ferris Baker Watts

They balance each other and acknowledge their individual strengths, with Lew Frankfort focusing more on the operational aspects and Reed Krakoff on the creative side of the business. They see each other as partners and have a very open and frank relationship, saying exactly what is on their minds, and thus setting a good example for the rest of the company. The trust factor also plays an important role.

We are partners in running the company . . .. We tell each other exactly what's on our minds, and that sets a good example for the rest of the company. Usually we don't even have to debate, but if we were to have a debate about an issue, we trust each other. Not only do you need to know your business and your customers, you need to understand the pulse points of your business, you also need to be nimble to adapt. I strongly believe in situational leadership—modifying my leadership style to fit the skill set and experience level of the person I'm working with—to appropriately "tell, sell, collaborate, or delegate" the project at hand. I am driven in part by a blend of striving for excellence and a fear of failure.

—Lew Frankfort

The leadership of Lew Frankfort has become legendary in the luxury world. His vision, planning, sense of the future, communication, and methods of managing the expectations of his staff and others led Krakoff to comment "the key to Lew's success as a dynamic and inspirational leader is in his ability to orchestrate a decision-making process that is both inclusive and incisive."

Lew Frankfort is a humble leader who is not afraid to admit when he has made mistakes. And he is proud of that fact. To him, the best managers are those who have experienced both success and failure. He considers every mistake he has made as a true learning experience, and he is always striving for excellence. He also adapts his leadership style to fit the person with whom he is working.

> *I'm flexible. I don't fall in love with my designs. . ... I'd rather not have an "It" bag; I'm very humble about our business. If no one says anything about [the perspective bags I am walking around the office with], I know they're probably not great. But if I walk by the catalogue people and [they] say "Oh my god, when is that coming out?," then you know you have something. It's a handbag; it's not your taxes. It has to be emotional.*
>
> **—Reed Krakoff**

Coach is a consumer-centric brand. CRM has played a major role in Coach's success. It's not that easy for a designer to set his ego aside and rely as much on consumer research as on his own creativity. In order to constantly innovate, Reed Krakoff had to be humble, focus on the business, and be creative at the same time.

In 2009, while still at Coach, Reed Krakoff launched a namesake line. In 2013, Coach and Krakoff parted ways. In 2014, Lew Frankfort was succeeded by Victor Luis. Frankfort then became executive chairman. He said in an interview, "I don't have a fixed retirement date." Under Luis, the company changed the name of the holding company to Tapestry, which included Coach. It added shoemaker Stuart Weitzman and millennial-focused Kate Spade to win new customers. In 2019, as the company struggled to integrate the brands and keep up with trends, Jide Zeitlin was appointed as the CEO but he stepped down a year after. Chief Financial Officer Joanne Crevoiserat, a former Abercrombie & Fitch executive, has been appointed as interim CEO of Tapestry.

Analysis

What was perhaps even more indicative of a good management style, however diverse, was that the companies discussed—LVMH, Hermès, Richemont, Rolex, Armani, Gucci, Prada, Coach—increased their revenue from 2010–2020, indicating a strong ability to recover from the global financial crisis. The most successful companies were LVMH, Hermès, Richemont, Rolex, and Gucci. LVMH, Kering, and Richemont had nurtured star brands in their portfolios, such as Louis Vuitton, Dior, Hennessey, Gucci, Balenciaga, Saint Laurent, and Cartier. They had always been in leading positions in terms of profitability. Gucci had its legendary boom due to its new designing style that made it an instant sensation in Asia and with millennials. However, Armani's and Coach's profit fell during restructuring. Though Armani had set up a foundation in his name and indicated that part of his high-end fashion empire should be transferred into a charitable organization, the designer had yet to name a successor for when he will finally step down. With a change of top management, Coach was having difficulty integrating its acquisitions and the growth of the brands it had acquired.

Another identified criterion to the successful management of a luxury brand has always been the notion of brand identity. It is vital to both the immediate and sustained success of a luxury brand. Each company analyzed had developed a strong brand identity. They all understood the importance of heritage and authenticity. They placed paramount emphasis on product and service quality, on creativity and innovation. Each recognized the importance of having a strong brand positioning and an excellent brand image that was required for their presence worldwide. However, it was worth evaluating to what extent each individual company was able to achieve this.

The family-owned companies had been able to develop over time at their own pace. After 170 years, it was rare to see a company still guided by the very essence of its beginnings, and to see the founding family still retaining the largest shareholding block and responsible for shaping the philosophy and performance of the business. Hermès focused on value rather than volume. They had a commitment to their craftsmen, allowing them large amounts of freedom so as to encourage as much innovation and creativity of their métiers as possible. The link to their heritage and equestrian theme had always been and will always be there. Yet it constantly evolved and mixed with an element of surprise. Hermès created innovative new products while maintaining existing favorites and bestsellers. Their motto, "Everything changes. Nothing changes," perfectly embodied the essence of the brand. Hermès took things slowly and gave time for its dream to flourish and spread, a path it was only able to take due to being a family-owned company. It was this elongated process of brand-building, production, marketing, and selling that had resulted in the timeless aura that characterized the brand.

Prada also was able to take the time it needed to evolve as a brand at its own speed. Mario and his brother ran the company at their pace until Mario's daughter, Luisa Prada, took the helm. Miuccia Prada joined the company and eventually took over from her mother in 1978, with Bertelli alongside her as business manager. Even then, Miuccia was allowed time to implement her creativity and transfer it into design. It was of no doubt that this freedom and encouragement of innovation and creativity contributed to its success. "Prada's originality made it one of the most influential fashion houses."[9] At Prada the technical acumen and commitment of employees was highly respected and Prada offered rewards and growth opportunities in order to retain talent. They had stayed true to their heritage as a producer of travel articles and accessories made with sophisticated techniques and the finest materials and extending their product range without losing sight of where they began. In line with succession, Lorenzo Bertelli, the son of Miuccia Prada and co-CEO Patrizio Bertelli, was given the role to lead marketing, communications as well as the group's corporate social responsibility function. As a former racing driver with little business experience, he settled in the company with his e-commerce and a sustainability agenda. In addition to digital investment, his focus on environment-friendly fabrics, such as nylon products made of recycled ocean plastic, fishing nets, and textile industry waste has likely benefited Prada's turnaround efforts.

In contrast, the brands that were owned by companies that have been successful were seeking growth and profitability. They wanted star brands that would be their cash cows. The cash generated from the star

---

[9]Carrie Grosvenor, "Prada: From Suitcases to Oscar Gowns, from Milan to the World." www.lifeinitaly.com/fashion/prada.asp.

brands was used to support the other brands and for acquisitions. LVMH, Louis Vuitton, Christian Dior, Hennessy, and more recently Sephora, were treated in this way. With the growth in China, it remained to be seen how the traditional Star brands could bring in the money. The brands were strong and resources were deployed preferentially to make them stronger, such that the brands could perform wonders with their consumers. In contrast, the brands within these companies that were not as strong might not be given the time and attention they needed or be overshadowed by the star brands.[10] One need only look at what happened with Michael Kors. "Was I mistreated?," Kors said in an interview. "No. Was I neglected? Yes. I never felt as though there were a strategy at LVMH as far as pitting the designers against each other or the brands against each other," Kors said. "It's just that I never felt anyone was watching the smaller companies at all, but everybody was spending their time on the two first-born children—Louis Vuitton and Christian Dior. In a way, if you're a nice kid, no one pays attention to you. If you're a bad kid, you get spoiled."[11]

At Kering, Gucci was their "star brand" and, during the era of Tom Ford, it completely lost sight of its heritage and its link to horses. The brand was promoted as having sex appeal and high-octane glamor. It was perceived to have lost its magic and the real story of Gucci was forgotten. When Tom Ford left the company the brand struggled, and his successor, Freida Giannini, had to go back to the archives for inspiration and draw again on the heritage of the brand. This illustrates the fact that luxury brands need time to develop both their image and their identity and sometimes with the way company-owned groups are managed this is not possible. And the management style was a key to develop and understand the brands. Another lesson was to say that brands were far more important than creators and managers; when Tom Ford and De Sole left Gucci, the brand did not suffer and growth continued. Following the previous duos, the next generation iconic team of Marco Bizzarri and Alessandro Michele had an effective response to the health crisis. They managed to completely relaunch the brand with a culture of

---

[10]Star brands are defined as those brands that are timeless, modern, fast-growing, and highly profitable.

[11] *Women's Wear Daily* (April 2004).

empowerment and a unique understanding of the historical codes. They renewed their focus on millennials, consumer engagement and creative partnerships once they took over in 2015. They reinforced the roots of Gucci to the next generation, that stood for inclusivity, diversity, self-expression, commitment to sustainability in more ways than one.

The common thread that was revealed during the description of the leaders and managers that run the houses, brands, or conglomerates was their dedication and the consistency in their vision, their passion for the industry and their brand, their relentless capacity to create, innovate, and at the same time to run their businesses globally. All understood the need to have a high level of in-house production and a high level of control over suppliers that resulted in high quality. All understood the importance of a powerful distribution network, the need for a strong global presence (particularly in the emerging markets of Asia, especially China), and to work toward optimizing all of these aspects as much as possible.

The dominant style, as seen from the above description, would be in the continuum from an autocratic to a laissez-faire style of management, but what remains a certainty is that all those at the helm of the luxury business have their own very special style of management. The autocratic yet hands-off style might be actually a variant laissez-faire style, because managers were not passively leaving decisions to their employees, but leading with a clear know-how of the industry. The conglomerates had pressures on their bottom line coming from their stakeholders every quarter. The family-owned brands had no such pressure and could take it slowly and focus on the long term. This made them less efficient and slow to respond to the changes in the environment. But in the end the industry demanded profits to sustain itself. The craftsmen and métiers also needed to be protected. This could only ensure that the skills of the craftsmen and their specialization were protected, nurtured, and encouraged to foster. This would ensure that innovation and creativity would be sustained to serve the ever-increasing number of wealthy people of the world.

Conclusion

The luxury market is characterized by complexity and diversity. At each corner lies a different managerial approach, from the large global multi-brand conglomerate to the small, exclusive family-run "Maison." As has been discussed, neither method has led to Eldorado. Certain brands are today successfully managed by these large corporations, but issues of neglect still, and will continue to exist. At the same time, the security and stability of joining forces had led many irreplaceable and unique labels to abandon traditional luxury ideas in favor of more commercial, global business practices through acquisitions and mergers. Despite this trend, some maisons, notably Hermès and Chanel, have managed to survive and prosper. It is the job of a leader to lead. The role to create a pathway into the future remains central.

Luxury is a world of detail. Details are what makes the difference, and this principle equally applies to a manager's work style and ethic. It is a world in which, in order to succeed, those at the top must adopt a hands-on managerial style. Finally, to have a vision one needs to speak the language of the brand, and never lose sight of the situation on a domestic scale. That does not mean neglecting the importance of global strategy in different markets.

Managers who were originally "outsiders" will succeed, and have historically succeeded.[12] Ambidextrous competence, multicultural leadership with European roots, French/Italian language skills, geographic flexibility, and managing creativity are the necessary factors that characterized the *luxury industry manager*. Furthermore, good people skills: listening and engaging aptly with a team or clients—both locally and internationally—are not just a bonus but a requirement if success and growth are desired objectives.

---

[12]Managers have replaced "chefs de maisons" on the luxury planet. They come from all horizons: Yves Carcelle from textile Descamps, for LV; Sydney Toledano from Lancel, where he worked for many years with the Zorbibe brothers. Patrick Thomas was with Pernod-Ricard, the famous French group, and was hired by Dumas to manage Hermès. During the 1990s, Dumas had chosen managers from outside the luxury world to manage Hermès, Mireille Maury, Gilles Duval, Christian Blanckaert, and Patrick Thomas. All of them had no experience in luxury. Mireille Maury came from Saint Gobain and Gilles Duval had been in the distribution of mass-market products. Christian Blanckaert came from Thomson. In the Pinault-Kering group, the artisan of the Gucci Group buy was Serge Weinberg, who had been a civil servant before his appointment as CEO of CFAO, a distribution company famous in Africa. François Pinault hired many managers from outside the luxury world and his son as well. Robert Pollet for Gucci came from a large food company. These managers succeeded very well, all of them. Some never stayed, like Fabrice Boe-Dreyfus who was the general manager of Hermès for a few months only, coming from L'Oréal, or Veronique Morali, a very capable manager who never found a position that suited her capacities within the Chanel Group.

One must remember that the key to succeed was to understand first that in famous houses, "no one is waiting for one to succeed." The designers and the managers are a blip in time. The brand will stay forever. When LV or Chanel or Hermès have been successful for more than 100 years, it is useless to come as a fighter or a Zorro to explain how to perform. The manager first needed to listen a lot to capture the subtlety of the luxury *game*, leave the creators aside, understand the product, spend a lot of time in the stores, and contribute to bettering business practices and processes. They have to change their orientation, put themselves in the mood of the brand, meet employees inside and clients outside, watch the reactions of everyone in various countries, and reflect. This is a long process of understanding; it takes time and modesty, humor and steadfastness to grasp every detail.

Different houses, brands, and conglomerates have different management styles that depend on the personality of their leader, the internal and external environment in which they are operating, the situation the brands are facing, and other specificities—such as size, expansion, retail network, and others. There are some successful practices that could be considered references. But there is no single recipe for the best managerial style within this industry. Thus, a mix of styles might be needed when implementing certain strategies, solving some problems, or managing complicated situations.

However, the human factor creates challenges for brands. The people behind these brands worked for decades; the brands survived through two world wars and multiple global fiscal meltdowns while building up their images and sustaining them. An economic crisis, or a health crisis like the pandemic of 2020, cannot fracture the values, principles, and standards that fuse the founding family or creator of the logo.

Each brand recognizes the importance of profitability while protecting the brand's identity and image at the same time. With very strong and unique leaders, managers, and owners dominating this industry, the two overarching themes are undoubtedly managing creativity and the bottom line, which seem sometimes to be at loggerheads, thus creating *homoluxus*.

In 1930, Gabrielle Chanel signed a contract with Samuel Goldwyn to be costume designer for United Artists. Gloria Swanson was one of the actresses who wore Chanel dresses.

Mademoiselle Chanel was always full of audacity. She dared to use an inexpensive fabric—cotton jersey—and even back then, she had no qualms about designing a suit for working women. Her tweeds were made especially for her in Scotland. Around the same time, she also started making costume jewelry. To Coco Chanel, fashion was on the streets. So, she dared to be different.

Chanel, Saint Laurent, Cardin, Courrèges—they were all daring and paid no heed to what others were doing. The luxury world abounded with people who dared, who were totally free and independent. Such people are simply themselves: they design as they see fit. Figure 7.3 depicts the characteristics of a leader in the luxury sector.

These people are everywhere in the luxury sector, because the freedom to design is not the privilege of a particular field. On the contrary, it is to be found in all luxury markets, from champagne to fashion, from cognac to hotels or watches.

Luxury products in all sectors simply need to be unique and extraordinary, like a Stradivarius violin. This is vital.

Figure 7.3   Characteristics of a Leader in the Luxury Sector

Chapter 8

Skills

Craftsmen are the major players hidden in the wings off the stage that is the luxury world. They come from extremely varied backgrounds, they are passionate about doing a good job, and perform their crafts with well-deserved pride. They are driven by beauty, perfection, a polished finish, and excellent handiwork.

They know they are the "Last of the Mohicans," but they are happy about this. Some are trained on the job, some in schools, some are the sons and daughters of craftsmen, and they all pull together as one. In the word "craftsman" there is "craft," and in "worker" there is "work"—as in a work of art. Craftsmen and workers are artists and they put their stamp on their work. Luxury craftsmen are committed to their works of creation: they mark them and they may see them again.

Craftsmen glean their knowledge by watching, certainly not by reading. They teach by demonstrating. They learn by observing and pass on their know-how.

Great craftsmen also know how to behave with clients, or in society in general. They know how to explain, listen, and demonstrate. They are passionate and demanding.

If they know how to *do* as well as how to *be*, then their futures are often mapped out with a major luxury house, but if they are on their own, then they could remain in the shadows their entire career. Luxury craftsmen are part of a team: they never cease to learn new things, they have to adapt to new models, new workshops, and new supervisors. They travel, learn from talking to others. Their lives are long discoveries. They are the true representatives of luxury and hold the key to the treasure trove: know-how!

It takes time to become a successful craftsman: time for learning, time for training, time to listen and to watch, time to try and try again. A work of art takes time and a luxury craftsman is part of a long-term investment.

Adam Smith (1723–1790)—the father of modern economics (*The Wealth of Nations,* 1776)—spoke about the four factors of production: land, labor, capital, and entrepreneurship. Karl Marx (1818–1883)—the father of the theory of the battle of the classes (*Das Kapital,* 1867)— spoke about labor as the most important factor. Capitalism has always been and is about optimizing the utilization and allocation of resources. The primordial resources being capital (to be understood here as *physical capital*: factories, machinery, etc.) and labor (the *manpower* or employees), this economic system that governs our world operates on the principle of maximization of output (what is produced by capital and labor) and profit (the surplus revenue accumulated after a firm has broken even in terms of its intermediary costs—otherwise known as the amount of money the firm invested in order to produce its output). While the luxury industry does operate in accordance with this principle of maximization of output and profit, due to its specific nature (craftsmen are rare and not easily replaceable by other employees or by machines), the relationship of the firm to its labor force has always been particular to the industry. This relationship is also an element to keep in mind when analyzing how luxury goods are priced. Rarity increases the value (intrinsic or monetary) of a good. Rare supply (as is the case with artisanal craftsmen) in turn increases the rarity of the good. Demand for the good thus increases (as consumers seek to own exclusive items), and as a result, the price increases.

This logic can be applied to the majority of luxury goods and services (from the Kelly bag by Hermes, to a cruise to Antarctica on a Ponant Yacht). As a summary, within this configuration, capitalism can squeeze only labor to maximize output and profit. Luxury, on the other hand, respects craftsmanship and thus can justify the price of the product.

With the rise of the luxury conglomerates, and the growing number of wealthy people around the world, especially in new distant markets, the luxury industry has experienced a phase of phenomenal growth over the course of the last three decades. As a result of the growth in foreign markets and the up-scaling of operations, the skills required to produce exquisite goods—in terms of economies of scale and economies of scope—had become a scarce resource. Scale and scope beg the question of how and where to find these special skill sets required for (1) craftsmen who have tacit knowledge of a brand's DNA, (2) designers who create while respecting that DNA, (3) salespeople who convey the brand's story to an increasing number of diverse consumers across cultures, nations, and continents, and (4) managers who run the business—not just domestically, but globally.

These four talent categories are comprised of individuals who have the skills to use their left and right brains effectively. The left brain uses logic, attention to detail, facts, figures, present and past, and complexity; it acknowledges reality, is strategic, practical, and safe. The right brain uses feeling, creativity, imagination, attention to the big picture, symbols and images, present and future, philosophy and arts, appreciates spatial perception, comprehends knowledge, and is open to possibilities and risk taking. In this industry craftsmen must master the balance between the right- and left-brain functions. On the other hand, to a certain extent, designers need to be particularly skilled in right-brain functions. Again, sales staff need to be extremely skilled in left-brain functions with skills development of the right brain. Managers, however, need to be skilled in using the left brain while acknowledging the right. It is a difficult balance, and it becomes more challenging with the expansion and growth of this industry.

Decades of phenomenal growth have caused some luxury conglomerates to outsource some of their activities to skilled labor in different countries, mostly countries with low-wage workers, to increase profitability. In this way the industry saw a period of transformation and renewal. But customers crave "Made in France," "Made in Italy," or "Swiss" watches. A key question to address is how to manage phenomenal growth on the one hand, scale up the production of goods while keeping the brand's DNA intact on the other, while at the same time producing in a home country where skilled workers are few and far between.

Bottega Veneta offered a good example of this. Tomas Maier, former design director for the brand, was committed to conserving Bottega Veneta's know-how, preserving jobs in the area where the company originated, and ensuring the survival of certain vital skills which might otherwise disappear. To do so, he had taken the initiative of creating leather-braiding schools in the Veneto region around Venice. Fighting hard to pursue what, for him, was a highly personal issue, he had succeeded in making his expectations of sustainability an integral part of Bottega Veneta's outlook. In other words, Bottega Veneta sought to make permanent a particular business and human resources quite beyond its current agenda and its own immediate interest.

In Chanel's case, it established a subsidiary, Paraffection S.A., in 1997 to preserve and promote the heritage, craft and manufacturing skills of fashion artisan workshops. Since 2002, Chanel has also held the annual Métiers d'Art, a runway show, outside of its traditional fashion calendar, to honor the fine craftsmanship that its artisan partners bring. The show is presented in a different city every year, and prompts a media frenzy wherever it pops up. It is a great tool to showcase Chanel's dedication to craftsmanship. In 2019, Chanel kicked off construction on the new site that housed its Métiers d'Art ateliers in Aubervilliers, a northern suburb of Paris. The site housed most of the 26 specialty ateliers Chanel controlled through its Paraffection subsidiary, which included the jeweler Desrues, feather maker Lemarié, embroiderers Maison Lesage, Atelier Montex, shoemaker Massaro, milliner Maison Michel, and cashmere specialist Barrie. In the same vein, the business of luxury was no longer a local business. It cannot therefore be run on a local business model. Gone were the days of one, two, or four shops in different regions of France or Italy. Emerging customers are educated, digitally savvy, and abreast of the changing ways in which the products and services were designed, marketed, distributed, and consumed. One of the undoubted strengths of the luxury industry was the power of brands' heritage and core values that attracted passionate and patient individuals. These individuals appreciated the creativity, craftsmanship, and cachet of working in this industry. But this is no longer enough. In order to thrive in the current transformative period, especially post-pandemic, the industry is seeking breakthrough talents with specific skill sets that are entirely new to luxury, while at the same time enabling the existing talent pool to adapt and change with the times, keeping them excited and motivated.

Following the Coronavirus disruptions, luxury brands' managements are facing the urge to redesign their talent strategy and establish "complete talents" in terms of skills. In this context, *complete* means a person *who has all the skills, requirements and preparation required for the type of activity he or she carries out, in its various possible applications (not limited to certain specializations).*

In fact, growth in the luxury industry requires that the workplace has no choice but to embrace the new reality, be flexible, and execute a reset in each area of the business's value chain. This will be essential not only to survive but to create a new experience for core customers and prospects, who are readying for the new norm. It would mean understanding the sociocultural context, nationalism, with its idiosyncrasies in its new digital knowledge of the well-informed consumers.

Craftsmanship Through History

Craftsmanship is the key to luxury, because I think the time has come back to restore the value of the expertise of craftsmen and to look to the solid foundation of the past to create the new.

—Fulvia Visconti Ferragamo

Luxury goods have existed for centuries as the royal and aristocratic classes around the world have spent their fortunes on extravagant handmade clothing and accessories. The luxury brands that are well known are around 100–200 years old. However, the industrialization of the luxury goods market has only taken place in the past couple of decades. Most fashion and accessories, jewelry and watch brands—such as Chanel, Louis Vuitton, Hermès, Boucheron, Cartier, Prada, and Versace—started out as small French or Italian family businesses, centered around a founder, a creative designer, or an authentic material. At that time, the required skill sets to work in luxury were simple and limited: the businesses were owned by families that served and satisfied local customers to a great extent, and in some cases regional or special-order customers. Skill sets mainly focused on a passion for excellent craftsmanship and creative designs that had their signature differentiation. For example, the story of Chaumet and the Swiss watch industry demonstrates how history had a part to play in the creation of the brand and of the sector.

Case Study: Chaumet

Chaumet was established in 1780, even before the most successful jewelry brands, such as Cartier, Van Cleef and Arpels or Bulgari. Its history can be divided into five periods: the Nitot period (1780–1815), the Fossin and Morel periods (1815–1885), the Chaumet Art Deco period (1885–1944), the Resurgence Period (1944–1987), and the LVMH Period (1987–present day).[1]

Marie-Étienne Nitot settled in Paris in 1780 after having apprenticed as jeweler to Queen Marie-Antoinette. His aristocratic clientele remained loyal to him. After the French Revolution in 1789, Nitot became the official jeweler to Napoleon I in 1802, from which beginning the Nitot jewelry house really took off. With the help of his son François Regnault, Nitot designed and set the jewelry for Napoleon's wedding to Joséphine de Beauharnais, and later to Marie Louise de Habsburg-Lorraine. He also designed and set Napoleon's coronation crown, the hilt of his sword, as well as many other pieces for the court. At the fall of the empire in 1815, Napoleon's exile aroused Regnault, a fervent royalist, to withdraw from the house and sell it to his foreman, Jean Baptiste Fossin.

(continued)

[1]https://en.wikipedia.org/wiki/Chaumet#Chaumet_Period:_resurgence_of_the _brand_(1944-1987).

(continued)

Helped by his son Jules, Fossin's elegant designs won him the family of Louis-Philippe, King of France from 1830 to 1848, as well as the Duchesse de Berry. The royal client list of the house went on to include Anatole Demidoff, a Russian prince, as well as many French and foreign artists. The French revolution of 1848 slowed the French business and led to its expansion to London, managed by Jean-Valentin Morel. At the London World's Fair of 1851, the house produced hardstone goblets with enameled mounts.

In 1885, Joseph Chaumet took control of the House and that was where the house got its name. Tiaras were trendy at the time, which Chaumet would make one of its specialties. Chaumet made over 2,000 tiaras from 1780, for monarchies and aristocratic families. Joseph's son Marcel Chaumet succeeded him in 1928, at the height of the Art Deco period. The house became a leader of the trend and participated in the 1925 Exposition des Arts Décoratifs in Paris. The house continued to excel until it had to close because of the Second World War. In the wake of the postwar years, Chaumet stood out as a precursor, embodying the taste and creativity of the Parisian woman. Its designs were marked by originality and unconventional combinations.

As mentioned in Chapter 6, in 1987 the house filed for bankruptcy, caused by failure of its diamond business. Its owners at the time, Jacques and Pierre Chaumet, were sentenced to imprisonment. The house was later purchased by Investcorp, an investment bank, and then by LVMH in 1999.

Within LVMH's jewelry portfolio, Chaumet holds the longest history and boasts many accolades, including "the jeweler of Napoleon," "rich artistic heritage," and "exquisite craftsmanship." Chaumet truly is a sleeping beauty. Its heritage is a valuable asset and a source of inspiration that the brand always refers back to. With innovation and reinterpretation of the brand image, Chaumet possessed potential for superior commercial performance.

After an unsuccessful attempt to penetrate the American market, in the late 1990s, the company opened stores in Asia to fuel growth. It entered China in 2007, much later than Cartier's 1992, Tiffany's 2002, and Bulgari's 2003. Admittedly, those early birds enjoyed an advantage in market performance and brand awareness in a relatively pristine market. But the market evolved fast. Jewelers and the rest strived to manage the paradox between heritage and market trend. It was a breakthrough time for Chaumet. Its choice of Yifei Liu, Disney's Mulan, as the brand ambassador, has been bringing wide exposure and eyeballs for the brand.

Usually, a special order or unique item requires 500 to 1,500 hours of work, representing a timeframe of two to six months. Each tiara undergoes many different steps: shaping, dismantling, preparation of the setting, polishing, re-cutting diamonds, setting, applying hallmarks, engraving, final assembly and final finishing. As a luxury product is the result of such painstaking efforts to meet the highest expectations of quality, it is not subject to the whims of style or season. Timelessness is not just about the beauty of the product, but also about its heritage and the vitality of the brand.

Case Study: The Swiss Watch Industry

The first mechanical clock was invented in Italy and England around the mid-fourteenth century. The oldest clocktower dates back to 1352. Over the course of 700 years, the mechanical clock epicenter moved from Italy to Germany to France to England to Geneva, and finally to Swiss Jura, where it remains today. The first wristwatch was a piece commissioned in 1810 by the

(*continued*)

(*continued*)

Queen of Naples from Abraham-Louis Breguet (1747–1823). Breguet is often thought to have been the greatest watchmaker of all time. During this time the rapid innovation from clock-tower to a wristwatch worn by the Queen of England paved the way for how watches were to be manufactured. Watches went through the manufacturing cycle of ad hoc local production, to division of labor between artisans who produced one-of-a-kind timepieces, to uniform assemblies of interchangeable parts. Switzerland, located in the alpine region, with high mountains and narrow valleys, has few natural resources. Conditions such as the terrain and the cold winter climate made agriculture difficult, so in-house handicraft industries such as textiles, cheese, chocolate, and watches were developed to supplement agriculture.

Watchmaking was introduced in the middle of the sixteenth century by the Huguenots—French refugees persecuted for their Protestant faith, among whom were many skilled watchmakers. These refugees settled in French-speaking Geneva. The Huguenots' arrival coincided with John Calvin's dominion over Geneva, who instituted a series of rules that essentially prohibited the wearing of jewelry. At that time, Geneva was renowned for its fine jewelry industry. However, wearing timepieces was not prohibited. So, watchmakers found themselves with a ready, and growing, market and jewelers saw an opportunity to change their trade. Soon, in 1601, the world's first watchmaking guild was established in Geneva. Over time, Geneva became crowded with watchmakers, many of whom branched out to the Jura Mountains.

Geneva became a city of merchants who understood trade and were skilled in watchmaking. Around 1785, some 20,000 persons worked in Geneva's watchmaking industry, producing 85,000 watches per year with another 50,000 watches in the region of Neuchatel. The long winters provided lots of idle time in this region and the relatively soft hands of cow herders were well suited to watch manufacturing. The herders were also willing to work for low wages, as watchmaking was relatively well compensated compared to farmwork. Watchmaking became synonymous with jewelry-making, due to the intricate complicated parts and the use of precious and semiprecious stones, enabling watches to withstand wear. The influx of Protestant refugees from France brought not only experienced workers but the commercial networks for export trade. At the same time, Germany, Britain, and France became involved in two world wars. Switzerland's location in the center of Europe, its multilingual population, 500 years of democracy, neutrality, peaceful trading, and export competency enabled it to trade across the world even in wartime. At the turn of the twentieth century Switzerland had overtaken Britain, France, and Italy, and become a leader of accurate and precise manufacturing of watches.

Entrepreneurial Designers

Family-run houses were entrepreneurs who started their businesses with passion and believed in what they did. For example, Hans Wilsdorf was passionate about watches and started a watch trading company when he was 22 years old, in London in 1903, as did Van Cleef & Arpels, Guerlain, Krug, Rothschild, the Chaumet brothers, Coco Chanel, Breguet, and others. They did not have any shareholders and maximizing shareholder value was not one of their business objectives; they did not feel the need to hire functional employees, for finance, HR, retail, marketing, and branding, nor did they set up a CEO, CFO, or COO.

The Sales Team

There are some unique features that separate luxury sales teams from those of other industries. They must have a mix of two contrasting traits.

Case Study: Hermès—Harness and Saddlery

Thierry Hermès, born to a French father and a German mother in the German town of Krefeld, was the youngest of six children. He moved to Paris in 1828. Having been trained and clearly possessing talent in leatherwork, he opened a workshop in Grands Boulevards of Paris in 1837 that specialized in horse harnesses, traps, caleches, and carriages. Hermès products were inspired by the dynamics of animal power and grace, movement and travel, nature and the outdoors. The business offered a model that was built on handcrafted stitching. The famous saddle stitch, which required two needles working two waxed linen threads in tensile opposition, was a fine, graphic stitch that would never become loose when done properly. Thierry's customers were socialites, the Parisian beau monde, and European royalty, including Emperor Napoleon III and his empress, Eugenie. But his real customers were horses. It was his passion to make horses and their riders comfortable with immaculate leather upholstery. Its richness lay in fine leather and elegant saddles that revolved around the life of a horse. After Thierry retired in 1880, his son Emily-Charles inherited the business, moved it to 24 Faubourg Saint-Honoré, and added a custom business that required measurements from both the rider and the horse.

Case Study: Louis Vuitton—Travel Bag

Louis Vuitton was born in Anchay, Jura, France, in 1821. He moved to Paris at the age of 16 in 1837 and was apprenticed to luggage- and trunkmaker Monsieur Marechal. With the apprenticeship he learned the art of fine-luggage creation; he also worked as a luggage packer for upscale Parisian families. This experience gave him insight into the world of luggage and the needs of wealthy travelers. In 1854 he opened his first store in Paris, creating Louis Vuitton Malletier, or Trunkmaker. He began by designing the first flat-topped trunks, which were lightweight and airtight, clearly innovating and differentiating his products from other trunkmakers, which had rounded tops for water to run off: rounded-top trunks could not be stacked in railway cars. To save trunks from water he designed the waterproof signature gray "Trianon" canvas. The "Trianon" trunk quickly became popular as a symbol of cosmopolitan living and elegant travel. The same year, Vuitton created innovative trunks to accommodate the voluminous crinolines worn by France's Empress Eugenie, wife of Napoleon III. The "Empress" trunk could be considered the beginning of Vuitton's carefully crafted image as a luxury and celebrity brand. By 1860, Vuitton was already sufficiently successful to open a larger factory in Asnières-sur-Seine to accommodate the increased demand for his goods. During the next decade, Vuitton created many innovative designs, including the first Vuitton wardrobe trunk, which contained a rail for hanging clothing and small drawers.

Case Study: Zegna

Angelo Zegna, a watchmaker by trade, started weaving wool from four looms. Of his 10 children it was the youngest, Ermenegildo, born in 1892, who was the young entrepreneur. Ermenegildo, at the age of 18, founded the Lanificio Zegna (wool mill) in Trivero, in the Alpine foothills near Biella, thus creating the Ermenegildo Zegna Group in 1910. His passion was to make fabrics that had to be "the most beautiful in the world." Following his passion, he started producing and

(*continued*)

sourcing fabrics of outstanding quality and designs that were avant-garde. Ermenegildo's skill was in sourcing that was way ahead of his time. He sourced quality natural fabrics directly from their country of origin that brought innovation to products in his homeland, Italy. This vision of integrated sourcing with highest quality weaving laid the foundation for a fully vertically integrated company and one of Italy's most acclaimed family-driven enterprises. Again, much ahead of his time, he understood the meaning of sustainable production and the importance of forging a relationship with the local territory and community. He understood that the beauty of the natural environment and people's well-being were indispensable. Angelo Zegna, son of Ermenegildo, described his father's achievements as "I see four forces acting throughout my father's life. First of all, he was born in the right environment to develop his business aptitudes. There were various small firms competing in a small area. Secondly, he was always determined to get the better of his British rivals, by offering creative Italian fabrics with an unbeatable quality. The third force was an exceptionally open mind, especially regarding the social welfare of the territory and redistribution of value to workers. Lastly, there was his fundamentally important relationship with nature, his awareness that natural resources are limited and that we must protect them. He was an ecologist long before the term even existed!"

One type of employee is trained for rigor and intelligence: to look into companies' financial positions; to be practical and understand the strategic underpinnings of a decision; to have a highly developed left brain: examples are bankers, doctors, lawyers, etc. The other kind of employee is creative and artistic: they think laterally, not just vertically; through their artistic talent and imagination, they create things; with a highly developed right brain such people include architects, musicians, dancers, and so forth. Luxury sales teams need to be practical artists, which sounds counterintuitive. The importance of revenue cannot be overlooked, but conveying a brand's DNA, and delivering art-level service, is even more crucial. Without them, brands will not grow sustainably. There lies the oxymoron that all luxury sales staff have to live with—they have to be strategic players with a dash of creativity. These two diverse skill sets are not easy to find in a single employee, and even if found it is difficult to manage such employees.

The challenge that luxury sales teams face is how to make profits without compromising brand DNA, grow without diluting the brand offer, be less accessible but still sell as much. For instance, Louis Vuitton expanded its reach to many remote parts of the world. Ninety-four percent of young Japanese women own a Louis Vuitton, making the brand less exclusive. The other extreme was Hermès, which was known to have much greater profit potential. On the one hand, Hermès can innovate, customize, and woo the Chinese and the Japanese. However, they are noted to stick to their cultural roots, their heritage, and it seemed they are not immediately interested in market share. They embody French aristocracy, deeply Protestant in their ways. Thus, they are unwilling to compromise on their craftsmanship, their excellence in quality, and their manual production process. They think for the long term and not for short-term gain. It was part of their family ethics. From the above two examples it is evident that the skill set required by LV was different from that required by Hermès. Another example to be noted in this regard is the Italian brand Bottega Veneta. They are known for the most exquisite craftsmanship. The striking feature about Bottega is that people are less aware of the brand than its competitors, such as Armani. And, in 2021, Bottega Veneta cut off all their social media channels, proving true to their DNA as a *stealth luxury* brand. This presaged a heavy upside potential for Bottega Veneta; the brand prides itself on its delicate subtlety. However, the discreet and no-logo brand image has worked well with its customers and, at the same time, boosted its bottom line.

Professional Managers

The first generation of entrepreneurs and designers had retired by the late 1970s and family businesses were inherited by their children or passed to immediate relatives. With the expansion of their businesses both new challenges and opportunities became prominent. The crafts-men, designers, and owners of the brands did not know how to embrace globalization effectively when more and more of their customers were from distant countries. They did not have the management depth to embrace growth, expansion, and profitability. That was probably the reason that, in the 1970s, many French firms, especially fashion houses, suffered from a variety of management and ownership problems. These firms lacked capital and were not yet mass-marketing their wares. The 1980s saw a revitalization of luxury firms. One reason was the use of celebrities to promote brand awareness, such as using the Academy Awards to showcase designer clothing. Another reason was the influx of capital to these firms. Leading this trend was real estate manager Bernard Arnault, who took control of Agache-Willot-Boussac-Saint-Frères and kept only its affiliate, Christian Dior. Arnault soon thereafter took control of Louis Vuitton and Moët-Hennessy. From 1985 to 2020, he took over 76 brands. With this came the consolidation and the business groups of Richemont in 1988 and PPR (now Kering) in 1999. This consolidation required distinctive skill sets drastically different from what had historically been needed. It gave rise to multibrand conglomerates whose business models incorporated globalization, professionalization, commercialization, centralization, digitalization, and profit maximization for their shareholders.

In order to deal with this new business strategy, the conglomerates needed to create new structures around the brands. They started employing line managers who had command of diversified skill sets—strong leadership, effective communication skills, efficient strategy-making skills, and financial skills. These line managers were used to managing fast-moving retail businesses and professional workforces. In fact, the luxury conglomerates forgot the position of Chef de Maison (Chief of the House) and began to hire CEOs, or other senior management staff, from other industries. For example, they hired Conchetta Lanciaux, Yves Carcelle, Lew Frankfort, Sidney Toledano, Christian Blanckaert, Tamara Mellon, Stanislas de Quercize, Daniel Piette, Michael Burke, Ravi Thakran, and others.

In the mid-1980s, this new group of professionals, who had no luxury background, was ushered into the luxury industry. They possessed some traits and skill sets in common, such as being educated in business schools of high repute, having proven records of well-rounded management, open communication, accounting and financial skills. They succeeded in recruiting, motivating, and retaining talent. They had a keen insight for change and development within the market vis-à-vis market entry, expansion, extension, and acquisition. They had a knack and an intuition about strategy formulation and implementation of skill sets across markets. For the past few decades, they have steered their brands successfully through cyclical environments by leveraging their advantages with an understanding of the luxury brands they worked for.

Perspective of the Conglomerates

In the last few sections, we discussed the skills cherished by the luxury industry. The three multibrand conglomerates specify somewhat different skill sets that are required to be successful in the industry, yet are also specific to the conglomerates.

The professional environment of the LVMH group is shaped by excellence and exacting expectations, reflecting our constant contact with the magic of creativity and with unique expertise in a tremendous number of different skillsets around the world. Our working environment is entirely focused on luxury, making it especially stimulating for people who are creative, passionate, and have an entrepreneurial mindset. LVMH is a veritable "ecosystem," counting over 100,000 people with an incredible wealth of experience and opportunities.

When people join LVMH they choose an environment that is fascinating and passionate, embarking on a professional journey that is stimulating and profoundly meaningful. Joining LVMH means being part of a Group that is the leader in its industry and enjoys a global presence, a Group where passion for aesthetic quality and creativity goes hand in hand with a commitment to excellence and to being the best. It means playing a part in an ecosystem that is constantly evolving and reinventing itself. It means contributing to the work of teams that are rich in talent and diversity. When people embrace the LVMH experience, their

*own story becomes interlinked with that of the brands whose rich herit-
age we represent as we perpetuate the "Future of Tradition."*
**—Chantal Gaemperle, Group Executive Vice President, Human
Resources and Synergies**

According to LVMH, it has a decentralized organization where each brand manages recruitment independently to meet its specific needs. The skill sets required are varied. It recruits *exceptional* people capable of combining *pragmatic* and *creative* thinking with an *entrepreneurial mindset* and *international vision.* They seek people who feel a *strong affinity with luxury products.* An unyielding commitment to *excellence* and an ability to *anticipate the future* while *respecting the DNA* of their brands are essential to a fulfilling and successful itinerary in the prestigious environment of the LVMH group. The LVMH group considers *diversity* to be a great asset.

Compared to LVMH, Richemont Group requires the following skill sets:

Richemont and its Maisons are committed to preserving the finer business values of entrepreneurship, integrity, and creativity. They offer talented and skilled people diversified and engaging development opportunities along their career path, both nationally and internationally. Moreover, they encourage them to build on their strengths, develop their skills and support the achievement of the Maisons' business success. They look for people who want to contribute to the successful history of our Maisons, who aim for excellence in whatever they do and share our long-term vision. They ask the best of our people and steer individuals towards achieving their personal excellence. We are committed to providing an environment where professional competencies are continuously developed; where trade skills are the finest in the industry and where professional development is considered a priority.

The Richemont Group manages by objectives, empowers people to take initiatives and expects the employees to actively contribute to the Group's success and show commitment to the Maisons and loyalty to the Group. They are committed to preserving high standards of performance and unsurpassed quality in their everyday business activities. They see it as a privilege to work for, and represent, excellence, tradition and prestige.

This is why their employees act as an ambassador of the Maison they represent and for the Group as a whole, just as Richemont is dedicated to providing excellence in shared services to our Maisons via our network of regional subsidiaries. They conduct their business in accordance with management principles that place value in our people's successes, namely: trust and loyalty, mutual respect. At Richemont they apply the word "Métier"[2] as an honorary term to credit those professions working at the heart of our luxury business, and which require a unique savoir-faire, expert qualifications and accomplished dexterity.

The Richemont values were: entrepreneurship, creativity/innovation, customer focused, learning culture, craftsmanship. Competencies required were entrepreneurial spirit, creativity/innovation, customer focus, learning culture, challenging partnership, team player, integrity and trust, self-management/leading by example, managing and developing teams.

The Kering Group has the following HR strategy.

The aim of the new Group HR mission, which is aligned with the Kering vision, is to empower our employees to fulfill their potential and creativity by fostering their skills and performance in the most imaginative and sustainable manner. Three main trends will support the Kering effect on HR: global, digital, and sustainability. The idea behind the HR strategy is to enable our brands to flourish through accessing and sharing among other things, a talent pool, expertise, standards and best practices. It means that brands, while benefiting from the created synergies and following the guidance of the Group, will be able to exercise their autonomy: a concept that can be summed up with two words: "roots" and "wings." Taking care of our employees in the same way as we do our customers and making talent development a managerial principle will inspire and guide Kering leaders.

—Belén Essioux-Trujillo, Senior Vice President Group HR

---

[2]Which in English means workmanship or "a highly skilled line of work."

As a conclusion, the interviews and surveys among luxury professionals show the following skill sets are being sought after by the luxury sector. They are diverse and have been clustered along three axes for the four levels in Table 8.1. The four axes are: (1) fit with the changes in the environment, (2) fit with the luxury sector related to the right brain, (3) fit with company culture, and (4) competency related to the left brain.

Managing Talent

Some of the main challenges that leaders face in the twenty-first century are globalization, an increased stress on the environment, the rapid dissemination of information technology, digitalization, scientific and social changes. But these weren't the only challenges the executive faced while managing a global corporation. From 2014–2021, the real growth of the luxury industry had gradually eased to flat, according to Bain and Company, confirming the new norm of slow growth. Luxury companies no longer benefited from a strong economy tailwind, but needed to navigate market volatility. Consumer confidence was hurt by Brexit, the US presidential election, terrorism, and finally the health crisis of 2020. From 2017–2019, there was a spurt in the real growth rate of the sector. It rebounded, boosted by revival of Chinese consumers and other regions. Local consumption rose while travel retail remained important. In 2020 the coronavirus brought unprecedented challenges. As the luxury industry changed, so did the role of its CEOs. Executives tried to understand the specificities of working in the luxury industry such as the need to manage creative staff and their egos, be strict about management discipline, and have the soft skills necessary in running a multicultural global business while locked in their specific countries. Travel retail was devastated. But these skills were not readily available inside the maisons that created the brands. Industry leaders always pointed out that there was a shortage of talent with the right skills, experience, and vision to navigate a crisis and steer luxury organizations through a period of transformation. The pool of talent within the industry is limited, especially in the areas of digitalization of luxury businesses.

Table 8.1 Skill Sets Sought After by the Luxury Sector

Figure	Changes in the Environment	Fit with the Luxury Sector (Right Brain)	Business Competency (Left Brain)
Craftsman	Training in the métiers Creativity Innovative Intellectual maturity Flexibility, humility, and willingness to learn Desire to build an effective succession plan Aesthetic quality	Understand the brand DNA Sensitive to the creative element of the business Creativity Autonomous Entrepreneurial Integrity Excellence Passionate Respect of the company culture	Commitment Trust Loyalty Learn-on-the-fly
Designer/ Creative Director	Design capability Ability to adapt Resilience Curious Adapt-on-the-fly Agile	Understand the essence of the brand DNA Understanding the six senses with keen interest in art, sculpture, music, theatre, museums, and walking the streets. Appreciation for different cultures such as Indian royalty and grandeur, French couture, German precision, Japanese sophistication, Latino flamboyance A great ambassador of the brand Able to manage cultural complexity Autonomous	Global Digital Sustainable Commitment Trust Loyalty

(continued)

Table 8.1 (Continued)

Figure	Changes in the Environment	Fit with the Luxury Sector (Right Brain)	Business Competency (Left Brain)
		Entrepreneurial	Drive sales around the world
		Integrity	Manage boutiques
		Excellence	Global
		Passionate	Digital
		Respect of the company culture	Sustainable
Sales Force	Agile	Understand the brand DNA	Learn-on-the-fly
	Ability to adapt	Sensitive to the creative element of the business	Trade
	Curious	Customer seduction at retail stores	Commitment
	Flexibility, humility, and willingness to learn	Ambassador of the brand	Trust
		Fluent language skills	Loyalty
		Able to manage cultural complexity	
		The art of storytelling, building personalized relationships, social confidence, knowledge, conversational skills, flair. Employees in the luxury sector should feel like stars themselves	
		Integrity	
		Excellence	
		Passionate	
		Respect of the company culture	

Manager			
Agile	Understand the brand DNA	Strong commercial sense
Ability to adapt	Sensitive to the creative element of the business	Understanding complex distribution systems
Open to change	Good rapport with the creative director and manage the creative process	Multifunctional experience in different companies and in different markets
Flexibility, humility, and willingness to learn	A great ambassador of the brand. The art of storytelling, building personalized relationships, social confidence, knowledge, conversational skills, flair, feel like stars themselves	Knowledge of retail and merchandizing—manage boutiques
Resilience	Able to manage cultural complexity	Good team player, able to delegate
Curious	Entrepreneurial	Global
Desire to build an effective succession plan	Integrity	Digital
	Excellence	Sustainable
	Passionate	Trading
	Respect of the company culture	Commitment Managerial courage
	Leadership skills of self-knowledge, solution-oriented, decisive decision making skills	Capable of working in an autonomous, destructured, corporate environment while establishing a coherent structure at the brand level
	Edgy and avant-garde	Open to mobility
	Manage celebrities	Learn-on-the-fly
		High employee engagement
		Trust
		Loyalty

Talent Pool

LVMH realized this back in 1991. With international expansion and scaling up, the major concern for LVMH was finding the right talent pool. The then HR Director, Concetta Lanciaux, confided that her primary concern was to "have the best managers who understood not only the business but also how to sell." Lanciaux's challenge was particularly difficult because there was no school from which one could get trained executives to manage luxury brands. Most firms were small, family-owned companies, without trained personnel or a proper succession plan. LVMH had to recruit and develop talent from different fields. Regarding the mobilization of LVMH's resources, Bernard Arnault commented,

> *In a global context, the progress of LVMH in 2003 was based above all on the excellence of the fundamentals and its capacity to mobilize its internal resources. We could rely on our traditional strengths, namely the talent of our managers and employees and their determination to make the difference, the appeal of our major brands, the certain values—more than ever in a difficult period, the creativity and excellence of our products and the power of our distribution networks. We are continuing to deploy the organic growth strategy [. . .] while still carrying out the sale of nonstrategic assets, we will maintain strict management focus, enabling us to reinvest the cost savings achieved in the driving forces of our growth.*

Talent Acquisition (Recruitment and Induction)

The three major conglomerates have developed in-house mechanisms to recruit talent that will be leaders for tomorrow. They consistently engage themselves to recruit from the best business schools in France (such as ESSEC, INSEAD, HEC, ESCP-Europe, and others) and abroad. For example, LVMH carried out various original initiatives for young people in France and abroad to develop talent for the luxury industry. It was through these initiatives that primary school children, high school students, art students, young artists, and designers, as well as those closer to the group's new work opportunities, such as college and higher education students, and MBAs, could benefit. In 1991, for example, LVMH partnered with Paris-based business school ESSEC to launch the luxury brand marketing LVMH ESSEC chair, funded with FF10 million equivalent to €1.5 million. Further partnerships were launched in Asia as well.

LVMH also instituted strong company-wide induction programs, as well as on-the-job training to introduce the world of luxury to its capable, bright novices. LVMH launched the SPRING program in 2020 to nurture fresh graduates (postponed due to coronavirus though). It also encouraged and passed on the know-how, skills, spirit of excellence, and attitude that conveys, through its creations and products, an exceptional art of living, which has been appreciated worldwide. The awakening and education of young people with these values has been considered an essential part of the Group's goal. External recruitment of fresh talent is a strategic pillar of LVMH's human resources policy.

In the case of Kering, the key goal of their relations with educational institutions has been to attract new talent while adapting recruitment to the prevailing economic environment and the diversity of activities and professions of the Kering group. It is conscious of its image and wants to position itself as a preferred employer. The group and its subsidiaries have therefore chosen targeted institutions (business schools, universities) with which specific actions and partnerships have been set up: participation in forums, conferences centered on the group, and the leading associated professions among the brands, and résumé-writing workshops to support students in their search for an apprentice position or a permanent job. For example, Kering has long been a partner of ESSEC within the program "Pourquoi pas moi? / Joining a business school—Why not me?" This setup is to help young people from modest origins and with high potential to access high quality education by developing their social capital and their self-confidence. Kering's entities (headquarters or outlets) open their doors every year to junior college students enrolled in this program to allow them to become familiar with their environment and professions, thus helping these students prepare for a future career path.

Talent Identification (High Potential)

LVMH invests in hiring people with experience in other industries, such as consumer goods, and selects people "who could understand good taste." Concetta Lanciaux cited engineering and business schools as specific sources of talent. In 1995, Lanciaux explained, "With some 40 brands potentially competing against each other in the group, recruitment and everyday business become complex. In the case of our group, what builds value and profits is the ability to act in an autonomous way and create new products. The business is built on the number of innovative products that come out every year—20% to 30% of the turnover is based on new products. Therefore, our companies' senior executives have to have a large dose of autonomy and creative capacity. People use these as aspirational products, so we need people who manage and dream—and make others dream."

In 2020, the Group had more than 76 brands in its portfolio. LVMH started its FuturA program to develop its high potential recruits. FuturA has been constituted as an international program to search and develop external or internal experienced high potential executives, enabling LVMH to deepen its lateral talent pool. The objective was to recruit and develop people who had the potential to take up key group positions within a five-year horizon. The selection process identified people with five to 10 years of professional experience and a proven ability to learn and adapt in increasingly complex environments. As future leaders within the LVMH group, High Potentials were supported by special initiatives to spur their development.

Data showed that 66% of the senior management jobs at group level are filled through internal mobility. Fifty percent of high potential employees are non-French and are trained through LVMH House, the training program for executives and LVMH Experience, the training for high potential managers who have recently joined the group, which is used as an integration tool and springboard for moving into leadership positions. LVMH Perspectives offers managers a way to speed up their career by learning from two different perspectives: the first is self-knowledge and the second is being aware of and facing strategic challenges.

In Kering group, Gucci was leading the way from 2015 onwards. The iconic duo Marco Bizzarri and Allessandro Michele was fundamental to Gucci's impressive response to the COVID-19 crisis. They managed not only to completely relaunch the brand with a culture of empowerment and a unique understanding of the historical codes, and to focus on consumer engagement and creative partnerships, but also, they planted the seeds for early evolution of the brand, demonstrably important during the crisis. Their strengthening of Gucci was built on the historical reference of Gucci's inclusivity, diversity, self-expression, and commitment to sustainability (the latter further reinforced after the newly launched collaboration with the resale platform TheRealReal). The special investment in employees' sustainability, social, and emotional skills over the years was nothing new. Such an investment was surely a feature of the company's culture that the brand could leverage the most during the pandemic. From a digital training and skill-building point of view, the implementation of the new Gucci long-term strategy was already leading to major cuts to its wholesale network, while investments were shifted to online sales growth through penetration in new countries and the offer of a seamless best-in-class client experience (including a wide range of e-commerce functionalities and rich storytelling).

As a further step to improve people development within the company, Gucci developed a partnership with Parks, an Italian non-profit organization supporting companies in the development of strategies and practices to promote diversity, by offering training, education, communication services, and consulting on pay policies and benefits, to finally guarantee an inclusive working environment. Marco Bizzari, CEO of Gucci, commented, "We are extremely proud to join Parks, and we could not identify a better moment to start the partnership with this inspiring organization. In the past two years, we have implemented a complete turnaround of our company, following our mantra of being the voice of self-expression. Attracting, retaining and promoting talent, while celebrating ethnic, age, sexual and gender diversity, sexual orientation and gender identity across the company, is our mission, which is completely consistent with the vision of our parent company, Kering."

Talent Development (Retraining)

The three groups tried to create changes within by training and educating their talent resources. LVMH, Richemont, and Kering all have put in place programs—LVMH House, LVMH Experience, LVMH Perspective, Kering University, Richemont Creative Academy—where they train managers to help them improve their core competencies.

At LVMH, training is distributed among the group, its business divisions, and the brands themselves, always focused on enriching the skill sets of employees and sharpening their performance. Training programs address needs that were identified and discussed during annual performance appraisal interviews. Technical skills are the responsibility of brands, which sometimes pool training across business groups. At the global level, the Group proposes a broad array of training in management, sales techniques, marketing, project management, and languages and cultural awareness, all centered on the distinctive LVMH ecosystem and its experience in luxury and serving specific clientele segments. Training is organized at the regional level—in Asia, Japan, the United States, France, the United Kingdom, Switzerland, Spain, and Italy—as well as by the brands.

For example, since 2000 Kering University has offered training development programs for its managers on various contemporary issues and perspectives in order to support and facilitate the deployment of the group's strategic positioning. Kering's University programs were in line with Kering's challenges, such as the Digital Academy, internationalization, performance, innovation and entrepreneurship, leadership, change management, personal impact, innovation and creativity, risk management, strategies and negotiations, and new buying behaviors. The subjects developed by Kering's University allowed the group's current and future leaders to stay ahead of change.

In the case of the Richemont Group, it promoted training and retraining of its employees in several different ways. Its 16 brands ran different programs, such as retail staff training at the Montblanc Academy, employment staff training at IWC, A. Lange & Söhne's in-house watchmaking school, Cartier's training center for watchmaking, and Piaget's "Les Ecoles de la rue du Louvre" in Paris, which is managed by the French Jewelry Association.

Among many other training programs, Richemont supports the Campus Genevois de Haute Horlogerie in Geneva, the Creative Academy (Master's Program in Arts & Design, which imparts specialized training in design for applied arts, in particular jewelry, watchmaking, and fashion accessories) in Milan, and the Richemont Retail Academy in Shanghai, China, which collaborates with WOSTEP (Watchmakers of

Switzerland Training and Educational Program) in world cities such as New York, Hong Kong, Shanghai, Tokyo, and London.

Talent Performance (Performance Appraisal)

One of the executive vice presidents of the LVMH agreed that the group sought to foster creativity not only among its design teams, but also with professionals throughout the business. He compared the process to mixing the perfect cocktail—LVMH tried to build a working environment that promoted creativity and at the same time adhered to strict business discipline.

At LVMH, Chantal Gaemperle, the group executive vice president, human resources and synergies, explained that the annual organizational management review plays a pivotal role in identifying talent and succession planning. This dynamic process is central to recognizing the contributions and talents of the Group's people. It ensures advancement within the Group by identifying key positions, internal resources, and the human resources needed to drive continued growth at LVMH companies. The operational management review is linked to the regular performance appraisals that identify employees' strengths and opportunities for improvement, as well as their personal goals. These appraisals serve as the basis for concrete action to enable people to achieve fulfilling career objectives. The LVMH group has focused on internal mobility—both geographic and functional—as a cornerstone of their talent management policy. This cross-fertilization of experience within their ecosystem, under the unifying umbrella, provides a space for development.

At Richemont, along with continued investment in learning and development, the Human Resources departments across the group work with managers to facilitate opportunities for employees to transfer between maisons. This internal mobility has mutual benefits, providing greater career development opportunities for employees and helping to retain skills and talent within the group. Regular performance management review and annual individual development plans have always been a critical element of the core strategy to retain, motivate, and develop its employees. The group saw it as a way to develop, recognize, and reward talent. It has also developed a specific Performance Management learning and development program for managers, aiming to support them in implementing the process within their teams. The program is designed to be an ongoing and incremental learning path that leads to retention and integration of high potential managers.

Talent Retention and Integration (Compensation and Benefits)

LVMH's aggressive growth-through-acquisition created both challenges and opportunities. On the one hand, the brand needed to be preserved while, on the other, the owners and managers needed to be absorbed, retained, and integrated until the time that the brand could be scaled up. LVMH tried to treat such moves sensitively, with a vision of integration. Lanciaux had commented: "First of all, it was about respecting, identifying, and then preserving all of the assets of the company—not changing everything at once. One of the mistakes that companies in this situation make was to change everything and bring in their own culture. When we buy these brands, we buy them to develop them. To develop the brand, the first thing one needed to know was what makes that brand. Very often it's a number of people who are behind it, often invisible. . .. One has to find them, make them visible. This means that we have been able to preserve the integrity of these brands. Our style is not to go in there and replace everybody—never." According to industry sources, LVMH's compensation policies for senior managers and high-potentials were much above the industry average.

While at Richemont, managers in maisons, regions, and functions were responsible for managing the performance of individual employees. They were guided by the Group's performance management process, which supports transparent compensation and rewards decision making using clear job responsibilities, annual strategic individual objectives, and the development of personal competencies. All managers and virtually all other employees at Richemont undergo formal performance management reviews leading to individual development plans.

To ensure equitable treatment across markets, Richemont's corporate Human Resources function performs a number of internal and external benchmark studies comparing reward and compensation practices. This information is used in an annual salary review to ensure equitable treatment of employees and that salaries and benefits remain competitive relative to their peers.

Figure 8.1   The Talent Cycle

In summary, talent management in the luxury industry requires creativity. It is not only the managerial talent that needs to be managed but also the designers and creative talent. Figure 8.1 depicts the talent cycle.

Talent Turnover and Right-Sizing

Talent turnover has been a key issue in this industry. The industry was always small, with a total of about 110 brands (excluding automobiles, hotels, yachts, and others). People usually move from one brand to the other. "Up-or-out" syndrome is prevalent as people working in this industry have to continuously reinvent themselves, be creative, be agile, and perform. Thus, the three big groups needed to plan the succession and the exit policy with precision and professionalism. For example, finding 75 CEOs and 75 creative directors, managing them, and planning their succession, if not thought out properly, could indeed be a challenge.

Research and data show that managers in leadership teams believe that it is important to share expertise and encourage talent mobility within the conglomerate. Sometimes, a top executive may reach the glass ceiling within an individual brand and it is always beneficial to look for mobility within the group rather than lose this person to the competition. For example, LVMH regularly hires ex-employees, while this is not so common in the other conglomerates.

At Richemont, with its 18 maisons and two online businesses, employee turnover and retention data are closely monitored by the applicable country, maison, functional area, and type of employee contract. Senior executives assess their subordinates on four metrics: mental agility (general intelligence), results orientation (ability to achieve goals), change management (ability to steer a business in a new direction), and people management (general skill at leading others).[3] Naturally, the turnover rates vary by maison, by country, and by function. Five broad carrier areas are mentioned: manufacturing, design creation, marketing, retail, and brand management. For example, secondary data suggests that in Switzerland, where one third of the group's permanent employees are based, the turnover rate was below 10%. This was in line with the market's average. The turnover rate was higher in countries where retail activities predominated, such as mainland China and Hong Kong. Richemont believed that through group-wide efforts with respect to new employee induction programs, and ongoing performance management and retention strategies, employee turnover rates in those countries will stay below the market average.

Richemont unveiled the group's Transformational Strategy in 2019. It reflected Richemont's aspiration for a more responsible and sustainable approach to luxury items production, a lifelong learning program to preserve their craftsmanship. It was meant to enhance the employability of their talents that promoted diversity, inclusion and well-being within their workforce. In 2019, the group started considerably focusing on technology in order to allow their employees to have access to company information, development opportunities and tools from everywhere. Richemont's early adoption and investment in digital infrastructure, integrating Yoox Net-a-Porter with Alibaba and Farfetch in China,

---

[3]https://hbr.org/2015/06/luxurys-talent-factories.

allowed the group to digitally support their workforce during the Covid-19 crisis. Employees were a part of a Learning Management System that had 700 active communities on their Social Enterprise Network, called Yammer, and had over 22,500 SharePoint users. A new initiative, called Oxygen, was put in place to modernize the global employee experience. It allowed pre-boarding for new hires that ran completely online, while the adoption of a global survey platform facilitated feedback and data analysis. Additionally, during the pandemic, Richemont revealed that digital upskilling initiatives were "continued through online certification programmes, coding workshops and masterclasses across the organisation with a focus on HR and manufacturing functions."

Conclusion

Over the years, the characteristics and skills of workforces have witnessed a shift, in the luxury industry as in many other industries: new roles have emerged that until a few decades ago did not exist, while other jobs have completely disappeared. This happened due to changes in technology, consumer trends, consumer preferences, and the business models of companies.

Following the COVID-19 disruption, the luxury brands' management geared up to redesign their talent strategies and establish a new portfolio of skill sets that would make the most sense to cultivate. It also considered what kinds of people skills would be needed most once the recovery had started. Research showed that leaders wanted to start training people across digital, cognitive, social and emotional, and adaptability and resilience skills. For example, 74% of Chinese luxury consumers revealed that they have been deliberately avoiding shopping in malls in the first weeks after the stores reopened.[4] This means that some offline sales could permanently migrate to the online channel, and therefore underlines the increasing importance of *digital skills* acquisition. It also requires the development of *social and emotional skills* to ensure effective collaboration, nurture customer relationships despite distance, and connect to peculiar and evolving customer needs. For example, luxury sales assistants at Louis Vuitton have been empowered to remotely close a sale

---

[4]McKinsey & Company, November 5, 2020.

with the same extraordinary relationship they used to have in-store. It also meant that, to thrive within a COVID-19-impacted environment, employees need to adapt not only to new working dynamics but also to new trends, cultures, and habits. Connected to this was the rise in local consumption, particularly relevant in Asia; *emotional intelligence and adaptability* would be required for a relocated setting that encompassed *stakeholder management and cultural fit.*

As a summary, the changing needs for hybrid skill sets reflected many new dynamics within the luxury industry: the digital revolution, globalization, faster and improved customer feedback, structural changes in the industry, new business models, nationalism and varied cross-relationship among governments. Hence, it can be reasonably predicted that the willingness to learn and the ability to successfully use new skills were increasingly attractive employee traits at all levels.

There has been an ongoing debate about ideal leaders for luxury brands. Are they supposed to be from within the industry or outside? Are they supposed to be formally schooled or is mere talent enough? Are their nationalities of any consequence? Is culture of any importance in this regard?

> **The question of industry:** Is it necessary to have a luxury background to lead a luxury firm? The answer is no. Having a luxury background certainly helps, as such leaders understand the industry well. However, if a leader from another industry walks into luxury, it is this ignorance in itself that can be used to the brand's advantage. The new manager will bring a fresh perspective and think outside the box; such managers do not have a fixed way of looking at things and can infuse a new lease of life into the company. The general conclusion is that employees grow mostly within the luxury industry and become leaders. However, mere talent is enough to make a way into luxury at any stage of one's career.
>
> **The question of family:** Luxury brands continue to be family held. Brands such as Patek Philippe, Richemont, Chanel, Hermès, Tod's, Armani, and Missoni are still closely held and follow the tradition of the children taking over the family business. Even LVMH and Kering are controlled by families. If becoming a luxury leader implies that you have to belong to a family that owns a luxury empire, the

answer to that question is no. One must remember that these luxury dynasties were started by men and women with no initial backing in luxury. They made these luxury empires from scratch. The Richemont dynasty was started in 1941 by Johann Rupert's father, Anton Rupert. He started out with a dry-cleaning business in South Africa, moving onward to tobacco. His son Johann was not too keen on the family business and initially became an investment banker with Chase Manhattan. It is evident from the story that the father did not have a luxury empire to start out with, but the son did. So, one can be in either situation and still manage to lead a luxury company to further success. It was the same in LVMH. Bernard Arnault always acknowledged that he came into this business due to family reasons as his family bought a fledgling asset, where they discovered the promising asset, Christian Dior. His daughter and three sons are in leadership positions in different brands—LV, Berluti, Tag Heuer, and more recently Tiffany.

The question of culture: In order to protect a brand's DNA, is it necessary to have a leader rooted in the brand's culture? Do French luxury companies have to be led by a French person? If an Indian led the French major Hermès, would Hermès become any less French?

Creating a tempest in the French haute couture world, Gianfranco Ferre, an Italian, was appointed creative director at Christian Dior in 1989. His appointment was criticized because the French haute couture world was uncomfortable with opening its tightly guarded door to other nationalities, which showed disrespect for French creativity that the French took a pride in. However, the industry realized only later that fashion was a common language understood by all. In today's globalized world, Italians appreciate French fashion as much as the French appreciate Italian.

The required skill sets to succeed in the luxury industry are changing fast. Figure 8.2 summarizes the skill sets that may be required to lead in the luxury industry.

Apart from these skill sets, one had to take into account that the new global challengers from emerging markets were playing prominent roles in global luxury markets. These challengers were rapidly globalizing their businesses and competing with luxury companies for market

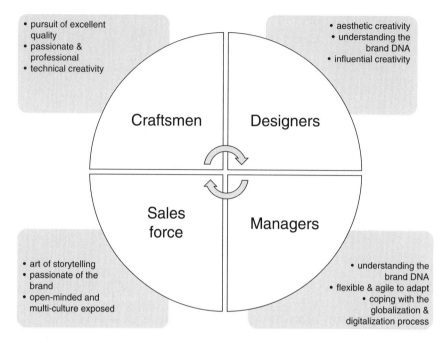

• pursuit of excellent quality
• passionate & professional
• technical creativity

Craftsmen

• aesthetic creativity
• understanding the brand DNA
• influential creativity

Designers

Sales force

Managers

• art of storytelling
• passionate of the brand
• open-minded and multi-culture exposed

• understanding the brand DNA
• flexible & agile to adapt
• coping with the globalization & digitalization process

Figure 8.2   Skill Sets Necessary to Be a Leader in the Luxury Industry

share, resources, and talent, both at home and abroad. The family businesses were fast dwindling. They were either eaten by the multibrand conglomerates or bought out by private equity companies or family houses. For example, LVMH Group bought Bulgari and Loro Piana, whereas the Kering Group bought Gucci and Brioni. Mittal bought Escada and had to sell to global private equity firm, Regent, after trying for 10 years to turn around the German brand. Labelux acquired Jimmy Choo, which later on was acquired by Mickael Kors. Eurazeo bought a stake in Moncler, which they divested subsequently, whereas the Qatar Foundation through its Mayhoola investments bought Harrods, Printemps, Balmain, and others. From the above mentioned examples, it is evident that, with digitalization, democratization, and growth in distant markets, gone are the days of standing alone with a few boutiques and delivering excellent results or being large without delivering. In both cases the brands will be acquired as it is time-consuming to create luxury brands. Will the future growth of the luxury industry be driven by the creative genius with traditional skills, or by business talents with new skill sets, such as leadership and strategic insight?

Chapter 9

Managing Operations and Supply Chain in the Luxury Business

The global outbreak of COVID-19 posed unprecedented challenges in managing operations at the back-end. Even before the pandemic, independent luxury goods wholesalers in Europe, and some of the large North American luxury department stores, were already struggling due to the complex nature of the business. To overcome this challenge, the large conglomerates were already on the way to vertically integrate their supply chain and control their e-commerce businesses.

In the carousel of city lockdowns all around the world, luxury companies have faced supply chain delays, factory and store closures, trade show and fashion week cancellations. Other issues, such as the rise of e-commerce, the drastic fall of travel retail, problems with long-term business agreements, especially in real estate, have also arisen. Uncertainties, including supply and demand across geographies, lead to a domino effect in which decreases in retail sales lead to delayed payments to suppliers, factory closures lead to order cancellations, and eventually, the entire supply chain is disrupted. In this situation, the smaller actors, upstream in the supply chain, have borne the worst consequences.

This crisis has forced some of these organizations into difficult situations: many employees have been made redundant; companies have faced bankruptcy. The damage can be observed across those brands that have not yet fully transitioned to a vertically integrated distribution model, and also fashion brands that need wholesale channels to reach new customers and finance their development. In order to survive, wholesalers have tended to adopt aggressive commercial and discount policies which could hurt the luxury positioning of brands in the short term.

The world has changed. During most of the twentieth century, one, two, or three shops had to be managed for each luxury merchant. Luxury goods were born due to the incredible competencies and savoir-faire of local craftsmen, mostly from France and Italy. Luxury was synonymous with small *ateliers* and *façonneries*. The craftsmen used to work in their workshops either above the shops or in the basement. The raw materials were processed and stored nearby and the finished products were brought from the shop floor directly to the stores. The owners could supervise the entire value chain from sourcing and procurement to sales. They themselves were also the designers, and supervised the operations and manufacturing. When a friend or a friend's friend visited their stores as a customer, they would come down, market the products, and sell them themselves. The owners alone guaranteed the service for the specially crafted goods that they made on the shop floors. The customer could in fact visit the shop floor and see how intricately the products were made and could even chat with the workers as they sometimes made special made-to-order materials. This way of doing things no longer exists.

However, in the past decades, the growth of demand and hence the requirement of volume production became so important that relying only on those local country-specific *ateliers* was not realistic any more. The global conglomerates started organizing a network of *ateliers* and local suppliers in order to face the new demand. The consolidation of the industry and the rise of consumerism only intensified this process and called for cost efficiency, higher volumes, and new geographies. To answer these challenges, the companies and conglomerates alike started considering new strategies, already employed by mass market companies, such as offshoring and outsourcing.

Outsourcing was not uncommon for luxury labels, though most of the production was completed either in France or Italy. They were using the global network of the best products and services available to craft their unique products. They have been outsourcing for years. For example, they outsourced embroideries from India and assembly of leather accessories in Eastern Europe. Brands like Louis Vuitton used an intricate strategy that allowed them to use the "Made in Italy" tag while most of the production was in Romania, for instance. Brands were also beginning to use outsourcing as a means to be closer to the final consumer. With the shift of global luxury goods consumption toward China, Gucci for instance considered relocating part of the production process to mainland China in order to reduce delivery lead time. It was also because the company had a difficult time keeping up with the 90-minute delivery schedule of local e-retailer JD.com.

With consumers scattered across the globe and sourcing done from multiple locations across the world, and manufacturing completed in Italy or France, the companies were grappling with the challenge. For example, crocodile skin had to be sourced from a crocodile farm in Singapore or Australia, while wool had to arrive from an alpaca farm in Peru, or cashmere from Inner Mongolia. And all the raw materials had to reach the shop floors on time. The processed products had to reach the Beijing or Delhi store on time, and that should coincide with the launch of the product in Paris, Milan, New York City, or London because the buyers were waiting. Customers already knew all about the products as they had browsed them on the Internet. The "See now, buy now" movement created another layer of complexity. Millennial consumers compared the products and were highly knowledgeable about the competition as well. They were not the earlier small groups of family, friends, and extended friends of the owners. They came for these exquisite products from faraway lands—from Japan, from China, from Nigeria, or from India.

But how does a company deliver products that are made in France, Italy, or Switzerland to customers all over the world within such a short time span? How does a company educate those customers twice every year with new offerings? How does a company track the products? It was not a shampoo that was the same product sold everywhere; instead, it was an exquisite pink python-skin bag. There were only two of them made this year. One was shown to an oligarch in Moscow, whereas the other one was being stored in Shanghai. It had to be brought back to London to be shown to a member of the royal family of Kuwait.

The challenge was something new. It needed to be managed with state-of-the-art logistics, a supply-chain, and customer management systems.

The Challenge

The luxury industry has evolved into a global industry which requires global systems and processes to manage the business. One could argue that this is why it is difficult to manage such a global operation. Procter & Gamble and Unilever are two firms that have successfully managed their products on an international scale. The difference is in the perception of brand value. The desire, hence demand, needs to be created; the story behind the brand and the company needs to be communicated; and the service needs to be delivered with the utmost care for products that requires such close observation during the production process.

Traditional strategies to satisfy the desires of high-net-worth individuals were changing every day. Expansion had created complexity and the speed at which it needed to be managed internationally was not an easy task. Along with such complexity, luxury companies faced additional challenges due to volatility in consumer tastes and spending habits, shortened product life cycles, a growing need for international compliance, and customer demands for sustainability and transparency.

Thus, these luxury firms had to look beyond the single global system, strategy, and structure to create new sources of value. The challenge then was to simultaneously focus on multiple strategic objectives in the search for efficiency, flexibility, responsiveness, and innovative solutions. Some of the key parameters that need attention for luxury goods are covered in the 10 Cs listed below.

1. **Content:** Luxury goods are by definition creative. Luxury goods companies design and deliver unique and handcrafted products. The way operational excellence and customer intimacy need to be delivered is through storytelling and the creation of content around the brand.

2. **Customization:** Customization, or making special-order products, has always been a strength for luxury brands. From the days of the Maharajas of India to today's custom-made products, limited edition products, special-event products, country-inspired products, Chinese New Year products, and others have always been a priority to make the customer feel special and cared for.

3. **Convenience:** The luxury customer went to great lengths to acquire what inspired him or her. Maybe the product that she or he was looking for was rare or unavailable. Creating convenience for the preferred customer, and thereby extending added service, is thus important.

4. **Cost or time value of price:** The real cost a consumer paid when the product was purchased usually exceeded what was printed on the price tag. It included the cost of transport, the opportunity cost of the time the consumer spent researching the location of the physical store, parking time, and so forth. Due to differences in tax structure and the constant fluctuation in exchange rates, the home location of a luxury firm—such as Paris, Milan, or London—most often offers the best price for a product, all things considered. The famous queue of Japanese, and now Chinese, tourists outside the stores of the Champs Elysées reinforces the power of the cost. So, to be sensitive to the time value of price, the systems have needed to evolve to embrace new trends, and respect consumers that come from far away to acquire an item they have dreamed of owning.

5. **Computing:** Back-end systems are also needed to process and generate data about billing, taxation, tax refunds, to identify repeat customers, coordinate functions, and track the process up to a sale, so that the customer's experience is seamless inside the store. Sometimes, intelligent systems allow sales personnel across the world to identify customers and thus give information about an individual's tastes and preferences.

6. **Customer franchise:** Customer franchises are the summation of all the positive feedback a customer had after the experience—be it the ability to trust the brand or the confidence (s)he has in the brand.

Customer franchise is the direct consequence of the branding efforts of a company—its positioning and the place that it then occupied in the customer's mind. It was imperative that this information be documented and available across the organization to better serve the luxury customer.

7. **Customer delight:** Customer service does not only mean well-behaved employees standing behind the service desk alone. A customer is definitely at ease if the salesperson speaks the same language. Figure 9.1 shows the six basic ways customer delight may be achieved.

8. **Community:** Building a community by inviting people to special events, regular mailings, keeping in touch with new product launches, and inviting people to brand promotion events go a long way to build and nurture a network of loyal customers. The network of people interested in the product discusses their experiences and also discovers what others from a similar social stratum are up to. This experience could potentially make or break the sale of a product. Once again, to use this type of information, aligned back-end systems are necessary that can enhance the total experience for the customer.

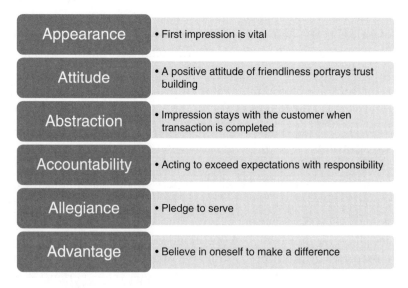

Figure 9.1   Six Ways to Achieve Customer Delight

9. **Communication:** The systems at the back-end should be able to code the brand offer and the feedback. Since the customers hail from multiple nations their expectations are diverse and different. Communication channels between the company and the consumer, and between consumers, become an important marketing input. The exchanges, social media, and clienteling help consumers to make up their minds about a product. The company database shows the buying pattern of return customers.

10. **Customer value:** Though luxury consumers are ready to spend a fortune on their purchases to address their emotional and psychological needs above and beyond their functional needs, they need to be assured of the product's value. The satisfaction that a consumer obtains from a product or, in economic terms, the "utility" that she derives, reveals the customer's values. One of the best ways to transmit customer value is by ensuring a powerful brand experience (in addition to the product) in the country where the purchase was made. Thus, the salesperson needs to be aware, not only of the total brand experience, but also the specificities of all product categories in the store. The stories sometimes go back to the life and times of famous personalities in a distant city, such as Paris or Milan.

To manage the Ten Cs simultaneously, the family-run houses needed a robust mechanism that would give them an advantage over their competitors. This system could not only track their products across the world but also give them data and reports to make professional decisions that were previously made on gut feelings. It would also let them control their operations from their home base and strategically plan for the future. To start with, one of the most important necessities was to secure their sourcing, the procurement of raw materials, and ship their products to their newly found distant customers.

The Global and the Local Supply Chain

The pandemic has taught us that the role of efficiency in supply chain management (SCM) is something that businesses cannot ignore. Previously, luxury goods had been manufactured by leveraging complex supply chains, involving manufacturing units that extended globally to reach the desired quality and exclusivity. This involved a multitude of suppliers, raw materials, processes, and distributors, all focused on producing an exquisite experience. As already discussed, in most cases raw materials were produced in one country, processed in another, assembled elsewhere, and the final product distributed worldwide. A case in point was the transformation of DeBeers in its value chain. The traditional supply chain was adapted with the blockchain technology. Blockchain, a distributed ledger technology, was used to improve traceability. DeBeers created Tracr, an inclusive mine-to-customer traceability blockchain solution for the diamond industry. This was implemented by transferring material data and tracking it across the supply chain. A secure and immutable digital trail was created for rough diamonds, starting from the mine to the cutter and polisher, and then to a jeweler in their retail outlets. A unique Global Diamond ID is automatically created on Tracr as the diamonds traveled along the value chain. This ID was used to store individual diamond attributes like carat, clarity, color, and type of cut by integrating with existing record-keeping systems. These facilitated the tool to consolidate data captured at each and every step into an immutable digital trail for each physical diamond, thus assuring its provenance and traceability from rough to polished. The system used stone images, planned outcome images, and the diamond's physical properties to verify and validate authenticity by the use of data science and physical identification techniques. Tracr verified the uploaded data at each milestone of a diamond's value chain and ensured its accuracy and continuity. It thereby enabled users to be in full control of what they shared with other participants through the use of privacy controls. The implementation of this technology didn't just boost confidence for consumers that the registered diamonds were natural and conflict-free, but also improved visibility and enhanced efficiencies across the diamond value chain.

The use of both local and global value-chain integration is increasingly important for companies to grow in highly competitive markets. A well-coordinated and implemented supply chain process gives a competitive advantage as supply chain efficiency is difficult for competitors to imitate in the short term. Sustained competitive advantage in the supply chain involves vertical integration across the value chain. A case in point is Rolex. The foundry is in-house. It has created its own formulae for three different kinds of gold and its own formulation (904L) stainless steel in its central laboratory on the outskirts of Geneva. Every alloy used by Rolex is produced entirely in-house. This is because they consider the composition of the metal to be the most important factor in determining a watch's aesthetic and functional properties. Formula 904L steel is resistant to rust and corrosion and slightly harder than other varieties of steel. Rolex has fully vertically integrated its foundry, watch case-making, and finishing. Its movements are in-house, made in Bienne lab, in the Jura Mountains, north of Bern. Each and every Rolex creation is completely produced in-house. All movements are hand-assembled. They have created a unique manufacturing system and the relevant machines to produce exclusive components for Rolex. Dial production and gem-setting are carried out in-house at Chêne-Bourg, on the border with France. Dials are produced, printed, and then set with indexes and other elements. Dial production takes place underground and gem-setting in bright white rooms filled with sunlight. At least 100 people are working on dial-setting at any point in time. Rolex has an in-house machine to filter out stones en masse to cull anything that is not a real diamond, although such cases are very rare—about one in a million. The focus on precision is under complete control. Final assembly and control take place in the headquarters at Geneva. Dozens of assembly-men and -women work in the pristine Controlled Environment Zones, which are totally dust- and humidity-free. Placing of all components from the other three facilities is done here. Dials and hands are set into the watch, movements put into cases, and serial numbers entered into a global database which enables Rolex to track the flow of every watch. Ensuring that the hands rotate with the right amount of tension and completely parallel to the dial and fit in the glass in the right way is an arduous process. Once the dial is mounted, a watchmaker checks to ensure there is no dust anywhere inside the watch. After final assembly is completed, they are turned over to final control for an intense set of tests.

The shift was predominant as luxury companies integrated their suppliers across the globe and started using more technology-oriented processes to reduce time to market their products globally. Collaboration and trust became important among stakeholders in the global value chain.

As luxury companies became global, they were forced to integrate SCM systems, which aimed at reducing manufacturing cycles and inventory levels (raw materials, semi-finished, and finished goods) to streamline the flow of information, remove bottlenecks (internal and external), and ensure rapid reliable delivery to customers—at the right time and to the right place. But they also aimed to increase profitability by making SCM more responsive and effective.

Some companies, such as Bulgari and Versace, believed just the opposite. They promoted localization of their supply chain. Bulgari was known for its "Made in Italy" manufacturing network, and its provenance from Rome. In 2017 it opened a 14,000 m² site in Valenza, Italy. Bulgari manufactured high jewelry in Rome, accessories in Florence, perfumes in Lodi, and silk in Como. It chose to manufacture its diamond jewelry only in Italy because it wanted to stay close to the roots and expertise that have been handed down over the centuries; Italy was once the heart of gold manufacturing. Bulgari has an excellent training system, which aims to create the very best craftsmanship in Italy. They recruit the best students from the numerous Italian jewelry and goldsmith schools, most specifically in the regions of Valenza, making it the local hub of jewelry production.

Versace has retained all of its production in Italy, too. Even after acquisition by the American group Capri Holdings, Donatella Versace announced the opening of more factories in her home country and showed no intention of shifting production to lower-priced countries, like other Capri Holdings brands. Donatella showed a commitment to further creating jobs in the Italian market, keeping production in Italy as an act of patriotism. Versace even attempted to go a step further, with the so-called "Reguzzoni-Versace" law, concerning the Made in Italy system. The law, proposed by a member of the Versace family in the Italian Parliament, aimed at avoiding items produced mostly outside Italy, but finished in the country in order to qualify for the "Made in Italy" label. It called for more of the production to be done in Italy for a product to be able to bear the label. Even though the law was frozen, it showed Versace's commitment to producing in Italy and the nationalistic feeling that went with it. However, it is important to notice that it is hard to determine whether consumers outside Italy so value Versace's patriotic feeling and commitment for it to be worth the high price of maintaining production there.

Over the years, high-end fashion houses have paid far more attention to product design, craftsmanship, and image than to the mechanics
of keeping their stores stocked. When new designs caught on they often
sold out, leaving the companies ill-prepared to speed up production and
distribution. Experience suggests that, with increasing costs of advertising, promotion, and retail space, synergies are not enough for profitability. Return-on-net-assets (RONA)—used to measure a company's
financial performance—also showed that sales per square foot have to be
monitored closely: shops should be stocked with products all the time,
and frequently replenished.

Many brands had long regarded limited-edition products as a way
to bolster their cachet. As a result, customers often found themselves on
waiting lists for popular merchandise. The popular anecdote about the
Birkin bag needs to be told. A journalist writes,

> *To fend off customers, Hermès had found an innovative policy. It was
> one of demand frustration and category segregation. Since the demand
> far outstripped the supply of Birkin bags, first they requested customers
> looking for Birkin bags to come to the store and try their luck. One had
> to reserve an appointment with a leather expert. Once the appointment
> was confirmed, the salesman was ready to hear the demand. Most of
> the time the Birkin or the Kelly bag was unavailable. Usually if the
> customer was a repeat customer the sales staff after asking the name will
> go and check the local database and perhaps the global CRM. Once the
> sales staff was satisfied that the person was indeed a high-value return
> customer, (s)he was instructed to tell that the customer needs to visit the
> store again-and-again till she was lucky or offer an alternative leather
> product. If the choice of the sales person did not match the demand, the
> sales staff was very kind to give him or her a visiting card. But once the
> customer called them with the number from the visiting card, they were
> instructed not to give the information about the product over the phone.
> It was somewhat an innovative marketing ploy whereby the customer
> had to visit the store to try her luck to buy a 7,000-euro handbag!*

But the market was changing, and the objective remained that products be readily available in stores. It is also true that Hermès increased

its production of Birkin bags, but demand still heavily outweighed supply. Fast-fashion labels, such as Zara and H&M, have thrived by spotting trends quickly and filling shelves with new products every fortnight by implementing a very efficient and sophisticated global supply chain. Their success has forced luxury and higher-end rivals to rethink their own supply chain model. Following in the footsteps of fast fashion, most of the luxury brands placed importance on speed-to-market. After decades of relying solely on their designers' instincts, for example, some luxury fashion houses, including Italy's Gucci Group, are now using focus groups to find out what consumers actually want in advance.

Progressively, luxury brands found themselves operating like successful modern retail stores, in order to better serve customers, by keeping their shelves fully stocked with popular merchandise. They educated their sales staff to be increasingly aware of the systems operating within their supply chain, including modification of the distribution system and the way salespeople serve customers in the stores.

However, tampering with production can pose a risk to a brand's image. Customers pay a fortune for luxury products, partly because they have bought into the notion that skilled craftsmen have made the goods the old-fashioned way. But the reality was somewhat different. There were limitations to doing things the same way they had been done in the olden days due to the sheer scale and scope of today's luxury business. Without a well-entrenched assembly-line production system, with skilled craftsmen alongside an efficient SCM, it was practically impossible to reach out to customers in hundreds of stores globally, keep the stores filled with both classic and new designs, and replenish them continuously.

For years, luxury goods makers have thought about supply and demand differently from other consumer goods companies. In most sectors, running out of a product when demand is strong would be considered disastrous. But production is limited for some luxury fashion items. However, the industry has begun to rethink that approach. For example, Hermès International has hired another 300 factory workers to reduce waiting lists for bestsellers such as the €5,000 Kelly bag. Hermès's craftsmen still stitched most of the bags by hand and signed them when they had finished. Louis Vuitton, which has annual sales upward of €10 billion, has announced that its supply chain changes will help it meet a goal of at least a 10% annual sales growth over the next several years. Versace S.p.A. hired a division of Computer Sciences Corp. and Giorgio Armani S.p.A. hired Oracle Corp. to help make their supply chains more efficient. Burberry PLC, Cartier, and Prada S.p.A. have retained German software firm SAP AG for the same purpose. As an example of the experiences of Louis Vuitton, the following case study illustrates how it implemented global SCM by introducing process reengineering, creating a logistics hub and training programs to accompany the new way of working.

- Summarizing, on the one side luxury brands have increased the efficiency of their SCM in different ways, due to outsourcing their activities. Companies like LVMH and Kering have sourced their embroidery to India, for example. Balenciaga and Burberry have started producing some of their iconic products in China. Balenciaga's iconic $850 Triple S sneakers came to the spotlight when it was found they were made in China, and not in Italy. Burberry stopped producing handbags and trench coats in China. On the other side, Chanel and Hermès resorted more to vertical integration and localization. In recent years, Chanel has ensured the control of its leather suppliers with the acquisition of different tanneries across Europe. Hermès has kept its production close by. It owns six fabric production sites and four leather production sites and exerts strong control over 11 leather goods suppliers. Out of the 52 production sites of the company, 42 were on French soil, emphasizing the importance of the country of origin and French savoire-faire. Hermès also owned a significant part of the French silk manufacturer Perrin. On the other hand, ready-to-wear, which was neither the core of the company nor its historic production, was completely outsourced. Axel Dumas, CEO of Hermes, had commented that they followed a meta-national strategy. "Nous allons là où les méthodes de production sont les plus authentiques possibles" ("We go where the production methods are the most authentic").

These two approaches had their own pros and cons. Outsourcing may cut the cost of production in France and Italy, where the workforce is more expensive, but may also reduce control over the brand's reputation. For example, it was exposed in 2015 that Hermès may be working with a crocodile leather supplier that was accused of unethical practices. Chanel has integrated many suppliers, increasing product margins. It committed to taking all appropriate measures to prevent human rights violations (including slavery and human trafficking) in its supply chains. Following pressure from animal rights activists, Chanel has banned furs and exotic skins from its collections. This commitment may presage a bigger challenge when it comes to meeting consumer demand and expressing creativity. Nevertheless, for luxury brands, ethical and sustainable missions and goal commitments are impossible to overlook or shy away from.

In conclusion, the post-COVID scenario will require supply chains that are agile, aligned, adaptable, and asynchronous. They also need to be integrated. Both global and local supply chains are needed, but in today's era of nationalistic feelings around the globe, and at a time when borders are closed due to the pandemic, local supply chains and supplier networks are a must-have. Finally, brands that produce in China, but do not fully disclose it or try to hide it, must now take a firmer stand. They must either try to pull back from production in China, positioning themselves closer to the French or Italian country-of-origin model, or they must embrace their Chinese production and create value either by being "proudly made in China" or by focusing on trend and lifestyle aspects of their brands.

Case Study: Louis Vuitton

Louis Vuitton, a unit of LVMH, implemented its global supply chain. With help from McKinsey, Vuitton made its manufacturing process more flexible, borrowing techniques mastered by carmakers and consumer-electronics companies. The new factory format was called *Pegase*, after the mythological winged horse and a Vuitton rolling suitcase. Under the new system, it takes less time to assemble bags, in part because they no longer sit around on carts waiting to be moved from one workstation to another. That enables the company to ship fresh collections to its boutiques every six weeks, down from 12 weeks before.

On the manufacturing side, it used to take 20 to 30 craftsmen to put together each Louis Vuitton "Reade" tote bag. Over the course of about eight days, separate workers would sew together leather panels, glue in linings, and attach handles. With the implementation of Pegase, clusters of six to 12 workers, each of them performing several tasks, can assemble the $680 shiny, LV-logo bags in a single day. Vuitton was releasing a new handbag each season. But the factories, which were working on long-term schedules, remained out of step. If a seasonal bag became a hit, the company wasn't capable of ramping up production.

Vuitton executives imported lean production processes developed by Japanese carmakers, which enabled their factories to react quickly to changes in vehicle orders. The Japanese approach seemed to offer a way for Vuitton to shift production to the handbags that were selling best. But Vuitton's manufacturing procedures weren't conducive to such flexibility. Each factory had about 250 employees, and each worker specialized in one skill, such as: cutting leather and canvas; preparing, gluing, and sewing; making pockets and stitching the lining; and assembling the bag. Specialists worked on one batch of bags at a time. Half-completed purses would sit on carts until someone wheeled them to the next section of the assembly line. Because craftsmen were specialized, it was nearly impossible for Vuitton to quickly switch workers from one task to another.

The realignment of the process to fit the SCM plan was carried out as follows:

The first step was to train workers to handle multiple parts of the assembly process. Gluing, stitching, and finishing the edges of a pocket flap, for example, became the job of one worker, not three. To minimize time wastage, the process for each product was apportioned: each worker would need the same amount of time to complete his or her allotted tasks.

(continued)

(*continued*)

The factory floor was reorganized accordingly. Mimicking the small team format used by Japanese electronics makers, Vuitton organized workers into groups of six to 12, depending on the complexity of the bags or wallets they made. For maximum efficiency, Vuitton arranged the groups in clusters of U-shaped workstations, with sewing machines on one side and assembly tables on the other. Workers simply passed their work around the cluster. As workers were less specialized now, they could produce more types of bags, which gave Vuitton more production flexibility.

The reorganization extended beyond the factory floor. Previously, a distribution center in France used to send products directly to Vuitton's stores around the world. Now the company implemented a global distribution hub outside Paris that shipped products to six regional distribution centers: two in Japan, two in Asia, one in the United States, and one near Paris for European orders. New products had been launched on a Friday morning so that stores around the world could feed three-day sales information to management teams on the following Monday. But now production was adjusted so that factories worked to a daily schedule, rather than the weekly arrangement prior to reorganization.

The reorganization's final stage—named Keepall—was implemented in the stores. In the past, salespeople advising customers would disappear into stockrooms when products weren't available on the shop floor. Now Vuitton assigns a few employees at each store to the stockroom. In the flagship Champs-Elysées store in Paris, items are sent via service elevator from a basement stockroom to the cash register. They arrive wrapped in tissue paper. Early indications that the reorganization is working have prompted LVMH officials to consider extending the new factory format to other divisions.

Customer Relationship Management and Customer Experience

With globalization and the expansion of markets, maintaining a database of customers across nations, engaging them, and keeping track of their spending habits present crucial challenges for the luxury industry. Slowly but surely luxury brands have recognized the intrinsic importance of customer relationship management (CRM) as it relates to short- and long-term brand success. Nine out of 10 luxury CRM executives believe that a customer-centric culture and values link to long-term growth and financial success for the brand. It was imperative that a system was maintained whereby managers could track the customer retention rate. Traditionally RFM (recency, frequency, monetary value) was the type of data most commonly found in luxury CRM systems and used in marketing campaigns for luxury brands. The luxury brands were slowly adopting more formal customer experience research. Before, the most commonly used source of knowledge about customer experience was from sales executives. As demand was always greater than supply, customers were pulled toward the brand; the brand was not pushed toward customers. But, with the expansion of luxury brands across national borders, a definite need arose to educate new consumers, who got wealthier as time went by. Thus, along with market access, the process of educating employees about different markets and the story of the brand is extensive. Once achieved, a true customer-centric culture would emerge. Also, key performance indicators (KPIs) were sometimes not aligned.

In order to understand why a customer-centric culture needed to be adopted by luxury brands, it was necessary to analyze how the luxury environment had changed over the last decade. Before, companies had goods that were sought after and each brand had its area of expertise, as did *ébénistes* (cabinet makers), *tapisseurs* (upholsterers), *menuisiers* (carpenters), and the other artisans who had made beautiful products for the court of Versailles. Competition did not exist then in the same way that it does today. Each "expert" had their own space, be it the jewelers or the perfume makers. Initially, luxury companies controlled what they made available to consumers, directing price and quality control. But today's environment is different. There is intense competition in both on- and offline domains. The bargaining power of consumers had increased with time. Technology, and access to information, had made consumers much more knowledgeable and products comparable.

So, with today's competition, luxury companies need to know more about their customers: not necessarily their consumption patterns, but definitely their aspirations and lifestyles. These companies seek to protect their customer base from that of their competitors by measuring *recency*, *frequency*, and the *monetary value* of purchase trends. These types of data are what is currently being used by luxury companies. For example, customers who have made a recent purchase are more likely to purchase again, compared with those who have not, or those who have purchased only one or two times. Customers who pay the most are more likely to buy again. The most valuable customers tend to become even more valuable the more they spend. The lifetime value of a customer is critical to developing an effective CRM system. Customers of high potential value may be young professionals, or up-and-coming, who spend now but will potentially spend more in the future as they mature and become loyal to the brand. Efficient CRM can help to create and maintain the "dream factor" for these luxury consumers. In mature markets, new technologies to track spending patterns within the brand or conglomerate universe are revealing a large potential for innovation and productivity gains within the loyalty landscape. In emerging markets, CRM systems have been easier to implement for two reasons. First, the CRM system was already in-place and had been time-tested in mature markets. Itinerant customers have usually had to provide the details of their nationality for value-added tax refunds. A CRM profile becomes possible once the system is globally integrated. Second, CRM knowledge is already integrated into the retail process.

CRM is intrinsically correlated to a brand's retail strategy. Luxury retailing demands a "hands-on" approach in terms of high service interactions, personalized communication, and superior service. For example:

> . . . *a member of the Kuwati royal family aspires to the Chanel brand. She usually shops in Kuwait and Bahrain. In those cities she has the status, not only of a repeat customer, but also of a member of the royal family who spends considerable resources in the Chanel store. She comes to Paris for work. She visits the Chanel stores at Rue Cambon, and then at Avenue Montaigne. Though she is clad from head-to-toe*

in Chanel products, the sales staff does not recognize her. She is just another wealthy customer visiting the store from the Middle East. In her mind there is no dearth of wealthy people from the Middle East who shop often in Paris. The customer is perplexed. She is not treated the way she is used to. She tells her friend to let them know that she is a regular customer and is looking for some specific products. The sales assistant is very helpful but she cannot do much. The customer's name does not appear in the database, or her passport details. Her friend then has to explain that she is from the royal family. The sales staff goes inside and calls the Chanel boutique in Kuwait. Once her identity is confirmed the whole shop wakes up.

In the luxury environment there is a low profile of customer behavior but the customers have high expectations of service. The challenge is to keep customer expectations consistent throughout all stores. The measurement of service interaction is a management issue as well. Micro-segmentation was the key challenge. If the focus shifts to macro-segmentation, the notion of personalized customer service might get lost in translation.

The state of the art in luxury CRM was to have diverse multi-channel practices to generate and foster customer loyalty. Data can be obtained from different sources: feedback from sales associates in-store during purchase, online browsing patterns, and cross-channel loyalty tools that align the customer with their cross-channel demand. The two most effective strategies that were usually implemented were customer affinity and preference, and personalized promotions across channels. This can measure, to a certain extent, lifetime customer value and the competitive advantage of the brand vis-à-vis their closest competitors in the category.

More real-time customer data allowed brands to understand the aspirations and trends of repeat customers, as well as new customers. This data slowly became a priority as it affected inventories and the resultant supply chain. It seemed that 30% of retailers were using real-time data and planned to fully implement POS tracking as well as online web traffic in real time.

In the luxury environment, control of the distribution and supply chains to get products to different markets was not shared: the supply chain of a brand was proprietary information. Its CRM system reflected how the brand was managing its exclusivity, and the consequent decision-making process drove value. This was because of the strong emphasis on controlling the supply chain and retail distribution. It was a top-down approach.

From the operations and system perspective, the key challenges were to improve customer experience, integrate demand-driven methods into product design, and execute and develop industry-leading innovative methods to maintain loyalty.

To achieve all of this, most luxury firms have already adopted an integrated enterprise resource planning system, like SAP, that manages all the business operations and customer relations. The concept of CRM has been around as long as people have been buying and selling. In the past, data were kept in diaries, notebooks, and ledgers—all of which were handwritten. With advanced technology the key to a good CRM remains the same. Effectively, it is to store information about customers. It was in fact a strategy to manage customer interactions and track the customer's profile—what they bought in stores. Using these data, stores could offer customers incentives and/or information about offerings so as to stimulate demand and sales. CRM software also helped companies to manage the customer relationship process. The key was in uncovering and storing information about customers. The more they know the better they can manage their product lines and product offerings. This involved acquiring the customer's contact information and keeping notes throughout the sales cycle. By tracking this type of detailed data companies could compile reports and data regarding the products that were purchased. They could send out "thank you" notes, birthday cards, and anniversary cards for a purchase, and more. During the pandemic, sales staff were the most important decision makers when closing sales. They had to be proactive on social media to keep in touch and support their individual clients.

Linked to CRM in the integrated value chain is the process of just-in-time (JIT). Stores need to be supplied with products in a manner such that there was neither a dearth of a particular product nor excess inventory, thereby controlling cost. It was also a way to move away from mass production to customization. The more customized the orders the stricter the control on inventory. Integrated enterprise resource planning software, such as SAP, enabled real-time processing that allowed companies to react to situations in their supply chain process. The integrated core functionality of the software tracks finance, production, planning, sales and distribution, and materials management. Product costing, human resource needs, and quality control were also integrated into the system.

Once the CRM strategy was selected and established, the next step for luxury companies was to focus on "speed to market." Whether a luxury product was destined for a company-owned store or offered in a higher-end department store, design leadership and speed to market continued to distinguish these brands. Making fashion ready-to-wear and getting it into the hands of eager shoppers required a well-integrated, coordinated, and thoughtful approach to planning and execution. Luxury retailers had significant success managing narrower collections of garments and accessories, producing smaller lots (albeit with much more detailed fabric, trim, and construction requirements), and simplifying operations. They also mitigated risk by removing most replenishment and limiting the product's on-shelf lifecycle. Luxury retailers continued to closely emulate supply chain giant Zara, which continued to break the conventional speed barrier with tightly controlled and integrated design, manufacturing, and demand-driven product management. Zara's latest innovations involved implementing store-level technology that gave managers more control over ordering products and choosing distribution options that would speed the shipment of in-demand products. The result was further reduced lead times that posed an even greater challenge to retailers hoping to compete. Zara's fast fashion, and use of information technology at store and corporate levels, have been studied extensively. The main challenge always remains to balance accessibility and exclusivity.

The use of appropriate technology—that speeds innovation and customer insight—was the next frontier in managing customer experience. In-store technology for luxury goods was more focused on simplicity and reducing the focal point during the transaction. Few engaged high-tech support, such as hand-held devices like tablets or kiosks. The checkouts were deemphasized, with registers hidden to the point of invisibility, such as was the case with Ferragamo and Bottega Veneta stores. These retailers deemphasized the commercial transaction to an extreme such that it added to the comfortable, exclusive nature of the experience. On the flipside, the ubiquity and familiarity of handheld devices meant that even luxury goods shoppers would likely be comfortable with an employee using a smartphone or personal digital assistant to access their customer record and tailoring the in-process shopping experiences in order to account for personal shopping history and previously observed preferences.

With so many stores to manage, luxury was moving toward the integrated retail experience. Retail was in the detail. Luxury goods retailers' focus on quality of design, speed to market, and comfortable, even simple, shopping environments with thoughtful, well-trained, and neatly dressed multilingual employees was a powerful model. It was a good baseline for aspiring midrange and upper-scale specialty retailers and vertically integrated manufacturers. This also reflected the luxury brand's requirement to maintain its exclusivity. Such was the case with Chanel, with well-dressed employees wearing Chanel apparel in all stores. Ferragamo also practiced this strategy: its employees wear black uniforms and Ferragamo shoes. Retailers that are truly demand-driven set themselves apart from the competition by choosing particular points of service at which to excel.

Conclusion

Researchers have argued that each cog in the wheel within the broad framework of the operational process—from the supply chain to CRM—should aim to lead an inclusive customer experience (Figure 9.2).[1] Managers have become increasingly aware of the need to create value for their customers in the form of experiences. In order for this strategy to work, luxury companies need to understand the "customer's journey"—from their expectations to the assessments they are likely to make. Analysis shows that, through the use of this data, companies can orchestrate and integrate a series of *clues* (anything that can be perceived, sensed, or recognized by its absence), which collectively meet or exceed people's

---

[1]Berry, Carbone, and Haeckel, 2002.

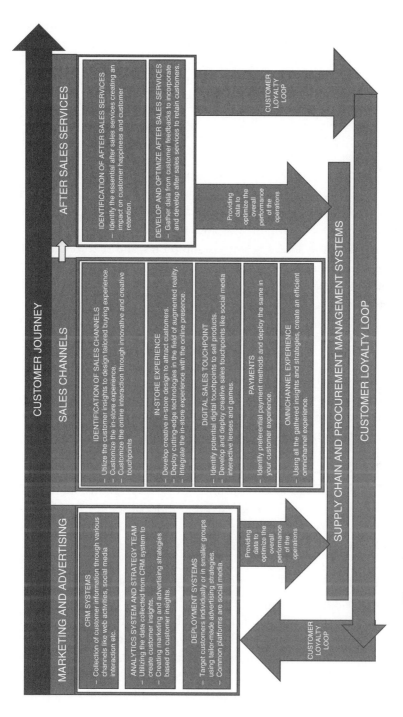

Figure 9.2 How to Create Value in Operations and Systems for the Customer Experience

301

emotional needs and expectations. The internalized meaning and value these clues symbolize can create a deep-seated preference for a particular experience—for one company's product or service over another's. Products or services for sale give off one set of clues, the physical setting offers more clues, and the employees—through their gestures, comments, dress, and tone of voice—give still more clues. Each clue carries a message, suggesting something to the customer. The composite of all the clues makes up the customer's total experience. For example, describing in detail the actual functioning of the product (the intricate story of the scales of the crocodile skin or the delicate python skin) was a clue. The services offered while showing the product and explaining the number of movements of a tourbillon was also a clue. The emotions and sensations, including the smells, sounds, sights, tastes, and textures, as well as the environment in which it was offered, were all clues.

The experiences the same customer has when visiting the LV Flagship store on the Champs-Élysées, the Hermès Faubourg Saint-Honoré store, and the Chanel store in Rue Cambon are entirely different. The feel of the leather upholstery, the tone of voice of the person answering the customer, the décor are all clues that envelope the functionality of a product and its service. This category of clues includes two types: *mechanistic* (clues emitted by things) and *humanistic* (clues emitted by people). Clues as these tend to effect and *affect* emotion, rather than reason, in the moment when the consumer considers whether to buy or move on.

To build on this competence—so that it becomes a characteristic of the organization—luxury companies would want to analyze their stores through the observation of consumer facial expressions, gestures, and body language in order to understand emotional states in various situations. To complement this information, it might be helpful to conduct in-depth interviews with customers and employees to find out how people on both sides of a transaction feel about different aspects of an experience, and the emotional associations that go along with it. For example, it is easy to monitor the growing anxiety of a potential customer over whether she will find what she has come for, having traveled all the way from China or the Middle East. People in this situation behave almost like a child wanting a product which she wants to buy at that moment. She does not need it, but the experience and the product will make her happy, her self-esteem will soar, and she will achieve a state of self-actualization. This experience can then be translated to the basic motif that reflected the organization's core values and branding strategy. The motif acted as the unifying element for every clue in the newly designed customer experience.

Regardless of the *a priori* conditions, customers always have an experience. It may be excellent, good, bad, or leave them feeling indifferent. What was important, however, was how effectively the company managed the experience. Management of both functional and emotional consumer experiences increases the chances of fostering an emotional bond between a brand and its customer base. It is this bond that then becomes a rare and expensive sustainable competitive advantage that cannot be imitated or copied. Without consolidated systems and operations, a satisfying consumer experience cannot be achieved. This may be the next frontier where luxury companies can strengthen customer loyalty for the next generation.

Chapter 10

Services: The Point of Sale

The welcome: *Sales assistants are chatting to each other in a corner. Luxury shopping is not what it should be. Even worse, an assistant greets the customer with a stare or a rude comment.*

"So, what do you want? I am busy at the moment."

"Can you make sure that the children do not touch anything?"

"What is that dog doing here?"

Or a sales assistant is putting away some articles while a customer waits to be attended to. Well, the customer could wait all day, because obviously she is not wanted.

A sales assistant sneers, saying: "You've never heard of this bag? How did you miss the advertisement campaign?"

The client is totally inept, poor thing!

A client walks into the store. The girls at the checkout counter are talking. He starts looking around until finally a sales assistant enquires politely, "May I help you with anything in particular?"

"No," responds the client. "I am not looking for anything in particular." And he storms out!

A customer returns a dress. "This dress has already been worn!" cries the sales assistant.

"No, it hasn't," replies the lady, "I simply tried it on again."

"Well, it is too late, it cannot be returned now, and where did you buy it?"

"Here."

"But who sold it to you?"

"I have no idea."

Skills in greeting customers are sometimes horrendous, or even blatantly non-existent. On other occasions, the reception is simply magnificent.

At the entrance to the store, a hostess greets you with a smile and ushers you in. Then she guides you around the shop. The customer has no obligation to buy, children are welcome—they even have toys for them to play with. Dogs are welcome too. Browsing through the store becomes a wonderful enchantment.

Greeting the customer is never a question of money; it is the result of motivation and pride.

Luxury becomes superb when it is dealt out generously, and welcoming a client is an act of self-effacing generosity. It takes little more than a simple, attentive look, escorting the customer to a counter or dressing room. There is absolutely no need for insincere flattery, just a light touch, a gentle sense of humor, without going too far.

The welcome epitomizes luxury; it flatters the mind and attracts the customer to the product, while complementing it.

The welcome to a luxury shop can be the best in the world . . . or it can be appalling. Just like luxury itself.

Luxury used to be "ordinary goods for exceptional people," but more and more it is becoming "exceptional goods for ordinary people." Service and luxury appear as intertwined and interdependent. In times such as now, major luxury brands are industrialized and converging in terms of the 9Ps—*product, provenance, paucity, persona, personage, price, position, publicity, phygital, performance*—therefore, the notion of service excellence becomes a clear differentiator that sets apart a brand, because service is one of the best touchpoints to convey the brand's DNA, history, and story.

The Luxury Service discussed in this chapter is the way in which employees of a luxury brand interact with a customer at various direct-to-customer points before, during, and after the purchase. While the retail department and online customer service team are those who serve at the front line, creative and manufacturing departments—even back-office teams such as marketing, omnichannel, training, logistics etc.—are all intricately involved in the product and service offering. Points of sale (POS) refers to channels where transactions take place, including brand-owned boutiques, stands or shops-within-shops in department stores, and online channels. While providing service the flow of the customer management process is intricately linked to how each brand engages with their customer.

Physical evidence encompasses the environment in which the service is delivered, both in terms of communication and service performance, but also in intangible experiences relating to the potential customer and to their satisfaction. The people and the process are explicitly and directly in contact with the customer, whereas physical evidence is implicit to the customer. Traditionally, brands have entered the global market via distribution models including, but not limited to: internal expansion, mergers or takeovers, licensing, franchising, joint ventures, or non-controlling interests. Complementing this, luxury brands also include flagship stores as the most prevalent and strategic method of market entry that provides controlled POS with ample brand-to-consumer benefits, no matter the market. Flagship stores and well-designed boutiques thus play an important role in the services offered by front-line personnel and reflect the productivity of the people involved in the sales process at the POS.

In light of this, brands have coherent strategies to differentiate themselves across markets by using their unique physical characteristics at POS. For example, they seek to differentiate their brand through concepts like pop-up shops, such as Hermès's pop-up scarf installation and Dior's Christmas lighting-up ceremony plus pop-up store, in order to make an unforgettable imprint on the consumer's mind.

Likewise, luxury goods consumers have evolved over the past decades. They are more aware of the range of choices available to them. They are also more knowledgeable, better traveled, and more experienced than their predecessors. They can easily compare and contrast brands and cross geographies when looking for luxury. At the same time, brands have extended their DNA and become more diversified, tending to be "generalists." For example, Louis Vuitton and Dior have extended their offers into high jewelry and watches, while Cartier have strengthened their leather goods range. Similarly, Berluti have extended from leather shoes and briefcases to ready-to-wear and a bespoke collection. Brands have also become cross-gender, with Dior and Celine going for men's wear while Hugo Boss has developed styles for women.

With designers becoming "generalists," the luxury industry has also significantly evolved in line with four major trends: globalization with access to goods, democratization with access to different segments, diversification with access to different product ranges, and digitalization with access to comparable and competing information. Due to these four phenomena, the place where customer and brand meet, the point of sale, appears to be the epicenter for significant impact. Beyond its influence on customer perception, satisfaction, and loyalty, the role of service is multilayered: communicating the true DNA of the brand; meeting and catering to new international customers' expectations; being different in design and style, timeless and yet modern; and being relevant to different cultures across national boundaries.

Issues at Point of Sale

With globalization, democratization, and digitization managers in the luxury industry are faced with the dilemma of bridging domestic and international clientele. From their home base they need to access foreign markets, not only in terms of geography, but also by welcoming foreign consumers from new and distant markets. As a result, managers have to do more than just manage a brand. What they in fact manage is a dynamic consumer base with different mindsets, cultural orientations, idiosyncrasies, and buying behaviors. For example, in emerging markets consumers often use the term "How much does it cost?" In mature markets, the consumers ask "How expensive is it?" Though the basic meaning of both questions is the same, the connotations are different. At the POS, a sales representative can interpret the questions from different points of view, according to her knowledge of prices and cost, and her life experience as well. Thus, in the luxury business more and more sales representatives are being hired from new markets while keeping the diversity of consumers in mind. This simple example of cultural connotation radically changes the foundation of luxury branding.

Michael Burke, the current CEO of Louis Vuitton and Chairman of the board of Tiffany, commented on managing people during the pandemic.[1]

> *The other thing is empowerment. When the crisis really accelerated, the only way to work [was] to fully empower people. The things that we've done in the last three or four months are good examples. The [Louis Vuitton menswear] show in Shanghai was cast locally and produced locally. The local teams were fully empowered to not just do a repeat show, but an original show. That show would have never happened before. We got away from this neo-colonial approach where everything happens in New York, London, Paris or Milan and gets trickled down through the various [markets] and they replicate; that's gone, that's finished. I also turned every one of our 10,000 sales employees into store managers. We went into the crisis with 450 stores, we came out of the crisis with 10,000 stores, because every single salesperson, when they were stuck at home, we empowered them through software that we wrote in 10 days to not just interact with the clients, but also to actually close the sale. Each client advisor became a self-standing store with access to all the inventories throughout the zone, they could sell any product to anybody. So, sales associates became store managers, a store managed by one person. This is how we were doing 30 or 40% of our business with all stores closed.*

Due to the issues in luxury branding with people, processes, and physical evidence, traditional luxury brands are faced with opportunities on the one hand and challenges on the other. Emerging markets bring high-net-worth individuals, exponential growth and consumption, low-cost production, and high technological advances, whereas the challenges are how much to democratize (embrace more customers), digitize, and globalize while keeping up with the development path without blurring their own identity.

---

[1] https://www.businessoffashion.com/articles/luxury/louis-vuittons-michael-burke-on-hardwiring-accountability-in-a-state-of-flux?utm_source=daily-digest-newsletter&utm_campaign=1685416498668386&utm_term=11&utm_medium=email.

At points of sale, where service takes place, the challenge translates to what type of image a brand would like to portray to its new generation of consumer: a parochial mindset, a diffused mindset, or a global mindset? A parochial mindset, at managerial level and POS, is blind to diversity across markets and cultures. There are few incentives in a foreign market, if any, to adapt processes to local conditions and by extension to foreign consumers in their home markets. On the other hand, a diffused mindset would mean that the managers and employees at the POS would have a deep understanding of the local culture and market. Finally, the global mindset understands and acknowledges difference and diversity of culture and markets, but is also able to synthesize across this diversity.

Dolce & Gabbana's incident in China was a wake-up call in the luxury world, fully displaying the harmful effect of a parochial mindset. In 2018, D&G planned to hold a fashion show in Shanghai on November 21st, which was supposed to be an hour-long tribute to China, featuring over 300 looks, 140 performers, and 1,400 people in the audience. Prior to the show, D&G posted three video ads on the Chinese social media app, Weibo. In these videos, a young Asian model, in a red D&G dress, appears to have trouble eating Italian food—pizza, pasta, cannoli—with chopsticks but finally figures it out with the aid of a male narrator. In the video featuring cannoli, the narrator asks the model "Is it too big for you?" Soon after, the blunder was compounded with screenshots online that appeared to show co-founder Stefano Gabbana's negative remarks about China. Later, the designer explained that his account had been hacked. Nevertheless, almost all the celebrities pulled out of the show. D&G ended up having to cancel it just a few hours prior to its start. The incident not only hurt consumer sentiment, but also reflected on D&G's sales. Its products were pulled from the major e-commerce sites in China, such as Tmall, JD and Secoo. The Asia-Pacific market shrank to 22% from 25% of total turnover in the fiscal year ending in March 2019, and sales in the Greater China region continued to shrink. In 2020, D&G opened a new store in Hong Kong amid the pandemic and protests. It was interpreted as a try of luck. The brand's business partners described its headquarters as highly controlling: "HQ never listens," said one. It may be difficult to require HQ to understand every market deeply. However, with the globalization of the luxury business, brands should realize the pressing importance of avoiding a parochial mindset, either by bringing more international talent into their HQ, or by giving more autonomy to local teams. D&G's China team might have prevented this incident if they had been given more say.

Cartier is a brand that has successfully displayed its wonderful global mindset. In 2019, Cartier held an exhibition themed "Beyond Boundaries," in collaboration with Palace Museum, a national Chinese museum housed in the Forbidden City, in Beijing. The exhibition showcased both Chinese imperial history and modern Western culture; in doing so, it made a connection between Chinese culture and Cartier's DNA. In the US, the Cartier Mansion was renovated and reopened in 2016. Its salons were named after some of Cartier's most prominent clients: Elizabeth Taylor, Andy Warhol, and Gary Cooper—names familiar to American clients. In 2017, the landmark building was used to hold Cartier's largest US high jewelry exhibition. The salons also displayed historic jewels related to each person. In an overly commercialized world, exhibition is not a fresh approach to enhance a brand's authenticity and build its connection with local clients. However, with its global mindset and sincere appreciation for local culture and clients, Cartier managed to use the approach in a way that is subtle yet effective. Consumers appreciate foreign brands' efforts to understand their country's history and culture. A global mindset throughout a company will reflect consistently in its marketing, retailing, and other endeavors. Brands should consider how to transfer their DNA through service at POS but also their appreciation and respect toward local cultures. This requires developing training procedures that include a global mindset.

The question that emerges—at both the managerial and POS level—is which strategic posture and communication method to adopt? Is it effective to be French or Italian, selling the finest French and Italian products in a parochial approach, or to have a diffuse posture like that of fast-moving consumer goods such as Unilever, or later on P&G, or to inculcate a global posture like that of Japanese firms, which are leveraged on the basis of standardized, highly efficient product–market structure? How brands answer this question will decide whether they can solve, on the one hand, the transnational paradox of managing local responsiveness and global coordination at the same time while, on the other hand, pursuing the meta-national mindset of sourcing knowledge and expertise from all over the world.

The Customer Experience Dimension

In addition to the beautiful products, the customer experience journey has become one of the most important factors to differentiate a luxury brand in such a competitive industry. An effective consumer experience involves two aspects. First, it must create positive emotions and memories to target customers and second it should deliver the targeted brand values. There are five elements that need to be taken care of from when a customer enters a store till the exit. These elements include store outlook and interior decoration, products, price, service, and a feeling of pride (Figure 10.1). Many luxury brands excel at store outlook, decoration, and product. However, their service level, and ability to pamper each customer's pride, may not work in their favor. Some brands' sales staff are known to be scornful of customers who don't look as though they can afford the products. This may cause loss of potential customers or neglect of customers' needs.

Figure 10.1   Elements of Customer Happiness

There are different kinds of relationship service that a luxury brand can provide to boost customer satisfaction and hence deliver a unique customer journey. These include services that raise awareness of consumers, enhance the shopping experience, give privileges to certain consumers to fulfill their pride, offer other value-added services, and provide timely after-sales service.

In order to raise awareness of consumers, a common tactic adopted by many brands is to place temporary artistic devices in luxury shopping malls, oftentimes accompanied by pop-up stores to highlight the latest collections. The physical environment of a permanent boutique has an important effect on a customer's shopping experience. However, a temporary artistic device is more like a manifesto, boasting of the brand's inspiration, and drawing traffic to boutiques in the meantime. In late 2019, Dior built a five-floor-high baobab tree in Plaza 66, Shanghai, an iconic luxury shopping mall. Interactive devices were set up within the hollow tree trunk, where customers could walk in and have fun. A light-up ceremony was also held, with clouds of celebrities invited. The baobab tree was the inspiration for Dior's 2020 spring collection, which was displayed in the pop-up store surrounding the tree. Sculptures of African animals, interspersed here and there within the scene, created a unique brand universe and unforgettable emotional experience for customers. Although the tree and pop-up store lasted less than a month, it became a hot-spot visited by fashion lovers and luxury shoppers. In Paris, Dior transformed the exterior of its store at Avenue Montaigne almost overnight. A five-story Christmas tree with African animal decorations lit up the store's exterior wall, spurring the holiday spirit all around the town and showcasing the spring collection inspiration.

Brands can enhance customers' shopping experience by proactively engaging with them. They can, on the one hand, push collective campaigns, using their CRM tools while, on the other hand, interacting at a one-to-one level. Consumers can be roughly classified into prospects, occasional buyers and VIPs, based on their purchase history and lifetime spend. Brands have their own way of further segmentation. Luxury brands have intrinsically excelled at serving VIPs; from the beginning of the industry they have been dealing with royals or rich clientele. Sales staff remember a client's birthday, their wedding anniversary, their likes and dislikes, culminating in a *wow* experience. For other consumers, brands leverage campaigns, such as emailing, SMS, purchase trigger, etc.

Two perspectives need to be catered to at all points of the interaction. First, the customer's view of what they want, and second, how the company wishes to define its products and services. Managing the perception of a service is always a greater challenge than managing the actual quality of service offered. In this respect, more so in the luxury and super-premium segment, the client needs to be the central priority. Selection, training, and development of personnel is the minimum requirement for an effective customer service function, but it is not the sole parameter. This is so because all the dimensions of service quality can be influenced directly by a company's employees.

Another tactic to enhance the in-store experience is to reduce the time that a customer spends standing in a queue, or looking for a particular product. In the old days, important clients would have appointments before coming to the store. They were the happy few, specially taken care of. Nowadays, the universality of luxury has significantly increased its consumer base. Luxury brands are simply not able to provide top service to everyone, creating the unhappy many. Gucci designed a picture-scanning function in their clienteling app. When customers come to a Gucci store with product pictures that they saw somewhere else, sales staff used to have to think hard, ask colleagues and managers, and appear ignorant if they could not find an answer. Now they simply scan the pictures with the app installed on their tablet. It will immediately show which collection the product is from, which stores have the stock, the price and other details. Prada once introduced a system in which every product and loyalty card carries an RFID chip, which is tracked on a Bluetooth connection. Through the chip, loyalty cards activated a database on the shop's computer to inform the salesperson about the client. It turned out that consumers were not comfortable with the amount of info collected, so Prada had to discontinue the system. Nevertheless, it was an innovative solution to tackle a problem. The challenge was always how to better serve the unhappy many in order to maintain their brand image.

Giving privileges to certain consumers fulfilled their pride and delivered the message that the brands cared about them. Some have defined a multilayered service offering, which categorizes customers based on their loyalty and/or spending in order to spotlight the VIP customers. The idea was to give greater attention to those customers, as opposed to excursionists, and to provide them with privileged exclusive services.

An example is to create an exclusive club such as platinum card holders for airlines, hotels, and additional services for those elite members. Many luxury brands, especially hard luxury, have CRM budgets that sales staff can freely use to pamper VIP clients. Organizing personalized tours, buying birthday gifts are basics. Louis Vuitton even monogrammed personalized garbage bins for Kim Kardashian! For prospects, inviting them to brand events and exhibitions can be a good way. The key to giving privileges is, on the one hand, it gives clients strong emotional and unforgettable experiences but, on the other hand, it's important to keep a close eye on return on investment.

To boost satisfaction, luxury brands offer other value-added services. For example, the brand could teach consumers how to drape scarves or use makeup. In 1991 Estée Lauder sought to capture the attention of their clients by providing a 25-minute free makeup video. This helped to teach their customers how to achieve better results. A special example is Make Up Forever. It is known in consumers' minds as a professional cosmetic brand. However, not many know that it owns makeup academies in Europe, Asia and the US. The founder of the brand, Dany Sanz, a former painter and sculptor, has always been passionate about teaching the art of makeup. She created the Paris Make Up Forever Academy in 2002, providing certified makeup education. It has since expanded to eight cities. Based on this unique brand DNA, Make Up Forever was able to create many tutorial videos on its official website. This was an example of how value-added services can be based on a brand's founders' DNA.

After-sales service has always been an important part of the whole service process, sometimes even considered the key to grade a brand's quality of service. Especially for jewelry and timepieces, customers are highly concerned about the turnaround time, the price, and the guarantee of after-sales service. A good after-sales service experience may win over the loyalty of a customer who will be likely to repurchase and to spread positive word of mouth. The satisfactory level of the after-sales service is not decided by the size or the position of the brand: unlike in-store service, which can be influenced by many factors such as size of the store and luxury facility, after-sales service is decided more by the strategy of the brand and by the formation of its sales staff. There are some successful practices in both big brands and small brands that can be learned from.

For example, Cartier's after-sales service is worth mentioning. The worldwide leader in high jewelry and star brand of the Richemont Group is established as the king of jewelry. However, this strength has brought difficulties for the brand in watches. Cartier is always thought of more as a "fashion" or "jewelry" brand than a real watch brand, although not considered completely "off-piste" in the horology world. The fact that their watch store is more often located in the jewelry section than the watch section also led to such an impression. However, Cartier has long understood the concept of "service" better than its competitors. The excellent quality of their after-sales service for their watches has won them accolades: customers experience the same quality of finish as from the finest jeweler. In their after-sales service for watches, Cartier offers several options for customers to choose from according to their own needs—from a rapid battery replacement service at £35, to a simple polishing service at £50, or a complete service that covers repairing parts, such as the water-resistant gaskets, polishing, and movement disassembly, which starts at £160. The jewelers also offer a more specific service: providing a wide range of straps for changes, a variety of colors, materials, finishing techniques, and styles—from lizard in matte and gloss finish, to alligator and Kevlar—to delight the customer. The service is not limited to watches and jewelry, but also extends to its writing instruments and leather goods, which are given the guarantee that "a Cartier should last for a lifetime." While its rivals, such as Rolex and Piaget, are often criticized for their expensive repairing services, Cartier wins over in the after-sales service, with extremely knowledgeable and helpful staff, guaranteed turnaround times, and a variety of services offered at reasonable price points.

Once an expensive product is bought it is expected that the consumer won't be in the mood to spend exorbitantly on getting it repaired in terms of both time and money. For example, many luxury brands, such as Rolex, Hermès, and LV, have universally recognized after-sales service. Rolex takes care of common problems faced by watch lovers concerning repairs and servicing. Rolex's service center in Singapore is known for its speed and rigor. One can take any Hermès product into any of its stores in the world either to return it or to repair it.

As summarized by Figure 10.2, there are a number of aspects that round up the customer satisfaction dimension. Luxury brands should strive to impress their clients in all these aspects.

Figure 10.2　Elements of Delighting Customers

The Service Dimension

Historically, luxury goods companies have neglected service, in the true sense of the word. They did it due to some inherent qualities of luxury goods explained in Chapter 2. Luxury goods, by definition, are of exquisite quality and craftsmanship, invariably aesthetic, rare, extraordinary and symbolic. The brand's equity is enough to sell such an article. Apart from the nature of the products, the power of the brand and low competition among specialized brands went against the common notion of service as a differentiator. With the growth of the sector and competition for new consumers from Asia, Latin America, and Eastern Europe, the aspirations regarding luxury goods have changed with time.

With the sector's expansion in both mature and emerging markets, the service dimension has become a key differentiator. With diversification in their product category more and more brands feel the need to touch the heart to increase their presence in the share-of-wallet of the customer. For example, Hermès was known for their saddles while Mont Blanc was famous for its writing instruments. But today they both offer accessories such as belts and watches. To be relevant to the customer in all segments, luxury brands have started to understand the necessity of focusing on each customer in terms of their satisfaction, their relationship, and ultimately their delight. This dimension is an act, an experience—a performance that is intangible, perishable, inseparable, and variable; and it does not result in the ownership of a tangible object, so it needs to be practiced and institutionalized.

The institutionalization may come through adoption of practices moving forward, from customer satisfaction to service quality. Essentially, to understand the process, there is first the notion of customer service. Luxury consumption in no way ends with the product. It consists of the entire experience: hearing about a product, going to the showroom, sifting through all the products, clarifying your doubts, and finally making the purchase. Also, the process does not end here. It is critical for a brand to offer an exceptional after-sales service. It is difficult to imagine authentic luxury without stellar service. If the service is poor, luxury escapes.

Second, with the economic crisis and the subsequent pandemic crisis, luxury companies have strengthened their ties with their customers as a means of differentiating themselves. The companies went back to their loyal customers, were attentive to their needs, and connected with them at an emotional level. Nothing is more valued by consumers than human attention. They want to be pampered while they are at the store.

Third, customer service needs adaptation to the changing behavior of the consumers. It is evident that with increasing knowledge and availability of more information consumers are becoming more discerning and demanding. The new consumers tend to ask more questions when they step into a store. One would expect luxury to be solely driven by pleasure and away from critical questions of customers. That was before.

Now they want to know where their money is going. They are influenced by press reports, tweets, and blog entries. A bad incident can reflect poorly on a company's service. When Oprah Winfrey was turned away by a Hermès showroom as it had been shut down for a private event, it reflected poorly on Hermès's service quality.

Service quality, by definition, is the consumer's perception of a brand, prior to an encounter, due to reputation and word-of-mouth. This is an interpersonal process that is culturally bound and relates to professional manners that speak about brand image. The concept of service quality rests on the different understandings of stakeholders. Five main gaps are usually identified. The first is the management perception gap. This is the knowledge gap that arises due to the difference between a consumer's expectations and the management's perception of the consumer's expectations. Management may think that they know what consumers want and proceed to deliver, when in fact consumers may expect something quite different. The second notion is the quality specification gap. This is the difference between the management's perception of consumer expectations and the actual service quality offered. Management may not set quality specifications or may not stipulate them clearly. Alternatively, management may set clear quality specifications but these may not be achievable. The third is the service delivery gap. It is the difference between service quality specifications and the service actually delivered. Unforeseen problems, or poor management incentives, can lead to a service employee failing to meet service quality specifications. This may be due to human error or mechanical breakdown while facilitating or supporting goods. The fourth gap is the communication gap. It is the difference between service delivery intention and what is communicated about the service to customers. Examples include promises given by promotional activities that are not consistent with the service delivered. It usually arises from a propensity to overpromise. A typical example would be first-class travel, which may have been promoted with glowing images and messages in glossy high-end travel magazines, but in the end falls below the level of service expected by customers. The fifth gap is about service quality. This arises due to the difference between what customers expect and what they receive: the service experienced is not consistent with the service expected.

The Phygital Dimension

Phygital simply means the fusion of physical and digital experiences and relates to the use of technology, which enables the connection of the digital world to the physical world. With this, the primary and overall purpose is to provide consumers with an interactive, unique, and pleasing sensory experience. This smart marriage between the offline and online environments at point of sale is what the customer is looking for, especially in the pandemic and post-pandemic scenario, when they cannot touch and feel in a brick-and-mortar environment.

Before the pandemic, customer experience relied essentially on the in-store experience and a personalized relationship with the customer. However, the pandemic has boosted the emergence of the digital age, which has disrupted the original characteristics of the luxury experience, such as exclusivity, personalization, or experience. This novel emergence of the phygital customer experience and sales touchpoints is probably one of the most crucial success factors for traditional heritage brands, which fosters desirability, innovation, and the bridge between timelessness and modernity. In contrast, newly emerging brands need to be authentic, credible, legitimate, with brand image coherence over time in order to be perceived as an original actor around the imaginary table, which mainly seats established and traditional players.

In the 2010s, in order to reach new clients luxury brands have strongly relied on emergent markets such as China. A customer from China who buys a luxury product expects to have an experience at least as valuable as the product they are buying. With time the customer profile has changed. Millennials and Gen Y, those who were born between 1980 and 1995, represented 35% of sales as reported in early 2021. The Z-generation, which gathers people born between 1996 and 2010, accounts for 4% of luxury sales (in 2021) but is expected to attain 40% by 2035. This age group can be targeted through digitalization as they were born at the beginning of the digital revolution; they have been immersed in new technologies from a very young age. They are sensible to digital technology. To maintain a relationship with these customers, point of sale means the meeting place, where it is important to create a magical experience, be it in a physical store or in the digital space. The phygital universe becomes an asset—a strong support, and complementary channel, which allows luxury brands to meet customers' expectations and provide a uniquely profound experience.

The phygital challenge is to build seamlessness of experience within the digital and physical environments. The goal of the new phygital experience is to transform stores, offices and industries so that they become smarter, more customized and more intuitive. Many brands have implemented different phygital solutions. For example, Hermès created its own pop-up store, called Hermèsmatic. This relied entirely on digital communication, coupled with a strong physical experience immersed in the world of the brand. For its part, Kate Spade introduced a connected storefront, which allowed purchase and delivery within the hour by remaining faithful to the brand image. Dior and Gucci created many different filters for its Social Media platforms Instagram, Facebook and Snapchat and enabled brand lovers to experiment by trying on apparel and accessories like sunglasses, shoes and hats, and many more—all powered by Augmented Reality. Burberry has created an Augmented Reality shopping tool through the Google Search technology, which allows consumers a genuinely realistic experience and interaction with Burberry's products by embedding them in the customer's current physical environment. Furthermore, the Augmented Reality technology improves consumers' online research results and overall shopping experience. Last but not least Augmented Reality windows have been proved to elevate a brand's narrative and storytelling by creating an art installation-like experience, which again can be perfectly shared over Social Media and contribute to virality and publicity. To provide the digital environment and make the customer feel at home in the physical stores, most brands have started offering screens, open Wi-Fi in-store, shelves for smartphones or tablets, fee-charging for hand-held devices. Services include appointment in-store via website, an app, in-store client recognition technology, seamlessness across store and website—such as exchange and return in store (declared in website), and others.

Research shows that American brands, such as Ralph Lauren, Coach, Tiffany, have adapted the phygital strategy much in advance, followed by European brands such as Burberry, LV and Gucci. For example, Ralph Lauren's shops feature fitting rooms with interactive mirrors that allow customers to request assistance, receive complete look suggestions, send a selection of pieces to their mobile phone, or escape the waiting lines at the checkout. Burberry, the leader in digital adoption from a decade before, has also shifted its entire business strategy to digital to ensure its customers a rich experience both online and at the store. Burberry recently opened its latest phygital boutique—an interactive and immersive shop, a so-called "social retail" store in Shenzhen, China, which truly transforms the future of shopping and showcases Burberry's pioneering spirit in the area of phygital innovation. Ricardo Tisci, Burberry's CCO, sees customers' behaviour on social media as a magic key for the design of future retail outlets: "Our social retail concept is just the next step in giving our community a truly personal, luxury experience. What I find so exciting is the ability [for our customers] to experience the Burberry world both physically and digitally." All this while Burberry has entered into a number of partnerships (with Snapchat, Google–Augmented Reality, DreamWorks Animation, Instagram, Tik Tok, We Chat and Apple TV) to strengthen its interactions with its customers globally through interactive windows and scannable QR codes, which provide information about Burberry's sustainability engagement, and offer consumers a genuinely personal and interactive experience in the new phygital store.[2]

Louis Vuitton was a pioneer when it came to digital transformation and customer-centric activities among the European brands. The French powerhouse had been the first luxury brand to integrate a WeChat messenger service for its Chinese clients, almost a decade ago, with the aim of building an even more personal and intimate one-to-one relationship with its affluent customers. With this, the consumers have the option to directly live chat with Louis Vuitton's salesperson, order online through their phone messenger, and pick up their new items directly in the store, which further enhances the personal relationship and the smart click & collect option and creates an additional personal aftersales touchpoint for the brand to excel.[3] Louis Vuitton recently introduced the innovative and agile order management technology "OneStock," which offers a high-end luxury service by allowing consumers to check real-time stock availability of different items through Louis Vuitton's e-commerce website. Not only did consumers have the option to get delivery on the

---

[2] AD Magazine, 2020.
[3] Jing Daily, 2018.

same day, but they were also free to visit the Louis Vuitton shop for an in-store purchase pick-up in under two hours. All these options—ship from store, click & collect, and return in-store—strengthen the brand's phygital capabilities and were rolled out across Europe in 2020. Furthermore, Louis Vuitton Chatbot on Facebook Messenger allows customers a more "sophisticated, personalised, visual and conversational online shopping experience for each client." In order to do so, it was necessary to implement Natural Language Processing (NLP) into chatbots, which allowed for a conversation between the customer and the brand in a natural way. During the quarantine of 2020–2021, Louis Vuitton offered a home-based experience to its clients by launching a series of virtual exhibitions (a visit to the Louis Vuitton Foundation) and cultural agenda to entertain them. Michael Burke, CEO of Louis Vuitton, had commented, "And, today, customers feel the need to be connected to the Louis Vuitton universe no matter where they are."

Gucci's e-commerce is directly operated and active in 35 markets and the brand also employs social media shopping features—to allow consumers to purchase the posted products. In 2018 already, the brand achieved 70% growth in the online channel, by investing in online customer experience tools, completely redesigning their website and increasing digital spend to 55% of their total media budget. Gucci enlarged the way they celebrate the brand's cultural foundations by investing in highly interactive and digital communication, to immerse completely the consumer in the House reality and create an emotional bond between Gucci and its clients, no matter the geographical location. By doing this, Gucci managed to increasingly shade the division between the physical store and the online environment and to provide clients with a truly exceptional experience across all channels and touchpoints, aligning the e-commerce side with the standards of excellence seen in its boutiques.

The early adoption of a digital focus, with the following development of digital infrastructure and talents in house, helped the brand recover from the consequences of the pandemic. To facilitate the delivery of this set of digital services and to bring a human touch to remote service, Gucci invested in the Gucci 9 project. The project, rolled out by the brand throughout 2019, consisted of a new global client service center headquartered in Florence (Italy) with regional hubs in the US, Korea,

Japan and Southeast Asia. A total of six service centers with over 350 dedicated online client advisors powered by the latest technology provided clients with a direct connection to the Gucci community through a seamless, always accessible and personalized experience with a human touch. The client advisors answered calls, emails and live chats and are trained to develop personal relationships online with callers, just as the traditional shop assistant would. The employees of these centers managed to replicate online their personalized in-store experience through a new video shopping service. The video service connects store staff with consumers via both mobiles and laptops and was designed to feel similar to an in-person visit, incorporating one-to-one interaction with a shop assistant showing physical products. The success of the project did not only require updated infrastructure, but also the employees' development of digital, social and emotional skills: in the CEO's words: "a precious human touch powered by technology." In 2020 Gucci made an essential but clear decision about the future of its fashion shows by representing a new digital narrative through a 12-hour live stream for the reveal of the spring-summer 2021 *Epilogue* collection. With 35.2 million views, the digital fashion show hit record numbers and is the brand's most viewed online event ever. Furthermore, Gucci created Gucci Equilibrium, a new online portal and Instagram site to highlight and engage consumers on the brand's Corporate Social Responsibility activities, labeling them as Gucci's *ongoing commitment to generate positive change for people and the planet*. By establishing "Gucci Live," a video service, physically distant clients were connected with sales personnel in-store, recreating a phygital trip to the Gucci shop. Furthermore, to showcase its heritage and roots, Gucci enabled brand lovers a virtual online tour through the Gucci Garden in Florence, allowing the visitor a digital deep dive into the brand's iconic pieces and culture. But the most promising phygital touchpoint was clearly the Gucci App, which enabled customers everything from virtual try-on (available for watches, sneakers, lipstick, eyewear, hats and décor) to a comfortable live streaming platform for runway features, over the playful exploration of the brand's aesthetics with the vintage style Game "Arcade" as well as Podcast, providing rich storytelling and candid conversation based on Gucci's philosophy. Gucci went even so far as to sell virtual, nonexistent goods through its phygital strategy to enhance engagement. The logic behind this idea shows some significant parallels to the gamification experience. Let's assume that the customer right at the moment cannot afford the desired outfit or a specific accessory. He or she has then the possibility to buy nonphysical products for an affordable price, and use the purchased virtual goods to dress their online avatars by playing the stylist. These online avatars will then have a big moment in the online community, which usually features some kind of interactive brand game. The chosen avatar is fully dressed in the priorly purchased virtual brand apparel.[4]

Marco Bizzari, the CEO of Gucci, was very clear about the phygital journey for Gucci.

> *Deepening the conversation with clients across all of the brand's touchpoints is critical for its long-term success, especially in a technologically connected society, where immersive and innovative digital experiences are paramount to lead the way and engage with consumers across the globe. This is achieved through the careful implementation of a qualitative content and platform strategy that is the source of an ongoing, authentic emotional and engaging narrative. . . Our clients are connected and mobile, constantly flicking between distribution channels, from digital platforms to brick-and-mortar stores. Our client relations strategy is epitomized by continuity on all communication and distribution channels. This holistic omnichannel approach is supported by targeted directly operated store extensions and strategies for distribution agreements, travel retail, e-commerce, social media and digital communication. . . The mission of our Gucci 9 global service centre is to provide our customers around the world with a direct connection to the Gucci community that is a seamless, always accessible, personalized experience. The service is delivered according to the values that define and differentiate our brand today: a precious human touch powered by technology.[5]*

In response to the phygital challenge, Dior created Dior Eyes, a virtual reality helmet that makes it possible to discover the "behind the scenes" of the latest fashion show. LVMH has strongly shown its interest in digitalizing their point of sale by investing in fully digital start-up such as the Memomi Mirror. It consisted of an in-store digital screen

---

[4]Cosco, 2020a, 2020b.
[5]Kering, 2019.

including augmented reality, which allowed the customers to try and visualize a product in all its colors. Other smaller, innovative brands such as designer Simon Porte Jacquemus, displayed a strong digital narrative and important digital customer touchpoint, almost representing a virtual personal diary, which featured the brand's latest collections as well as the designer's individual thoughts and inspirations. In July 2020, in the middle of a wheat field, the designer organized a fashion show one hour away from Paris and invited a hand full of guests. As one of the first designers to put on a runway show during the pandemic, he titled the event as "a magical moment, we couldn't have done without it, and we all needed it."[6] Right afterward, the phygital short film "Amour" was created and published, showcasing how a real-life physical event can be harnessed to maximum effect for the digital world, emitting an authentic feeling of connection and local onsite presence.

To summarize, phygital customer experience is a way to entice digitally savvy customers to be at ease with the brand universe. And this is an essential part of the omnichannel retail. The use of websites, e-commerce, social media as well as new technologies is accepted as a necessity. Gens Y and Z are looking forward to omnichannel interaction with luxury brands. It represents the future of luxury sales to reach out to this generation. The gaps can be bridged by assurance, empathy and employee engagement in both the physical and the digital world. The assurance is dependent upon the employees' ability to convey credibility, and inspire trust and confidence. Showing empathy means to be attentive to the customers. The service quality ultimately depends on the frontline employees who deliver the firm's promises, create an image and promote those services. Frontline employees in that sense are the real face of the brand. Research has shown that new customer services are about the total customer journey that can be provided before, during, and after the consumption and interaction with the brand. For example, the experience before could be of website, hotline, catalogues, design, colors, social media, PR events, launches, press, advertisements, and others. Both Burberry and Ralph Lauren were further advanced in the digital space than other competing brands but others like Gucci, LV, Dior are catching up. The sales experience could be appealing to the six senses in

---

[6] *Vogue*, 2020.

the store, through design of the store, in-store welcome, product knowledge, and contact with the salesperson in-store and through the digital
media. It could be the words used, eye contact, body language, special
attention, and others. After the consumption, the interaction could be
either at the place of sales, VIP club, virtual community, maintenance
advice, after-sales exchange, the exchange process itself, special attention
during the discussion of exchange and others. This phygital customer
experience is all the more essential as Generation Z and the Millennials
will be the main consumers of luxury products by 2025. These digital
natives are looking forward to a customer experience that is both digital
and human. We can mostly agree with Claudia d'Arpizio, consultant at
Bain, who sums up the future outlook on this subject with relevance:

> *By 2025, 100% of luxury purchases will be influenced by digital. In
> this context, the role of the seller will be completely different. The shop
> will become an important place of contact between the customer and the
> brand, the place where the image of the house will be deployed, where
> passion will be created around this universe and, above all, consideration
> for its products. It is therefore the place to invest and seek to innovate.*

Figure 10.3 summarizes the discussion.

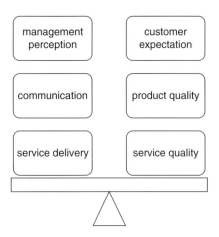

Figure 10.3   Management Perception versus Customer Expectation

Conclusion

The world's population is more digitally connected than ever before, as a consequence of the COVID-19 crisis. Some companies have had to go digital and change their business plans, which should have taken years to implement but only took a few months in order for them to avoid damaging their business. The customer journey has to be rethought. Phygital consists of creating bridges between the digital activity and its physical points of sale, in integrating digital technology and methods in the stores. A trend that responds to a strong insight on the part of consumers, juggling indifferently between the two points of contact. The options are many. There are different types of technology, and tools are used to create these phygital experiences. The examples of Ralph Lauren, Burberry, Gucci, LV, Dior and others make us rethink the in-store experience. It is perhaps not enough.

It has become imperative that brands develop dedicated, knowledgeable and empowered sales forces who understand how to bridge this gap in a seamless fashion. Salespeople are the face of brands and it is the human interaction that helps in converting a purchase. Consumers of today and tomorrow would like to have the options of interacting with the brand before, during, and after the purchase in multiple environments. They expect to get varied experiences that live up to their expectations. It is again imperative that such channels are made available to the consumers and consistent high-quality services are delivered across channels. This is easier said than done. Figure 10.4 depicts the challenges, the service dimension, and the customers' expectation for luxury experience.

Challenges	Services	Customers
• globalization	• enforce communication in pre-purchase phase	• attention
• democratization	• enhance the in-store & on-line experience	• pleasure
• diversification	• ensure the delivery of the POS service	• convenience
• digitalization	• guarantee the after-sales-service	• pride
		• trust

Figure 10.4   Challenges, Service Dimension, and Customer Engagement

Customer experience and engagement is more than customer relationship management. Revolving technology to aid the understanding of their buying behavior is being developed. The consumer behavior is also changing due to the nature of interaction at many levels. A database of their likes and dislikes can go a long way in maintaining the relationship. Gucci and LV understood that much earlier before the rest. The retail spirit has always been one of the key values in the company's roots. Luxury salesmanship is not about the price but about assisting customers in their experience of fun and enjoyment during their purchase be it offline or online through any channel. They are purchasing something they want, something that serves their own passion. They are looking for an indulgent, luxurious experience. They want to connect and feel at ease when they come in to spend a substantial amount of money, so the transaction needs to go seamlessly without too much anxiety over pricing and negotiating. The process of seamless sale is very important as without good customer service, there are no referrals or repeat business. Since the luxury goods are purely aspirational, switching to another brand is also seamless.

At the heart of sales is the sales staff, who need to show their passion and be informative when selling to clients. The process needs to be involved and ideally should be fun and exciting for everyone involved. This will let the sales staff and hence the brands stay in touch with their customers, or potential customers, and build a relationship by following up and staying current. Perhaps the best way to stay in touch is not by bothering people but by informing them about something they've already expressed interest in. Customers looking for an experience need to feel welcome in a comfortable setting. It's an art to take customers through the numbers of any particular transaction and get them to understand without being assertive. Then, it becomes more about sharing the experience, building the relationship and helping the sales to happen. What a luxury customer wants from the salesperson is not a sales pitch but assistance in making a decision that demonstrates that the customer and the salesperson are on the same team. It is important to let the customer know that it is okay to spend money and enjoy their life with the products. The products are special. It is neither about the money nor about the product characteristics. It is about the feeling, the experience, and the feelgood factor about owning the product. The channel does not matter. There's nothing bad about it—that's what luxury is all about.

Case Study: A Man in a Wheelchair—the Extra Mile

As he glanced casually through the window from the inside of the boutique, a Hermès sales assistant noticed a man in a wheelchair across the street, in front of a shop that belonged to a competitor of Hermès.

The sales assistant observed the situation. He opened the large door of the boutique that gave access to the side street, Rue Boissy-d'Anglas.

He could see that the wheelchair was somewhat jammed, and that its owner was stuck there on the other side of the Rue du Faubourg-Saint-Honoré.

He crossed the street and asked the man, who appeared to be an elderly British visitor, whether he needed any assistance.

The man in the wheelchair nodded and replied, in faltering French, "Oh, yes, please, I think my wheel is broken."

The sales assistant immediately called his colleagues to come and help. He and two others carefully lifted the gentleman from his wheelchair and settled him in a plush chair inside the Hermès store. Then they offered to mend the wheelchair on site.

The gentleman looked as if he could not quite believe his eyes.

Twenty minutes later, the wheel was repaired and the man safely seated in his chair again.

He bid them good-bye and left, thanking them profusely.

One month later, they received a letter. The gentleman, who turned out to be an Irishman, claimed that he had "never seen anything like this." He wrote: "I had never imagined that Hermès could be a place where they do not deliver some kind of sales spiel or try in one way or another to push their products because it is their job to sell. I was amazed that they would go the extra mile and help someone on the other side of the street, taking the trouble to carry me back to the store, with no

(continued)

(continued)

concern for names or details, and that they would be prepared to mend a wheelchair, no questions asked. Among the staff present, no one knew that I am a loyal customer and have been for as long as I can remember. To me, your approach reflects the quintessence of a luxury brand: showing patience and respect, offering help, and not going all out to sell."

That day the Hermès store displayed long-held values, showing a different aspect of luxury in which selling is not the issue. Acting in such a manner was purely and simply an expression of family business ethics. That day, the staff at Faubourg Saint-Honoré made their team, indeed the whole company, very proud.

They had done the right thing, at the right time, and with the right attitude. That day, the word *luxury* regained its true depth of meaning.

Part III

CONTEMPORARY ISSUES AND THE NEW FRONTIERS

Chapter 11

Digitalization of Retail— E-commerce, Platforms, and Omnichannel

Introduction

We have to find the middle path (between digital and physical), but it cannot be mediocrity.
—Alber Elbaz, AZ Factory, Richemont Group

We need desire, to dream, to live. Desire and dreams bring emotions. Emotions are part of our experiences. Emotions with all the six senses cannot be fully realized through digital. That is why stores, concerts, museums will always have a place. For example, a standing ovation after a concert brings emotion. That moment cannot be replaced through digitalization. But one can relive those emotions during and after through digital streaming. That is different.

—Ashok Som

The business world in the twenty-first century is heavily reliant on the world of internet and technology to foster its growth and development. Whether to ply the internet as a part of the business strategy particularly to attract sales and brand awareness is no longer a question; it now is about how effectively it is deployed in the strategy. The internet offers the utmost interactive and integrative communications system. It has been a game-changer for all scales of businesses, whether it be Les Maisons or Petite Boutiques, and going online in a way means making it global. For consumers who are cash-rich but time-poor, the web is a perfect channel to meet their needs and wants.

There has been resistance from some luxury houses to embrace the internet because they feel that e-commerce in itself is not luxurious, which lays the foundation for the experience of luxury. Luxury is about the experience, not just the product giving the consumer a sensation of upliftment of status or identity by instilling feelings of exclusivity, richness, uniqueness, culture, or quality. For the average luxury shopper e-experience is a requisite. Yet few brands showed resistance in embracing complete digital integration. One reason for the same was the added fear of tarnishing the brand positioning by breaking with traditions. On the flipside, the digital marketing has proved that cultivating digital could not only revive a declining profit but also aid in reaching new targets.

Due to the pandemic, the years 2020 and 2021 were challenging for most businesses, including the luxury retail segment. Still, adapting to the demands of social distancing and safety norms, digital transformation helped brands to survive the global health emergency and slowdown. Businesses that made the digital transition and experimented with social media during the crisis witnessed a substantial increase in their reach and engagement, as more audiences were present online than ever before.

The coronavirus pandemic has reignited the debate for luxury brands to either digitize or perish. Firms have leveraged digitalization and social commerce to thrive in the middle of a pandemic. Diego Della

Valle, president of Tod's group commented, "Covid-19 hit us in the middle of our digital transformation that today is always more important. Heritage, alone, it's not enough anymore. It has to be conveyed with a language and specific channels to speak with a new generation of consumers which have a web's religion but they can ignore the Italian lifestyle and buy a sweater just because a famous rapper wore it."

This accelerated the need to digitalize the approach to new consumers, not just to sell goods but, most important, to communicate the image of the brand and to educate users and consumers about quality; all of this leads to the sell. In order to do so nowadays there are two schools of thought: one wants to build a digital department in-house, the other wants to outsource. In the long run, of course, the in-house solution would bring more benefits to the firm in terms of growth, profitability and control but at the same time it requires important investments and knowledge about technology and data science. Outsourcing, on the other hand, would bring know-how and experience as soon as the contract starts but with less control and typically with the payment of a fixed expense plus fees.

During the initial period of globalization, in the early 1990s, luxury brands could not control all the value chain. They were focused on creation and production. Thus, they had *neogtiants* or wholesalers for wine and champagne, a wholesale retail model for watches, franchises and licensing for leather goods and accessories, and so on. With an increase in revenue and margins, the 2000s saw luxury brands slowly vertically integrate their value chain. This was to have full control of the whole value chain, even to the extent of buying crocodile farms for exotic skins. Since the pandemic, the debate is now about digitalization and how to go about it.

With the pandemic, the digitalization of luxury retail has become an irreversible trend: new consumption habits and consumption patterns have developed. At the same time, as GenZ has gradually emerged as the main consumer of luxury goods, their expectations and evaluation standards for digital shopping are also higher. Among consumers, how to attract new consumers while maintaining the feeling of exclusiveness for loyal users is the key to the entire digitalization experience process. For enterprises, although digitalization was a strategy forced to grow rapidly in the health crisis, some sustainable strategies in the post-Covid era can provide long-term support for brands or enterprises.

A key strategic question in most people's minds is how to maximize the consumer experience in the internet environment. Each experience is different; this makes a one-size-fits-all dilemma as brands need to rely on their own experience, which they have been at their physical stores for years. Language, currency, and transportation issues have improved to a large extent. The areas that can still be explored in the future include online one-to-one service relationships, social customer relationship management, on-site services, and even VR experiences.

Evolution of Distribution and Retailing

From the late 1980s, with globalization and the rise of wealthy consumers across the world, distribution was one of the key elements in the value chain of the luxury goods industry. Previously, it had been different. Most producers of luxury brands harped on their aspirational value. It was all about the brand and thus related to branding of their goods and brand management. With the spread of luxury aspiration across consumers and across geography the focus for most shifted to efficiency in the distribution of the products. Distribution is about execution. The brands had to make their goods available to consumers in distant lands at the right place, the right time, within the right environment, and at the right cost. How to reach them and at what cost were the key questions that the business of luxury goods had at top of mind.

During that time, luxury houses decided to focus their attention on their distribution channels and redefine ways to efficiently reach new customers through diverse ways. The distribution channels were categorized into five main areas: directly operated stores, franchises, wholesale distribution, travel retail, and licensing (Figure 11.1). Simply described it is a function of control, capital required and profitability. Directly operated stores (DOS) were the most costly to maintain and had full control, whereas licensing was the least costly and had negligible control. Of course, if the control and capital required was high, the profitability was also high. For example, LV, Chanel, and Hermès all have 100% control of their DOS, whereas brands such as Calvin Klein and Lacoste depend mostly on licensing.

With the booming era of travel, from the 1990s, the luxury retail sector began reaching its consumers by the aforementioned ways or

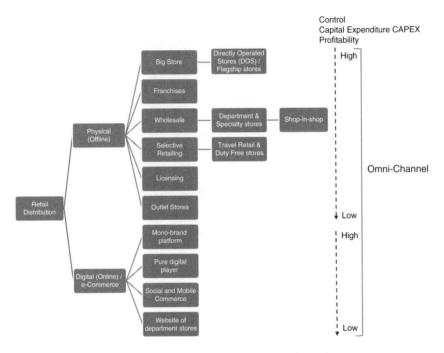

Figure 11.1 The Various Distribution Channels

a combination of them. They intensified their distribution methods through direct retail formats with an increased number of stores, innovating as they went on different store formats such as flagship stores, large format stores, multistoried stores inside prestigious malls and department stores, shops-in-shops, and others. To disseminate information across different geographic locations they developed a minimalistic online business model with selective and still limited revenue generation. Also, they bolstered shops in duty-free areas for travelers. To supply products to these diverse clienteles they had to evolve their production methods from manufacturing a few pieces to hundreds or thousands of pieces depending on the number of stores they had. To keep in line with this model they had to innovate their supply chain, their structure of inventory turnover that depended financially on extending their product line to accessories such as handbags, perfumes, cosmetics, and others. This product and distribution strategy enabled them not only to target a wider customer base but also to democratize the luxury goods industry, keeping in mind future consumers.

Many argued that this global distribution strategy on crafts and art would reduce the perception of exclusivity, aesthetic and technical superiority, distinction, and singularity, and ultimately threaten the legitimacy of the brand. The challenge was to redefine, rethink and reevaluate how to balance broader distribution while reasserting the singularity of the offerings.

To address the issue of brand legitimacy with a global distribution strategy, luxury brands such as Vuitton, Dior and Chanel linked traditional legitimacy based on craft skills and know-how to charismatic legitimacy. This was based on an exceptionally charismatic persona together with the creative director, who designed the products as they reinterpreted the codes of traditional legitimacy within the context of the changing environment of today. Charismatic legitimacy for example has been based on creating devotion to (adoration of) the exceptional character of a leader, dramatized in his or her persona, and the compliance of followers with the leader's mission out of affectionate devotion to this persona, such as Louis Vuitton, Miss Dior and Coco Chanel. Charismatic legitimacy was combined with the creativity and artistic interpretation of Marc Jacobs for Louis Vuitton (till 2013), John Galliano for Dior (till 2012) and Karl Lagerfeld (till 2019) for Chanel. The interpretation of the charismatic legitimacy by the artistic director was communicated extra-organizationally to create its strategic value in marketing of the brand within the different channels of distribution.

Physical (Offline) AND Digital (Online) Distribution

The pandemic has witnessed an evolving nature of consumer behavior. It implied a changing demand. On the demand side of the luxury industry, consumption trends were changing. It was first linked to the new austerity attitude. The crisis tends to decrease the luxury industry's attractiveness with shops closed, travel ban, different countries under different waves. Consumers were rethinking their spending priorities and tended to prefer buying a product with exclusive features and a high return on investment potential in case of reselling and renting rather than focusing on the aspirational values luxury brands have always played on.

As the demand side evolved, the persona for the luxury industry also evolved with the continuation of the health crisis. The new persona for luxury brands was younger and Asian. In fact, the industry faced an affluence of Chinese consumers as China came out first from the lockdown. In 2019, Chinese consumers accounted for 35% of industry revenues, but in 2025 they could represent more than 50% of the market.

> *China has really succeeded because of its stability. So my feeling is, how they are going to maintain this fantastic stability in a very fast changing economic situation. I think this is a challenge we face, how the global region will evolve in stability with such a fast growth. If they succeed to do that, no doubt, in the next generation it will be the major area of the world, economically.*
>
> **—Bernard Arnault**

With China taking center stage as a growth engine, the new luxury goods customer is also much younger. A few years ago, luxury was mainly reserved for successful and wealth consumers above 30. Now it is also adopted by the younger generations. Gen Y and Gen Z were responsible for 40% of the luxury goods revenues in 2019, and it is probable that it will grow to 60% in five years. These consumers are tech savvy and mostly prefer online to offline access to luxury retailing channels.

Characteristic of Luxury Retail

Pre-pandemic, with global expansion, an integrated global retail distribution strategy was a necessity. The integrated distribution system created the satisfying and unique shopping experience in the stores. It was not only to differentiate each brand from their competitors but also to communicate the unique features of the brand to their respective customers. In retailing, the most important criterion is execution. This can be best done through directly operated stores. It is about bringing the best designed product to the right kind of shop at the right time. It is said that "retail is in the detail." It is important that during the retail experience, the perceived value of the product with better quality and higher prices is transmitted seamlessly. With seamlessness, the cultural authenticity and historical heritage of the brand is transmitted the same way as the country-of-origin. Compared to fashion, which is subject to short-term cycles and perpetual change, luxury is for long-term traditions. In a way there is no intrinsic luxury good to sell. It is for the retailer to organize and govern the access to luxury goods for consumers. Organization and access have to be in the same way in which luxury evolved and expressed in a particular cultural context. The access or the retail outlets thus in a sense needed to be hedonic and multi-sensorial to connect with customers on an emotional level. Physical retail outlets thus ideally provided for a high *ratio* of intangible value to price. The successful luxury retail strategy relied on the logic of adoration, a charismatic bias. For this reason, mature markets witnessed a growing presence of luxurious shopping districts that remained highly sought after. High-end department stores continued to expand internationally through physical stores and online. Premium department stores opened in new markets. Several department stores started offering international delivery.

Physical Distribution Direct Operated Stores (DOS): The Flagship Store. From 2000 onwards, as part of the integrated global retail strategy, there has been a rise of numerous impressive flagship stores, not only in established markets such as Europe and the US, but also in emerging markets. Luxury brands used to choose Paris, London, Milan, New York, or Tokyo for their biggest flagship stores as these cities provide more credibility and visibility. Many of them have moved to cities in mainland China, such as Shanghai and Beijing, for their new flagship stores, after Tokyo, Hong Kong, and Seoul. They chose what is known as the luxury business districts (LBDs). The role of a store in an LBD is very specific. They are like a temple: a sacred place. Luxury brands use the codes, symbols, rituals to create an in-store sacred experience—almost mystical, religious.[1] This includes the architecture but also interactions with the salespeople, and the layout of the products. Indeed, a store can go beyond the utilitarian meaning of the space to go into the symbolic and incarnate the heart and savoir-faire of the brand; the store helps cultivate myths, the myth of the brand and the myth of luxury as a whole. In the same way, many authors explain how stores (especially flagship stores) provide an insight into the personality and soul of the company, which

---

[1]Delphine Dion & Stephane Borraz (2014). Managing heritage brands: A study of sacralization of heritage stores in the luxury industry. *Journal of Retailing and Consumer Service*.

is reflected in the development of a working relationship between the stores and the clientele. All in all, stores help build the image of the brand and its legitimacy through storytelling. They should not be about products available everywhere, they should be about products that generate the most desire, create more dreams than any other.

Opening flagship stores is expensive, especially when the price of rent per meter square on luxury streets is $15–$20,000 per year. On the positive side this investment lets the brands have full control and market data on customer profiles and the needs of specific clientele in these mature markets. The proximity to these cities gave the brand a strong knowledge of the clientele and made it easy to closely monitor the response, the visual presentation, and facilitated the logistical preparation for training and planning in-store events. In that sense, the retail space was also about communication—a crucial communication vector for luxury brands. The space had to provide the element of fantasy, charisma, and an aura while maintaining the cultural heritage of the brand. To provoke this feeling, and the emotion, the retail space plays an important role. The shopper needs to be seduced with the lavish surroundings—a Disneyland of desire. To build this desire and the context has driven Louis Vuitton to design stores with famous architect Peter Merino to open flagship stores in markets at an incredible pace.

Yet the stores need to portray a consistent image both geographically and spatially. The retail space must correctly evoke the codes of the brand, with no disconnect from what is going on in the advertising or on the runway; otherwise it risks the consumer becoming disenchanted. For example, Aldo Gucci defined the appeal of authentic luxury goods in 1938, when he hung a sign in the brand's first store in via Condotti, Rome. It read: "Quality is remembered long after price is forgotten." Ironically, few people can remember what the store's original interior looked like, because it has been redesigned to reflect each incoming designer's interpretation of the Gucci brand. As each successive designer tweaks the codes of the brand, its original values disappear under layers of artifice. But it is not only about the store, it is also about the location.

Upscale stores are invariably located in elegant districts that create an elegant, sophisticated microworld of their own. Examples abound. Paris has the Champs Elysees, the Avenue Montaigne, the rue du Faubourg Saint-Honoré, rue Cambon, Place Vendome, and others. London has its Regent Street, Tokyo has its Ginza. As luxury shoppers want to reinforce their perception about quality, emotional reward and then price, exclusivity or status of the location of the stores becomes a key differentiator.

Future luxury stores will be different. It would be a place to enjoy, for entertainment, to spend time. The store will be the extension of on-line experience. Free Wi-Fi, digital mirrors, augmented reality features, a place to sit and discover, will be the norm in some way as more and more discovery will be online. For example, Berluti has a salon inside the store for men to relax, sit, shower, have a drink. Tiffany and Co.'s prototype concept store has vending machines fitted with tiffany blue fragrances, big neon signs, and huge flat TV screens that let customers design their own jewelry the way they want. Gucci established a perfect mix of art, music, technology and even social and environmental activism in its "Gucci hallucination" campaign where it used interactive window displays and digital illustrations to create a virtual reality experience for users in select stores to witness an artist's vision of Gucci. LV is experimenting with stores such as Bags Bar, lounging space on Rooftop in Los Angles, Haute Maroquinerie salon for bespoke experience. The new store will include super-sensory spaces, private areas, it will be a social hub with enhanced digitally enabled assistance features. It will cater mainly to locals, including millennials, Gens Y & Z, HENRYs and hipsters. It will cater to ultra-VIPs and mass VIPs. And it will cater to Chinese clients.

Franchises The DOS and the Flagship store (referred as Big-Store) retail strategy may not work out easily and can be a challenge even for big brands due to the high level of investment, the difficult choice of location and high rent in those locations. For example, many brands fought court battles during the pandemic with their landlords and many had to close down their stores. The flagship stores demanded more input at both financial and managerial levels, such as CAPEX and knowledge of local lifestyle and shopping trends, especially in emerging markets, which are more complex to manage because of different cultures and business environments. Thus, the markets which were given to franchisee partners were essentially Eastern and Central Europe, the Middle East, and Asia.

Ideally, franchising partners in key markets, such as Dubai and Moscow, consist of larger and more established luxury groups such as Al Tayer (representing Kering group), Chaloub (representing LVMH group), and Mercury (representing both) among others. These groups run their operations as an extension of the luxury brands they serve. During the initial years, most of the luxury boutiques in the Middle East and Asia were located off the lobby of five-star hotels, making it easy access to tourists and safe and discreet places to shop for local clientele. There are franchisee groups, such as Al Tayer in Dubai, who own Bloomingdale's and Harvey Nichols, while Mercury in Moscow own the local department store, Tsum.

As Big-Store retail strategy has its pros and cons, some brands have downplayed this strategy and concentrated more on a mixed strategy. One example is Ralph Lauren. Ralph Lauren has been relying heavily on franchising and licensing in most markets, where they have no DOS. Their low retail presence in important markets such as Europe and China may be why the brand was witnessing a dilution of brand value there. In China, many consumers associate the brand with only the Polo and Denim lines. That is also reflected in the brand's travel retail performance, which explains why Chinese tourists account for less than 2% of Ralph Lauren's Paris flagship store sales, while its rivals have been benefiting by up to 50% of sales from Chinese tourists, such as Burberry.

More and more, luxury brands have opted for a directly operated boutique presence in certain markets, notably China, or converting their franchised partnerships into a Joint Venture (JV)—a temporary partnership.

The reasons for opting for a JV today are many, including the response to globalization, change in technology due to which the environment is now more complex and competitive, risk limitation, and bilateral management.

The franchise model of the 1990s still works for emerging markets, where state regulations do not allow brands to own wholly operated stores. In addition, this gives an option for small to medium-sized brands, which cannot afford the heavy investment required to develop a network of directly operated boutiques. Partner selection is key: partners should be professionally managed, financially stable and experienced

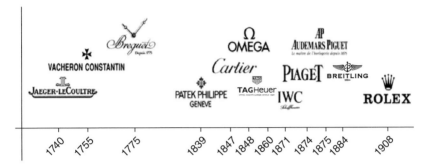

Figure 11.2   The Birth Years of Brands

with luxury goods. With technology at the forefront during the pandemic the singularity and convergence of the physical and digital shopping experience will be the key challenge of the future.

Wholesale   The concept of wholesale is rare in the Luxury industry. It is mainly prevalent in the watch, wine, and champagne sectors. Luxury watches were born as early as 1740. Figure 11.2 depicts the timeframe when the 10 well-known luxury brands were born. Their birth was not entirely sporadic. Three brands—Breguet, Vacheron Constantin, and Jaeger-Lecoultre—were from the 1700s. The brands Omega, Cartier, Patek Philippe, Audemars Piguet, Piaget, and IWC were from the 1800s. Rolex was from the 1900s.

The fact that these three clusters existed in the watch industry suggests that gaps were identified in the industry by owners of companies. This led to multiple brands targeting the various emerging segments. It gave an idea about how the market segmentation evolved based on watch complications, the advent of newer technologies, and changing consumer preferences. It indicated how important heritage and legitimacy were for the watch industry.

All watch brands follow a wholesale strategy as part of their distribution strategy. They book orders at watch fairs like the Basel Watch Fair, which has evolved to Watches & Wonder from the pandemic. These fairs provide multibrand retailers with their brands, which are pre-booked during the fair. In this way, with a concerted strategy of owned stores (DOS) and multibrand retail chains, they can reach their customers with ease. The watch brands using this strategy can be present in Italy, USA, Germany, Japan, China, and France with DOS and multibrand stores in New York, Singapore, Hong Kong and in some other Asian cities. Some brands, such as Rolex, Cartier, Vacheron Constantin, Patek Philippe, IWC, and Jaeger-LeCoultre, have made a strong presence with both DOS and multibrand stores in mainland China. Patek Philippe is the only brand that has been following a consistent US-centric retail strategy, and its expansion plans in China indicate that it does not plan to expand like its competitors in Asia.

Travel Retail and Duty-Free Stores   Travel retail has been worst hit during the pandemic. Travel retail refers to the sales done in outlets at airports and duty-free shops, plus shopping on airlines during the flight and on cruise ships.

Travel retail was the darling of the luxury industry. It had a consistent growth story from the 2000s, barring occasional dips when travel was restricted. It had its growth as there was high taxation on luxury goods in frontier markets in Asia, Eastern Europe, the Middle East. Due to considerable price differentials, customers from these regions tended to shop overseas for luxury goods. For example, during the pre-pandemic days, Europe profited from travel shoppers, especially from China. Twenty to thirty percent of the industry's revenue comes from overseas consumption. In 2018, the total number of Chinese outbound tourists exceeded 150 million. According to a McKinsey estimate, the purchase of luxury goods outside of mainland China accounted for more than half of the total luxury expenditure of Chinese consumers. Asians go abroad to buy luxury goods, not only because the prices in Europe are lower, but also because shopping has become an indispensable travel experience— shopping where the brand originated feels reliable and exciting. With over 2 million Chinese travelers in France spending an average of 2,000 USD per capita, in Triangle d'Or it was about 4 billion USD of revenue.

However, due to the continuous implementation of travel restrictions by various countries, this important engine of luxury consumption has suddenly stalled. In 2020, due to the ban on travel the Chinese government pivoted their strategy to take advantage of the more than 110 billion USD of luxury spending trapped on the mainland by focusing on local consumption. Hainan, a subtropical island in the South China

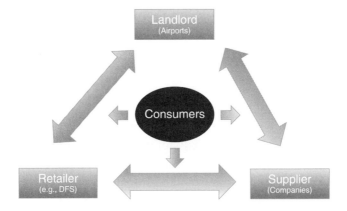

Figure 11.3 Trinity Stakeholders

Sea, with hundreds of beachfront resorts, has allowed duty-free shopping for domestic visitors since 2011 and become an increasingly popular destination during Covid. This way the pandemic has helped achieve the Chinese government's goal of bringing spending back home to China.

Retail success in the duty-free sector is dependent on contributions from the three major actors, known often as "trinity" stakeholders. The trinity stakeholders are the landlord, the retailer, and the supplier. Figure 11.3 shows the relationship between trinity stakeholders (the landlord, the retailer, the supplier) and the consumer.

The Landlord: These are the airports. They are like the shopping centers: they provide access to the passengers and the retail space for duty-free retailing. Their expertise lies in promoting the airport as a destination for shopping. The exclusive and highly sought-after nature of the retail space that the landlords own or manage means that risks to the landlord are low. They are responsible and play the important role of boosting passenger flow and therefore retail footfall. Thus, any duty-free business models will link the landlord's rental income to passenger numbers in one form or another. With limited duty-free retail space available, most privately owned/managed airports will invite bids from retailers in an attempt to secure the highest possible rental income. The airports at Dubai, Singapore, Hong Kong, Macao, Hawaii, Hainan, Frankfurt, and NYC have some of the most sought-after landlords in the travel retail world.

The Retailer: Retailers provide the store expertise and knowledge that is required to operate duty-free stores profitably. Sales revenue is the most common performance indicator for retailers. The trinity is a very specific model as so many airports adopt minimum annual guarantee (MAG)-based rental structures.

The Supplier: The supplier provides the product expertise and insight into consumer preferences that is required for duty-free shops. As a result of the global and high-income nature of traveling passengers, suppliers benefit from brand exposure, resulting in relatively low risk. Currency fluctuations in various international travel retail channels may reflect retail price points and pose difficulties to margin and wholesale price management. Also, with a high loyalty rate for hot traveling areas, where airports hold more power in price negotiation, brands sometimes do not have direct control over the travel retail price and promotions, which could be inconsistent with the brand's strategy and image. Suppliers need to keep an eye on the overall offer in travel retail.

The Consumers: The ever-changing mix of travelers, the consumers, flowing through airport terminals provides unique challenges and opportunities. Some of the key challenges that can be overcome are as follows.

Licensing The luxury goods industry took the licensing route from the beginning of retail expansion. Licensing was a favored option as it lets a brand enter a new market with relative ease and minimum investment. During the initial years, licensing contributed a significant portion of total revenues for many luxury goods companies. For this reason, the luxury goods companies selectively disclose and investors carefully review data on the mix of owned and franchised or licensed operations. For example, groups such as LVMH have no strategic licenses while Gucci had a limited number of strategic licensing partners. Specialty apparel brands, such as Polo Ralph Lauren and Armani, rely on a greater mix of licensed sales. Compared to that, Hermès has no licenses at all and Chanel only for eyewear.

Though a licensing distribution strategy has proved to be a quick and efficient way to increase the scale and scope of luxury businesses, in many cases it has come at the price of a tarnished brand, particularly for those who overextended their licensing activities. This is because the risk of diluting the brand with time exists if the license agreement cannot be controlled and the partner cannot be trusted with the licensing agreement. The experience of each luxury brand is different, but the trust issue has consistently emerged to be one of the most painful experiences. It is clear from these experiences that an appropriate mix and structure of licensing activities is crucial for a company to be successful within the luxury goods industry. As companies mature, they seek full ownership of the licensed business to increase control and provide a platform for greater value extraction. Writing-instrument companies, such as S.T. Dupont, Montblanc, and eyewear businesses relied heavily on the licensing business model. The well-known licensing companies were Safilo and Luxottica for eyewear, Fossil and Swatch for watches, and L'Oreal for beauty and cosmetics. The infamous cases that had destroyed brand value through licensing were those of Gucci, Polo Ralph Lauren, Calvin Klein and Lacoste, among others.

The Digital (Online) Era in Luxury

The pandemic has strongly impacted on the physical trade of luxury goods, whatever the sector. The various global lockdowns have led to store closures and a complete shutdown of tourism. The share of luxury sales linked to tourism is considerable in Europe; 70% of purchases in France are made by foreigners, including 30% of Chinese consumers. In addition, unstable economic conditions have led to a strong recession of around 8% in the Eurozone, directly impacting purchasing power. The only way for luxury players to save their sales was therefore to turn to the online market, a strategy adopted by all consumer sectors. As a result, there was a generalized increase in online purchases of 18% and 13% in the world of luxury goods. Why a slower rise in Luxury? To quote a consulting firm, "For many players in the sector, digital was not compatible with the idea of hand-picked customers and scarcity." Indeed, consumption habits in luxury goods are not the same as in other sectors. The consumer has an emotional connection when buying a good of this type, as well as being sensitive to the customer experience, to the touch or to the feeling of the product. These elements, which seem to be exclusive to luxury goods, are until now difficult to transcribe online. Moreover, this should be compared to the relative decline in luxury-related research on the Internet, reaching the lowest point ever recorded in Europe, China and the USA. This means that the conversion rate has undeniably exploded on luxury online sales sites. A real change has also taken place in terms of the type of product purchased, especially in China where sales of products at less than 1,000 yuan (about 125 euros) have taken up more space, at the expense of higher priced products. This has been associated with a change in the profile of buyers, with the share of people over 30 years old rising from 49% in early 2020 to 60% during the crisis. Such a large gap shows a change of mentality regarding online commerce and a better confidence on the part of these buyers, especially in luxury goods which cannot be considered as essential. This sudden transition allowed the online luxury business to take over. Many of the brands, whether from conglomerates such as LVMH, Richemont or Kering or the independent ones, had implemented digital development plans in recent years. The objectives for several years were beaten in just a few weeks. "In six months we have accelerated more than in the last four years," explained Ian Rogers, ex-digital manager of LVMH. Same for Celine, for Bulgari. In the same way, Chanel has doubled its online sales.

The Transformation of Online Distribution and E-Commerce

No man ever steps in the same river twice, for it's not the same river and he's not the same man.

—Heraclitus

Electronic commerce, or e-commerce in short, means a business model that sells or purchases various goods or services on the internet. E-commerce ranges from the area of transactions between companies and consumers to the realm of transactions among corporations. It can be conducted over smartphones, tablets, or computers, which suggests that it looks like a digital version of mail-order catalog shopping.

A difficult challenge for senior leaders in the luxury industry was maintaining ambidexterity. It would be many times so in the digital world. It is the balance between exploration and exploitation, between clarity and disparity, between resilience and rigidity, between stability and agility.

The paradox senior leaders face is that they must create a corporate culture which structurally embraces constant changes, like a large App Store,

while ensuring stability when a structural transformation is necessary. If you need to undergo surgery, you must stop all activity until you have recovered. Similarly, strategic transformations require management and policy stability. Impermanence is the norm, but change requires stability.
—Cyrille Vigneron, CEO, Cartier

The digital channel is accelerating its growth, especially during the pandemic. In the same vein, post-pandemic physical channels need to be rethought. Internet retailing is a growth story in the luxury sector, with North America and Western Europe vying for the title of top internet consumption markets, but with a long way to catch up in China. The original idea of e-tailing was to sell a large range of brands, and to liquidate old or surplus stock at discounted and often cheap prices. Thus, luxury versus e-tailing is an interesting paradox of accessibility.

An ensuing debate that once raged within the luxury industry was the notion of online distribution. Historically, luxury brands were successful in their delivery of elegance and exclusivity in their stores, the retail space. Luxury goods and services have been reluctant to embrace e-tail, fearing that it will cheapen their brand's image in the eyes of affluent customers. The internet, after all, was synonymous with no-frills "accessibility" and bargain hunting, which seem to clash with the discriminating nature of luxury. But it may be a lucrative option. As a thriving medium, used by an estimated 95% of luxury buyers, more savvy luxury brands are seeing it as an opportunity to engage in efficient niche marketing while harnessing the internet's incredible reach. Slick production websites are an opportunity to extend the exclusive service experience of luxury purchasing online, while websites are ideal backdrops for customization and obviously could never be understocked. Moreover, it may be that an online retail presence is a way to stop counterfeiters from "filling in the gaps."

E-tail has its advantages and disadvantages. The key challenges in e-tail are the following. How to tell the story of the brand? How to provide in some way the touch-and-feel of the brand? How to convey the brand DNA? How to live in the ecosystem and transfer a unique interpretation of service that would not only listen but would also act as an effective sales driver?

The experience factor: Those in favor of e-tail propound that design and concept are also the key in e-tail. The believers put forth that although online and offline experiences aren't the same, the goal is the same. The main purpose of the boutique and the website is to bring a unique, memorable experience to the affluent customer. The moment they land on the doorstep or the homepage, the exclusiveness of the brand needs to be reflected to entice them in a world filled with aspirations. It is possible to make purchasing online a sophisticated, unique process.

The sites, though very different from brand to brand, often have many of the same features in common: high-quality images, multimedia, an element of surprise and an appeal to the imagination of the user in order to enter a typically bland homepage. The storytelling is celebrated through brand rituals and ceremonials and can be integrated by videos, short movies and pictures. This provides scope for consumer interpretation, musing and dreaming, especially in markets where consumers are still being educated. Embedded video features and streaming enable customers to view an item from multiple angles, which helps overcome the disadvantages of not being able to feel the cloth. For example, Chanel's podcasts and video of catwalks and fashion shows add story elements to the mix. Gucci takes a bold step at capturing the sensation of the in-store experience on their website. Instead of providing search and navigation like most e-commerce sites, the brand instead displays handbags and watches on shelves just as in their offline shops. By displaying the product in this light, the designers are able to bring some of the emotion that one might get from shopping in-store. Gucci has its online sales for consumers in France, Germany, Austria, Belgium, the Netherlands and Ireland as well as the UK and the USA.

The accessibility factor: The sites can be accessed by one-and-all and provide instant reach to customers in far-off places, especially in large emerging markets where any number of physical stores is not enough. Among the most visible international brands providing access are Net-a-Porter, Guilt Group and Yoox. Yoox, for instance, is a virtual boutique, with about three million visitors a month. It sells Armani, Roberto Cavalli and other top designers from its website. It has developed some very clever features, including the zoom-in functionality offering visitors a good "feel" of the fabric. Designer Marc Jacobs launched his e-commerce site to generate new revenue opportunities via online and mobile with a playful, unique and innovative feel combined with whimsical illustrations, photography and video to bring the experience to life as in his own retail location. When the online shop first loads, shoppers view a colorfully illustrated storefront and click the front door to enter the main site.

The analytical factor: Instead of a physical store the consumer experiences a virtual store with much more information to process, compare and decide at their leisure from home. Potential customers will spend significant time dreaming of a luxury product and should have ways to talk with the brand online. The purchase decision is much more analytical in that sense as the decision has been processed. For example, the Apple site provides the cue. Its homepage and e-commerce section consistently benefit from luscious photography and design. It provides the consumers all the details and provides them with an option to buy online or visit an Apple store with all the information beforehand.

Thus, most luxury brands stand by their in-store experience rather than fully integrate their offer by combining it with e-shopping convenience for their niche markets. The inherent risk associated with leveraging e-commerce platforms to generate sales is in a way the cannibalization of sales from the brick-and-mortar stores. But this is not such an important issue. The discount-oriented stigma in the e-commerce space is the more important issue that may in turn dilute the prestige associated with the brand. In addition to this, one also has to acknowledge that digital and mobile internet are the fastest-growing channels of retailing. Any web search will reveal that each and every luxury brand has its own website with information on products, and even a catalogue, and retailer/dealer locations, but stopping short of selling their products online. For example, LV and JD.com has a singular model catering to their Chinese consumers. Designed by JD.com for Louis Vuitton, it redirects users from the JD app directly to Louis Vuitton's official Mini Program.

E-Retail and Platforms

On the Internet, E-commerce companies are scale businesses, characterized by high fixed costs and relatively low variable costs. You can be two sizes: You can be big, or you can be small. It's very hard to be medium. A lot of medium-sized companies had the financing rug pulled out from under them before they could get big.

—Jeff Bezos, the founder of Amazon

If you're going through hell, keep going!
—Sir Winston Churchill, the former British Prime Minister

The pandemic is emerging as a growth lever in e-retail. The lockdown caused by the crisis has accelerated the digital transformation, drastically changing consumer habits. It is highly likely that many consumers will keep their new habits after reopening. For example, luxury pure digital player Farfetch has seen its stock increasing continuously since the beginning of the pandemic, which illustrates the strength of their platform business model.

The major advantage of the platform business model of e-tail companies is connecting the luxury brand, its sellers, to its luxury customers. It could be a marketplace model or a consignment model or a mix of both. The marketplace model is where the platform connects buyers and sellers, be it individual sellers or luxury brands. The consignment model is when the platform buys, curates and holds the inventory of the products. The platform model generates *network effects.* This is the phenomenon where the value of the platform rises as the number of users expands. And this can be distinguished through different effects: direct network effects among the same kinds of stakeholder; indirect network effects between different stakeholders.

These effects are common to all platforms of this type (Amazon, Facebook, Uber . . .). The more users, the more reviews and comments available. Here, *more* is key as higher interactions generate increasing value for other users. Other users benefit from this effect when they engage in the comparative experience on the platforms. The more brands on the platform, the more value for other brands to have their product appear alongside exclusive offers. Similarly, there are indirect externalities. The more users, the more value for brands to enter the platform (potential clients), and the more brands available on that platform, the more value for users who can compare and shop for different brands at the same place and with even more convenience. Similarly, negative network externalities exist, although they tend to be minor, and the reinforcing mechanisms strengthen the platforms as they grow, and help explain their success in recent years. To harness the network effect, it is evident that each platform should have the same level of brands on their platform to attract a likeminded clientele. But the pandemic also revealed that markets are after all local, with local institutional and national specificities.

Overview of the Current Luxury E-Commerce Platforms
Platforms have taken luxury retail by surprise during the pandemic, among customers as well as luxury brands. For customers, online retail platforms gave them an opportunity to shop for their desired products in the comfort of their homes. This digital transformation has accelerated, while changing drastically consumer habits of having the leisure to shop from home. For luxury brands with insufficient online capabilities or logistics networks, they could rely on the platforms to continue to operate even with store closures. Partnering with the online platforms is an efficient and cheaper alternative to use their expertise than developing in-situ expertise, at least in the short term. Alliances of this sort are new terrain for luxury brands, which are obsessed with preserving total control over design, manufacturing, and distribution. It is a new era of inclusivity and signals a more accessible and balanced attitude that is in line with the needs of young, hyperconnected consumers, especially Chinese consumers.

Three types of online platform have evolved from the 2020s. The first is third-party multibrand luxury online retailers, such as Yoox Net-A-Porter (YNAP) and Farfetch. These purely digital players have been growing rapidly in sales over the past years. The second category is composed of luxury brands' own official websites through which brands have been investing not only in content-creation and storytelling, but also in driving online sales. Luxury brands are leveraging more and more their own monobrand websites and social media to create a 360-degree omnichannel experience through digital prelaunch, personalization and click-to-buy. The third category is made up of multibrand e-commerce portals owned by offline department stores which are investing more and more in their digital platform to compensate for offline losses due to closure of physical stores and a huge decrease of tourism in Europe. Online platforms, such as those of the Galleries Lafayette and Harrods, all adopted innovative strategies in response to the pandemic.

It is interesting to note that, for luxury brands, the lack of digital development experience has also led to their cooperation with pure digital players. In 2018, even while still resistant to selling online, Chanel signed an innovation partnership deal with Farfetch in an attempt to develop digital initiatives to make its physical stores more attractive. Bruno Pavlovsky, Chanel's president of fashion, had explained that Chanel is not starting to sell on the Farfetch marketplace. Their position on e-commerce was the same. Chanel wanted to connect with its customers with their own products and the Chanel boutiques are the best way to do so. Chanel had been always very consistent with their strategy, but Chanel is using Farfetch's know-how to accelerate this. Table 11.1 details the benefits and challenges of the three models.

Farfetch   Farfetch is one of the leaders today in the online retail platform market. Founded in 2007 by Jose Neves, a Portuguese entrepreneur, it is an in-season luxury platform based in London, with 2 million active users and 4 million visitors per month in 2021. The website offered products from more than 1,300 boutiques, brands and department stores, to customers in more than 190 countries, and in the meantime charges brands an important commission fee. With the vision to be the global platform for luxury fashion, connecting creators, curators and consumers, it aims at offering a unique online shopping experience and access to the most extensive selection of luxury on a single platform. Its revenues have grown significantly over the past few years and the pandemic has accelerated its acceptance in the luxury industry with brands such as Harrods and Harvey Nichols partnering with them. Jose Neves, CEO, Farfetch commented:

> *We really envisioned Farfetch as a platform for boutiques that are strug-*
> *gling to keep afloat in light of crisis. We launched just as the financial*
> *crisis was happening [in 2007]—two weeks after we launched, Lehman*
> *Brothers collapsed—so we know what it's like. Right now, what our*
> *partners need most is a platform to sell their stock, and that's what we're*
> *trying to provide. . . . In the future, digital transactions are expected to*

represent a significantly larger proportion of the overall luxury industry. The current situation, with current store closures and travel restrictions, may serve to further accelerate the secular shift to online shopping.

Arriving in the early stage of the online luxury market, Farfetch understood quickly the missed opportunity to bring products in brick-and-mortar stores all over the world into customers' homes. Its success

Table 11.1 The Benefits and Challenges of the Three Models

	Pure Digital Player	**Monobrand platform**	**Website of department stores**
Benefits	Accumulated experience in digital operations Technology knowledge and expertise Wide range of offers and diversity of choices Economy of scale in terms of logistic, technology and operation Control of the curation, price and display Contacts and resources for contemporary designer brands	Strong brand DNA and differentiation Exclusive brand offer with digital pre-launch and personalization Guarantee of authenticity Full control of the selection, price and display Potential for storytelling via digital channels	Wide range of offers Long history and legitimacy in luxury retail experience Huge retail area to reimagine the future retail best practice via technology Expertise in customer services to offer a personalized service Brand direct operated stores and retail space to differentiate one brand from another Partnership and long-term relationship with various famous brands
Challenges	Lack of physical presence Lack of brand DNA in front of customers Difficult to differentiate from one brand to another on the platform	Lack of technology expertise to innovate and operate digital channel Limited range of choices Lack of experience to connect online and offline inventory	Lack of technology expertise to innovate and operate digital channel Lack of brand DNA in front of customers

arose from four distinct competencies. First, it was primarily a logistic technology company. Farfetch developed a technology which allowed it to keep track of retail inventory worldwide. By doing so, it not only ensured quick delivery for its clients, but also facilitated the logistic work behind each order and reduced related cost, which eliminated one of the gaps between physical and online stores. This model did not require Farfetch to hold inventory. It gave all the power to the brand to interact directly with its customers while using Farfetch's logistic and technology services. For example, the technology allowed Farfetch to know in real time that a certain pair of shoes existed in five shops around the world and is available in certain specific sizes. Second, Farfetch participated in unique product selection. It curated unique products on behalf of the brand by predictive data analytics, taking help from the big data that was generated from the site. Hiring an internal team to do so, Farfetch developed a unique competitive advantage in face of its competitors such as Net-a-Porter and rising competitors such as Amazon by having an overlap of only 4% in terms of product offer with Net-a-Porter. Third was the weekly drop. Each week, around 1,000 new items were posted on the platform, offering a brand-new inventory for its regular customers, which was favorable for repetitive purchase. It avoided market saturation. The fourth was its acquisition and collaboration strategy. Farfetch acquired Browns, a London boutique retailer as part of its omnichannel strategy following which it also acquired Stadium goods, a premium streetwear and sneaker marketplace.

In 2019, JD.com Inc. announced buying a stake in Farfetch for US$397 million and Farfetch agreed to merge its Chinese business with JD.com. In the same year, Farfetch acquired New Guards Group, which includes luxury fashion brands such as Off-White, Heron Preston and Palm Angels. In 2020, Farfetch announced its partnership with Alibaba and Richemont to accelerate the digitization of the luxury industry. The new China joint venture enabled Farfetch to operate on Alibaba's Tmall luxury pavilion and luxury soho with 75% of the ownership with Farfetch and the remaining 25% with Alibaba and Richemont group. A total sum of US$1.15 billion was committed to be invested by Alibaba, Richemont and Artemis into the new Farfetch China joint venture.

Farfetch has unveiled its Store of the Future, which leverages technologies such as AR shopping experience, emotion-scanning software, and innovative payment solutions to blur the gap between online and offline experience. The scanner installed on customers' phones when they enter the store will enable sales associates to read client's profile, their wish list while browsing online catalogs, record the items they picked up and save them in an application where they can review them in the future. Finally, Farfetch also created a holographic display that allows self-creation, customization and virtual try-on.

Farfetch is yet to reach its breakeven. However, with the evident growth in the field of online luxury and traditional brands showing interest in venturing into this space, Farfetch will gain from its expertise in the field of technology. Investments by luxury conglomerates into the platform signals the promising growth of the online luxury business and, in particular, of the Farfetch business model.

YNAP YOOX (founded in Milan by Federico Marchetti) and Net-a-Porter (founded in London by Nathalie Massenet) were both launched in 2000, being the pioneers of the online luxury marketplace in Europe. YOOX was the representation of men (Y) and women (X), linked by infinity (OO). YOOX specialized in buying renowned fashion brands' overstock or unsold products to sell them at a discounted price. The advantage for the brands was to get rid of their stock without undermining their image. The idea of the company Net-a-Porter was to publish fashion magazines online and the client just had to click on the product to be able to buy it.

In 2018, the two companies were merged into YOOX Net-a-Porter Group (YNAP), which was then acquired by Richemont group. The combined entity operated four multibrand online stores, such as Net-a-Porter.com (offering women's luxury goods), MrPorter.com (focusing on men's products), Yoox.com (offering a wider range of discounted products, from fashion to art and design) and Outnet.com (dedicated to discounted high-end luxury). It offered service to 4.3 million active customers worldwide in 180 countries. YNAP's competence was its unique ecosystem with one technology and logistics platform. Their experience of 20 years in the luxury e-commerce space is also a key strength. Their primary strength lay in the balance of technology with a human touch to redefine the ultimate luxury experience, keeping the customer at the heart of the business. Their ability to provide customers with a personalized experience through its NEXT ERA model, including personal shopping, was a key differentiating criterion. Further, as seen with their strategic joint ventures, they strove to take a localized approach which could help connect with customers better.

In 2018, Kering ended its partnership with YOOX to create its own shopping sites and further invested through Artemis in Farfetch. Companies such as Armani.com, Valentino.com, jimmychoo.com joined YNAP due to its services like setting up online stores, assistance on e-tailing operations like customer care, shipping, invoicing, and others. It was also a one-stop for the Chinese market. As part of the joint venture with Alibaba, Net-a-Porter was launched on Alibaba's Tmall Luxury Pavilion, bringing the latest collections to customers in China.

The differencing factor of YNAP group was its technological expertise to establish online stores for respective brands. Leveraging on its technology innovation, its aim is to eliminate the gap between online and offline experience. Thus, the group keeps investing in the development of artificial intelligence, augmented reality, voice and visual search. Federico Marchetti, before stepping down as CEO in 2021, noted that YNAP is like a tech company, a digital company. It was always 50% technology and 50% luxury.

Alibaba Tmall Luxury Pavilion Formerly known as Taobao mall, Tmall.com is a spin-off from Taobao and is a Chinese online business-to-consumer (B2C), contrary to Taobao, which is a consumer-to-consumer (C2C) retail platform founded by Alibaba group in 2008. Further, Tmall has differentiated platforms, namely, Tmall Classic, Tmall Global and Tmall luxury pavilion. Tmall is completely a China-focused platform for brands to sell in China that serviced the needs of the Chinese consumers. With over 200 leading luxury brands and a vast pool of buyers, the platform is expanding itself by adding more up-market brands and offerings.

Tmall luxury pavilion, launched in 2017, is Alibaba's response to the growing concern of traditional luxury brands around digitization of luxury customers' buying experience. The platform hosts over 200 prestigious luxury brands such as Cartier, Prada, Balenciaga, Bottega

Veneta, Givenchy, Baccarat, Burberry, and 22 brands from LVMH group. Tmall luxury pavilion also offers luxury soho, an outlet version of luxury pavilion.

The strategy of Tmall is not to interfere with brands' DNA but to help them increase their influence and improve their brand value. They promote China-limited editions as a responsive mechanism for brands to reach more customers, especially Gen Y and Z in China. For example, Loewe launched the exclusive Barcelona Collection for Chinese Valentine's Day on the luxury pop-up store Tmall Space. As a company owned by Alibaba, it enjoyed the database obtained from the entire eco-system of the group, including a life-streaming platform, food delivery, e-payment through Alipay, GPS, and others. Through big data, digital analytics, and its new technology "Uni Marketing," it aimed at analyzing customers' lifestyles based on their past consumption behavior. Moreover, it has worked with Sesame Credit to offer its customers interest-free installment, a temporary increase of the credit quota and pre-authorization reservation.

The strengths of the platform are varied. It provides partner support such as marketing tools, incentives, highlights and campaigns. As a service, it provides multiple benefits to luxury pavilion customers. The benefits are included under a loyalty program launched as part of New Retail initiative. Platform members are provided with access to bespoke offerings, latest payment options, priority delivery, a door-to-door return service and invitation to events. Premier members are provided with additional benefits like personal shopper service, a concierge service and access to premium spas. Also, at additional cost, services such as running of daily operations, customer services, logistics and e-commerce are provided. The platform charges an annual fee along with the sales commission based on category. This way the platform provides brands a safe space with reduced risks of overcrowding and expert fashion and beauty curating. In less than a year from the inception of Tmall's luxury pavilion, a record 100,000 users were attracted to over 50 luxury and high-end labels on the platform.

24S   24S is the e-commerce platform of LVMH group. It was launched in 2017 to compete with established platforms such as YNAP and Farfetch. YNAP had participation from Richemont and had tie-ups with

Kering. The name was 24 Sèvres that aimed at a new shopping experience by offering fashion and beauty brands representing the French art-de-vivre. It was time to take LVMH's expertise in visual merchandising, which the Maisons have long brought to their stores, and transform it online. The name referred to the famous Parisian department store's address, Le Bon Marché, located at 24 rue de Sèvres. In fact, the platform was the perfect representation of Le Bon Marché's spirit, which has existed since 1852. 24 Sèvres became 24S, a simpler name, in order to be easier to identify internationally.

On the occasion of its launch, 24S presented a capsule collection created with Le Bon Marché and 68 other Parisian and international brands. The capsule was composed of 77 limited-edition pieces which were each Maison's iconic products that they have revisited with the collaboration of famous celebrities. The platform sold all the group's products as well as some products from outside the group, such as Jimmy Choo, Balenciaga, and Max Mara, offering more than 300 fashion and beauty brands. It was launched with high ambition with an exclusive, curated selection of over 150 womenswear brands with state-of-the-art virtual windows offering the most innovative and attractive online presentation on the market. 24S is the only platform to propose Dior, Celine, Moynat and Louis Vuitton, which enabled the website to attract high-end luxury consumers. But in a mix-and-match policy, they also offer some emerging and more confidential brands. It boasts excellent customer service with shipping to over 100 countries and personal stylists available at disposal. Stylists were available for live one-on-one video consultations or live chat on the website as well as on the mobile application. It has a Style Bot on Facebook Messenger, which recommends upcoming products, connecting customers instantly with the retailer fashion experts in Paris.

Designed to be complementary to the offline shopping experience at Le Bon Marché, 24S aims to offer a matchless shopping experience. Firstly, the packaging is customized. The design of the box is recreated each quarter and inspired always from different visions of Paris in cooperation with various artists. What's more, being an extension of in-store experience, human touch was also considered important on e-commerce. Working on the legacy of Le Bon Marché, the platform shared the loyalty program that provided a seamless experience and benefit utilization.

The benefits included bespoke services, private events, member days and others. 24S offered a range of state-of-the-art services, such as express shipping to over 100 countries, with 24-hour delivery to New York, London, and Milan, as well as same-day delivery within Paris. The customer service team was available 24/7 and the expert personal stylists are at the customer's disposal for tailored selections and shopping assistance. Furthermore, the return service in Paris was simplified with the valet service, which enabled customers to reserve a 30-minute appointment to try the product with the well-mannered delivery sales associates waiting outside to pick it up if a return is needed.

After the pandemic, there was a restructuring at the top-management level. LVMH group had not yet made it clear how they wished to position the online platform, as the individual companies in parallel were also developing their own e-commerce business through their website and other social media channels. However, Bernard Arnault in various meetings showed his optimism toward the relevance of the e-retail platform and its potential to capture the future growth in the online sales, while being cautious that the online platforms still did not make money.

JD.Com JD.com Inc., which formerly went by the name 360Buy, is a Chinese e-commerce platform headquartered in Beijing, China, that was founded in 1998. The company was founded in 1998 and its retailing platform went online in the year 2004. The platform had diversified offerings from selling electronics to selling luxury products. JD.com is regarded as one of China's biggest tech giants that boasts of over 362 million active users and has a market share of 24.4%. Some of the participating brands are Delvaux, Salvatore Ferragamo, Proenza Schouler, MSGM, Gucci, Prada and Miu Miu.

JD.com targeted mostly millennials and Gen Xers across China, especially north China and Si Chuan Province, as well as low tier cities. The brand capabilities include "JD Luxury," which is a branch growing out of its luxury portal Toplife and "JD Rubik's Cube," which is JD's gateway for product debuts. As part of its service JD.com provides a classic e-commerce curation which is reliable and offers fast and high-end delivery services. On the logistic front, the orders are shipped from JD warehouses or brands, and shipping facilities like JD luxury express and White Glove delivery are provided to the luxury brands.

JD.com provided brands with a built-in infrastructure, which enables luxury brands to quickly become operational in the Chinese market. The company invested in advance technologies and artificial intelligence delivery using autonomous technology and drones. Initially, in 2017 the platform had partnered with Farfetch in a bid to position itself well in the luxury e-commerce market but in 2019, Farfetch decided to merge its business in China with JD. com. In 2020, Farfetch joined Tmall with the tripartite funding from Alibaba, Richemont and Artemis. In 2021, JD.com designed, for Louis Vuitton, a singular model that redirects users from the JD app directly to Louis Vuitton's official Mini Program. Visitors only need to type "LV" into their search bar on the JD app, and they get automatically redirected. JD handed Louis Vuitton 471.9 million annual active customer accounts and in return, the Chinese e-commerce won French mystique, glamor, elegance, prestige, status and partnership with LVMH. This move has positioned JD as the leader of a high rivalry, fiercely fought marketspace.

JD.com operated in a highly competitive space against its main rival, Tmall by Alibaba group. Also, the platform is receiving intense competition from social e-commerce platform Pinduoduo, which is reported to have surpassed JD.com's GMV value. Messaging applications like WeChat allowed luxury brands to cut out wholesalers like JD.com and link the brand's profile to its direct-to-consumer e-commerce sites. For example, over 70% of luxury brands included in Gartner L2's China luxury index operate a WeChat mini program of Tencent.

Mytheresa.Com   In 1987, Susanne and Christoph Botschen opened a women's multibrand luxury boutique named Theresa in München, Germany. The couple wanted to offer the "finest edit of luxury fashion" to its customers and proposed brands like Prada, Miu Miu, Saint Laurent, Balenciaga, Céline, Valentino and others. Their success was such that they became one of the most famous addresses in Europe for high luxury brands and designers. In 2006, the couple launched their website mytheresa.com to sustain their growth. The website catapulted its growth and mytheresa.com started delivering in 120 countries worldwide by 2021. In fact, the platform was very successful in Germany and in the rest of Europe and had plans to extend to the Asian market. The platform hosts products in various categories like clothing, bags, shoes and accessories. Mytheresa.com had a restricted portfolio of 250 international luxury brands. It keeps its portfolio small to enable superior service. This choice has helped the company maintain strong relationships with its retailers who are able to sell capsule collections on mytheresa.com. And as a result, the platform proposes some products that cannot be found elsewhere. Moreover, mytheresa.com has quick checkout on its e-commerce platform, which is deeply appreciated by its users. As part of its service offering, the platform ensures authenticity of products, fast reliable delivery, and exceptional customer service available 24 hours a day, six days a week, and in 13 different languages.

Mytheresa.com concentrates on developing new categories with a strong focus on active wear and the launch of a skiwear category. In 2020, the company launched children's wear at the beginning of the year and not long after launched its menswear section. The latter category is the response to the fact that there is a strong male client base internationally and especially in Asian countries. Those new categories forced the company to invest in back-end services to support the firm's international growth.

In 2014, mytheresa.com was acquired by Neiman Marcus in the USA. The health crisis saw its e-commerce activities boom with a 20% increase. However, its parent company Neiman Marcus had to file for bankruptcy in 2020. The platform, led by Michael Kliger, the CEO of mytheresa.com, successfully completed its IPO on the New York Stock Exchange in early 2021, with a valuation of $2.2 billion.

Matchesfashion.com The first Matches store was opened in 1987 by Tom and Ruth Chapman in Wimbledon Village and offered global luxury retail for both men and women. The founders devoted 20 to 30% of their store to welcoming their customers with unmatched hospitality. They had sofas to relax and coffee was offered to their clients. In the 1990s, new boutiques opened across London and proposed high-end luxury brands like Versace, Prada or Bottega. In 2007, the company opened its e-commerce platform and Matches became Matchesfashion .com. In 2012, the couple sold stakes of the company worth $20 million to Scottish Equity Partners and Highland Partners. This money contribution helped reinforce the platform's presence online. In 2017, the company was sold to the private equity firm, Apax. In 2021,

Matchesfashion.com represented more than 450 brands, delivers in 176 countries and 95% of its sales are made online.

The key element was hospitality that they started with. It remained one of the key pillars of its strategy today. Even with the digitalization of their offer, Matchesfashion has remained close to its customers. Only 3% of their customers account for 35% of the company's revenue. Matchesfashion cherishes them by reaching out to them wherever they are. In their concern to always improve their customer relationship, they keep working on how to enhance the delivery system, the aftersales service and the advice given to clients. For example, the company is able to deliver in 90 minutes anywhere in London and is aiming at reducing that time to an hour in each big city.

Matchesfashion invested in research and digital innovations. For example, it invested in social shopping with the creation of Style Social on its website. This new tab allowed clients to buy directly from Instagram and Twitter pictures posted by other customers with the hashtag #MatchesFashion. It was a first in the e-commerce luxury business where social commerce was integrated in their platform. Furthermore, each Wednesday it published The Style Report (one for women and one for men) which presented fashionable designers, interview of creators and related content. It was available online, as well as in paper format (100,000 copies four times a year). The advantage of the online version was that it was possible for a client to buy directly the fashion product without having to stop reading. It helped the company know which products are bestsellers.

Due to its close proximity to its clients and the brands, Matchesfashion is an important actor in the luxury retail business due to its capacity to detect creative talent and the needs of new customers. The digital strategy of Matchesfashion.com has already shown success. Clients spend on average 778 euros per purchase. The website has shown increased resilience during the health crisis. However, even if digitalization has been a success story for Matchesfashion, the company did not want to put an end to its physical stores.

SSense   At the origins of SSENSE are three brothers: Rami, Bassel and Firas Atallah. In 2003, in Montreal, Canada, they decided to launch their streetwear retail store to implement a new vision of retail where streetwear and luxury could coexist. Their philosophy was that everyone would mix luxury and streetwear. At SSENSE they had been doing it for 15 years. From the start, they refused to categorize everything. They had ready-to-wear and sportswear or accessories in the same place. The coherence of the whole seemed more important to Rami Atallah. The platform primarily works on creating its own technological solutions by working from scratch. SSENSE was born on the idea of offering accessible luxury e-commerce, contrary to the traditional luxury retailers. The platform has moved beyond just the e-commerce setup and is expanding its focus toward the nexus of content, commerce and culture.

In 2006, SSENSE launched its website. When the brothers launched the website, they decided to focus first on menswear and to propose confidential and original fashion labels. For example, they were among the first to propose Marine Serre, Vetements or Off-White right from the beginning. To promote their view of fashion, they added portraits, music, architectural and art content to their website, not always relating it to fashion. Their first ambition was not to sell their products but to build a relationship with their potential clients and, one day or another, they hoped it would result in a sale.

The founders were millennials. Nearly 80% of their clients were between 18 and 34. The pricing was adapted to stack all the odds in their favor and reach their target. For example, 90€ for a T-shirt, 260€ for a coat. To support their strategy, 80% of their employees are also millennials. The platform works on the idea of accessibility.

In 2017, they opened a five-floor physical store in Montreal. The opening of their boutique in Montreal was an illustration of their pioneering spirit. Beyond the fact that the store was ultramodern, a personal shopping service allowed customers to make an online selection of what they wanted to try on 24 hours before coming to the store and all would be prepared for their arrival. This new and unique phygital strategy has encountered great success among SSENSE's customers who sometimes travel to Montreal only to go to SSENSE's retail store. In 2019, they launched their mobile application, offering the customer a personalized experience. SSENSE delivered in 150 countries generating an average of 88 million page views. It is so because they keep focusing on understanding the world through its innovative content. The website's content aimed to be more relevant and meaningful than what can be found elsewhere on the web.

Secoo Richard Rixue Li and Zhaohui Huang launched Secoo in 2008 to sell second-hand luxury accessories and clothing for men and women. In the last decade, it became one of the most famous Chinese luxury e-commerce companies that sells both online and offline.

In 2011, Secoo started with 10 shops in Chinese provinces and opened its first flagship store in Beijing. It was also in that year that the company decided to launch its website and the mobile app followed two years after. In 2014, Secoo was recognized as the largest website in China for customers selling or buying luxury goods. In 2015, Secoo revealed its plan, Fashion+, which was to open its website to European fashion designers. In 2017, the company was listed on the NASDAQ stock exchange. In 2018, it made a collaboration with Parkson Retail Group, which is an important department store operator in Asia. In the same year, LCatterton and JD.com invested $175 million in Secoo with the objective for JD.com to become its online retail partner and for L Catterton to share its expertise. Following the growth story, the company has more than 3,000 brands and has physical stores in Shanghai, Hong Kong, Tokyo, NYC, and Milan.

The company's omnichannel strategy was based on consumer desire. First, the company only sold second-hand luxury products and had recruited a specialized team to detect counterfeits since this was the main bottleneck for luxury brands in China. Then, to respond to Chinese consumers' growing desire for a luxury lifestyle, the platform started proposing luxury cars (Bentley, Porsche), yachts, personal jets, hotel reservations, travel packages and others. Due to this diverse strategy from second hand to lifestyle, Secoo managed to build a loyal customer base with 18.7 million registered members among the well-educated middle to high income population in China. The membership system helped maintain the client's loyalty by offering them benefits according to the amount they already spent and upgrading them as they spend more. For example, in 2020, Secoo participated in the inaugural 616 shopping festival with a short-video on the video platform Kuaishou by launching a 24-hour livestreaming channel on its new account. The channel sold for over $14.8 million in the first five hours by opening different theme rooms such as vintage, fashion, handbags or brands themselves.

Secoo offered its customers a high-quality service with delivery on the same day of the order by a courier in costume and white gloves. That explains why a customer spends around 570€, which is 20 times the average basket on Chinese e-commerce platforms. Tod's, Versace and Salvatore Ferragamo sell on Secoo. In the last few years, Secoo has signed many partnerships with different brands in distinct sectors to develop its product and service offerings. All those partnerships, going from collecting data to innovative luxury retail to a unique shopping experience, formed a strong base for Secoo to maintain its position among the leaders of the e-retail luxury industry. In 2021, Secoo expressed its intent to secede from the NASDAQ, as its net income had dropped to abysmally low levels. The competition has intensified, with Farfetch on one side, JD.com and the social commerce players on the other.

Table 11.2 provides a detailed comparison of luxury platform business models.

Discussion on the evolution of e-commerce platforms

When having a closer look at luxury e-commerce platforms, it is not obvious that there are considerable differences between the platform when it comes to the phygital customer experience they all provide. Even though their business model may all be similar by offering a wide range of luxury brands online and delivering parcels straight to the homes of their consumers, it becomes clear that some luxury e-commerce platforms excel in terms of traffic and revenue.

In 2021, Farfetch, YNAP, JD.com are leading the online luxury retail market by not only providing a platform for brands to sell their products, but also providing technological services to luxury brands to enable their digital transformation specifically in building their in-house luxury online retail store. With time, it will be interesting to see if the luxury brands will continue working with platforms or move toward using their own digital capabilities in the long run. In the short term, however, it is clear that most of the players would partner with one of these platforms to get their products to the online customer base.

Table 11.2 Summary Table of the Platforms and Their Business Models

Platform	Services & Competencies	Business Model
Farfetch • Founded by Jose Neves. • 2+ million active users across 190 countries. • 500 brands and 700 boutiques. • Brands include the likes of Chanel and Saint Laurent. • Boutiques include high end retailers such as Harrods and Harvey Nichols.	• Online luxury fashion marketplace for customers. • Asset light with technology-savvy nature and start-up flexibility. • Online selling platform for luxury brands. • Logistical services. • Technological solutions in the field of innovation for luxury, digital expertise, support and solution. • Contacts and relationship with contemporary designer brands and boutiques worldwide. • Weekly drop system. • Unique and widest range of product selection. • Control of curation, price and display. • Uses sophisticated 3-D geometry algorithms, combined with neural networks, that identify the location of the shoe in space and apply it to the users' feet. • Introduced the revolutionary phygital "Store of the Future"—a physical store featuring AR, connected mirrors, clothing racks, RFID, ultrasound technologies as well as interactive holograms with innovative payment methods as well as intelligent software, which is able to scan customer emotions and connect the offline world with the online world by leveraging data for an ultimate and personalized customer journey.	The main activity of the company, the e-commerce platform provides an online presence to the traditional luxury brands and boutiques, enabling them to sell online without incurring the added responsibility of operating the online marketplace. The platform is an inventory-less business providing a rapid distribution system for purchase delivery by collaborating with different brands. Farfetch extends its technological expertise in providing additional business solutions on the supply side, i.e, to the brands. Through Farfetch platform solutions the company services enterprise clients with e-commerce and technological capabilities. Some of the services include setting up WeChat stores, end-to-end digital customer experience and digital stores. Other businesses are Browns and stadium goods, which offers luxury products to consumers and New Guard, which is a platform for the development of the global fashion brands. Farfetch effectively monetizes its services by charging a 25% commission on each purchase made through the platform and an additional 8% if the seller outsources the order fulfilment to the platform. Also, as part of its strategy, Farfetch has locked in 98% of its retailers with an exclusivity contract.

Yoox Net-a-Porter (YNAP)

- Founded in 2015 as a result of merger between Yoox and Net-a-Porter.
- Currently owned by Richemont group.
- Comprises e-commerce shops—Yoox, Net-a-Porter, Mr. Porter and The Outnet.

- Online retailer providing multibrand online stores, selling directly to the customers.
- Access to a vast number of luxury consumer data, which represents the currency of the future.
- Online flagship stores, a suite of B2B luxury services, helping brands meet their customer's every need and desire.
- YNAP integrated WhatsApp messenger and Instagram Checkout in its personal shopping operation.
- YOOX made use of artificial intelligence by incorporating the YOOXMIRROR, which allows consumers to create their own customizable digital avatar and try on different looks out of 50,000 individual pieces.
- Off-season discounted luxury items.
- Offer luxury brands digital support and solution.
- Offer one of the widest ranges of offers among competitors.
- Unique eco-system with fours websites covering second-hand and discount outlet that create synergies.
- Ability to diversify and minimize the risks.
- Control of curation, price and display.
- The service "You Try, We Wait" implemented in London and China for VIP clients allowed clients to receive a selection of products proposed by stylists and then return any unsuitable items after try-on.

The main areas of operation for YNAP group are online luxury retailing, through its multibrand shops like Net-a-Porter, Mr. Porter, The Outnet and Yoox, and online flagship stores division, where the platform partners with different designers and brands to power their own e-commerce and omnichannel solutions.

All four online retailing shops are uniquely positioned into the market. Net-a-Porter serves to the taste of style-savvy consumers through its curated content and higher-end non-discounted items. Mr. Porter works similar to Net-a-Porter but is focused toward men's fashion. On the other hand, Yoox and Outnet offers off-season discounted items. Yoox follows the approach of buying overstocked and unsold items which are off-season directly from the luxury brands and authorized distributors and selling it online at discounted price.

As part of its flagship online stores, YNAP group empowered brands through its technological expertise to establish online stores for respective brands. YNAP group comprises services like setting up of online stores, assistance on e-tailing operations like customer care, shipping, invoicing etc. Some noteworthy online stores powered by Yoox are Armani.com and valentino.com, and by NAP, jimmychoo.com. It implemented customer-centric tools, like an image-recognition function, virtual personal styling and natural language search.

(Continued)

Table 11.2 (Continued)

Platform	Services & Competencies	Business Model
Alibaba TMall Luxury Pavilion • Owned by Alibaba group. • Tmall was founded in the year 2008 and Luxury pavilion was launched in 2017. • Over 200 prestigious luxury brands. • Brands include the likes of Cartier, Prada, Balenciaga, Bottega Veneta and Burberry. • Greater than 750 million annual active users controlling more than 90% on the online fashion market in China.	• Online marketplace to sell luxury goods by being luxury brands' sole luxury partner in China. • Brands control pricing and merchandising, Tmall is the kitchen, brands are the chef. • Luxury pavilion is an App within the Tmall App. • Icon on Tmall home screen is only visible for select customers. All customers can search for "Luxury Pavilion." • Unique database of Chinese most affluent customers under the ecosystem of Alibaba. • Client service, logistic expertise, resources and technology curation owned by Alibaba. • Ability to build and operate the platform, providing customer services, quick delivery worldwide. • Contacts and relationship with luxury brands. • Ability to track the origin and guarantee the authenticity via blockchain. The blockchain technology allows it to register the manufacturing process and circulation process, which enables customer to track the product. It's a tool to minimize counterfeiting. • Big data and Analytics support for fine tuning responsive marketing strategy.	Tmall luxury pavilion is an invite-only service and the platform provides partner support such as marketing tools, incentives, highlights and campaigns. Also, at additional cost, services such as running of daily operations, customer services, logistics and e-commerce are provided. The platform charges an annual fee along with the sales commission based on category. The platform provides high level of customization and personalized platform space for each brand. The platform introduced a new "Maison" tab, an invite only option for brands, and is meant to enhance the luxury experience of the site. Tmall luxury pavilion also integrated luxury soho, an outlet version, in order to maximize the lifecycle of products on pavilion. Tmall also provides multiple benefits to the luxury pavilion customers. The benefits are included under loyalty program launched as part of New Retail initiative. Platform members are provided with access to bespoke offerings, latest payment options, priority delivery, a door-to-door return service and invitation to events. Premier members are provided with additional benefits like personal shopper service, a concierge service and access to premium spas.

24S

- Owned by LVMH group.
- The platform was launched in June 2017.
- The platform offers the finest selection from over 300 fashion and beauty brands. 24S is also the exclusive partner of Louis Vuitton, Dior, Celine and Moynat globally.

- High reputation and image of LVMH and Le Bon Marché.
- Exclusive offer from brands of LVMH group. Limited editions, exclusive models and co-branded models that are hard to find elsewhere, such as Loewe's Hammock bag, Miu miu's Miu Lady bag, Jil Sander's white floral shirt and other 77 capsule series.
- Synergies within the LVMH group.
- The most Parisian romance of 24S lies in the full-time online professional stylist service, which has always been committed to creating an immersive Paris shopping experience for consumers.
- Ability to guarantee the authenticity of the products.

Building on the legacy: For over 160 years, Le Bon Marché has existed as a destination store at 24 rue de Sèvres in Paris. 24 Sèvres aims at building upon the legacy and bringing the experience of shopping there online, giving customers all over the world access to a curated and distinctly Parisian perspective on fashion. 24S also hopes to capitalize on the existing in-store customer base by efficiently integrating the shopping experience and loyalty program.

Targeting niche consumers: The platform typically targets consumers in the age group of 28 to 45, who possesses real interest in the chic and effortless style of Parisian women.

Visual leading merchandising: 24 Sèvres focuses more on visual elements than editorial or content-driven features as part of its user interface design. The UX is combined with pleasantly intricate animations, giving the feel of a slick and playful UX.

Technology for customer relations: The 24S app includes a video chat feature allowing users to connect with a stylist based in Paris. This means that customers can get the same service as in-store—perhaps even better, due to the focused nature of a video call. The platform also utilizes Facebook messenger chatbot to provide personalized fashion advice.

(Continued)

Table 11.2 (Continued)

Platform	Services & Competencies	Business Model
JD.Com	• The platform caters to over 362 million active users and has a market share of 24.4%. • Some of the participating brands are Delvaux, Salvatore Ferragamo, Proenza Schouler, MSGM, Gucci, Prada and Miu Miu. • Leading technology driven e-commerce company with strong competence in retain, logistics, health, and customer service. • Started as retail infrastructure service provider in the area of 3C (computer, communications, and consumer electronics) industry in China. • JD.com is an online retailer with brands having less control. • Focused on China's fast-growing lower-tier cities. • Has its social e-commerce platform, Jingxi. Jingxi is available to consumers via Jingxi app, Jingxi mini program and a WeChat first-level entry point.	JD.com targets majorly to the millennials and Gen Xers across China, especially North China and Si Chuan Province as well as low tier cities. As part of its service JD.com provides a classic e-commerce curation which is reliable and offers fast and high-end delivery services. On the logistic front, the orders are shipped from JD warehouses or brands, and shipping facilities like JD luxury express and White Glove delivery are provided to the luxury brands.
mytheresa.com	• The online platform became operational in the year 2006. • The platform led by Michael Kliger, the CEO of mytheresa.com. • Successfully completed its IPO at New York Stock Exchange in January 2021 with an evaluation of $2.2 billion. • It started as an online mall and later on converted to online platform to sell luxury goods. • Provides women around the world with an online fashion luxury shopping experience like a boutique. • Connected to at least 7 social platforms, including WeChat and Weibo.	The unique selling proposition of mytheresa.com is its exclusive, curated and tightly edited offerings. The platform realized the challenges of online retailing in the field of luxury and strategized its value proposition accordingly. The platform ensures exclusive rights to sell limited edition products offered by luxury brands to become a differentiator and the only platform providing such products. The company projects a 48-hour shipping commitment and even provides same-day delivery in the US. Resonating with its idea of luxury, the platform states bearing of addition delivery cost, in cases of unsuccessful delivery attempts due to unavailability of a receiver.

- For the year 2020, mytheresa.com serviced its clients spanning across 130+ countries.

SSENSE
- Founded in 2003 by three brothers Rami, Bassel and Firas Atallah.
- SSENSE is a privately held company and is financially backed by Venture capital firms.
- Rami Atallah holds the position of the CEO, whereas Firas Atallah and Atallah Bassel hold the position of CFO and COO respectively.
- The e-commerce platform serves around 150 countries, generating an average of 88 million monthly page views.

- Online platform to sell luxury goods. Started in Canada.
- Customer services.
- Logistics.
- E-commerce.

- The founder of the platform envisions to offer a platform which is in contradicting nature to the traditional luxury brands. The platform works on the idea of accessibility.
- SSENSE aims at providing distinctive in-app experience through the capitalization of unique capabilities like data-based personalization, efficient navigation and a sense of immediacy. Delivering such experience means combining buying data, styling comprehension, customer browsing patterns, and their intent to insinuate a personalized user journey.

Facing the opportunities and threats brought by the pandemic, it seems the digital players have three strategies for growth. Firstly, either invest in developing of technology or partner with third-party platforms. Technology such as big data, blockchain, artificial intelligence and voice searching offer clients a unique online shopping experience. Technology could make clients feel that shopping online is even more confident and convenient than shopping in physical stores. Secondly, continue to offer luxury brands digital solutions and provide technology and logistic services during the development and operation of brands' websites. YNAP's online flagship store division supported 41 brands in website operation and Farfetch Black & White runs digital retail operations for luxury players, including Harrods. Lacking in-house digital talents to keep up pace with the digital times, traditional luxury brands except for conglomerate groups who have the resources prefer to outsource the design and operation of their digital platform to the digital expertise of third-party digital players at a lower short-term cost. It provides necessary tools and features of online platform such as customer service, international payment, Click and Collect and in-store returns by linking offline stocks to their websites. Jose Neves, founder of Farfetch, commented:

> Some brands will want to have complete control over design, build and day-to-day operation of their website, while others can ask us to manage everything for them, from customer service to payment, to online marketing. If a brand wants to sell on WeChat in China, they just need to use our API code and integrate their operations.

Thirdly, pure digital players are opening offline stores and reimagining the modern physical shopping experience by integrating advanced technologies such as augmented reality to connect online and offline experience. A 360-degree omnichannel approach would be the future of retail. The main drivers for that move can be explained by the following reasons. Not only will the face-to-face service and in-person experience boost sales by increasing conversion rate but they also will help the sales associates to understand better clients' needs through interpersonal communication and maintain long-term relationship. According to studies, when opening a new store, the digital retailer will increase its traffic by 45%. Physical stores also improve brands' awareness, recommendations, satisfaction and consumer perceptions. Moreover, experience has always been the key in luxury shopping, creating immersive and unforgettable memory. Even though with more and more advanced technologies such as augmented reality (AR) and virtual reality (VR), there's still a long way to go before the gap between online and offline really disappears, and seamless phygital becomes a reality.

The key to success for digital platforms in the future lies in a seamless omnichannel experience that integrates online and offline channels, during which the power of data will be used in order to create unique and personalized recommendation and styling service. The present offline is indispensable to maintain an emotional and personal relationship with customers. The decision of YNAP is not to prioritize digital channels to virtually try on clothes, but to try physically and then offer the possibility to return for free.

On another note, the battle against counterfeiting will remain the key concern for future customers. Sustainability was found to be another key issue. Leveraging on big data and blockchain technology to track the origin, producing places and transportation information will be one of the solutions that digital platforms are harping on. As for monobrand websites, apart from creating a seamless experience and solving sustainability issues, luxury brands find it difficult to propose a unique customer experience to differentiate themselves from other brands via their digital channel. It is a challenge to make the websites complementary to their physical stores in terms of services, visual and assortment merchandising, product offers and experience.

By way of conclusion, there are challenges. It is a challenge for luxury brands to stay exclusive and attractive as they venture out to online access. Third-party platforms had constant lingering issues of counterfeited goods, lack of experience and service and the notion of control. It is predicted that luxury brands and digital platforms will continue to innovate and reform their digital strategy to better perform in the digital age. Several innovative ideas have been put into reality such as the use of augmented reality to eliminate the gap between online and offline experience, personalization options to create value added to online sales, and digital prelaunch to privilege online purchase of exclusive luxury goods. The key to success for digital platforms in the future lies in a seamless omnichannel experience that integrates online and offline channels, during which the power of data should be used in order to create unique and personalized recommendation and styling service. Thus, the presence offline is indispensable to maintain an emotional and personal relationship with customers.

E-commerce: Social Commerce and Mobile Commerce   Social and mobile commerce (S-commerce and M-commerce) is the fastest growth area in the e-commerce space. It is catapulted by Chinese consumers who are trained and digitally evolved to navigate super-apps such as Alibaba and We Chat. It is predicted that the Chinese consumer will account for 50% of the market by 2025, who will use only digital modes to search, shop and embrace singularity. In 2021, 80% of the sales in China was influenced by online touchpoints. There won't be any cash transactions in the very near future in China.

China's third generation of social media is driven by a mixture of Social operating systems and AI content, which produces feeds based on content rather than networks. China has moved away from the aggregated, network-based social feeds that defined second-generation social media, such as Instagram, Facebook, Twitter, Pinterest or WhatsApp (all blocked by the great firewall). They have moved toward more content-focused approach via super-apps like WeChat and Weibo. In 2021, WeChat had 1.16 billion monthly active users with 79% penetration in China, whereas Weibo had 500 million active monthly users with 93% on mobile. Unlike second-generation platforms, these third-generation ones don't require users to build a network to engage with this content because their feeds are driven by a mix of social networks and Artificial Intelligence content engines. These content-based feeds benefit creators and sellers much more as they can appear on anyone's "for you" page without the need for paid promotions. That is a stark difference from what we've seen thus far on Western social platforms.

China is now home to a growing number of short-form video platforms, the most popular being China's version of TikTok known as Douyin (over 600 million daily users), Kuaishou (over 257 million users) and Xiaohongshu (Little Red Book over 100 million users, mostly younger women). On these platforms, the AI-driven "swipe" replaces the need to click through and follow individual profiles. Algorithms provide recommendations based on user content preferences.

The analytics derived from this machine-powered learning is based on a combination of the user's likes, comments, shares, watch time, "dueting" videos (those that require user-generated content), and "stitch" videos (those that begin with up to five seconds of another creator's video). This format has become so popular that a growing number of platforms, like Weibo and Xiaohongshu (The Little Red Book), are integrating short-video and livestream features into their feeds. But it's also because these third-generation platforms also contain e-commerce features that link feed content directly to shopping.

Short-form video platforms may seem "low-fi" compared to expensive and thoroughly planned campaigns, but they have become crucial to successfully resonating with Chinese audiences. Chinese luxury buyers are younger than Western luxury consumers, so they need to be targeted through different channels, which Cartier has done with its recent campaign. Luxury brands like Cartier have already embraced this change in China by creating fun campaigns on short-video platforms such as Douyin. Cartier did a successful campaign called Make Your Own Path, released in 2020 to promote the brand's new PASHA DE Cartier watches. While luxury brands almost always try to be exclusive, Cartier invited everyone on Douyin to participate in its user-generated content campaign. The premise was simple: show off your dance moves in a video, apply Cartier's special filter to it, and post it under the campaign hashtag. This simple-yet-effective campaign brought in 1.1 billion views and inspired thousands of users to boogie! Cartier even upped the ante by launching a livestreamed clubbing event by partnering with a hip-hop dance crew and the famous trap artist DJ Anti-General at a Shanghai club. The fun, refreshing campaign smartly tapped into China's creative consumers, club-going youth, livestream lovers, and social media content creators. Cartier also invited celebrities to participate in the campaign. As a result, the platform's algorithm boosted the campaign widely on user feeds and generated considerable organic support.

Embracing an all-inclusive social commerce on third-generation platforms in China has been rewarded. The equalizing and embodiment of mass appeal for a high jewelry brand such as Cartier was something new. They came down from their pedestal, became more experimental to resonate with younger audiences. Brands that are creative and innovative on third-generation platforms had done well both in engagement and sales. The Italian down jacket brand, Moncler, created a series of online and offline events on Weibo livestream as a way to maximize exposure for a new collection drop. They also witnessed impressive results. The release, featuring designs by the godfather of Japanese streetwear, Hiroshi Fujiwara, was from Moncler's highly regarded Genius Collection. Ever since Louis Vuitton's public livestream flop on the platform Little Red Book, luxury brands have been careful about optimizing their presentations on this burgeoning format. Another example was Christian Dior. After Burberry's success, Christian Dior couture launched a limited-edition Lady Gaga bag on Valentine's Day in China through a WeChat mini-program. The bag was sold out in a few hours. Christian Dior was also the first brand to launch on Tik Tok and Bilibili primarily focusing on the next generation of Chinese consumers. The brand saw an increase in engagement during the pandemic.

The flagship store of Louis Vuitton in Shanghai with its innovation on phygital online and offline runway witnessed record-breaking sales in the second half of 2020. This was primarily driven due to the men's spring collection 2021 show. It was one of the first to introduce an online/offline runway model. This initiative was a success as it generated a viewership of 100 million people across multiple platforms.

M-commerce It is mainly driven by a digitally savvy very young generation. It is a crucial indicator that Generation Y and Z do not respond to the same stimuli as the older buyers in mature markets. They are looking for vibrant, status-enhancing artifacts, and they prioritize distinctiveness and modernity over timelessness. In addition, they are much more tech-savvy, which has big implications for the marketing: they respond very well to the use of influencers, online presence and technology-enhanced in-store experiences.

In China there are currently almost 720 million smartphone users and the use of smartphone apps, from chat to digital wallets to M-Commerce, is like nowhere else in the world. It is no coincidence that the world's first online fashion show was held in Shanghai, broadcast on Tmall, the Alibaba Group's e-commerce platform. There were also live-streaming and online events where the designers described the collection and showed the work backstage. The popular "See now, buy now" format was also used, allowing viewers to buy clothes from the current collections or pre-order those from the new autumn–winter collections. The opening showcase on the first day attracted 2.5 million views. The success of the show highlighted the need for brands to take seriously the m-commerce generation in order to gain the attention and loyalty of increasingly sophisticated and digital consumers as well as being managed to democratize the most exclusive event in the sector.

Omnichannel Omnichannel realizes the environment where various channels including physical stores and online stores are integrated, which enables customers to purchase products or goods from such various channels. For instance, suppose one customer wants to buy a bag. However, the customer finds that the bag is not available at physical stores. Then, the customer purchases the bag from the designated website but receives it from a nearby physical store. The omnichannel strategy makes it possible for customers to receive goods anytime and anywhere they want to do so, which leads to boosted turnover due to an increase in user satisfaction.

There is a similar channel called multichannel. The difference between multichannel, which simply increases a channel to purchase, and omnichannel, lies in whether the information of customers, goods, and inventories are all integrated. In other words, in the multichannel, it's not possible to receive goods from physical stores if a customer purchases them from websites. There is a clear border between shopping on websites and that in physical stores.

The main challenge to shift from multichannel to omnichannel is the digital transformation. Omnichannel companies are capable of developing, managing, and maintaining an inventory management system, an information system so that customers will be able to access the same information regardless of physical stores or online stores. This integration is difficult to achieve but once integrated the customer journey can be seamless.

The reverse is also true. Even as the global luxury goods market gradually moves toward online retailing with digital revenues quickly outpacing brick-and-mortar, digital-born luxury companies such as Warby Parker, Bonobos, and Glossier are now opening physical stores of their own. Interestingly, these stores are not only temporary pop-ups but also permanent showrooms. Even though this move may seem to be counterintuitive at first, there are many complementary benefits to be derived from it. Even though online shopping offers convenience for luxury shoppers, it does not satiate their need to touch and feel a high-end product before buying. The stores provide a platform for consumers to have a more immersive brand experience than what is possible online, thereby enabling the e-commerce companies to have control over the entire customer journey.

It has been seen from intelligence studies that an omnichannel strategy also increases traffic with increase in brand mentions and searches online. While online shopping remains highly transactional, it is the brick-and-mortar stores that are leveraging the interpersonal interaction to drive conversion rates and enhance average purchase values.

The network effects generated by online retailing platforms create a winner-takes-all situation, where it is very likely that one or two platforms will emerge victorious and end up dominating the market. In this regard, an important factor is going to be the omnichannel experience. It has become clear with e-retail platforms that customer experience is a defining factor in the luxury retail sector. Let's note that once again, the two biggest players, LV and Gucci, are the ones with the highest number of digitally developed solutions, confirming the importance of integrating e-retail into the gambit of luxury fashion. In order to become dominant, e-retailers have already started thinking about how to diversify their offer, notably through the creation of physical stores. YNAP tried the experience in 2020 during Vogue's Fashion Night Out event, by opening two interactive, digital pop-up stores, and it was a great success. While e-commerce sites offer convenience, physical stores offer a unique advantage that is missing online: human-led personal service and multi-sensorial experience. This unique and tailored experience creates trust toward the brand, and tends to boost sales. Furthermore, physical stores make it possible to engage the digital customers on even more touchpoints, and really be part of the customer journey all along, from the discovery of the pieces to the actual reception of the item, whether at home or in a store. This human experience of interacting with store associates cannot be replaced, and greatly contributes to make the shopping experience even more emotional, and thus unforgettable. Finally, online and offline presence and interaction with the customers can be mutually beneficial, and help strengthen the assets of the platforms. Data collected online can be leveraged by store employees to better advise and create links with clients, boosting the quality of the shopping experience. At the same time, having human interaction adds context to the data collected online, creating even more value for said data, allowing brands to create deeper bonds with their customers.

Conclusion

The post-pandemic luxury brand has a lot to do. It needs to invest in a seamless omnichannel strategy by integrating touchpoints across all channels and enhancing the user experience. Through a phygital model, the brand can combine physical and digital channels to expand the customer's flexibility. These flexibilities will allow consumers to try out the products while appreciating the unique in-store experience and purchase online afterwards. Due to the digital shift to e-commerce caused by the pandemic, it is expected that, in the post-Covid-19 scenario, many customers will remain online. Moreover, by focusing on digital distribution, the brand will, on the one hand, save the high rents of store locations, and on the other hand be able to reach more customers worldwide. Partnership and collaboration are here to stay. Being available on those platforms is the only way in the short term to reach consumers, especially in China. Michael Burke,[2] Chairman of LV and Tiffany, in an interview, sums up the discussion in a very transparent way:

Louis Vuitton, seven or eight years ago, was, I would say, more introverted, in its bubble—very successful but a bubble. In the meantime, I think, Louis Vuitton has become a much more diverse environment, embracing diversity wholeheartedly. Vuitton is much more plugged-in with what's happening outside its own ecosystem, which nourishes the creativity that we see and which creates not just great PR and images, but also great relationships with clients that are truly high-end.

This has to do with opening up Vuitton to the world. Success breeds insularity and one of the things that you have to be very mindful of

---

[2]https://www.businessoffashion.com/articles/luxury/louis-vuittons-michael-burke-on-hardwiring-accountability-in-a-state-of-flux.

when you're in my job is to ensure that insularity does not become stifling. Insularity is good when it has to do with your provenance, where you come from, your uniqueness, but you have to battle to make sure that you stay plugged-in with what's happening around you all over the world.

That's why we embraced the digital world. Six, seven years ago, we were attempting to use the digital world to maintain one-directional communication from the brand to the client. Now, these social platforms have been absolutely embraced by Vuitton, but they're not run out of Paris. You can't; it's culturally impossible to do, logistically impossible to do. The clients, they want immediacy, they want that transparency, they want authenticity and they want to be in the context. They want to hear the message through their loudspeakers. So we went from being a fairly insulated, insular, successful company to a much more diversity-embracing company that is extremely successful in the digital world, which means being totally contextualised, totally empowered locally and extremely agile and quick, and not fixated on controlling every last piece of information, because that's just not possible.

From the above discussion, it is certain that these digitization strategies will continue for many years to come. In this fast-moving market, with new regular players, the consumers will be more knowledgeable, evolve in their attitudes, their skill sets will evolve and all the above will change their habits. The KASH will evolve over time. It seems logical that during confinement an increase in confidence in the marketplace is observed. In the same vein, on the one hand by the habituation of the elderly, and on the other hand by the arrival of the millennials. This new generation is a strong argument for brands to continue to invest in digital technology. For this evolved population of consumers, looking at products on the Internet has become intuitive. So, the convenience of e-commerce is here to stay.

The phygital dilemma through onmichannel, S-commerce or M-commerce strategy will also find its way through webinars, livestreaming, virtual shows and events, movies to accompany brands in their digital transition. Should brands be careful not to desecrate themselves, their history, their ethos with content that is too mainstream? This eternal paradox is likely to be more current than ever with the arrival of these new modes of advertising.

This effervescence can be seen in the positioning and strategy of the various companies as each and every one tries to find the right balance. The departure of Ian Roger from the digital management of LVMH, the replacement of YNAP founder Federico Marchetti by Georoy Lefebvre, digital director of the luxury group Richemont, the Farftech decoupling from JD.com, the joint venture of Farfetch with Alibaba, LV choosing JD.com, and so on and so forth. Each player is positioning its pawns to prepare for the next digitally enabled chess game, which promises to be crucial for the future of luxury.

As a conclusion, the $247 billion luxury market overflows with new opportunities. If the coronavirus pandemic was considered as a threat for the sector, which counted losses during the first months of the lockdown, sales are now recovering and growing back exponentially. The consequences of the pandemic have forced luxury businesses to accelerate their digital transformation and to adapt more rapidly. Some brands were able to anticipate the outbreak and were agile enough not to lose any time. For others, the transition from physical to online was perceived as very difficult as luxury does not only focus on delivering an excellent quality but also an excellent service. Brands could ask themselves how they would be able to bring satisfaction by being 100% online. This leaves room for additional innovative ideas that could thrive in the near future. Nonetheless, if in some countries some stores have reopened and this leaves an opportunity for brands to sell their products physically, it is necessary not to forget that still some consumers are reluctant to get to physical stores as they might still be afraid. Others may also have adopted this new way of purchasing, as they are now able to order from their favorite brand without the need of leaving their own place.

Faced with the consequences of this current crisis and taking into account observed consumption trends, headwinds in the luxury industry are now to be expected. The shift to digital will become central for any brand, and a sense of sustainable development will also be expected from consumers. New economic models, linked to the second-hand market and the rental of luxury goods, should emerge as winners as luxury brands try a step further in their quest for vertical integration.

Chapter 12

Sustainability, Circularity, and the New Era of Luxury

Luxury is anything that can be repaired.

—Jean-Louis Dumas

Introduction

In the year 2019, the global personal luxury goods market size totaled over 281 billion euros. Within these figures, the luxury apparel sector made up 23% of the personal luxury goods market. Increasing disposable income in emerging countries and the rise of awareness among millennials and Gen Z played a considerable role in the luxury fashion industry's growth. The stories they tell, the experiences they provide and the way they take accountability for trending social and environmental issues immensely influence their consumers. With the growth of the market and the market size within the luxury fashion industry, brands are largely scrutinized over factors such as their carbon emissions and waste management. There has also been an unprecedented increase in acceptance in the concepts of renting and reselling within the industry. Therefore, social responsibility and sustainability initiatives from brands act as important drivers for consumers' attraction and preferences. Several renowned brands, such as Stella McCartney, Burberry, Gucci and Louis Vuitton, are now actively participating in sustainability measures in different ways. These arise due to definitional issues of their own concept of sustainability.

The fundamental definition of sustainable practice is the idea of meeting the needs of the present without compromising the needs of future generations. As the idea of sustainability differs from person to person, company to company, and country to country, the extensions to this concept have been discussed extensively in research and the press.

The growing concerns around climate change, animal cruelty and working conditions have led to greater scrutiny of different industries. Luxury products in particular possess significant vulnerability toward such consumer scrutiny as they may be perceived as nonessential. Time and again the luxury industry has been criticized for generating significant waste, destroying unsold products as a marketing gimmick, animal abuse, and damaging biodiversity. On the other hand, the slow production cycle along with extreme exclusivity of such products, pay homage to the concept of sustainability. With multiple contrasting and complementing characteristics between luxury and sustainability, it is challenging for the brands to follow "the right strategy."

Definitional Issue and "the Right Strategy"

In some ways the words "sustainable" and "luxury" are synonymous while at the same time paradoxical. The contradiction begins due to the definition of traditional luxury in contrast to current luxury. Let me explain. Luxury often connotes excess, fashion, pleasure, showing off, wastefulness, whereas sustainability is synonymous with ethics and restraint: it invites consumers to meet the needs and desires of the current generation without compromising the ability of future generations to meet theirs. It is often forgotten that luxury also denotes sustainable products with the same essential qualities of luxury goods; they call for extraordinary creativity and design, they need to be made from exceptional materials, with good quality, and they place an importance on durability in the concept of less is more. Luxury goods have implicit sustainability built in as they don't go out of fashion and are lifelong products. Such products from yesteryear have always been sustainable, but have not been seen as such. As social and environmental stresses increase and global resources come under greater pressure, the luxury industry has started to embrace environmental and labor norms. Why is this so? One reason is that the current generation demands a shift in mindset. The word *sustainable* creates desire. It means products are created ethically, are less wasteful, and last longer. Educated, conscious and culturally aware consumers are keen to express who they are in terms of being ethical, creative and connected. They are less keen to simply possess more goods. They are keen to know about the origin of ingredients and raw materials, animal welfare, and the social and environmental impact of products more broadly. On the supply side, for products to be desirable, brands need to emphasize the sustainability factor. This is about preserving the art and savoir faire, and respecting the environment, thus creating a product with sustainable values which is by definition rare. It is another way of saving the planet since we would be channeling our purchasing power to where we might do the least harm.

The relationship between luxury and sustainability is, hence, no longer one-way, but rather an interdependent relationship in which one cannot exist without the other. It had to be so, for failing to acknowledge the scarcity of these resources would mean not only their eventual disappearance but also the end of the businesses in question and, in some cases, of more than century-long traditions. Indeed, through limited production, strict control of demand and supply, high prices, the decision not to delocalize or subcontract production, the limited use of machinery, and the preservation of craftsmanship, as well as the production of high-quality products, these companies have survived the onslaught of globalization and democratization.

Social, Environmental, and Economic Challenges

The concept of sustainability is often described in terms of three interconnected pillars: one social, one economic, and the third environmental. Following this illustration, sustainability can be achieved at the intersection of these three pillars. This view is the foundation of the UN's 17 goals for sustainable development. First, *environmental sustainability* is often (wrongly) used interchangeably with *sustainability*, although it is only one of the three dimensions. Its goal is to maintain ecological integrity and keep all of earth's environmental systems in balance, while the natural resources within them are consumed by humans at a rate where they are able to replenish themselves. Economic sustainability aims at ensuring that communities across the globe have access to the resources that they require—financial and other—to meet their needs. Economic systems should be intact, and activities should be available to everyone. Social sustainability is based on ensuring that universal human rights and basic necessities are attainable by all people, who have access to enough resources in order to keep their families and communities healthy and secure. Healthy communities have just leaders who ensure personal, labor, and cultural rights are respected and all people are protected from discrimination. Fine jewelry brands need to ensure that they act based on these three pillars in order to become more responsible businesses. Figure 12.1 shows the relationship between the three pillars.

The fashion industry, as reported by the World Economic Forum, is the second most polluting sector in the world after oil. The challenge to be relevant is real and rationally justified especially when the pandemic has shown that wastage can be saved and can be ploughed back in to the bottom-line. More and more customers are intellectualizing, even more than before, their relationship with consumption, as the health, social, environmental, and economic crisis impacts their daily lives. Their quest for meaning is more than ever inscribed in their acts of consumption. If they are ready to spend a large amount of money on a luxury product, they demand in return to be informed of the initiatives taken by the brand to build this "world after" to which they aspire.

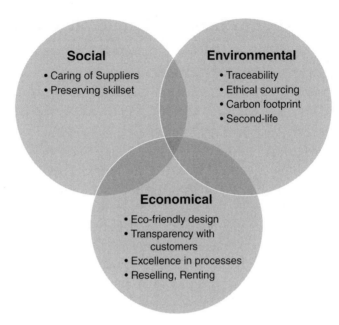

Figure 12.1 The Three Pillars of Sustainability

The Social Challenge

In the past, luxury businesses have been criticized for their minacious working conditions in the production and sourcing facilities, extremely low wages when compared to price and margins, and indulging in gender inequality. The challenges faced by the industry on the social front have the potential to shape the brand image and hence, brands with focus on social sustainability may achieve a brighter presence.

On another front, a luxury brand may adopt a market-oriented approach, where it ensures the well-being not just of its employees but also of every resource associated with its value chain, within or outside the firm's boundaries. Given the prestige of a luxury brand, it is worthwhile for the image of the brand to only associate itself with best practice followers and project itself as a responsible organization. A market-oriented approach is also required where a brand ensures the well-being of the overall market and society. Due to the nature of luxury goods, which create positivity and feelings of happiness and desire, it's desirable to maintain a broader perspective of the market, contrary to a firm-specific narrow perspective. To ensure this, brands constantly observe and implement practices that are in line with trends, such as consumer behavior, government policies, and emerging innovations in various fields. For example, Kering prides itself on having incorporated sustainability into its core values:

> *Bottega Veneta is committed to conserving Bottega Veneta's know-how, preserving jobs in the area where the company originated, and ensuring the survival of certain vital skills which might otherwise disappear. To do so, it has taken the initiative of creating leather braiding schools in the Veneto region around Venice. In other words, Bottega Veneta now seeks to make permanent, a particular business, and human resource, quite beyond its current agenda and its own immediate interest . . . . A Boucheron sapphire necklace. A jewel of this kind requires infinite patience to seek out the finest stones; it then requires some 500 hours of labor to assemble; all on top of the 14 years of study to master the skills required to make one . . . . A Boucheron necklace becomes a family heirloom, a tuxedo by Yves Saint Laurent will be a classic for generations.*

The Environmental Challenge

Various environmental challenges are believed to have a direct impact on the cost and availability of natural resources utilized by the luxury industry. With a growing population, increasing animal rights activism, decreasing biodiversity, and climate change, the industry's challenges are only intensifying; brands have vertically integrated wherever possible to secure access to rare and exquisite raw materials.

To remain sustainable while retaining access to their unique raw materials, brands often go the extra mile to restore and regenerate the ecosystems for these materials. Preserving natural resources, while extracting the materials necessary for the production cycle, is key to sustainability. For example, Ermenegildo Zegna, Brunello Cucinelli communicate how they take care of their suppliers and are proactively involved with the community from where they source their finest fabrics.

Reliance on creating a sustainable supply of raw material may still be prone to uncertainties beyond the control of the brands. In order to mitigate such risks, in 2021 it has been observed that a brand may also innovate to find alternatives for its raw materials, such as mushroom leather for Hermès and recycled scrap leather for Loewe. These innovative ways may be a way to restore and regenerate the ecosystem for the raw materials.

When products are not sold and cannot be discounted the luxury brands have been notorious for destroying their excess inventory. In July 2018, a scandal erupted when it was revealed that Burberry had incinerated more than USD 38 million worth of unsold items in order to preserve the prestige and rarity of its products. Numerous critics have spoken out against this act. Burning excess inventory was very common in the world of luxury goods. It is also totally contrary to the eco-responsible practices in which consumption is trying to be embedded today. Earlier, the independent group Chanel had been under fire for cutting down trees in a forest in the Perche region of France to create a decor for a fashion show at the Grand Palais, provoking strong reactions from several environmental protection associations. On similar lines, the social and environmental impact of gemstone mining, the use of animal fur or skins in the fashion industry, or the overconsumption of luxury cars are all subjects of exploration, which also point to a contradiction between the world of luxury—whatever the sector—and responsible consumption. For example, most brands have already taken distinctive steps toward responsible consumption. *Kering is not an isolated example. Many other luxury houses are working toward the same goal. Hermès is an obvious case in point—they have made considerable savings in water consumption in the production process for their silk scarves. Another instance is Loro Piana, which is engaged in protecting the vicuña living on the high plateau of the Andes. Cartier originated the Responsible Jewelry Council, which has become a benchmark authority for sustainable jewelry and includes Boucheron among its members.*

Richemont has made significant efforts in recent years, which are described in their annual sustainability report. Their "Movement for Better Luxury" includes four areas through which they want to address sustainability: People, Communities, Sourcing, and Environment. These are commitments defined at the group level and implemented within the Maisons. In 2021 LVMH released their Eco-design pledge, which stated that it has no plans to take on the resale market—a meaningful frontier in the sustainability movement—and is instead focusing on what it calls "creative circularity." This involves eco-design practices that will be implemented across all of the group's businesses, from Fashion & Leather Goods to its Selective Retailing arm. Creative circularity is driving the second life for the products—both for clients and the group. The shift to eco-design includes plans to bulk up services for clients, such as repair and polishing, as well as upcycling and recycling leathers and furs. LVMH asserted that "sophisticated repair services, upcycling, reuse of precious raw materials, and efforts to find alternative materials all feed into the Group's circular economy strategy." By 2030, LVMH pledges to have a specific traceability system for each type of primary material, using blockchain technology—from the field to the store. In 2021, it says, upcycled sneakers designed by Virgil Abloh for Louis Vuitton's spring collection, and a woven leather handbag from Loewe made from leather scraps, would be the first steps in their eco-design strategy of creative circularity.

Mini-Case:

Solantu and Yacare Pora have been preserving and nurturing the crocodile trade in Argentina. As reported in Design for Biodiversity, this trade is a great example of the balance and interdependencies between business, habitat conservation, and local livelihoods. Crocodiles play an important role in their wetland environment: they help maintain a balance within the ecosystem by regulating other species and fertilizing water plants, and yet are threatened by illegal hunting and the high mortality rate they experience as hatchlings. In an effort to support the habitat and population of Caiman Crocodiles in Argentina, breeders have collaborated with local Gauchos (legendary Argentinian figures and master horse riders), who work on ranches and hold a strong connection to wildlife. To protect the eggs from predators—both human and other animals—the Gauchos

(continued)

(continued)

harvest them from the wild, marking the nest as they go. The Gauchos bring the eggs back to their homes where they are able to care for them until they are transported back to the breeding station to be hatched and grown. Once big enough, half of the crocodiles are returned back to their original nests, while the rest are kept for trade purposes. By educating and offering the local community an opportunity and incentive to be part of a legal trade, illegal hunting has decreased and the population of Caiman crocodiles has dramatically increased—essentially fostering both economic and ecological resilience for the local environment. The imperative for fashion brands to think about the natural resources they rely on is clear—the luxury accessories market is worth around €57 billion, and exotic animal skins make up almost 10% of luxury handbag sales. Despite the surrounding controversy, the demand for exotic skins like snake, crocodile, and alligator has been rising: with a croc bag selling for 30 times more than its bovine counterpart, it is easy to see the business incentive. While it can be difficult to understand the desire for exotic skins in fashion—and there are many who consider it immoral—they remain an important and valuable resource for communities across North and South America and South East Asia.

Chopard, which was taken over by the Scheufele family in 1963, is another example worth mentioning. An integral part of their sourcing strategy is the commitment to 100% ethical gold. They use Fairmined-certified gold, and diamonds sourced only from suppliers certified by the Responsible Jewellery Council (RJC) for all the Maison's creations. Chopard has partnered with the Swiss Better Gold Association (SBGA) in a project to source gold in a responsible way from Barequeros in El Chocó, Colombia. El Chocó remains one of Colombia's poorest regions, despite being the nation's second-largest gold producer. The Barequeros are artisanal goldminers who employ local traditional mining techniques, such as sluicing and panning with handheld tools. They don't use mercury in the process, which helps conserve the locale's rich biodiversity. The project contributes to the supply of gold as part of a fully traceable and responsible international supply chain. Tiffany is another brand worth mentioning. What stands out in Tiffany's approach to sustainability is the vertical integration of their business. This enables the company to create full traceability, which is integral to social and environmental responsibility and hard to achieve in fine jewelry. "Nobody used the word 'sustainability' when Charles Lewis Tiffany cofounded this company, in 1837, in New York. But in his own way, Tiffany was ahead of his time," selling as well as designing and manufacturing their own jewelry with a control over their value chain. Tiffany owned diamond workshops, where stones were cut and polished. Jewelry-making or polishing facilities were in-house. They bought directly from source and owned mines, cutting out the middleman, and thus could pinpoint who provided each stone. Tiffany laser-inscribes every stone larger than 0.18 carats with a microscopic code indicating its provenance. For its positive economic and social impact, they pay a fair living wage—factoring in variables such as family size, housing, and transportation costs—adapted to local realities as well as fair working conditions. Furthermore, Tiffany is putting efforts into educating their customers about sustainable practices implemented by Tiffany. As an integral part of their storytelling, salespeople are trained to talk about how sourcing methods differ from those of competitors; customers are encouraged to consider these practices when making a choice in their spending.

Since 1976, Rolex has recognized an award for companies or projects that have made a positive environmental change. It demonstrated Rolex's desire to move toward improving the sustainability of their industry and its commitment to greener consumption. Projects were judged on their feasibility, originality, potential for sustainable impact and, most importantly, on the entrepreneurial spirit of the applicants. Over the past 44 years, Rolex has supported a global network of pioneers. The winning projects ranged from scientific and technical inventions to initiatives to protect rare and endangered species—from the tiny seahorse to the giant whale shark—and habitats—from the Amazon rainforest to forest ecosystems in Sri Lanka. Some were reviving ancestral practices, from agriculture in the Andes and Africa to medicine in the Himalayas; others provide water, energy, shelter, food, and safe, low-cost medical care in developing countries. The main idea of the Rolex Award is to maximize the impact of the projects and, through initiative and ingenuity, to benefit humanity.

The Economic Challenge

Minimizing pollution and reducing environmental impact do increase the sustainability of goods and services. However, these are not the sole pillars of a luxury brand's sustainable business model. Other examples are: innovation in the production process and all operational processes, such as packaging, waste management or raw materials, reuse of available resources, less is more, bespoke production, and switching off lights in flagship stores, which can also lead to sustainable products. For example, Paris-based On The Spot is just one of a number of parkour collectives around France trying to raise awareness about light pollution and energy consumption as part of the Lights Off movement. They do that regularly on Fridays on the Champs-Élysées, putting off the signs of Sephora and others.

In recent years, interest in environmental issues has been increasing, and the pandemic has made the need for change even more visible by emphasizing the importance of sustainability. Clients are increasingly aware of environmental issues. Brands actively share these values. Those who allow "responsible consumption" may have a competitive advantage. For example, Giorgio Armani wrote an open letter to *WWD*, in which he promoted the idea for "an approach to design and making clothes that suggests a way to buy them: make them last."[1]

Sustainability discussion is not new in this luxury and fashion business as for generations the brands have survived the test of time and remained relevant. For example, Stella McCartney has been at the forefront of sustainable fashion for years and recently launched the "World of Sustainability," a platform entirely dedicated to documenting the brand's sustainable practices. The brand is very demanding with its suppliers,

---

[1] L. Zargani. "Giorgio Armani writes open letter to *WWD*." *WWD*, April 3, 2020.

controls the entire ecological impact of its production, and works with several environmental protection organizations. It integrated a practice called "Clevercare" into its products, a simple five-step approach to help customers keep their product as long as possible in a sustainable manner. In Italy, Gucci with its Equilibrium campaign, Ferragamo, Versace, Burberry, and many others have joined the sustainability issue. Marie-Claire Daveu, chief sustainability officer of Kering Group and a member of the brand's board, is of the opinion that "with Millennials and Generation Z consumers making up 30% of all luxury shoppers and on track to represent 45% by 2025, luxury brands need to accelerate their work towards sustainability and conscious living if they want to stay relevant."

Kering deals with a strategy of Care, Collaborate and Create. With the help of PricewaterhouseCoopers, they developed an Environment Profit & Loss (EP&L) statement which measures the various sustainability elements in their supply chain in order to further use it to develop their sustainability targets. LVMH launched its LIFE "initiatives for the environment." LIFE speaks about nine-step process that starts from eco-friendly design, sourcing, traceability and compliance, supplier responsibility, preservation of skillset, impact of carbon dioxide emissions, second life and reparability, transparency with customers, and excellence. Figure 12.1 (page 388) depicts the three challenges of sustainability.

The Three Challenges

The intrinsic values of the luxury sector seem to go in the direction of more responsible consumption. Firstly, the production of the luxury industry is often small, which by no means exhausts the rare natural reserves, and some brands make it their core marketing strategy, such as Hermès and its limited number of bags available for sale. The low demand in terms of number of customers in the luxury market will always limit the quantity of products created. It stands in marked contrast to fast fashion, which is adept at hyper-production and offers an ever-increasing number of products in gigantic quantities to the four corners of the world. Even in terms of figures, the turnover of LVMH (44.7 billion euros in 2020), the largest luxury conglomerate in the world, represents only half of the turnover of Carrefour and one fifth of that of

Apple, showing the reduced size in value and therefore quantity of this extremely high-priced market.

Secondly, the desire to preserve an often historic know-how, whether in the leather processing, textile, watchmaking or jewelry sectors, is often very strongly emphasized by the various brands in the luxury industry. This strong identity is then borrowed from a quality, local and non-robotized craftsmanship that goes in the direction of sustainable development both socially and environmentally. The preservation of the savior-faire of ingenious craftsmen and -women, with unique skill sets for the various luxury brands, is a way to emphasize their strong brand identity while claiming to support a limited carbon footprint and fight for the preservation of local craftsmanship.

Finally, the demand for quality, specific to the luxury sector, goes hand in hand with products that last a long time, with reasoned and limited consumption. This trend to consume less but consume better is gaining traction within the new generation. Less waste, less clothing thrown away by consumers, consume less but consume better, experience more—is the new logic that entices the leap toward creativity in the circular economy.

Forces Shaping the Sustainability Model for Luxury Business

The Circular Economy

> *A Circular Economy is a regenerative economic system with the goal to minimize waste by re-using, repairing and recycling and keeping resources in use for as long as possible, withdrawing the maximum value from them while in use, then recovering and regenerating products and materials at the end of each utility life.*[2]

The circular economy may be a way forward if a brand wants to ensure sustainable profitability, though brands have previously been critical of the concept since it is believed to work against the principles of

---

[2]https://www.knewin.com/en/blog/circular-economy-in-the-luxury-retail-space-expectations-vs-reality/.

the luxury industry. The circular economy practices the extraction of raw material, manufacturing of products, consumption of products, and finally, rather than disposal of the product, its repair, reuse, recycling and reconsumption. There are 16 key principles in this domain that cover the lifecycle of a product, from design and sourcing to production, transportation, storage, marketing, sales, and the final stages—i.e., the final discarding of the product. During these phases, the product is not wasted, and its value is maximized. A relatively easy way to become circular is to focus on three key aspects of the fashion and luxury business. They are *product design*, *infrastructure*, and *business models*. This is because the term *circular fashion* stems from two main words, *Circular Economy* and *Sustainable Development* (Figure 12.2).

In simpler words, during the design phase, fashion products could be designed with the sole purpose of high longevity, resource efficiency, nontoxicity, biodegradability, recyclability, and implementing ethical practices during the value chain. It also means that products should be designed in a way that reselling, refurbishing and sharing among multiple users is feasible over time. These products could be utilized until the user deems them no longer usable. In such a circumstance, the product must be recycled and reused for the manufacturing of new products. If unfit for recycling, the raw materials need to be composted, in order to become raw materials for plants and other organisms. Circular Fashion only points to how the resources must be consumed and discarded on a daily basis.

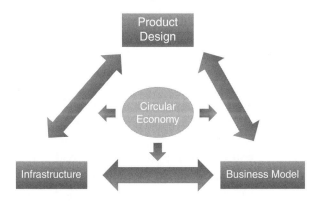

Figure 12.2   The Circular Economy

In terms of infrastructure, the common practices to extend the life of a product are reselling, renting, donating, repairing, and redesign. For example, in the case of infrastructure, the bag owner could have consigned the unused item on a luxury resale platform and, by chance, the second customer, looking for the same model, could have bought the bag second-hand, wasting fewer resources and saving money. At the end of the usage phase, if the product has deteriorated, it can be properly disposed of; otherwise, the materials can be recycled to start the cycle again.

Fashion and luxury brands have long followed the business model of a linear economy: extraction of the raw materials, production, consumption, disposal of the product. Such practices were not surprising given the reputation of luxury brands to provide only the finest quality and exclusive products. It may initially seem that the idea of recycling and the circular economy is entirely working against the core principles of traditional luxury brands where luxury must be inaccessible, and the price paid for the product must strongly be controlled by the brand. Such apprehensions are logical; hence, a lot of traditional luxury brands have remained critical of the circular economy. They were not ready to compromise on their control over the product cycle, which entails the brand reputation.

For the design and infrastructure phases and the business model to work together the alignment of industry forces would be a necessity. Traditionally, luxury brands were battling against two forces, which were counterfeiting products and second-hand products. Counterfeiting products were bound to provide no incentives to the luxury brands, whereas careful structuring of the second-hand luxury market may bring benefits to the luxury industry. A second-hand luxury resale business requires the support of brands to be authentic and create a sense of trust in buyers. For example, TheRealReal platform, selling fake products, was a good example of noncooperation between the brands and platforms. Another example was the lawsuit filed by Chanel against TheRealReal for selling counterfeit products. What we must understand is that counterfeit products are the real threat to luxury. Luxury brands can't control the proliferation of counterfeit product business but can exert control over the second-hand luxury industry, as the industry sees growth and legitimacy in this business model.

The Sharing Economy: Circularity and Singularity

As a designer, I think it's the biggest compliment for your designs to have an afterlife—to me, that is luxury.

—Stella McCartney

The fashion industry can no longer continue with a take, make, waste approach—brands need to disrupt their linear model by embedding circular thinking across all aspects of their business. The thirst for constant newness has led to incredibly high levels of consumption which has pushed up mass overproduction, making the fashion industry one of the most polluting. Decoupling economic profit from the use of natural resources is a way forward for singularity. Singularity in the thought process and circularity is really a key solution to building a more sustainable fashion industry: it allows people to access fashion without the production of new pieces, supporting the industry in moving away from reliance on vital natural resources such as land and water.

The rising importance of the concept of a circular economy indicates that luxury fashion consumers are educating themselves about recycling fabrics and upcycling garments. Moreover, with increasing mergers and acquisitions, the luxury fashion industry is seeing an increasing trend in the sharing economy. Apart from the business benefits, the sharing economy also paves the way for companies to share their resources, logistics and retail real estate. This reduces the environmental impact and creates employment opportunities, thus proving to be beneficial for all stakeholders involved.

One can say that the luxury fashion industry is being redefined and there are therefore possibilities for new and different kinds of competitors to disrupt the market. While traditional brands, known for their heritage and craftsmanship, are conflicted about adopting the new trends, it is only a matter of time before adapting to what consumers want will determine their standing in the market. For example, Kering claims some of its materials are already circular and has developed a Circularity Index based on the recommendations of the Ellen MacArthur Foundation. On similar lines, H&M has specific goals on cotton, packaging and water use in the supply chain, but no timeline for becoming fully circular. LVMH has launched an e-commerce marketplace for its brands' unused fabric and leather.

An edited wardrobe, where less is always more, is a way to achieve singularity and circularity. The clothes that are not worn can be recirculated by reselling or donating them. From a singularity point of view, buying fewer pieces, but quality pieces, can achieve this goal as they would be long-lasting and command a resale value. Another way is to achieve a capsule sustainable wardrobe and follow a strict one-in, one-out policy. Another way of achieving the desired goal is to follow a transparency route whereby products are only bought when the production process and the conditions under which the production was done can be traced and documented. With respect to unsafe working conditions and unfair pay for many garment workers, the Rana Plaza disaster in 2013 really brought this into public awareness, demonstrating how important transparency in the production supply chain is.

> *(The resale market growth) is the reflection of a much bigger trend that goes far beyond the resale space. Number one factor is the drive towards sustainability (. . .). Secondly, (. . .) everyone is looking for a good deal, regardless of how big their wallet is. Resale is an affordable way to access luxury goods. Finally, I would mention the trend towards less ownership, (. . .) consumers move toward less assets and more experiences.*
> **—Charles Gorra, Rebag CEO**[3]

During and after the pandemic, as some countries return to immediate normalcy, resale and renting are seen to be two important trends in the luxury industry. Consumers enjoy the variety of products they can consume this way. It is consumption freed from the notion of possession. These products by definition are also carbon neutral. The stigma once attached to second-hand luxury products is now seen as sustainable consumption. New generations are no longer satisfied with accumulating items in their wardrobe, wearing them once or twice, and disposing of them when they fall out of fashion. Pre-owned experience means consuming as many high-end bags and accessories as one

---

[3]https://fashionunited.uk/news/retail/fashion-resale-a-booming-market-interview-with-charles-gorra-ceo-of-rebag/2019092445408.

wants and then reselling or returning them (if rented). The perception of pre-owned luxury is rapidly changing, evolving from the "accessible" option for those who cannot afford to buy directly in the stores, to the "experiential" option for those who never want to wear the same outfit twice while saving the planet—even the Kardashians launched a luxury resale platform (Kardashian Kloset) featuring their designer clothes and accessories.

On the other hand, due to the Covid-19 pandemic period, a considerable portion of Americans and Europeans have started considering selling their luxury products that they no longer use. An example of such are the designer clothes unused in their closets. They perceive opportunities to make some extra money in light of the pandemic period's economic challenges. As a result, there has been an increase in the number of people selling their pre-owned luxury products.

Reselling: Shop, Use, Consign

Reselling promotes the circular economy and thereby sustainability. The key drivers of the resale business are the movement to be minimalistic and the notion of less-is-more. There was always resale, be it in the corner shops outside the museums, the famous and infamous vintage shops, the auction houses, and the C-to-C sites such as e-Bay and others. Thus organizing this business of resale with digital platforms, providing collectable, vintage items while reaching out to customers, usually the millennials and Gen Z, who are unable to travel during the pandemic, with affordable prices has seen this business model grow at a pace that was not witnessed before. Additionally, success stories of resale platforms like RealReal, Vestiarie Collective, Fashionphile, Chrono24, Watchfinder & Co. and others have proved that the new wave of reselling of luxury fashion is a concept here to stay.

How does consignment work? The e-commerce luxury resale platforms' business model is based on a circular value chain that balances supply and demand. On the first side, there are private sellers; without any costs, they can ship the luxury item they want to consign directly to the company's facilities or, if possible, find a brick-and-mortar store to drop the item physically. On the second side, there are the buyers that, as in a classic e-commerce model, have at their disposal a free access platform where payment is not based on bundles or subscriptions, but reflects the single price of each product in the shopping cart. In some cases, brands have also physical stores for a classic brick-and-mortar customer experience. The circularity of the model is preserved given the flexible status of the players involved; indeed, buyers can become consignors and, vice versa, sellers can turn into buyers. The brands stand in the middle, between the supply and demand side, allowing the exchange process to happen. The most complex and costly process to deal with is authentication. Certifying an item's originality requires a dedicated team of highly skilled authenticators for each product category; plus, the more the platform takes the shape of a managed marketplace (moving from the peer-to-peer model), the more experts will be required for the successive phases of product photography, description, and pricing decisions.

Due to their durable and timeless nature, luxury goods are suitable for the consignment model. For example, resale of fine jewelry provides an opportunity to support long-term sustainable goals. Fine jewelry pieces that were sometimes barely worn can be sold for considerably less on resale platforms in a transparent way with authentic certification. Luxury brands could see this as a threat to their business or convert the threat to an opportunity. Instead selling vintage and rare pieces of fine jewelry could be a way for heritage brands like Tiffany or Cartier to engage with the resale trend. The luxury watch brand Richard Mille has opened stores in London, Tokyo, and Singapore where the brand sells rare and sought-after pre-owned watches. A similar concept is also gaining traction for the fine jewelry sector. It could add to the brand value and promote the timelessness of their designs. Wearing vintage pieces is the most sustainable way of consumption of fine jewelry. Luxury brands have traditionally moved away from the second-hand market for fear of diluting exclusivity and reducing sales. But partnerships and collaborations between Vestiaire Collective and Selfridges, Vestiaire Collective and Kering, The RealReal and Gucci, Burberry, Ralph Lauren and Depop demonstrates the growing interest in luxury used goods. "We've talked with many brands over the years, especially brands at Kering, it's only a matter of time until more brands start to realize that resale is a big part of how people will shop going forward."[4]

---

[4]Allison Sommer, senior director of strategic initiatives at The RealReal.

Renting: Rent, Use, Return

Renting is another trend within the logic of the circular economy, with platforms like Rent the Runway, Front Row Tribe, Les Cachotières (renting among private consumers), Le Closet (clothes-box renting), L'Habibliothèque (targeting the young), Sac de Luxe (for leather goods) and 1 Robe pour 1 Soir (event-based) targeting a market that has emerged. An item can be rented to several people throughout its lifetime and can create value for each one of them without the need of creating new items. While consumers really enjoy the way it enables them to consume more products, the impact this has on sustainability remains debated. For example, jewelers have always been willing to lend items to loyal clients but engaging in renting on a large scale could be risky in the fine jewelry industry. First, fine jewelry is very precious compared to clothing. If the product gets harmed when rented this could lead to high costs for the brand. Also, there is a risk that fake products will be returned, there would thus be the need of an authentication check by a specialist after each return. Renting could also lead to a cheaper brand image as the precious items become more accessible.

How does rental work? In the luxury rental managed-marketplaces platforms work as an intermediary between the vendor and the buyer. In contrast to the peer-to-peer model, the rental process does not perfectly match supply and demand. The seller, indeed, does not keep the ownership of the item, but it is the platform that selects the inventory and buys the products deemed trendier and more rentable from the vendors. On the demand side, the buyer has at his disposal a classic e-tailer site providing a vast choice of luxury items to rent in subscription or single-purchase mode. Most of the time, rental companies rely on a subscription-based business model and offer their customers different packages to choose from. The price of the subscription bundles varies in respect to the number of items that can be rented simultaneously and the length of the rent. Some brands also provide two other purchase options: reserve one single item without paying monthly fixed fees, and the price would depend upon the original retail value of the item, and purchase the product after the rental period.

While the most expensive and complex procedure in the resale model is authentication, for rental e-tailers, it is necessary to efficiently manage two fundamental steps of the value chain: inverse logistics and repair and cleaning services. A robust and quick shipping and return process, supported by valid partners, is vital to win over competitors and to survive the burden of logistics costs. Let us assume that a beautiful pair of Louboutin have just been rented by a customer; the company needs to organize not only the delivery, but also the return, which in some cases happens in a time-period as short as five days. Plus, once the shoes return to the facilities, the first objective is to limit the time they rest unused in the inventory to increase the return on that product. The process of cleaning and repairing, therefore, needs to be optimized in order to make that pair of shoes available again on the platform in the shortest time possible. As explained previously, the major sources of income for online luxury rental services are subscriptions, one-time rentals, late return fees, and item purchases. In comparison to US-based e-tailers, for Chinese platforms like YCloset, logistics costs are six times less expensive, usually accounting for only 20% of the subscription fees.[5]

Renting could become a promising way to promote sustainable consumption while at the same time building further brand value. Renting seems to be more complex within the fine jewelry and watch industry, but less so in the leather and apparel industry.

Upcycling: Accept, Redesign, Sell

There is a movement toward conscious consumption and production. Conscious consumption embeds circular thinking across all aspects of the process—from recycled fabric, to upcycled pieces and designs that are crafted with circularity in mind, whether for longevity or to enable more recycling. Many companies are experimenting with upcycling as part of their sustainability efforts. For example, fabric innovation in the search for more environmentally friendly substitutes for cotton and leather. Some trends that have been driven specifically by the impact of the pandemic, such as an increase in more casual and sportswear. Overall the main trends prior to the pandemic have further escalated, such as the growing popularity of sustainable brands, vintage, streetwear and leading designer brands such as Gucci, Dior and Prada. For example,

---

[5]https://www.theharbingerchina.com/blog/rent-to-buy-the-chinese-runway-with-ycloset-coo-michael-wang.

TheRealReal launched the ReCollection program, a series of collections upcycled from old garments donated by brands such as Balenciaga, Dries Van Noten and Stella McCartney. With these donations they plan to develop their own line of 50 pieces. Its second drop was an in-house range of cashmere loungewear. The upcycled garments will include no virgin materials, zero-waste production and be manufactured in America for a fair wage, according to The RealReal. The above examples show that the mere quality of the products is no longer sufficient. Millennials want to be involved in the front line and live unique experiences. Millennials are a generation that cares about sustainability and values authenticity and transparency. Technology is part of this category that has a digital singularity. Figure 12.3 shows the circular fashion business model.

Figure 12.3   The Business Model of Circular Fashion.

The Blue Ocean of Singularity

There are several reasons why luxury brands are interested to navigate into the luxury second-hand blue ocean. First, resale and rental platforms actually incentivize luxury purchases. Resale of luxury items allows a significant income in view of the different prices of luxury products. Thus, a customer who resells a luxury item that he bought in a luxury store has a high chance of using the money collected to buy a new luxury item, which is a double win for the luxury brand in question. As a matter of fact, second-hand consignors are usually first-hand buyers and because of the possibility of reselling the items, it has been observed that 44% of them are purchasing more expensive products first-hand. On the other hand, 62% of consumers buy a luxury brand for the first time on the resale market, but, when they get loyal to the brand or have enough purchasing power, 57% of second-hand buyers turn to the first-hand market to purchase again the same brand.[6]

Second, it allows many customers who would never have had the pretention to try a brand, to appropriate a luxury good. From this second-hand acquisition can be born a real craze, a better loyalty on social networks, a special attention to commercial events. Thus the second-hand can be seen as a gateway to a brand-new market which could be presented as excellent news for the big luxury brands. One out of every two Millennial luxury consumers buys second-hand luxury products, whereas only 35% of Baby Boomers do so.

Third, traditional brands may benefit from partnering with e-tech platforms because of the huge amount of data they process about customers' preferences and purchasing behavior, in order to deliver a better customer experience, improve the marketing efforts and address clients' needs. An example worth mentioning would be the collaboration between Rent the Runway x Marriott Hotels. By anticipating the needs of business travelers and their painpoints, all the Rent the Runway's customers traveling and staying at a Marriott Hotel are coddled with a personalized closet concierge service. Before arriving at their destination, they can select the items they want to find in their

---

[6]https://www.bcg.com/publications/2019/luxury-brands-should-celebrate-preowned-boom.

wardrobe, from working attire to elegant gala dresses, and travel without heavy luggage.

Fourth, second-hand promotes sustainability and by collaborating with resale or rental platforms, luxury brands encourage a more ecological way of doing business and demonstrate their concerns about the planet to the growing eco-generations. Participating in the circular economy stands for a greener image of luxury that goes hand in hand with the expectations of increasingly changing behavior of younger consumers.

Changing Customer Behavior

It is now more or less certain from the above discussion that the pandemic will have long-term social and economic repercussions on the luxury industry. These include behavioral trends that arose during the lockdown due to the confinement measures and travel bans. These behavioral trends are going to settle and evolve in the future, remodeling a new era of high-end consumption. High-end consumption is at stake due to the underlying behavioral change of future generations. The next generation is as concerned about sustainability as it is about meeting the needs of the present without compromising the ability of future generations to meet their own needs (WCED, 1987). Given this premise, some researchers and authors argue that there is no human economic activity that can be completely sustainable, that every business does some damage. However, there are degrees of damage and it makes a difference to do less harm. This stream of literature proposes responsible business rather than sustainable business practices.

Therefore, the consumers of fashion industry are educating themselves about responsible business. It is gaining gradual but noticeable popularity. This has resulted in fashion consumers shifting from fast fashion toward fashion engineered from technology and materials that last longer. Many luxury fashion brands have incorporated these suggestions to foster better methods, create cleaner product lines, and open a channel of communication with their consumers on social and mobile commerce. Adapting to the "conscious consumer" and their environmental sensitivity is in the very near future a key determinant for changing industry dynamics.

The consumption patterns today indicate that businesses and consumers alike are going through what is called an "ethics era." The millennial and Gen Z consumers demand transparency from the companies and brands they associate with. They are making informed purchasing decisions based on the implications of the products in the market, through their entire supply chains. In a world where physical and mental health are of the utmost importance, consumers' decisions on what they eat, the transportation they take for commuting, and the products they use are being highly scrutinized. These "conscious" consumers are also looking beyond themselves, at the environmental and social impacts of their purchasing decisions.

On this note, for the luxury business, the concern about sustainability and responsible business is now mainstream: both brands and consumers can no longer ignore this behavioral aspect of younger customers. This concern has implications on businesses which were peripheral to luxury business and were ignored before. They are the luxury secondhand market, the resale market, the rental market, and the vintage market clustered around the category of pre-owned goods.

Climate Change

Climate change is an immediate threat to various industries and luxury is no exception. The climate change poses at least five types of risk for the luxury industry. Research shows that these could be input risks, physical risks, market risks, stakeholder risks and regulatory risks. It may not be necessarily in that order. That is what circularity is all about. For instance, the input risks can be associated with the availability, quality and cost of raw material. Climate change has impacted habitats on all scales. Overreliance on specific raw materials and reluctance to embrace the new technologically fabricated materials may not ensure a steady flow of supplies. The physical risks can be associated with the risks of security and access to the company's own operations and assets. An example of such a risk could be extreme weather due to climate change. Such an event has the capability to impede the manufacturing operations and disrupt the mobility of humans and goods alike. The market risks can be associated to the change in market preference that can ask the question of who is the product for and what are the questions that the customer is asking. Such changes are necessary to track with every change in the environment. The stakeholder risks entail failure to deliver against stakeholders who care about the climate change. For example, the divestment movement has shown how many stakeholders are holding investment portfolio managers and companies accountable for climate impacts. Investors themselves, a key stakeholder for luxury, are increasingly including climate risk in their decision making by considering metrics such as the Dow Jones Sustainability Index 5 and transparency. The regulatory risks are the risks of changing regulations that result from a rising price on high carbon sources and the energy intensive activities that depend on them. These regulations, though they concern climate primarily, have an effect on the broader regulatory landscape, too, including policies on air quality and on the protection of biodiversity, natural systems, and water. There is a movement from regulators to penalize for nonconformity in regulation but it should move to incentivizing for conformity. It is for sure, and more so after the pandemic, that a sustainable value chain strategy is of great importance if such risks are to be mitigated.

Due to the above risks, the climate change crisis has stirred up major conversations in the fashion industry over the past years and more so since 2015. The fashion industry's impact on the environment accounts for over 10% of carbon emissions and the energy consumption amounts to more than that of the aviation and shipping industries combined. The industry is also infamously known for its poor waste management and reports about 20% of wastewater generated globally. Although it gets complicated to calculate the precise number of emissions produced from a single unit of apparel (from transportation of raw material to final distribution to the consumer), the cyclical and seasonal nature of the fashion industry can be seen as the primary contributor to the problem. Fashion trends come and go, but the environmental damage caused is long-lasting. Thus, there have been several initiatives taken by brands in both the fast-fashion and luxury fashion industries. These initiatives have focused on the sustainable business model that has created some model best practices.

Sustainable Business Model Best Practice for the Luxury Business

More and more discussion is taking place in the realm of best practice that relates to environment, social and governance (ESG) issues. Investors and stakeholders are increasingly interested in transparency that highlights best practice in different ESG issues, such as diversity in the workplace, women in top management teams, gender equality at the workplace, work–health–life balance, and others.

Environmental Best Practice

Securing raw material supplies in an environmentally unstable situation is among the prime concerns. One way is to extract the smallest number of natural resources from the planet. Another way is to reduce transportation, or transportation through waterways or by train and at least by airways. A strong vertically integrated brand has the potential to mitigate such risks due to its total control over the value chain. It has the ability to create a sustainable practice. Most luxury brands already demonstrate strong vertically integrated infrastructure, giving the brands ample control over their supply chain. Those in France, such as LVMH, Hermès, and Chanel, believe in the notion of full control: they would like to control their full value chain and probably are much more advanced to pursue full vertical integration for their entire portfolio of products and brands. On the other hand, Kering group, with mostly Italian brands in its portfolio, although it has strict control over its value chain, is more democratic in working with different suppliers, partners and third-party platforms on sustainability issues.

A shift toward eco-friendly material can be a much-welcomed move into a sustainable business model. Its application has the potential to preserve biodiversity and create a responsible image of the brand. For example, Kering group's support of the Sustainable Cashmere Program allows for regeneration of pasturelands, maintaining healthy Mongolian grasslands, and controlling the proportion of goats and sheep.

Ensuring availability of material without harming the environment is a pressing topic and multiple best practices could be adopted to remain ahead in the game. Innovation with vegan material is one such best practice which has the potential to address multiple concerns of a brand. Some luxury brands have successfully adopted this idea and can be seen in their initiatives. A leading example would be Stella McCartney, which is using a technology called Mylo and is created by Bolt Threats (a breakthrough biotech company). Mylo is a sustainable material that looks and feels remarkably like animal leather and uses mycelium fiber, the underground root structure of mushrooms; it can be produced in days rather than years without the material waste of using animal hides. Stella created Re.Verso, a regenerated cashmere produced from cashmere leftovers from the factories in Italy. The brand also used recycled nylon, ECONYL, which is made from industrial waste such as plastic, synthetic textiles and even fishing nets found in oceans. Other examples are the sustainability practices adopted by Gabriela Hirst, who has joined as the creative director of Chloe, in addition to managing her own namesake brand.

Another way to address the best practice issue is to extend the life cycle of its products and address the second-hand and rental market for luxury as discussed before. Extending the product life cycle can have economic consequences, which may work in favor of the luxury brands and their consumers. The best example in this domain is the jewelry industry, where the life cycle can be extended over generations. For example, the gold can be melted and with it a new piece of jewelry created.

Jewelry production models in the past have consistently received criticism for using toxic pollutants for raw material extraction and inhumane working conditions for the factory workers. Now, though, claiming gold without considering the underlying consequences of the sourcing methods has great potential to take a big toll on luxury brands' reputations.

A luxury brand desiring to position itself as a sustainable brand must understand the overarching purpose of ethical gold. Goldmining produces significant amounts of debris, which includes highly toxic chemicals such as mercury, lead, arsenic and cyanide, which eventually enter into the water cycle. Another shortcoming could be the growing restrictions on goldmining, as can be seen in the case of The

Democratic Republic of Congo (DRC), where goldmining is declared illegal. Anticipating restrictions on future supplies of gold may not seem like an unreasonable assumption for the luxury brands. Combining the adverse effects of goldmining, the possible restraint on gold supplies and finite gold reserves, it can be assumed that rethinking gold supplies and shifting focus toward ethical and recycled gold can bring about a level of sustainability for the brands.

One way of ensuring ethical gold is through recognition of ethical mining practices. "Fairminded certification" is awarded to the brands to identify ethical gold. Some conditions for the certification are: strict working regulations, child labor prohibition, special social development standards, environmental criteria for goldmining, and fixed monthly wages for workers. Other such initiatives are the Swiss Better Gold Association, which is a part of the Fairmined and Fairtrade gold initiatives.

It is interesting to see how luxury brands are taking these issues with great sincerity. For example, the brand Chopard can be seen as an advocate of ethical gold. Since 2018, it has been utilizing 100% ethical gold for the production of watches and jewelry. New York designer Kimberly McDonald is another great example. The designer uses reclaimed gold, recycled diamonds and naturally formed one-of-a-kind geodes handcast in New York.

In the jewelry industry a moot point for sustainability issues is the use of lab-grown diamonds. The hypothesis behind this discussion is whether sustainability is possible when the raw materials are sourced unethically or the source is uncertain. And as a corollary the question of traceability of all stones, especially diamonds, has been a point of concern due to the tricky heritage of DeBeers and mining companies across the world. The answer to this question is a clear negative. The luxury industry thrives on aspirational services and the foundation of such aspirations seem incompatible with unethical practices. On the other hand, unethical practices attract uncertainty, which questions the consistency and coherence of a brand.

In order for brands to weather such uncertainties and unethical practices, shifting focus toward achieving precious gems through technological advancements may sound like a viable strategy. DeBeers, the world's largest diamond company, ventured into the lab-grown diamond market in the year 2018 by launching a product line by the name of Lightbox. With deeper understanding of its consumers, the brands can discover if such practices are alternatives to the natural diamonds or a way to create a different market. Lab-grown diamonds are one such artificially created mineral that has structured and segmented the market. A gem formed through time and discovered from the womb of nature is a lot more than just a beautiful stone. It has a heritage, rarity, legacy, and authenticity. It is timeless. It carries the idea of commitment, credibility, and legitimacy. Can lab-grown diamonds bring about the same emotion? They can be the answer to the question of how brands can become sustainable and ethical. However, it doesn't necessarily replace the natural diamond market and the high jewelry created from them. Segmenting and creating a new market of custom jewelry may legitimize the use of manmade diamonds. The high jewelry brands are careful to consider it as a fashion accessory and not a luxury item.

Brands like KBH Jewels and Courbet prefer to use lab-grown diamonds instead of mined diamonds to not contribute to the detrimental impact that mining has on the environment. Some argue that the energy needed to create lab-grown diamonds can lead to significant carbon pollution if the energy source is not renewable. Also, mined diamonds provide a lot more jobs than lab-grown diamonds. Ultimately, the question of whether lab-grown diamonds will sell depends on the effectiveness of marketing and positioning. Natural diamonds create emotions. It is about the sentiment, the time, the event. The miracle of nature. Lab-grown diamonds are made today. In the laboratory. They will mostly be flawless, better in clarity, cut, and color for every carat compared. It portrays a different value to the younger generation. Purchases could also depend on the type of emotion. To hold value. Mined diamonds will stay relevant for engagement rings, high jewelry, whereas lab-grown diamonds could be acceptable for more occasional or casual use.

Courbet is a young French startup of the new jewelry ecosystem that is built on the use of synthetic diamonds and online sales. The company distinguishes itself from its high-end neighbors through the use of recycled gold and manmade diamonds. With equivalent optical and physical qualities, the synthetic stones manufactured by the young company in the United States and Russia are on average 40% less expensive than mined diamonds. Courbet recently raised €8 million in capital. The Covid-19 crisis allowed the small structure to consolidate and to leverage their 20% share of online sales. Manuel Mallen, founder and president, aims to reach 70% of online sales and €30 million in turnover within 2023. They have plans to invest part of the capital raised to enrich the platform with functionalities based on 3D video and augmented reality. The new digital experience focused on the customer to personalize their purchase and choose a ring in conditions close to a physical store. The brand is betting that the new generations are open to acquiring jewelry online. In Asia and the United States, this is already largely the case. China is also on their radar for expansion, with about nine million weddings a year and at least as many engagements, together with multiple festival occasions throughout the year.

To conclude, the jewelry industry and its glamorous image often overshadow the sustainability supply chain practices. It has its impact on the social, environmental and economic level. The main sustainability issues that the fine jewelry industry faces are the finite aspects of many jewelry raw materials, a lack of traceability, damage to the environment, and unethical production and treatment of people, including health issues. For example, the issues of conflict diamonds, ethical sourcing of silver, gold and platinum as nonrenewable resources are being questioned. While diamonds and gemstones might be created in labs once natural sources are depleted, this is not the case for silver, gold and platinum.

Social Best Practice

As part of an organization-oriented approach, the most fundamental of social best practices can be the creation of a dignified working environment with a focus on the well-being of employees, in which no gender gap exists. A good example of social stewardship is Ermenegildo Zegna. In the early life of the brand, the founder ensured the welfare of the company's wool mill workforce by investing in essential infrastructures such as roads and schools. Another example of social best practice can be noted from the year 2017, when LVMH and Kering group committed to the well-being of all the models associated with promotions and fashion shows.

As part of a market-oriented approach, the brand can project its humanitarian initiatives through philanthropic activities as well as through social movements. With many examples during the pandemic, a noteworthy pre-pandemic example of such a social best practice was demonstrated by the brand Balenciaga in the year 2018. The brand collaborated with the World Food Programme to actively fight against world hunger.

Animal Rights Activism

The reliance on animal farming for exotic skin has consistently attracted criticism for the luxury industry. However, with the growing demand for such products and the idea of supporting third-world countries and their animal farmers by following all the international farming standards, such criticisms were countered. PETA remained at the forefront, with their efforts to convince luxury conglomerates to give up exotic animal-skin based products. The organization found their way into the shareholder's meeting of LVMH and Hermès by buying shares of the respective groups. Such acts were not entirely welcomed by the groups. However, the organization remains active in their effort.

It is worth noting that luxury brands are giving up certain animal-based raw materials, and are actively switching to alternatives. It would not be entirely correct if the credit was only given to animal rights activism. The uncertainty and overreliance on animal-based raw materials were a matter of concern for various brands and hence, such a shift was evident. With brands like Gucci, Prada, Balenciaga, Versace, Valentino giving up fur and Chanel committing to becoming a vegan brand, the drift from animal farming is the new reality.

Some of the major factors contributing to this shift are technological advancements in fabrication, consumer attitude toward animal cruelty–based products, animal rights activism and company-wide sustainability plans.

Conclusion

The analysis above gives us a clear understanding of how luxury and sustainability can coexist and can share compatibility within their business models. The forces shaping the sustainability efforts of luxury brands carry a holistic significance as they touch the three social, environmental and economical pillars of the luxury and fashion ecosystem. Sustainability efforts can be viewed from different points of view. On the one hand, such efforts can be in the form of very specific action; on the other, they can encompass society as a whole. This dilemma of focus creates uncertainty. Forces like climate change are too broad in scope for individual companies to tackle in its entirety. It poses an immediate threat to the industry due to the increasing awareness of a new generation of consumers. It is also a function of the availability of resources that companies can deploy throughout their entire value chain. Another approach is piecemeal: some sustainable efforts can be adhered to, but not all due to the non-viability of the economic model. The country of origin creates this dilemma. If the raw materials are sourced from all over the globe— manufactured in the country of origin, packed, and shipped all across the globe—the business model already has a built-in carbon footprint that is difficult to remove in totality.

Another force of great significance is the circular economy. Luxury brands are already battling against counterfeit products and may have to heed the third-party platforms that are engaged in the second-hand and rental businesses. One way of addressing the issue is to integrate a product's second life into the business model and fully or partially control the second-hand and rental markets. Kering and Richemont are experimenting with this business model. The other is to ignore that second-hand and renting business like before. LVMH, Chanel, and Hermès have taken this option for the short term. But one must not forget, going by the changing behavior of consumers during the pandemic, organizing second-hand and renting businesses is an opportunity. For the industry to maximize its profitability and adhere to controlling the value chain, it may want to explore the concept of the circular economy invoking singularity in the business model. Overall, a holistic sustainable business model in the luxury business must address issues on three broad fronts: social, environmental and economical.

While the luxury fashion industry, though late, is slowly adapting to become a socially responsible industry, there are still debates on multiple fronts. For example, after adhering to most stringent ways of sourcing natural materials such as cotton, cashmere, and linen, converting to eco-friendly materials does not necessarily imply that companies are entirely sustainable in their production process. They could still require large amounts of water, dye, and transport. Thus, the carbon footprint of the industry may reduce but for all practical purposes will never become nil. However, the industry's efforts to innovate and create low-impact fabrics and processes are an inspiring future to look forward to. Another issue that has been repeatedly discussed is about greenwashing. Transparency here is the key issue. Several companies have already been accused of only carrying "sustainable" tags but actually providing misleading information about how they are eco-friendly. "Are these brands really in control of their whole value chain?" is a question often put. Along similar lines, what should the brand communicate and what not? Historically, brands have differed in the way they communicated their sustainability practices. It used to be common practice not to communicate supply chain activities to clients. The big brands did not need to as they were highly profitable, with double-digit margins and demand exceeding supply. The smaller brands were not in total control of their supply chain and more often than not depended on intermediaries and partners. However, in a global battle against climate change, and an environment where the issue of sustainability is more important than ever, brands can use their influence to shape consumption patterns. If brands avoid discussing sustainability, the consumer is left unaware and uninformed. Not being transparent with clients could eventually create a barrier to enabling responsible consumption practices. While leading luxury brands tend to keep their communication about sustainability very discreet, there are many new brands in the sector that define themselves as sustainable brands. The concept of "sustainable brands" is thus misleading in some sense. It more often than not harms the sustainability efforts of the entire industry. Another debatable topic is which way the brand should go. Should it go all the way to adhere to what the customer wants? Some opine that it may dilute the essence, the DNA, and the heritage of the brand. The aspirations on which the brand's storytelling has been built through decades may be at risk. There are conflicting opinions on losing the heritage and dream factor due to growing demand for what the "conscious" consumer desires. Should the luxury brand listen to the customer and get embroiled in the technicalities of sustainability or provide their customer with their heritage, their savoire-faire, their story, create the dream and let the customer follow, as they have been doing for generations?

Chapter 13

New Markets and the Future

D ata from 2000–2019 suggest that luxury goods are no longer an exclusive attribute of Western societies such as France and Italy. This is corroborated by World Bank Data on the growth of gross domestic product (GDP) and purchasing power parity (PPP), which shows how emerging economies are fast gaining importance as luxury markets. Following in China's footsteps, such economies now account for roughly 60% of worldwide luxury spending. Sensing high growth opportunities, luxury companies had heavily invested in the decade of 2010–2019 in brand-awareness campaigns and opening flagship stores in these promising markets. There was a race to be the first to conquer these new frontier markets. This radical evolution of the global luxury map was part of a wider shift in the industry. The tectonic shift of the global luxury map enabled the brands to discover the ever-changing tastes and preferences of new consumers in these frontier markets. These new consumption trends became more and more important as these markets now influence the major part of the business. The heritage brands focused their efforts on appealing to a young, tech-savvy clientele and thus underwent decisive rebranding-focused campaigns through social and mobile commerce. The health crisis from 2020 opened the eyes of the brands as the global economic scenario threatened the survival of long-lasting luxury icons by compromising the traditional retail experience. The future of established, and not-so-established, brands lies in the expansion of untapped markets and new, agile distribution models while reimagining democratization through digitization in an otherwise strongly consolidated industry.

A Consolidated Industry

The luxury industry is unique and cannot be compared with any other. Its propensity to rebound and grow from strength to strength after each crisis has been well documented. The luxury market has represented an important driver of GDP, especially for Europe. By 2024, personal and experiential luxury alone was estimated to be a €1,1260 billion market—a significant increase from €845 billion in 2015. The total of luxury consumers was estimated to reach 496 million by 2024. To a unique industry there are unique challenges which may explain the high degree of consolidation in certain countries of origin that are linked to the current tourism industry. The luxury sector records some of the highest profitability margins among mature economic segments, and has proven to be quite resilient to global economic downturns in the past, as explained in Chapter 1. As a further indication, pre-pandemic the LVMH group had reported a gross margin of 66% and an operating margin of up to 21.4% (2019). For this reason, leading luxury groups have remained extremely attractive for investors. In 2020, European brands traded at 70% on the MSCI index. This unfaltering attractivity had arguably two origins. The first is the premium that consumers are ready to pay for a unique, status-enhancing product, and the second the extremely high barrier to entry in this sector for newcomer brands with limited heritage.

For this high barrier to entry, this very lucrative pie is still shared by a limited number of dominant players and well-established iconic brands. Despite the acceleration of the worldwide spread of luxury consumption and the sustained standards of performance of the industry, examples of successful market entry for newcomers remain scarce. This phenomenon can be explained by the core attributes of a luxury brand—status and heritage. As the often-called "pope of luxury," Bernard Arnault, founder and president of the LVMH group, had declared once, "star brands" share the fact that they are "timeless, modern, fast-growing and highly profitable." This timelessness is precisely one of the reasons that explains why top-selling brands are often more than a century old, and why brand image and reputation is so hard to build from scratch.

As a result, old European countries such as France, Switzerland or Italy, reputed for their refined culture and manufacturing "know-how," control seven of the top 10 bestselling luxury groups in the world. It is worth mentioning that other regions have specialized in certain luxury activities with some degree of success, such as Southeast Asia and South Africa for the jewelry market (DeBeers, Chow Tai Fook), the United Kingdom for car manufacturing (Aston Martin, Jaguar), or the United States for personal affordable luxury items (Coach, Michael Kors). This geographic concentration of the industry has further repercussions on the production and sourcing of luxury items. In 2019, research reports mentioned that "Made in Italy" represented 29% of personal luxury items produced worldwide, ahead of "Made in France" with 21%. By comparison, China, which has become the "factory of the world" in almost any other manufacturing market, only accounted for 5% of the global supply of luxury goods.

The Frontier Markets

The Paradox of Impermanence

In Japan, the old gardens of Kyoto have existed for centuries, but change colors every season and must be cared for every day. To further bring us the same emotions, impermanence must be fully accepted. Everything changes all the time. The philosopher Heraclitus said this a long time ago. Despite this, we tend to see stability as the norm and change as the exception. Yet the world evolves faster than ever. To live in this world serenely, we need to embrace impermanence. Most of our management concepts assume stability, but app stores have fully integrated constant changes. Apps evolve all the time and the updates are pushed in continuum, letting us update when we are ready or forcing them when necessary. One of the biggest breakthroughs in modern technology is based on an old principle of impermanence.

— **Cyrille Vigneron, CEO, Cartier**

China: The Growth Engine

I don't see many reasons that would prevent Chinese consumers from representing a larger portion of the luxury goods market in five years. . .. The luxury market has become dependent on China. If the Chinese sneeze, the luxury sector gets pneumonia.

—**Luca Solca, senior research analyst of global luxury goods at Bernstein[1]**

The luxury industry in China grew in parallel with the country's economy in the first two decades of the millennium. The most populated country in the world represented the largest market for luxury in the world after surpassing the US. It has grown at a compound annual growth rate (CAGR) of 16.5% from 2016 to 2020.[2] China's share in the global personal luxury market increased from 19% in 2012 to 35% in 2020 and reports from consulting practices predicted it to make up 50% of all luxury purchases globally by 2025.

LVMH and Kering entered the country in the late 1990s and other luxury brands followed. The key players across all segments have entered the Chinese market through holdings in the shopping hubs of Hong Kong and Shanghai. Initially the companies focused on Tier-1 cities and more influential demographics, but as incomes in mainland China have

---

[1]https://jingdaily.com/china-luxury-spending-stalls-travel-policy/.
[2]MarketLine Industry Profiles.

caught up, Tier-2 cities are slowly becoming the next prime target for the luxury companies. This strong expansion and continuous opening of stores was halted by the pandemic and the focus shifted to improving the quality of existing outlets and increasing penetration across digital channels.

In keeping up pace from the supply side, China's demand for luxury goods is by far the highest in the world. The increase in the demand for luxury goods in the Chinese market can be attributed to the fact that this market was previously isolated and unconsidered. When it was embraced and targeted by the luxury industry, it experienced exponential growth. This demand is fueled majorly by the aspirational middle class and millennials (the four-two-one generation, with four grandparents, parents and a single child), who have considerably higher wealth than the previous generations. They perceive luxury goods as reflective of their social status. Multibrand conglomerates enjoy high sales due to the creation of an illusion of choice. Ten percent of the country now has wealth between 100,000 USD to 1 million USD and there are 390 billionaires.[3] The demand for luxury goods can be easily correlated with economic prosperity on an individual level.

This astonishing importance of China, especially from 2014 to 2020 and with its V-shaped rebound of 2021, is of increasing importance to the luxury world. It was even more true as China recovered at full steam from the pandemic, while Western economies struggled to relaunch. Luxury purchases made online increased throughout the crisis and the online channel could represent up to 30% of China's market by 2025.[4] Their purchasing power parity (PPP) is on the rise and sooner or later most Chinese in mainland China will be able to buy luxury goods on demand. It is very premature to assume that China could become the largest internal market for luxury brands, as soon it commands the largest market by size, overtaking the USA. With China's high Gini coefficient,

---

[3] Bain-Altagamma luxury report 2020.
[4] It is predicted by the research reports from consulting companies that Mainland China will account for 28% of the luxury goods market, up from 11% in 2019. Online channels have achieved double-digit growth in 2019, and will continue to gain share and occupy 30% of the market by 2025. The younger generation (Gens Y and Z) will drive most of the luxury goods market.

the wealthy will become even wealthier, and they will increasingly seek not only *real authentic value* from luxury brands but also the ability to *command their choices* and even grow local brands. In this scenario, the next question that will be evident is how to keep on growing in China. How to access the new generation, whose values are evolving. How luxury brands can keep up with the change. Is there a need to change their European values over time and with specific localization? How should this change be communicated through the digital channel, as more and more of the population becomes digitally savvy?

According to research reports,[5] Chinese citizens born in the 1980s contributed to 55% of turnover, compared to 23% of those born in the 1990s. These two groups have disposable income that made them ideal for targeting by luxury goods. They contributed to approximately 60% growth in total spending within the country. It has been seen that Generation Y or Millennials pay more attention to personal experiences and the habit of "showing off," while Baby Boomers who have consumed luxury goods are also beginning to show an interest in "experience."[6] It may be expected that the positive momentum of experiential luxury goods will continue, but this may weaken during the initial post-pandemic period in the short term as consumer interest temporarily returns to physical goods. As inequality grows, the second generation of China's ultra-rich class would definitely avoid conspicuous consumption as an object. The new "fuerdai"[7] class is less inclined to signal status and wealth and prefers to "play the low-profile card." The new generation of luxury consumers is college-educated, modern, conscious about environmental and social issues, and less dependent on transitory trends. It thus appears that the Chinese market has novel characteristics, and should push brands to reevaluate their strategies for the twenty-first century. With a growing wealthy middle class and a booming industrial power, the International Monetary Fund has already considered

---

[5]Bain 2020, BCG 2020, Mckinsey 2020, Deloitte 2020.
[6]The Silent Generation (born 1928–1945); Baby Boomers (born 1945–1965); Generations X (born 1965–1979); Y/Millennials (born 1980–1996); Z (born 1997–2009); and Alpha (born 2010–2024).
[7]https://jingdaily.com/luxury-wealthy-chinese-millennials/.

that China became the world's new economic powerhouse. In addition, Chinese brands are making the competition harder.

India: The Sleeping Giant

> *The land of dreams and romance, of fabulous wealth and fabulous poverty, of splendor and rags, of palaces and hovels, of famine and pestilence, of genii and giants and Aladdin lamps, of tigers and elephants, the cobra and the jungle, the country of a hundred nations and a hundred tongues, of a thousand religions and two million gods, cradle of the human race, birthplace of human speech, mother of history, grandmother of legend, great-grandmother of traditions, whose yesterdays bear date with the moldering antiquities for the rest of nations—the one sole country under the sun that is endowed with an imperishable interest for alien prince and alien peasant, for lettered and ignorant, wise and fool, rich and poor, bond and free, the one land that all men desire to see, and having seen once, by even a glimpse, would not give that glimpse for the shows of all the rest of the world combined.*
>
> **—Mark Twain's description of India**

India has historically been a country rich in culture with an outstanding heritage, but a majority of the population has lived in desperate poverty due to the colonial regime of Great Britain. However, currently the country is going through a significant transformation in terms of the amount of wealth that is being created.

Historically, India was a rather socialist country due to its agrarian roots. The country opened to foreign investment in 1991 but policies have not evolved as predicted due to a complex bureaucracy and regulations. The country has not been receptive to luxury and has continued to impose high import tariffs on luxury goods. Furthermore, the political climate of India was controversial in the decade to 2020, with radical governmental policies which had a negative impact on the growth rates due to poor execution. Recent interventions, such as demonetization and the introduction of a goods and services tax (GST), further impeded the number of potential luxury consumers in the short- to medium-term, who had the propensity to use cash or black money to provide gifts. Geopolitical tensions with its neighbors China and Pakistan added to India's uncertainties about international trade policy. Certain measures, such as increasing ATM cash withdrawal limits, may help increase the sales of accessories.

Due to its wealth generation, the luxury goods market in India has shown potential. It exhibited a growth rate of 25–30% per annum in the first two decades of the millennium. But it has not exactly developed proportionally to the other emerging markets in Asia. Foreign luxury goods had to overcome critical challenges due to India's cultural diversity, economic inequality, infrastructure challenges, and the constrained rise of a price-sensitive middle class. For the above four broad reasons, distribution of luxury goods has been largely concentrated in the metropolitan cities, New Delhi, Mumbai, Hyderabad, and Bangalore. With the infrastructure development of the 2010s, stores that had existed only in five-star hotels are now (2021) in specialized luxury retail malls, such as the DLF Emporio mall in New Delhi, the Palladium in Mumbai, the UB City mall in Bangalore and the Quest mall in Kolkata.

Though inequality is rising in India, middle-class incomes have steadily risen. India also has the most rapidly growing number of high-net-worth individuals in the world. Because of a lack of supporting infrastructure, the outreach to Tier-2 and -3 cities has been low but luxury consumption has increased. Despite the low outreach and accessibility, 44% of the luxury industry's revenue can be traced back to Tier-2 cities and townships. Despite a few attempts by luxury brands to democratize and localize their offerings by collaborating with Indian designers such as Sabyasachi Mukherjee, to appeal to the reluctant Baby Boomers, the industry still has not seen growth as experienced in China and other Asian countries. One reason for this outcome is that traditional handicrafts, artisans, and Indian designers provide an alternative to foreign couture labels. Traditionally, the Indian consumer has chosen to spend on "hard luxury" goods, such as watches, jewelry and automobiles, which constituted about a third of the total revenue of the industry. This is due to changing demographics—young people are increasingly less conservative: experiential luxury segments such as fine dining, travel, and wine & spirits have reported increasing sales. Luxury beauty, skincare, and prestige fragrances have been the largest growth drivers of revenue in the industry.

Despite these positive figures, India remains one of the toughest luxury markets in the world, mainly because of the lack of suitable luxury retail spaces. There are multiple drawbacks to opening a luxury store in India. The country's largest cities lack proper street retail locations or the ability to create shopping districts within an appropriate environment. Luxury retail development is impeded by less than desirable surrounding neighborhoods, cleanliness, and security, which don't show signs of improvement in the near term. One of the reasons that organized retail has not taken off is due to the previous regulations on retail ownership, which has considerably delayed the penetration of luxury companies in India. For example, Tiffany still does not have a store in India, and Louis Vuitton—the first entrant in this market and an arguable benchmark in the case of luxury retail—has six points of sale that are not even located at street level but within upscale hotels or luxury malls. As a matter of fact, Hermès is currently the only luxury brand in the country to have a stand-alone store at street level, following its 2011 opening in Horniman Circle, Mumbai.

Even though society is largely patriarchal, the Indian woman is increasingly becoming a top priority for luxury brands as they are driving the growth of the luxury industry through skincare and cosmetics purchases. With the repealing of homophobic laws, the LGBTQ community is no longer taboo and social stigma around homosexuality has reduced, leading to more gender-neutral offerings in clothing as well as makeup. This has seen the rise of "seenagers" (senior teenagers) in metropolitan cities, who are highly influenced by western media, informed about luxury brands, and finally are able to afford and access them.

If a luxury brand decides to embark on significantly increasing its brand exposure in India, one of the keys to success is to properly understand consumers' needs and how they differ from those in developed countries. It is common knowledge that there is a wide disparity in style between the Indian community and that of developed nations. For example, it is widely known that Indian women wear saris to formal events and therefore the luxury ready-to-wear market has yet to be developed. Another peculiarity that sets India apart from other emerging markets is its huge cultural legacy in clothing, jewelry, and accessories, which dates back centuries. More and more luxury brands have recognized the importance of creating Indian-inspired items, such as limited collections to show connectivity with the taste and lifestyle of the locals. To cater to such local tastes and preferences, Hermès has created a limited-edition collection of saris made in France that will be exclusively available in India. Bottega Veneta launched its limited edition "Knot India" clutch, which blends conventional embroidery with a signature Bottega weave and has "India" embossed on a sterling plate inside, just below "Made in Italy." Italian luxury men's fashion brand Canali has designed a *bandhgala* (closed-neck) jacket specifically for the Indian market, inspired by jackets worn by India's first Prime Minister, Jawaharlal Nehru. However, this may change in the future with the influence of Western culture.

India is notorious for a lack of supporting infrastructure and institutional voids and that's one of the main reasons most foreign companies hesitate to invest in the Indian market despite its huge potential. Currently, in the early 2020s, Narendra Modi's government is trying to bridge this gap through policies and initiatives which improve the ease of doing business and position India as a manufacturing hub of the world (especially for companies looking to switch base and develop contingencies after a catastrophic supply chain bottling in 2020 due to the pandemic in China). The 15% rise in Internet penetration and increased accessibility can be attributed to Reliance Industries and its rock-bottom rates of "Jio" data bundles with highly affordable and functional smartphones by Chinese manufacturers such as Xiaomi. This has implications for the luxury industry and could explain the paradox of low visibility but high sales in Tier-2 cities.

Showing respect and understanding of the local culture is important also for those foreign luxury jewelry brands that want to succeed in this country. India has a long tradition in high-end jewelry, especially gold and diamonds, and emphasizing the use of local precious metals and stones could be an additional factor to break through in this market. There is no doubt that India has its own unique set of challenges. However, given the country's rapid growth in the luxury market, the inflexion point is not far off and chances are that the initial time and effort required to establish a brand will pay off in the near future. Can such a strong heritage in so many luxury product categories contribute to the beginning of an era of homegrown Indian luxury brands? Patrizio Bertelli, Chairman and CEO of Prada Group, commented in 2004, "India is potentially interesting for us, not now, but in the long term. You need to look 50 or 100 years into the future."[8] After 17 years, this is still true.

South Korea: The Promising Frontier

The luxury industry in South Korea has exhibited resilience in fighting off the financial crisis of the late 1990s and bouncing back in the decade up to 2021. Consequently, this market represents one of the three pillars of luxury in Asia. The presence of luxury brands in the primary channel—i.e., department stores—has grown from 20 to over 300 in the last decade. The luxury market grew by rates between 15 and 20% consistently from 2010 to 2020, one of the highest in the world and second only to China. The South Korean consumer is emotion-driven and successful luxury brands in the market exhibited two characteristics: great after-sales service and enhanced customer relationship management practices. Compared to its western counterparts, where the sale of clothing and accessories had shrunk, South Korea continued to be one of the driving cultural forces behind the boom of the cosmetics and fragrances segment due to the following reasons.

The South Korean government has been extremely pro-business since the country adopted a more capitalistic market structure much earlier than its neighbors, such as Vietnam. The country is culturally and politically very similar to Japan, which has historically been one of the most receptive to luxury goods. The country had benefited from being a part of free-trade deals and export-oriented strategy. The government had also been known to launch initiatives which augment the cultural dimension of the country, by supporting cinema, couture and other art forms.

The South Korean economy has been booming at a steady pace and disposable incomes have risen, which has had a direct impact on the sale of aspirational products. The country is consistently ranked among the top-ten Asian countries with ultra-high-net-worth individuals.

South Koreans celebrate luxury and do not view it as distasteful. There is high peer pressure in South Korea to conform with neighbors.

---

[8] International Herald Tribune Conference, November 20, 2004.

This pressure is a growth driver for the luxury market because luxury goods reflect social status. Previously, middle-aged women were the highest spending segment, but lately the younger Generation Z, whose parents are first-generation millionaires, has become the focus for luxury brands. Korean culture exerts great influence regionally as well as globally. The progressive culture doesn't have any taboos: men shop and male K-Pop stars have been huge cultural influencers globally, in cosmetics as well as fashion.

South Korea also boasts a highly educated society and the technological infrastructure is advanced and on a par with western markets. Also, South Korea has one of the highest internet penetration rates in the world (96%) and thus represents a potential for proponents of M-commerce looking to expand their digital and e-commerce stories. Extremely innovative and functional dermatological formulations have been the reason of the success of K-beauty in its golden age.

South Korea set an example for the world by handling the coronavirus outbreak in the most efficient way possible without imposing any lockdowns and with an end-to-end contact tracing capability. Social distancing measures adopted throughout the country led to a decrease in footfall at the country's primary luxury channel, department stores. While manufacturing and logistical activities did not halt, due to a drastic reduction in inbound tourism, duty-free sales reduced by 95%, as in most countries. South Korean consumers are risk-averse, though, and retained their cash savings to weather the financial impact of the pandemic. The rebound started in late 2020, and was attributed to revenge spending, whereby consumers who could not spend due to the pandemic came out in full force to spend and consume. It was also attributed to wedding season sales as couples splurged heavily due to disposable cash from canceled honeymoons and events. The wealth of millionaires has largely been unaffected. However, for ultra-high-end customers the most influential factors of luxury purchases have changed from momentary exclusivity to durability and quality. South Korea's millennials have been the dominant segment: their luxury goods purchases have increased sevenfold between 2010 and 2020. Online channels have registered double-digit increase in sales and digital channel expansion will be a central tenet of the strategy of all luxury conglomerates. The Korean populace has been very compliant to guidelines and has thus emerged as the fastest recovering economy after China and remains the most promising Asian market after China in the short to medium term.

Middle-East: A New Hub for "Big Spenders"

The hubs of Dubai, Abu-Dhabi, Doha, and now Riyadh have transformed themselves as destinations for tourism. Spending a few days there is enough to understand the scale of the ambition of Middle-Eastern governments to grow the cities of tomorrow. With skyscrapers flourishing from the ground and paradise leisure resorts in the region, these countries have undergone, and are still undergoing, a transformation from resource-based, closed economies to international hubs for the tertiary sector. During the pandemic they were among the first countries to vaccinate and open for business. Within these cities, the concentration of extremely wealthy individuals is almost unparalleled. In 2020, the standard Saudi Arabian consumer spent six times more than the Chinese consumer's average basket for luxury goods. The growth of the luxury sector is estimated by Bain to remain at 5% in the region, with Dubai accounting for about a third of the turnover. The authorities have opened their gates to many foreign luxury brands, with advantageous tax regimes. In addition, the recent trend toward female emancipation is expected to guarantee prosperous days for the local luxury industry.

Africa: The Untapped Continent

If there is one region that represents the future of the world economy, it is Africa. With the sub-Saharan population expected to double by 2050, it is already the main attraction for many industries. But luxury leaders remain hesitant to address this market just yet. While Maghreb economies and South Africa already host some luxury brands, for their wealthy elites the rest of the continent still remains a longstanding promise. However, the landscape is changing surprisingly fast. For instance, French champagne producers realized way back in 2014 that Lagos, one of the world's most vibrant cities, had become one of the top 20 champagne markets in the world, and the fastest-growing. Moreover, there is a deep underlying connection between luxury and the African continent. Some of the tribal crafts, arts and styles have become cornerstone inspirations for Western designers over the past century. For millennials, African civilizations have developed a real affinity with working on precious materials (gemstones, metals) and have stood out for their authentic artisanship. In this sense, we are seeing the emergence of an authentic African movement called "Luxe Ubuntu," which goes back to the core inspirations of African styles.

The solution to long-term growth also necessitates searching for other promising markets. Many economies show promise, or at least some promise, that the luxury industry could expand rapidly in the coming years. They may succeed or fail. For example, who would have thought Mongolia would be the next frontier market? Back in 2009, Yves Carcelles did. The then-CEO of the iconic brand came across numerous LV handbags on the arms of elegant ladies when he visited the capital, Ulan Bator. A few months later, Louis Vuitton opened the first true luxury store in the city center, quickly followed by Ermenegildo Zegna. The expectation was that the country was about to enter a period of exceptional growth, driven by the exploitation of its natural resources. And indeed, the country's GDP went up by 18% in 2011 following the flourishing rise of the mining industry. For a few years, Louis Vuitton enjoyed their leading position there. With this early move, they had imprinted their image into the customer's mind and they were starting to create strong loyalty. However, this risk did not pay off in the long run. In 2016, Mongolia entered a severe economic crisis. Moreover, the logistics for LV's distribution network in the remote capital were not worth the investment. Louis Vuitton closed its store in July 2017. The key takeaway is, although first-mover advantage gives a real competitive edge, the macroeconomic fundamentals must be strong enough to support such a high-value industry as personal luxury goods. A contrasting example would be Porsche in South Africa. Despite Covid-19, luxury car manufacturers performed rather well. Due to sales by Mercedes-Benz, Tesla and Toyota, US luxury-car sales grew by 44.3% in 2020, compared to the 40% growth in the same period a year before. The automotive industry in South Africa has long remained relatively underdeveloped. In the 1960s, General Motors owned around 70% of the automotive industry; but as the country's economy bloomed, Porsche saw an opportunity. The German manufacturer entered the market in 1952, becoming the first European luxury car brand to set foot in Africa. With this move, Porsche started to strengthen its consumer base, and ensured a market leadership position by exporting new models at the same time as they came out in Europe. As a result, the company has remained to this day an iconic brand in SA, the Porsche Cayenne Turbo being the most popular premium SUV in the country. The brand went further in 2008: it opened its biggest car dealership in the world in Johannesburg, at almost 20,000 square meters. The center is equipped with a state-of-the-art customization workshop, as well as a private test track. It shows that one of the keys to ensuring success in emerging markets is cultural awareness, but also bringing the same level of experience to new consumers as in older, richer markets, a strategy that is too often overlooked by industry leaders.

An important point to note is that the average customer in these regions is very different to those in traditional luxury markets. Scholars have defined these new customers with the term HENRYs (High-Earners-Not-Rich-Yet), young people who earn between $100k and $250k per year and are likely to become wealthy clients in the future. Although they do not individually spend as much on luxury as the super-rich, they represent a substantial volume opportunity. They often respond very well to targeted marketing.

The Pandemic Aftermath

Luxury has been a golden business since 1995, with big groups showing double-digit growth year after year. For decades, the luxury industry has been synonymous with sustained growth, exceptional margins and resilience to economic cycles. Only the sky seemed to be the limit. Who could have anticipated the stock market success of Prada, LVMH, Kering, and Richemont, and then the fall, and rebound almost immediately, during and after the pandemic?

The 2008 global crisis unfolding had reinforced the common belief that luxury brands were relatively immune to financial recessions, at least in comparison to premium (but non-luxury) retail segments. Even during the years of recession in 2009 and 2011 most luxury companies rebounded with an annual growth of between 10% and 20%, sometimes even more. However, these figures declined overall in 2013 due to a strong euro and a decrease in real consumption. Some resisted decline more than others. So why not after the pandemic of 2020? There is hope.

Early analysis of Covid-19's impact tells a totally different story. It was forecast that global luxury revenues would fall to between 25% and 40% by the end of 2020. For China, South Korea, and Japan it was not so bad as they were able to turn the situation around. On average the impact in 2020 was closer to 15–20% across sectors. The reasons for this shock were mirroring the factors that used to make the strength of the sector. It was tourism. Shopping while traveling came to a brutal stop; the all-important in-store experience disappeared for most of the year and consumers' willingness to pay for luxury in these challenging times decreased overall.

The future is positive, though not as before. Buoyed by a burgeoning middle class in emerging markets across China, Asia Pacific, and Africa, luxury goods sales were close to €281 billion (about $310 billion) in 2020, down from $320 billion worldwide in 2013. The reason was the health crisis that the pandemic brought worldwide. The growth engines in the last five years were Gucci, LV, Chanel, Hermès, Sephora, Dior, and Bottega Veneta for the personal luxury goods industry. Gucci, like Louis Vuitton, was pushing for sales of non-logo products while accelerating sales of expensive leather bags—in four years Gucci bought 60% of the turnover of Kering Group, which accounted for 80% of their profit. It is remarkable that both Louis Vuitton and Gucci are now moving in a new direction, with more expensive products, upgrading their quality to place themselves at the top of the luxury market, especially with accessories catering to Gen Z and the HENRYs.

This is in line with the policy of extremely high quality and a staggering price tag that for many years has proven successful for brands such as Hermès, Chanel, and Bottega Veneta. Bottega Veneta was one of the brands that outperformed all other brands during the pandemic of 2020 and reported a growth of about 3.7%, compared to Gucci, which was down by 22.7%, Yves Saint Laurent, whose revenues fell 14.9%, and other Houses that decreased by 10.1% on a comparable year-on-year basis.

Brands did everything possible to adapt. There was immediate development of click & collect measures, e-commerce sales, and sanitary measures in stores. But the crucial customer link, in this highly experiential industry, was drastically weakened as travel came to a standstill. For example, in Paris before the pandemic, the four main fashion weeks brought roughly €1.2 billion per year to the brands and local authorities. In 2020, the city tried to organize a reduced version of the Fall Fashion Week, but it failed to get the expected momentum and received some backlash. The restrictions of movement, combined with a lingering fear to go in to public spaces, meant that 2020 was particularly tough on high-end restaurants, hotels and bars, which led to lower opportunities for cross-selling products such as fine wine or travel accessories.

All was not looking desperate, as companies took to engage in one-to-one customer relationships on social media. With advice from the sales staff in individual markets, clients moved toward spending on luxury goods through e-commerce sites and platforms. Moreover, e-commerce was a chance to acquire new customers who were browsing from their homes. The eagerness with which consumers flooded in the stores after periods of quarantine also exhibited the strong resilience of the sector. Many brands had used these opportunities to strengthen their customer loyalty programs, call their clients, rebrand their websites, like Louboutin in Paris, who more than fully recovered from 2021 by showing a 5% year-on-year growth. It also raised capital from Exor NV, the holding company of Italy's billionaire Agnelli family, which acquired a 24% stake in Christian Louboutin for 541 million euros ($642 million), valuing the famous maker of sky-high red soles at 2.3 billion euros.

It was one crisis, but it had multiple consequences, both at the industry level and geographically. There was *hyper-polarization*. It meant that different subsectors and related industries were affected to different extents. A closer look at the market segmentation revealed that luxury shoes, beauty products, and leather accessories had better chances to rebound after the pandemic. It was because historically these categories of goods had established a better performance on digital channels and were not prone to follow seasonal purchase patterns. On the other hand, hard luxury with more "unique" or "experiential" products, such as jewelry and luxury watches, was predicted to have a tougher time to recover. For such items, the purchase decision was usually made in-store after fitting and trial of alternatives. In the same vein, different countries exhibited different responses to the sanitary situation. For example, in countries in Asia, especially China, South Korea, Vietnam, Singapore, and others, the Middle East, Israel, the UK and the US, the rebound was much faster that in continental Europe, which was heavily dependent on tourism.

To summarize, some of the immediate trends that could have been foreseen were:

The necessity to help governments during the pandemic became paramount. Being from the cultural industry it was important to stay relevant to customers and increase corporate social responsibility by actively participating in epidemic prevention actions. For example, LVMH donated 2.2 million USD to Red Cross in China and promised 40 million masks for France while converting production lines into hydroalcoholic gel production. Hermès donated 20 million euros to Assistance Publique—Hopitaux de Paris, and produced over 31,000 masks early in 2020. Through the "Coach Foundation," the Tapestry Inc. group distributed over 3 million USD to small business owners in the United States. Kering donated funds to the NAACP to support the Black Lives Matter movement together with €2 million to medical and health institutions in some Italian regions, such as Lombardy, Veneto and Tuscany, a ¥5 million donation to the Red Cross Foundation in Hebei Province, China, and Prada donated 1.1 million euros to Italian medical workers.

Local became king. Without travel, all brands focused on catering to their local markets, with China leading the way. Stores in Europe, with no tourists, were instructed to reconnect to their local customers, gathering a wealth of data and renewed connections—advantages that would continue even as international travel resumes. Before, brands had not kept track of whom they were selling to; they were relying on tourists. It helped that Japan and China, the second- and third-largest luxury markets by sales, recovered quickly from the virus, and the rise of "revenge buying" (shopping sprees driven by pent-up demand during lockdown) and "reunion dressing" in China increased purchases. For example, it was reported that at Hermès' second-biggest boutique in Guangzhou, China, the sales volume broke through 2.7 million USD for a single day. In the same period, it was also reported that for Louis Vuitton sales in mainland China grew by 50%. The US luxury market also proved surprisingly resilient. With stock indices reaching record highs and fewer opportunities to spend on international travel, restaurants and spas, the wealthy shopped with renewed interest for handbags, fine jewelry and cashmere tracksuits. Thus, expansion of the main flagships in China, and the opening of additional locations in less populous cities, is bound to occur.

Logos could be back. Logos had been conspicuous during the previous crisis of 2011. There was a guilt factor. After prosperity based on the proliferation of logos and visible ornaments (as evidenced by the success of Louis Vuitton), it seemed that luxury might once again focus on rarity—the founding principle of its value. Designers such as Virgil Abloh, Jacquemus, and Olivier Rousteing embodied this new rarity, reconciling the modernity and authenticity of their houses and building the loyalty of young people to luxury fashion through capsule collections. Yet, this new modernity differs between Western and Eastern markets. It seems that, after surviving this pandemic, consumers may be flaunting their logos to reward themselves to increase their self-image and confidence. Chinese consumers still prefer logos and other visible adornments and this polarization may remain.

Benefit of size. The luxury goods industry has proved its ability to rebound time and time again. However, some brands will become stronger after the crisis and some will struggle. The difference depends to a large extent on whether the company can deal with short-term challenges while focusing on the future and planning for the long term. The multibrand conglomerates which were already increasing their market share at the cost of the smaller players, through the integration of their value chain, may capture more market share with their deep pockets and ability to renegotiate. That will make things tougher for independent, family-owned houses—some of which are likely to be put up for sale.

M&A is predicted to intensify. Baron Rothschild, an eighteenth-century member of the Rothschild banking family, commented that "the best time to buy is when there's blood in the streets." For the past 10 years, European luxury brands and private equity firms have been vying for attractive acquisition targets, and American fashion groups and Middle Eastern investors have joined them in their search. After the outbreak of the epidemic, some of these acquirers (especially those outside the luxury goods industry) may realize that they do not have the core capabilities and patience to cultivate these high-potential brands, so they intend to sell these assets. Therefore, acquisitions that were once extremely expensive may become more "affordable" after the epidemic.

This situation is expected to promote further integration of the industry and even spawn new luxury goods groups. For example, right in the middle of the pandemic, VF Corp agreed to acquire streetwear brand Supreme for $2 billion, Moncler took a majority stake in rival Stone Island, Exor N.V. took a stake in Shang Xia and Louboutin, and LVMH completed its acquisition of Tiffany. Oncoming questions to ponder would be whether Kering and Richemont will merge to compete with LVMH. What about Chanel and Armani, as their owners approach their long-awaited retirements?

The department store has changed forever. Prior to the pandemic, tailoring was enjoying a comeback, steadily replacing hoodies, track bottoms and other streetwear-inflected designs on catwalks and on garment rails. A year of mostly working from home has changed all of that. Department store buyers are investing in "soft tailoring" for the future as seen at MaxMara's SS21 show; Prada's SS21 men's collection offered a timely take on "waist-up dressing."

Adaptation in fashion shows without a live audience for a period of time. Innovation in fashion shows, live streaming and digital streaming of fashion shows will somehow be the new norm for the initial years until people are ready to travel without fear. Travel restrictions and social-distancing rules forced fashion houses to rethink the traditional catwalk show in 2020. For example, Chanel staged its December Metiers d'Art show at a French château for an audience of one. Cartier released its latest Pasha watch in China, two months before the rest of the world, and Moncler moved its Genius show from Milan Fashion Week to Shanghai in 2021.

Circular fashion, sustainability, inclusivity and diversity will be under the radar. Collections will continue to be customized, bespoke, smaller, and more designers will opt for certified-sustainable fabrics in response to climate concerns while reducing wastage. Even before Covid-19, collections were shrinking as brands moved away from trendy, seasonal products toward more dependable sustainable items. For example, Hermès produced its first vegan leather handbag made from mushrooms during the pandemic. There was backlash suffered by Dolce & Gabbana over a perceived racist advertisement in 2018 in a call for cultural sensitivity, Gucci's black mask backlash in the USA, Balenciaga's handbag release for the Qixi festival, and China's Valentine's Day was criticized for its poor rural design—far removed from European aesthetics.

The marriage between luxury experiences through digital play is here to stay. The impact of luxury platforms and their renewed business models will keep innovating. Technology and its interface are supposed to help consumers interact on the digital platform. This is geared toward renewing their appetites for luxurious products. It is also supposed to facilitate local engagement. It entails a phygital and personal touch that appeals to the majority of high-end luxury consumers. Recent findings have revealed that society has leaped at least five years ahead with regard to consumers' and businesses' adoption of digital technology during the pandemic. Digital product placement in games, 3D deployment in stores with immersive experiences and entertainment, virtual showrooms, social and M-commerce, CRM programs relying on AI, e-commerce internalization and non-fungible tokens (NFTs) are the new inspirations to look forward to.

Polarization in performance differentiation and its dependence on geographic diversification. The differentiation in the luxury goods industry is intensifying in the latter stages of the pandemic. The following three factors will further intensify polarization. The health of the brand's balance sheet before the crisis, the elasticity of the operating model, and digital capabilities, supply chain agility, and reliance on wholesale channels and targeting measures taken to deal with the pandemic. The goal to survive will be to maximize short-term financial, operational growth and brand resilience. Even before the outbreak, the average performance data of the luxury goods industry was not very meaningful because the growth rates and profit margins of different companies were very different. Even in the same market segment and price, the growth rate of luxury brands varied greatly (some as high as 40%, while some are negative); the distribution of yields could range from single digits to 50%. Thus, the rebound is dependent on the waves of Covid-19 in different markets, speed of vaccination, the speed at which international travel can resume, as well as the resilience and confidence of local customers. These scenarios depend vastly on geographical situations and how individual governments respond to the crisis. It will have an effect on the decline in revenues. It will have a disproportionate impact on profitability. This is driven by the requirement to continue to spend and sometimes even accelerate the pace of investment on most cost elements such as store rents, running costs, marketing, digital investments and others, despite a deterioration in sales. It is thus predicted that full recovery can gain momentum over the next three years and the market might return to 2019 results by the end of 2022, or even 2023.

The Future

Business as usual does not exist anymore. The game is becoming tough, forcing many brands to scrutinize their business and ask themselves questions, such as why consumers who used to be satisfied are now disappointed.

The years 2013 and 2020 show that the luxury industry is not immune to the effects of external factors. The world—and the business of luxury—has changed because the crisis is everywhere, the political landscape is unstable, currencies are uncontrollable, and the tourism flux was almost at a standstill in 2020.

The luxury industry was also concerned with, and affected by, its own weak points: slow-paced innovation, too little effort in R&D and a naïve belief in infinite success. Some brands opened too many stores, which were too big, forgetting that *small is often happiness, dreams should be an obsession, surprise is the motto, detail is a must.*

In fact, the pandemic was an opportunity to reflect. The brands went back to basics and asked themselves what luxury is now and what luxury will be in 2030. What are the ingredients necessary to be a luxury brand in the future? Brands were forced to renew their communications and their way of serving clients.

How will luxury brands use new technology in the digital age? To what extent will digitalization find equilibrium with bricks and mortar? Will they be able to seamlessly support each other by reinforcing the dream factor of the luxury brand and helping consumers to buy the right products instead of diluting the brand? It remains a challenge.

Just as too much CRM can affect a luxury brand negatively, too much digital threatens to kill the desire of the brand—ultimately, one of the most important aspects when discussing luxury. But change in the luxury ecosystem after the pandemic is inevitable. Traditional and authentic luxury houses will probably remain a little bit reluctant to make such transformations for a while but there are significant elements which show they are progressively changing their mind. Through his family office, Artemis, François-Henri Pinault, a wealthy owner and executive of the Kering group, created in 2017 the dedicated venture capital fund Red River West and endowed it with 100 million to bet on technological gems from the new ecosystem of luxury startups and hope for returns and synergies with the group's brands. Its main competitor, LVMH, built LVMH Luxury Ventures the same year with the same perspective. With an investment ticket of between 2 and 10 million euros, the fund aims to leverage the growth of young and promising brands, with great visibility on social media, and to boost technological startups, which are likely to shake up consumption and purchase habits among the luxury industry.

Thus, the most important question remains: *How does one stay unique when all brands use the same technologies, the same method of digitalization, and the same training program for salespeople?*

On top of this, more questions arise: *How to be exceptional? How to find the stars of tomorrow? How to define the new level of services that ensures that luxury is fancied and recognized by consumers?*

The years 2021–2030 will be the beginning of a new era for tourism, the rise of the nomads, which will contribute to redefine the luxury industry. Until now the flux of tourists has been relatively stable, with Chinese being the main group buying luxury when abroad. Will this pattern change? Will the tourists stay in their own country and shop there? Will luxury brands embrace localization as consumers force the brands to integrate local beliefs, norms and specificities?

In 2013 more than 100 million Chinese traveled abroad; in 2020 there were none. Data shows that Chinese consumers bought 47% of the world's total luxury goods in 2013,[9] which translated into 102 billion US dollars' worth of luxury goods, with some 28 billion in the domestic market and about 74 billion in the overseas market. But the purchasing behavior of Chinese consumers was always difficult to predict as they shopped for luxury goods in countries with a favorable currency. The

[9]Statistics released by Fortune Character Institute, Bain & Company, in conjunction with the Italian luxury goods trade organization Altagamma.

pandemic was an eye-opener for countries such as France and Italy, with the absence of tourists.

In 2021, to attract tourists, European and Middle Eastern countries, and even the US, are making more of an effort. To promote Miami as a luxury shopping destination, and to attract tourists from South America, the US is issuing visas valid for 24 hours. Europe still remains their most popular destination, accounting for 35% of all global luxury sales, followed by the United States at 31%. Dubai announced a one-year work visa for those who want to relocate to Dubai while working from home (WFH).

In Europe, France and Italy are expected to be the top-two countries benefiting from tourism. With the late response to the pandemic and vaccine politics, the strong euro can be an obstacle for European countries, turning clients and tourists toward the US due to the weaker dollar. For example, in Paris the four main fashion weeks previously brought roughly €1.2 billion per year to the brands and local authorities. In 2020/2021, the city tried to organize a reduced version of the Fall Fashion Week, but it failed to get the expected momentum and received some backlash. Crucially, designer brands cannot advertise their new collection to fashion-savvy customers as efficiently as they did before. To attract these tourists, consistent efforts have to be made in areas such as visa regulation—multiple entry visas, quicker dispensing of visas—better and more efficient security, and new ways of welcoming tourists.

Furthermore, it is no secret that the American market is an emerging market for luxury brands. The potential is promising: more and more rich women are buying luxury goods both on the internet and by visiting stores. The challenge of expanding in the American market is similar to that in China—to have enough capital to invest in a market of that size. America is becoming the number-one target for the luxury industry, both as a market and as a destination. A case in point was the acquisition of Tiffany by LVMH, as referred to earlier.

Only rich and powerful brands, with strong top-lines and strong enough to resist problems and drastic changes, will be able to survive in the business of luxury. Though this may not be fully true. The impact of the pandemic cannot be fully understood just by looking at global luxury revenues. The industry hosts a wide variety of specific sectors which have been impacted to very different degrees; even within sectors, between similar product categories, outcomes have been very different. Both geographic polarization and hyperpolarization will be there to stay as performances within the industry in different sectors will vary across different countries. Of course, the capacity to cope with the ripple effects of Covid-19 will depend on the financial health prior to 2020, the agility of the value chain (including sourcing and manufacturing), as well as the staying power of the brand. On a closer look, it appears that luxury shoes, beauty products and leather accessories will have a better chance to rise again after the pandemic. This is because these categories of goods have established a better performance on digital channels, and are not prone to follow seasonal purchase patterns. As such, they are better equipped to catch up in the coming months and to minimize the 2020 losses. On the other hand, it is predicted that more "unique," "experiential," hard luxury products, such as jewelry and luxury watches, may have a tougher time to recover. For such items, the purchase decision is usually made in-store after fitting and trial of alternatives. Moreover, they are more associated with one-off spending patterns and are thus more seasonal.

Similarly, different countries have exhibited different responses to the sanitary situation. For many observers, the reactivation of the Chinese market has been exceptional. It was in part the city-by-city containment approach of the government that slowed the proliferation of the virus. Several brands have declared that the return to the stores has exceeded last year's equivalent sales figures—a phenomenon referred to as "revenge shopping" by some. In other countries, such as the old European guard of Italy, France or Switzerland, the prospect for 2021 was bleaker. These depend heavily on tourism, and struggled to contain the propagation of the virus. As I write in early 2021, "business as usual" is not right around the corner.

The New Frontier

In China, as well as India, funds and creators like Shang-Xia from Beijing—now with a presence in Shanghai and Paris—are thinking about the concept of luxury brands. Why should the French, Italians, English, and Americans have a monopoly of luxury brands? Why shouldn't an Indian or a Chinese brand be a competitor to the Western brands in the future? Luxury brands are not in a safe haven anymore. The country of origin, "Made in France" or "Made in Italy," is not a strong barrier any longer. Tomorrow's luxury brands can be made in India as well as in China and be as credible as the European counterparts. As the "Made in France" and "Made in Italy" loses its meaning, brands should push toward more innovative products and greater improvements in the service level. Innovation is key at the product level, but it is crucial in terms of service. Not to take it into account would be a very big mistake.

It is an illusion to believe that luxury will keep meaning "foreign" and will only be a forte for mature customers from developed nations. Take Ralph Lauren as an example. The brand represents an American success story. A similar success story is with Coach. Another success story is Supreme. They are affordable luxury and lifestyle brands, showing that the market is open to foreign luxury brands coming from many countries. The new trend suggests that affordable luxury brands such as Michael Kors and Black Box Wines (from USA), Uniqlo (from Japan), Top Shop (from UK), Havaianas (from Brazil), and others have consistently shown high growth and have successfully captured the generous spending of young affluent. The young affluent, who are younger than 45 years of age, are reported to repeatedly spend about 50% more than mature affluent on luxury. These young affluent are turning away from brands that primarily are used as status symbols with the Made-In mark. Instead, the young affluent as of now want brands that reward them with pride of ownership and show them off as a smart shopper.

The "Made in France" or "Made in Italy" tag should be understood as a means to connect with the consumers and to become a love mark in different ways, including new technologies. However, it is important to stress that it is not an asset that guarantees a lasting credibility and advantage over other brands; that would indeed be arrogant and foolish to believe. Before, the luxury brand was the privilege of families and of rich customers and it was either French or Italian. Now it is open to millions of consumers in the middle class, there are only few families left in charge of their brands and the business is now "financial"—requesting both managerial skills and a creative genius. All these factors combined generate a highly complex business model.

Luxury has a mission. It is to be part of a new sustainable development policy and should embrace circularity, which would give more nobility to this very profitable business. Luxury enjoys continuous growth, and the limit of the growth is not clear; it seems impossible to say where the end is, so big, so huge are the market potentials. It is predicted that soon Europe will remain a stable market, full of tourists from everywhere—China, India, Africa, and South America. Crowds of tourists will again make Europe a paradise for shopping in luxury shops. Japan is, for example, a country for luxury foods; China and America will continue to provide tourists for the world. China, Brazil, Africa, all Asiatic countries have not yet revealed how they will contribute to the growth.

Luxury has a seemingly unlimited territory. This is why luxury has obligations to contribute to the sustainable development of the planet. Luxury brands need to develop, train and retrain artisans from underdeveloped countries in Africa and Asia, where so many talents have not emerged. A nationwide program for each nation has to be put in place to give space to craftsmanship, and find a way to include new talent in the process of creation. It is a must.

The development of craftsmen around the globe will help brands to be more creative, will help artisans to escape from poverty. Luxury brands should share their bounty with others, protect the planet, and develop education programs. They can be leaders to develop craftsmanship worldwide and give birth to old practices like *savoir-faire* in India with textiles, lacquer in Vietnam, porcelain in China, silvercraft in Africa, jewelry artisans in Africa, and others.

Luxury is guilty sometimes of being too successful; it is wrong to think like that, but anyone can understand social reactions. This is why the future of luxury is so linked to its capacity and the will to join the clubs of sustainable companies. LVMH has many programs. Save the Children in Japan, "pont neuf" in France, "fondation Claude Pompidou," "Institut Pasteur," and others; LVMH also sponsors many artistic events such as the Richard Serra exhibitions in New York and Paris, Anselm Kieffer, and others. Louis Vuitton has the Fondation LV; Hermès has created "Fondation Hermès" to help young talents all over the world. L'Oreal is very active, Gucci partners with Unicef, and Kering is at the forefront of the movement of sustainable luxury and particularly concerned about women's leadership.

Sustainable development forces luxury brands to show their utility, to explain what they do, and show how they contribute to beauty, innovation, and creation. Luxury is a business model which is successful due to its innovative capacity. It opens doors for others as innovation is today the most important means to succeed. Luxury has obligations to think how to employ people, how to recruit new talents, how to go further in creativity, how to innovate, how to find new usage of raw materials, how to better treat animals, and how to make better use of skins. Luxury is obliged to see the world with new eyes, to contribute more, to open the doors for the rest of the world, to be part of its universe.

The consequence for luxury brands is to modify governance. More and more creators will have to travel, see the planet, get ideas everywhere, and they will work from all parts of the world, in-house, outside, with others. The challenge will be to communicate, to grasp their ideas and transform them into products and services. Managers will learn to work differently to share views with people traveling, to put together all talent, some being "nomads," some stable, some remote.

It is a dream that, through digitalization, management by community, without hierarchical orders, will replace the classical type of governance: each problem, each idea will be discussed through digital tools by interested citizens the world over, who will bring their own experiences, ideas, history, to the subject. It will mean that, to develop a luxury brand, classical management rules will not be able to fulfill the request for more innovation, as innovation is, and will become, the key element of differentiation. How to be leaders in innovation while remaining hands-on with the strategy? How to create more to surprise consumers, keeping the brand DNA alive, without compromise? Luxury has a future bounded only by desire. But not for all brands; some will emerge and continue to grow, some will disappear. Brands such as Louis Vuitton, Burberry, Tommy Hilfiger, Dior and Estée Lauder have already begun to leverage Big Data and AI-based technologies, such as machine learning and analytics, to deliver more timely and personalized services to their customers.

If the coronavirus has put a historic halt to almost all segments of the luxury goods industry, it has also highlighted the gap between certain organizations and the new demands of consumers, embodying new growth areas. An ROI approach, which has become imperative in the current crisis, has also led us to deep-dive into value chains and the possibility of rethinking production methods to make them agile, adaptable. This is a key requirement, given the increasingly volatile demands of consumers, whose purchasing incentives are now much more transparent thanks to the data they generate. The advent of digital technology presents luxury with a major dilemma, which it will have to resolve with a balanced strategy: combining authenticity and an innovative experience, reconciling visibility and scarcity.

Among those that will emerge most are today's unknowns: Iran or Nigeria. But a lot of them are already open—India, Brazil, Qatar, and South Africa. Why mention Africa when referring to luxury? Africa remains a land to be conquered by a certain type of luxury, based on authenticity and genuine quality. The combination of rapidly growing economies and youthful populations shows promise. Countries with oil and gas have the potential to breed a new generation of high-net-worth individuals (HNWIs) within a short period of time. The countries showing promise are Nigeria, Angola, Ghana, Mozambique, Kenya and Tanzania.

In fact, luxury usually sets in as soon as a middle class starts to emerge, as has been the case in Asia—in countries such as Vietnam, the Philippines, Indonesia—and in Latin America. However, why open a store in Mongolia's Ulan Bator and not in Dakar? That's probably for Louis Vuitton to find out.

Some questions that luxury companies should ponder include: Which will be the next growth markets? Will it be the young nations or the nations where the middle-class is fast expanding? What type of products and goods will these markets like? How far should luxury brands extend in search of new markets or rejuvenate existing markets? How many stores should one open? Where? What needs to be the footprint for success? As markets will shift in the next 15 years, should luxury brands try local tastes and preferences or stick to global products? Will they follow the nomads? What would be the characteristics of the nomad of tomorrow? Should the creator anticipate the consumer's demands, their choices, their preferences or should they create only the best and let the nomads choose? How should brands renew the trust and loyalty from the old customers while remaining relevant to the new generation? How does one transfer the values, the savoir-faire to the new generation? How does one know what the millennial will dream about and aspire to? Should luxury companies follow the demographic dividend route or should they promote European roots while delivering global products? What is the future of affordable luxury? What about lifestyle? Is affordable luxury here to stay? With the digital age, what about time as a function to build a brand? Who will be the first mover capable of capitalizing on the launch of meaningful NFTs (non-fungible tokens) that resonate with the audience? Who will emerge as the leading digital marketplace for fashion NFTs? How does one reconcile the past and the future? What about European leadership in the luxury goods business? And then there is everything to do in space, be it space tourism, space voyage, to know the unknown. Is space the new frontier of luxury?

European brands will definitely have to face new competitors; the future of luxury will show new faces, new survivors, and new talent, we hope. The future is open. It can be bright, but it will be difficult and one thing is sure: it needs new priorities and talented people, and includes risky decisions and high profits or losses.

It is a new frontier for luxury: the easy times are now behind us.

Chapter 14

Epilogue: How to Create a Luxury Brand

Luxury goods are the only area in which it is possible to make luxury margins.

—Bernard Arnault

The famous quote of Bernard Arnault has seen many companies, start-ups and venture capital funds take interest in this industry. But they rarely succeed. The important question thus is to understand what sets them apart from traditional retailers? There are certain characteristics that do this. These characteristics are a must-have but still may not be enough to qualify a company as a luxury brand. Historical analysis suggests that most, if not all, the luxury brands (here distinction has to be made between fashion brands and luxury brands) were *family-owned for generations*. Almost always they *bear the name of the founders or the creators or the designers.* Each one of these brands was created, nurtured and maintained by their founders with *extraordinary creativity and design* for a *considerable period of time.* They continued nurturing this aspect as a way of super-differentiation and specialization. They made the science of *craftsmanship* into an art. With time they perfected it in such a way that they became legends in their category. Almost always they were *made by hand and had proprietary savoire-faire.* They chose *exceptional material* from across the world and with it came *exceptional quality.* Since it was made with such care and precision and in limited quantity, only for the very few who could afford it, *the discerning clients,* they were *rare.* Due to the above conditions the products were *expensive* and those who could afford it demanded *exceptional services.* For example, Chanel (1910) and Dior (1946) were known as couture fashion houses; Louis Vuitton (1854) was known for its luggage; Gucci (1906) was known for its leather handbags; Cartier (1847) for jewelry; Hermès (1837) for its saddles; Burberry (1856) for its raincoats; Christofle (1830) for silver; Krug (1843) and Dom Perignon (1670) for Champagne. All were the names of people. Rare exceptions are Mont Blanc (1906) for writing instruments and Rolex (1908) for watches.

The above brands have their own quality, style and authenticity. They are credible and legitimate in what they do. Each symbolizes the pinnacle of craft and taste in their domain and is revered in each and every society where they are known. Such is their brand power. For this reason, for decades, this sector has fascinated scholars in marketing and brand management literature for its unique appeal; after all, luxury is not essential, but it carries a symbolic meaning, cultural roots and heritage, and nonverbal cues, while capturing the sincerest aspirations and fantasies of consumers. The consumers are also special. Usually they fall into two groups. The first is more introvert, researches his or her preferences, is selective, discreet, and stays in a more intimate environment. They consume for themselves for their self-actualization needs. The second group belongs to a tribe, a group, a community. They share similar ideas and wants to look similar and be recognized within the community. What works for their community also works for them: they are extrovert, they communicate. Both groups exist. The challenge of luxury brands, as discussed before, is to cater to both or select one and excel. For example, the strategic choice of Gucci has been the second group while that of

Bottega Veneta has been the first group. These decisions are from two brands in the same group (Kering). From this decision all other decisions as brand management will flow. The metrics of measurement will be different for two diverse strategies, on one hand, but the final performance measures will be the same on the other. For example, the similar metrics will be same-store sales, which will drive realignment of retail footprint. Being discreet will mean less exposure: absence from social media, store closures, relocations while retaining the intense brand and store experiences. Similarly, Gucci will still measure customer retention, conversion, unit per transaction to help boost same-store sales. The final performance measure will entail personalized experience to result in the top-line. With the reset brought forth by the pandemic, only time will tell which strategy will work better after the pandemic.

Researchers and industry experts argue that it is difficult to create and nurture a luxury brand. But they also agree that, once created, it is in the realm of the blue ocean,[1] where competition is negligible in the new market space, unlike in the fiercely competitive red ocean. One can move out from the red ocean through their value innovation by reducing competition, eliminating conventional wisdom, raising the barrier for new entrants, and creating a space where superior profits are possible.

The next section describes through some examples how brands have been created, designed and turned; it shows the creation and re-creation process of luxury brands in real life.

Case Studies on Luxury Entrepreneurship

The Perfume and Cosmetics Sector

Anyone could rightly say that the luxury perfume cosmetic market is super-saturated. There are global diversified giants such as Unilever Prestige, Procter & Gamble, Johnson & Johnson; pure players such as L'Oreal Luxe, Estée Lauder, Clarins, Shishedo, Amore Pacific, Coty; luxury players such as Chanel, Hermès, LVMH, and numerous local players. However, most customers do not have only one lipstick; they have a

---

[1] Chan Kim, W and Mauborgne, R (2005). Blue Ocean Strategy: How to Create Uncontested Market Space and Make Competition Irrelevant, Harvard Business Review Press.

variety of different colors. Incorporating the concepts discussed before, creating a new product of color or super-specialized luxury products for this sector may not be part of the rivalry in the red ocean; it may be considered part of the blue ocean, as it creates a new market. Any new brand needs to fulfil a desire to be successful. One fascinating story is that of six women entrepreneurs who created multimillion-dollar cosmetic brands by focussing particularly on the woman's face. Anastasia Sores focused on Brow Kit; Jamie Kern Lima on the forehead skin with CC+ cream; Kylie Jenner on the Lip Kit; Kim Kardashian on the cheek, with creme contour and highlight kit; Huda Kattan on the eyelashes; and Rihana Fenty on the lips with multiple shades of lipstick.

Huda Beauty In 2013, Huda Beauty was founded by the beauty blogger and makeup artist Huda Kattan, the majority owner. Huda gained prominence on social media when she started posting makeup tutorials and tips on the advice of her sister. Together with her sisters, she launched a false eyelash collection as Huda Beauty's first product at Sephora in Dubai Mall. Huda Kattan had reported that "working as a makeup artist (for Revlon), I wasn't satisfied with the style and quality of lashes that were available at the time so I often ended up stacking and customizing the lashes myself to suit the client's eye shape." Her blogs became so popular that Huda was ranked #1 on the "2017 Influencer Instagram Rich List," earning $18,000 for each post of sponsored content and due to this reason was chosen as one of "The 25 Most Influential People on the Internet" by *Time* magazine in 2017.

In 2017, the three sisters decided to sell a small part of the brand to the strategic investor TSG Consumer Partners. All Huda Beauty's products are cruelty-free, and some of them are vegan. Not much is said about the sustainability activities of the brand. But Huda achieved popularity on Instagram, attaining more than 47 million followers as of 2020.

The Huda Beauty blog reported about how to make beauty eco-friendlier and surprisingly, promoted sustainable brands like Lush. In 2020, Huda Beauty Investments invested in a sustainable resale platform, "The Luxury Closet," which attracted public attention. This investment was a big step in the sustainability direction.

Huda Beauty's phygital challenge was that the brand's primary customer touchpoint was their website and social media channels, as it was an initially digital brand. Besides their website, the products were sold via multi-brand online retailers and physical stores. To solve Huda Beauty's phygital challenge, the brand opened its first pop-up store in London in 2019 to close the online and offline gap. Huda Kattan donated $100,000 to makeup artists who suffered due to the Covid-19 pandemic. The brand announced delivery delays caused by the pandemic on their website.

Fenty Beauty and Fenty Skin

Fenty Beauty by Rihanna was created for everyone: for women of all shades, personalities, attitudes, cultures, and races. I wanted everyone to feel included. That's the real reason I made this line.

—**Rihanna**

The famous singer Robyn Rihanna Fenty closed a contract with LVMH to create Fenty Beauty in 2017 after her success with 40 shades of foundation, later on expanded to 50 shades of skin types. The strategic intent behind having so many shades was to create the differentiating factor from other makeup companies that do not cater to such a broad and diverse market. Fenty Beauty was named one of *Time* magazine's best inventions of 2017.

Rihanna's promotion strategy focused on her social media channels to advertise her products and popular beauty influencers, like Nikkie Tutorials with over 14 million Instagram followers. The products are sold via the brand's online shop and multi-brand physical and digital stores. To improve the online shopping experience, the Fenty Beauty website offered a foundation shade finder. Fenty beauty focused on the current trend of inclusivity. Moreover, Fenty Beauty and Fenty Skin were embracing sustainability while focusing on reducing, reusing and recycling. The company promotes its effort in having refill systems to reuse packaging, and eliminate excessive packaging to reduce and recycle as many materials as possible. Even the shipping boxes were entirely recyclable. It was widely reported that Fenty Beauty's sales reached almost US$570 million in 2018. Although Covid-19 decreased sales, she nevertheless launched Fenty Skin in 2020.

Maison Francis Kurkdjian   Maison Francis Kurkdjian (MFK) was founded in 2009 following the encounter of perfumer Francis Kurkdjian and Marc Chaya. Before starting his own house, Kurkdjian had created of a number of bestselling perfumes, notably Jean-Paul Gaultier's Le Male, but had not gained the recognition that Chaya believed he deserved. He had also been the author of oversized installations that combined olfactory senses with art in order to offer the public multidimensional experiences. The duo subsequently opened their own fragrance house to bring back to light the savoir-faire and genius behind the making of a scent. Positioning the maison in the higher spectrum of the perfume industry, the co-founders targeted the niche luxury fragrance segment. The emerging brand grew steadily over the following years, reaching sales of about $44 million in 2019, up from $7 million in 2015, before joining LVMH in 2017. According to Marc, this "human decision" enabled the small luxury fragrance house to have higher ambitions with the access of the group's "synergies and best-practices."

Building a luxury brand from scratch meant building symbolic value, as well as elaborating differentiating elements that would bring the sense of exclusivity that was omnipresent in the luxury industry. Maison Francis Kurkdjian successfully did so, starting with a strong identity built around a master perfumer who had a story to tell through his creations. Not only did he find inspiration in art, culture, fashion, and past experiences, but he also knew how to create a special bond with the public by using scent as a component of greater artistic expression. The perfumer had the ability of making the customer dream, linking the scent with emotions and personal experiences. By selling a product that was essentially experiential, MFK had the quality of developing deep connections with the client, which facilitated customer loyalty. The brand also built exclusivity by adopting an ultra-selective strategy as its distribution was concentrated only at a small number of retail points. In addition, the founders defined a contemporary vision that guided their every move: *highlight the creative genius behind the creation of perfume and the use of perfume as a means of expression*. The fragrance house distinguished itself with its innovative concept of an "olfactory wardrobe," to offer men and women the freedom to choose the scent most adapted to a mood or occasion, adapting to modern active lifestyles. Moreover, MFK's slow production pace stayed relevant with sustainability trends, as perfume creation took on average of about 18 months. This rhythm also corresponds with new-generation mindsets, as they wished to take more time for the important things in life.

Like most, the pandemic has taken its toll on Maison Francis Kurk-djian, with 2020 sales hitting lower numbers than in 2018. People were not perfuming themselves as much during confinement, and alcohol, the principal raw material for fragrances, has become less available with the increased production of sanitizers. However, recovery perspectives are positive for the fragrance house, with more than 100% growth in the United States, despite the health crisis, in a market that already accounted for 40% of their sales. MFK continued making its way through the crisis with the launch of a new masculine fragrance, L'Homme à la Rose, as well as a new scent for Fendi's leather goods. The maison has also been embracing digital platforms as a way to continue selling a dream virtually; as part of their strategy to improve its digital content, MFK launched the "Paris as a Gift" Christmas campaign to invite customers to bring Paris into their homes as an alternative to travel. Finally, the brand planned to address lockdown lifestyle changes by launching scented soaps, candles, and home fragrances, products that made working from home a little more pleasant.

The Luxury Home Furnishing Sector

Shang Xia

> We do "Chinese style," but it's not a case of using one technique this season and another the next, it's not a one-off application but an accumulation. Working for two years can only enable us to understand the history and basic development of the craft, there are still many depths behind the craft that can be studied. And the more you use it, the more familiar you will become with it, and the more surprises you will get after three, five or seven years.
>
> **—Jiang Qiong Er, CEO & Art Director of Shang Xia**

As above, as below, the name of Shang Xia is simple but profound.

The Shang Xia brand was established jointly by the world-famous designer Jiang Qiong Er and Hermès in 2010. It was sometimes colloquially known as the Chinese Hermès, where Hermès owned 90% of the shares. It was a sophisticated brand which delivered a contemporary fine living lifestyle. It represented the oriental philosophy pursued by China over its long history, which linked tradition and the present, Oriental and West, human and natural—a symmetrical, balanced beauty between seemingly diametric poles.

One of the greatest works of Shang Xia was a two-and-a-half-meter-long Ming-style desk gathered in the collection of the National Museum of Decorative Arts in France. This desk was made with carbon fiber textures but painted with the most traditional pineapple varnish in Chinese culture. It was a complex piece of work that took a year and a half to produce. Referring to this, Qiong Er reported that,

> *It combines traditional construction with new technological materials. A national museum doesn't just go for a "good idea," their collection would have already spanned thousands of years, they are looking for a work of art that is representative of contemporary China: a work of art that reflects the highest level of craftsmanship of the day, that synthesizes lifestyle, aesthetics and craftsmanship, that is a record of a historic phase.*

Such tables cannot, of course, be mass-produced. It was within their means to leave some pieces that belonged to the highest level of our time. In the beginning, the products of Shang Xia were mainly concentrated on a limited number of categories such as clothing, accessories and tea sets, but going further its production apparel, footwear, furniture, homewares, leather goods, jewelry and accessories which the brand described as centered on home and representing a perfect melding of tradition with modernity.

> *There are some products that can only be orphaned in extreme editions, they are challenging the technical difficulties and the production process and are not suitable to be commercialized, but they can be turned into a mark of the time. There are some products that can only be limited editions due to the scarcity of raw materials, the technical difficulty of the production process and the long-time cycle. There are some high-end products that are not limited edition but have limited overall production in the cycle. These are all "as above."*

Shang Xia had a design team of about 20 people, mostly Chinese with Western living experience, which gave them the strong ability to integrate Eastern and Western thinking. It was their spirit not to discuss the differences between East and West, but to let them flow naturally in the designer's body just like blood. The purpose of Shang Xia was to bridge the gap between the tangible and the intangible, tradition and present. The brand continued to use its distinctive combination of contemporary design with exquisite hand craftsmanship, Chinese culture, and the highest quality standards to champion the dazzling grace of everyday modern life.

Shang Xia opened its store in Shanghai, followed by Beijing in 2012 and Paris in 2013. In 2020, private investment company Exor NV, the investment vehicle of Italy's Agnelli family, invested US$97 million to become the largest shareholder, while Hermès still represented an important investor alongside Jiang Qiong Er. Jiang commented after the acquisition,

> *Though we operate as two independent brands, Shang Xia and Hermès share the same philosophy: celebrating the heritage of craftsmanship of our respective countries and combining that with innovative, contemporary design. For Shang Xia, it's also about redefining what "made in China" means to the rest of the world. . .People now favor simple, timeless designs that transcend cultural boundaries. We see Shang Xia as a long-term project: we hope to connect past traditions with today's world, and then carry it on for the generations to come. . .*

Watches & Jewelry

Baume

> *Baume is the synonym of reinvention. Baume is a new way of doing things. We root ourselves in the history, legacy and watchmaking expertise of Baume & Mercier, our mother company but with another approach to watchmaking. . .We put the human being and the environment at the centre of our creations while having always in mind that we want to do great things for a better tomorrow.*

In May 2018, after more than 18 months of hard work, Baume was launched in Los Angeles, California. It was the work of a dozen people, directed by the former CEO of Baume & Mercier, Alain Zimmermann. Together, they created a new watch, along with a new brand, something that had not been done by the Richemont Group since 2009. The group of people who worked on the project started from scratch, and therefore worked as a start-up, while keeping in mind the heritage and the quality standard of a Swiss watchmaking brand such as Baume & Mercier. However, even if the brand was created by a Baume & Mercier team, Baume operated completely independently.

The philosophy of this new brand, more affordable than the other brands of the Richemont Group, was to respond to three new trends in the luxury watch market: the sustainability of the components, the customizability of the watches, and the digital experience. In addition, it was still of great importance for the brand to keep the watchmaking craftsmanship.

To promote the launch of the brand, Baume hosted special guests and organized events in the Baume Beach House in Malibu, which the brand created. Several influencers were invited, such as famous photographers, YouTubers and rappers. In addition, the new brand was presented at the Vivatech salon in Paris in 2018. Baume watches were not directly targeted toward millennials,[2] but rather toward people with a millennial mindset.

The head of the brand, Marie Chassot,[3] was previously part of the Baume & Mercier team. Baume was created around the idea of designing a better tomorrow. The actions of the brand were driven by two pillars: mindfulness and collective intelligence. One of the brand's most important goals was to limit its environmental impact. To do so, they used upcycled, recyclable and natural materials. The watches were entirely made of sustainable and recyclable components, such as cork, linen, upcycled PET or cotton for the straps and aluminium or stainless steel for the cases. In addition, Baume did not use any animal skins, conflict minerals or precious materials. Usage of complete sustainable material made it a born vegan brand.

The production also decided to opt for a made-to-order strategy, that limits inventory, and thus limits waste. In addition, the brand operated from offices where 50% of the cement was recycled and worked

---

[2] Born between 1985 and 2000.
[3] Marie Chassot was born in Switzerland and started working for the Richemont group, and more particularly for Piaget, in 2000. After working for Dinh Van for four years, she joined Roger Dubuis. In 2015, she became the Marketing Director of Baume & Mercier.

together with its suppliers in order to help them reduce their CO2 emissions. Baume's slogan, "It's About Making Time," summarized very well the brand's goal of shaping a better future.

In accordance with the wish of the brand to limit its environmental impact, Baume collaborated with different NGOs and universities. For example, Baume collaborated with Waste Free Oceans, an NGO committed to transforming the plastic they collected in the ocean to make innovative products. The brand also sponsored the Material Futures MA Course at Central Saint Martins that aimed at developing sustainable processes and materials. Moreover, the brand donated 2% of the company's turnover to the partners, in order to support their projects.

Concerning the Baume watches, they were not produced in Switzerland, which made the brand different from other Richemont brands, and in general from other luxury watches, as most of them are Swiss Made. The creators of Baume decided to locate the production of the watches in the Netherlands, and more specifically in Amsterdam. However, Baume's quality control was still in Switzerland, even if they were trying to move it closer to the assembly line, in order once again to limit the environmental impact of the brand. The Baume watches were therefore, as different as they may feel, not "Swiss Made."

The watches were unisex and entirely customizable, with more than 2,000 possible combinations. The process was the following. First, one could choose between four basic designs (two 41mm and two 35mm). Then, one could start customizing the case, the dial, the hands and the strap. One could also add a personalized engraving. It must be noted that the customization did not change the price of the watch.

Baume watches were more affordable than other luxury watches. They ranged from €490 to €560 for the Custom Timepieces. They were the entirely customizable watches. Special editions were more expensive, such as the HRS Limited Edition, which retailed for €1,200, or the Iconic Edition, which retailed for €960 (those editions were not customizable).

In addition to a new watch, Baume created a unique buying experience. At first, the brand wanted to sell the watches only through their online platform. Therefore, the brand had a strong online presence, with the watches available to buy in more than 85 countries around the world. However, the team quickly realized the need of having a physical presence, as customers liked to touch and try on the products before they buy them. Therefore, Baume decided to sell its watches in pop-up and concept stores, in addition to their online stores. The first Baume pop-up store opened in Paris in 2018 and lasted one week. The aim of Baume was to open pop-up stores in cities all around the world. In addition, the concept store "NOUS" in Paris offered the BAUME HRS Limited Edition watches. As of 2018, Baume was present in pop-ups and concept stores in Paris, Bordeaux, New York, and Geneva.

However, as Baume watches were completely customizable, the challenge was to make it possible to try on the watches in-store. As every watch was made-to-order, and thus the company had no inventory, it was not possible to physically try the watch that one had customized before buying it. In order to address this problem, Baume presented during the Viva Tech Salon two scenarios. The first one, in partnership with Hapticmedia, offered the possibility for the customer to customize his or her watch on a large screen and then visualize the watch on his or her wrist thanks to augmented reality. Baume was already working with this company as they collaborated on Baume's website in order to create the customizing tool, presenting the watches in 3D. The second scenario was developed in partnership with Smartpixel: the customer could project their customized watch on a white wax watch. Hapticmedia and Smart-pixel were two French companies which specialized in digital technologies such as 3D visualizing.

At the end of its first year of existence, Baume had opened in concept stores in three additional countries—Belgium, Hong Kong, and Italy. The further success of Baume depended a great deal on how customers would respond to this new product, but also the new buying experience that went with it.

Ganjam Indian luxury jewelry brand Ganjam is among the few jewelry brands in the world which has a house (workshop) of artisans and remains in the hands of the original family. With a heritage stretching back over a hundred years, Ganjam has carved a niche for itself as a master of jewelry design and production (crafting). The company was established in 1889, and can be traced back to the Vijayanagar Empire. Ganjam Nagappa founded the company in Bangalore in 1889 and was appointed jeweler to the Maharaja of Mysore, and by the early 1900s, he was invited by the King of Nepal to train his goldsmiths. The jewelry crafted by Ganjam has been desired and worn by Maharajas and Maharanis and continues to grace the men and women of modern India and countries beyond. Inspired by South Indian temple architecture, these pieces, with sheer intricacies of design and flawless craftsmanship, are true to their traditional roots. Carnatic jewelry is not merely gems and gold crafted into ornaments, but a symbol of human spirituality over the centuries. This is what drives Ganjam to preserve and continue the extraordinary tradition.

This legacy of fine and exquisite craftsmanship has sustained the excellence with which Ganjam is associated today. Expertise in diamonds, precious gems, and traditional Carnatic jewelry has made Ganjam a cultural reference of Indian jewelry design. In creating these refined and elegant pieces, Ganjam has ventured into new terrains: not just in the use of precious gemstones, where it is one of the very few Indian jewelers to use only hand-selected "f" color diamonds in all its jewelry, but also in the introduction of new weaves and techniques to India. The emphasis on innovation, design, quality, craftsmanship, and heritage has made Ganjam jewelry not only fascinating but also highly desirable, as it combines the best in international trends with the richness of traditional Indian craft.

Ganjam's flagship location is Bangalore, where it was founded. The company operates through directly operated stores in New Delhi and in Mumbai's Taj Mahal Palace, a popular destination for luxury tourists. The brand also promotes itself internationally. A private exhibition of handmade and heritage jewelry was held in London in June 2011. The company launched a line of jewelry to appeal to the Japanese market in 2010. Although the collection retained the "Indian essence," the line was modified to meet customer expectations in Japan and to have a contemporary treatment. The company planned to use this venture, pursued in collaboration with Japanese Citizen Jewelry, to enhance its brand awareness and presence in the Japanese market. Ganjam also expanded its reach to the United States.

The challenge for the brand has been to handle the paradox of maintaining a balance between the classic and the contemporary in terms of designing—from creating jewelry with deep historical religious significance to crafting cultural pieces with references to the contemporary world of today. With the tagline "Heighten your senses," the brand aims at creating an exclusive image among high-end consumers, but is yet to face the test of time of being globally accepted against brands like Cartier and Van Cleef & Arpels.

Wine & Champagne Sector

Turnaround of Krug   Founded by Joseph Krug in 1843 in Reims, France, the Krug champagne house was one of the most prestigious in the highest segment of the market. However, in the 1990s the French group Remi Cointreau, then owners of Krug, faced financial difficulties. This meant the house faced less investment and fewer opportunities to develop its potential, in turn creating a situation of a certain stagnation. In 1999, the French group Möet Hennessy, belonging to the luxury conglomerate LVMH, acquired Krug with the intention of developing its potential. The descendants of the Krug family still held a representative role within the house, but its management had already been professionalized. Initial efforts achieved hopeful results but, despite this, the situation was complicated by the realities of the year 2008, revealing Krug's problems were even more complex and profound than what had been previously understood. By 2008 the situation was critical. The house lost over 45% of its business with a fall that appeared to have no end. The subsequent economic crisis only sharpened problems. While the fall in industry was an estimated 10%, the situation at Krug was much more worrying.

In 2009, Maggie Henríquez took over as President and CEO of Krug with the mission to turn around the iconic brand. But she reported that,

> My previous successes in complex restructuring processes paved my way. But this was different, I was expert in mass market products and not luxury, which is a totally different approach. My approach was wrong the first year and sales fell by another 35%. In only two years, the company had lost over 64% of its volume and 95% of its results. I understood I had had the wrong approach and I had to do differently.

Coherence was understanding the primary source. This experience highlighted the need to understand the house from its very roots, from its founder. It was essential to understand how and, above all, why Joseph Krug founded this house in 1843.[4] This story would have been lost in the mists of time, had it not been for the care with which Joseph described his philosophy in a small notebook. A notebook which had remained forgotten and out of sight, in the safe of the house.[5] In it, Joseph wrote to his son how a good champagne could only be created with good elements: "We could create champagnes which appear to be good by using regular or even mediocre elements. But these are the exceptions upon which one must never rely, or we risk damaging the operation and losing our reputation."

Moreover, he annotated how all good champagne houses should produce only two types of champagne:

All good houses must create only two types of champagne of the same quality. Number 1. Its composition must alter from year to year. If in one year the wines have too much body, one must use more wines from fresher years. And to the contrary if the wines of the year are lighter, as in 1848. Number 2. In accordance with the circumstances. Its composition

---

[4]Joseph Krug, born in Mainz in 1800, began his career as a wine salesman. When he arrived in France in 1834 he began working for one of the leading houses of the time, Jacquesson. His excellent work soon opened doors to greater responsibilities. In addition, his marriage to the sister-in-law of the president of Jacquesson handed him a comfortable social position. But his work in a house focused on sales volumes clashed with his true passion, that of experimentation and quality. In 1840, Joseph began to collaborate in secret (to avoid family disruptions) with Hippolyte de Vives, a wine merchant with his own small champagne house, but who was more interested in his political career. Enthused by Joseph's ideas and his search for quality, he gave him free rein to develop a champagne of his own. Finally, in 1843 the House of Krug was founded. At last Joseph could develop his own particular understanding of quality champagne.

[5]The value of the notebook was much greater than that of a mere antique document. Opening the notebook was like traveling through time to meet Joseph Krug himself. The notebook had been written in 1848, as Joseph feared not being able to transmit his knowledge to his son, Paul, born in 1842. Years later, after his father died, Paul kept the notebook in a wooden box, where it would remain for the next one hundred years. In the 1970s, the notebook was found in the archives of the house by Paul II who, realizing its importance, kept it in his safe, where it would remain until the group's historian would find it again.

is based on wines of only one year and it should only be created when the history of the year needs to be expressed.

After two years of research, and profoundly following its founder, the house confronted its problems. The first step was to clearly define the philosophy and the distinctive know-how ("savoir faire") of the house. As such, the three essential principles of the house were defined: a focus on the individuality of the elements, the art of blending, and time itself. This was the original purpose of the house, to create a champagne of the highest possible quality and it was the true basis of its reputation and legacy.

In the second place, careful work was undertaken to recuperate the codes of the house, lost with the new personality introduced following the year 2000. The typography, color schemes, and visual identity, as well as the tone of communication, had not corresponded with the authentic elements of the house. This was about an introspective process of understanding its true nature.

In addition, the client needed to understand that each edition of Krug Grande Cuvée was a unique creation, the result of a process of individual selection and of a blend of base wines that was different every single year. Through understanding the need to inform the consumer of their philosophy, the Krug ID was born. This was all of the information of each edition (such as the characteristics of the year, the years which created the blend and the chef de caves' notes explaining the process of creation). This would help the client to understand the philosophy of Krug. The Krug ID was indicated on each bottle from 2011 onwards, as well as being available via the web and on the app which was created with this purpose in mind.

After two years of dedicated labor the DNA, which defined the personality of the house, was decided. This was about showing what the house of Krug really is, a house where each year is different, but always utterly refined. A house which pored over the tiniest detail while never compromising on excellence, or focused on greater volumes, nor permitted grapes of a lesser quality, or less time in the bottle, all of which served to focus on the ideals they held sacrosanct. In this way Krug would always remain true to be a house guided by the pleasure of champagne and by a desire to ensure their clients feel truly at home.

Furthermore, a decision was made to collaborate with different musicians so they would choose the music for each type of champagne created. This musical selection would be available to clients via the Krug ID. In 2015, we found that there is science behind the connection between hearing and tasting; a foundation was established to invest in research which contributes to humanity's well-being. It is called Fonds K pour la musique and invests in research, education, cultural activities and solidarity, taking music where there was none. Musicians are paid to play music in schools, hospitals, etc. In this way, Krug helps musicians to make a contribution and boost people's well-being.

> *The results of this transformation have been spectacular. However, achieving coherence took time. Krug had positioned itself as the only house which only produced prestige champagnes from its very origins. It was centered on pleasure and not on status. Something which the house described as the "power of choice" as opposed to the "choice of power." The turnaround was complete. It seems as if a new page has been written in the history of Krug. In 2020, the world has not stopped advancing. The arrival of new generations of clients and new modes of digital business place new challenges on the table. The year 2020 has been a challenging and meaningful year, we have gone through the crisis protecting our strengths and building on our weaknesses. The house has shown its solidarity and we will get out of the COVID crisis stronger, this is for sure. These have been 12 very rich and extraordinary years for me, and 11 years of transformation for the house. We can say with pride, the House of Krug, a house where everything has changed and nothing has changed.*
>
> **—Maggie Henríquez**

Revisiting the 9*P*s as the Essentials of Building a Luxury Brand

Good business leaders create a vision, articulate the vision, passionately own the vision, and relentlessly drive it to completion.

—Jack Welch

Provenance, Country of Origin, Heritage of the Brand

Its heritage and story is usually the starting point for any brand to succeed. Otherwise, the best way is to build a story around the brand. From the examples discussed above, Krug had its provenance but the story of its founder was lost in time. It was rediscovered and became *the* essential part of the turnaround. Storytelling the heritage of the brand is important as it inspires desire.

Some general country associations can be leveraged to a great extent to build the brand's reputation. For example, champagne and perfume in France, watches in Switzerland. This is well known. Instantaneously it brings credibility and legitimacy to the brand. Another example would be Carlos Miele or Lenny from Brazil. The brands are associated with what is perceived by the West as a very glamorous part of Brazilian lifestyle. The ads with the Ipanema beach in the background evoke the idea that Brazil is a colorful place with beautiful women who are familiar with this beach lifestyle and who like to have fun and party—hence the colorful designs. This is also part of the reason that Brazil's Havaianas brand did so well and became the world leader in flipflops.

Positioning and Historical Association

New luxury brands might be successful outside their home markets if they are associated with a time that was considered "glamorous." The example of Shang Xia is relevant here as it was made from China's roots and historical associations. The same can be said for India's jewelry brand, Ganjam. The brand is associated with what is perceived to be a beautiful period of India's history, where the Maharajas were very opulent and wore jewelry specially ordered, not only from local craftsmen, but also from brands such as Cartier and Chaumet.

To be successful internationally it is almost mandatory that a new brand needs to be successful in its home market. To do this, it must be associated with the traditional techniques and craftsmanship that are unmistakably associated with its country of origin. One example would be MFK, where they built the story around the perfumer while innovating custom-made perfumes which targeted the niche luxury fragrance segment. Shang Xia used luxury positioning in association with Hermès while going back to the roots of China's heritage, to a time when China was considered a world leader.

Persona and the Brand DNA

Each brand discussed above had its unique brand identity, its personality and character. This was conveyed through visual advertising, consumer touchpoints, offline and online, and by the events of brand communication. The codes were either clear and defined, or had to be redefined. It is time-consuming and delicate. Once the persona has been defined it has to endure until it resonates with consumers. Changing the brand persona quite often leads to brand dilution and confusion. For example, Baume created its persona from scratch, which unambiguously catered to millennials. Over time the persona of Krug had been lost and it took painstaking dedicated research of two years to recreate it. Shang Xia took ten years, and is still not profitable. It takes time.

Personage, the Physical Face of the Brand

When building a luxury brand, there is a choice. The face of the brand, the story creating the desire could be the founder, the creator and/or the designer. But there should not be any confusion. For Chanel the whole enigma is about Coco Chanel. The story revolves around her and her only. Karl Lagerfeld was a genius interpreting and reinterpreting the ideas of Coco Chanel while mixing his creativity into the story. MFK is about the creator. Krug is about Joseph's passion which burst out of his little red diary. The other way is to make the designer the face of the brand. For example, Celine was reinterpreted by different creative directors in their own way. Phoebe Philo had complete freedom to re-create Celine. She did it with great success. Her successor Heidi Slimane is doing it now. Alessandro Michele redefined Gucci. Daniel Lee, Virgil Abloh, Kim Jones, Maria Grazia Chiuri and others are reinterpreting their brands while keeping true to their DNA. On the other hand, on the face of it Moncler and Hermès do not have a definite personage. It is the brand image that supersedes the creative director. All the above brands use public figures, celebrities and notable personalities from different walks of life and in different geographic locations to promote the brand.

Paucity, Rarity, and Exclusivity

The success of a new luxury brand also depends on its capacity to convey a feeling of inaccessibility. The more difficult it is to obtain a product, the more desirable it becomes. For example, brands like MFK, Krug, Ganjam demonstrate the know-how and savoir-faire that requires time and expertise, and their products are therefore produced in limited quantities. Moreover, their distribution is concentrated to a few selling points, adding to the sentiment of product rarity.

An interesting point to note is that the new pandemic-induced trends are putting pressure on luxury brands' capacity to develop a sense of rarity and exclusivity. Customers are now asking for more products at accessible price points, and the rise of e-commerce is forcing brands to expand their distribution online, making luxury goods more accessible and thus lowering their exclusivity. Furthermore, while sustainability concerns are pushing brands to rethink their production pace, younger generations like to experience constant change and fast innovation. New luxury brands therefore need to be able to satisfy diverging wishes while trying to maintain the desirability of their products. To this end, technological innovations might be a solution to increase the rarity of luxury goods, as the time and R&D requirements increase reproduction difficulty. Exclusivity also used to be about rare and private events, but luxury brands need to think out of the box to use new technologies and digital platforms to offer unique experiences that correspond with new phygital trends.

Phygital

Due to the pandemic, consumer trends have changed. For instance, pre-Covid-19, 85% of cosmetic products were purchased in-store. With Covid-19, due to store closures, this behavior changed to online shopping. The crisis led to lifestyle changes that provoked an increase in the need for phygital experiences. This entails having to bring the experience to the customers through digital platforms. The future of luxury will be about using digital to bring people to stores but also developing physical exclusive experiences to boost the brand's visibility online. For example, Baume and MFK adopted a more digital-based communication to overcome lockdown obstacles, while Krug experimented with music and champagne drinking.

Publicity

Luxury brands distinguish themselves principally by their capacity to sell a dream, which they achieve through storytelling. Luxury houses draw from their history and heritage to elaborate an authentic story that gives life to the brand, going beyond the product. It creates a personality and an identity, which then act as a guiding thread for all of their activities. A unique story is an asset that is nurtured carefully for engaging in *coherent* publicity in different channels. This publicity, through different channels, allows a recognizable interaction that stands out from the competition and connects with customers at a deep level. Heritage brands such as Krug, Baume & Mercier, have successfully emerged in our contemporary world as luxury brands because they recrafted the brand's mystique around iconic founders and historical creations. More modern brands Huda Beauty, Fenty Beauty, and MFK are also constructing an aura around the founders, who make use of their creative genius to tell their story.

Contemporary trends have driven luxury brands to digitalize the entire storytelling process, enabling them to spread their aura to millions of consumers through online platforms. Chanel, for example, regularly releases videos about its history, heritage, and savoir-faire, which helps increase admiration and emotional connection from the customer point of view. While digitally storytelling is an useful asset for new luxury brands, the challenge lies in maintaining the right balance between heritage and modernization. With the acceleration of sustainability concerns due to the pandemic, emerging brands can use a storytelling strategy that is oriented toward environmental and social responsibility.

Pricing

While exclusivity used to be solely about price and accessibility, recent trends have shown that millennials now ask for more novelty. As such, personalization, collaborations, and limited editions prove to be a successful approach to create exclusive products. Francis Kurkdjian masters this notion particularly well as he offers perfumes that customers can adapt personally to their mood. Krug pairs its champagne with specific music. Additionally, the objective of unique and superior experiences is to make the consumer feel that they have an exclusive relationship with the brand. This is key for building client loyalty. And then the price is no longer a concern.

Performance and Opportunity for Conglomerates

A nonnegotiable condition to start a venture in the luxury industry is to offer an exceptional experience that will make the customer feel special. First, it is but natural that to compete in this category the product is a guarantor of the brand's superior quality, and should combine aesthetic and functional attributes. This ensures the durability of the product, so that it might be perceived as a timeless object that can be passed on to future generations. Luxury houses rely on remarkable craftsmanship, unique materials, attention to detail, creativity, and innovation to stand by their promise. For instance, Moynat still uses ancient trunkmaking techniques and Maison Francis Kurkdjian highlights the genius behind the process of fragrance creation.

A brand's performance is reflected by its customer's journey. The purchasing experience is an important part of performance measurement. A sense of surprise and seamlessness goes a long way to astonish the customer. As discussed before, this is particularly true for Generations Y and Z, who have higher expectations in terms of experiential luxury. Combining digital with physical experiences is a way for young brands to appeal to young customers.

It is observed that the post-COVID world is marked by a strong shift to experiential luxury and an increase sustainability concerns, which bring new challenges to brands wishing to deliver the finest performance to customers. This means that new brands need to start by prioritizing sustainability at every level of the product supply chain, starting with production, where materials should be as sustainably sourced as possible.

Usually, conglomerates wait until brands prove to be profitable by themselves before acquiring the brand. Emerging market luxury brands present an opportunity for conglomerates. Purchasing an emerging market luxury brand allows the conglomerate to increase its competition and presence in emerging markets. It would be able to develop and grow these emerging market luxury brands in Western markets, where it may already possess distribution networks and influence with retail space opportunities. Finally, the conglomerate would be able to increase distribution and manufacturing capabilities in these emerging markets, as well as create synergies between businesses. The conglomerate would also gain knowledge and expertise about doing business in these emerging markets. Examples abound in the perfume and cosmetics sector. Fenty Beauty has been supported by Sephora of LVMH; Huda Beauty has been supported by private equity firm TSG Consumer Partners, who acquired a small minority stake; MFK was partially acquired by LVMH; Kylie Jenner and Kim Kardashian West (KKW) sold part of the business to Coty Inc.

Expanding into International Markets as a Way of Growth for Emerging Brands in Frontier Markets

Unlike markets in Europe, the US, and Japan—where customers have reached a certain level of understanding and sophistication—frontier markets are still in their branding infancy. China is the market to look for in the decade from 2021 to 2030. This is due for the following reasons. On the one hand, information asymmetry, misguided political regulations, inefficient judicial systems, a lack of proper IPR rules, and complex labor laws make it difficult for brands to thrive, innovate and create. On the other hand, the mindset, the complexity of business structures, the diversity of demographic composition, and the geographic spread requires a certain unique branding philosophy. In this context, what are the conditions and competencies that can help homegrown luxury companies flourish?

Once successful in their home markets, there is an option for brands to expand into international markets. It is in one way easy now with luxury platforms and e-commerce. But the competition is steep. This is a difficult process given the amount of resource, network, and franchise value required to start from scratch in a new market. There are four key steps to this process.

First is to make sure the brand has recognized excellence, is differentiated from similar products within the same category, and portrays a set of distinct and unique value propositions, both in its product and service offerings, in their home market. For example, LV proposes its roots are in travel bags, whereas Hermès proposes that its roots are in its craftsmanship in leather goods and accessories. The promising luxury brands of tomorrow not only need to capture the unique spirit of the respective region, their country-and-place-of-origin, but they also need to lead the way by creating that spirit. An example of this type of expansion route was followed by Shiseido. The new brands have to overcome their liability of foreignness. For example, the negative perception of the "Made in China" tag, and the associated linkage to Intellectual Property Rights and the counterfeit market, remain a challenge and are detrimental to China's aspirations to become a branded giant.

Second, new brands need know-how and legitimacy in Western markets: especially France and Italy, where the industry was born. At the same time, they need to balance local specificity. Thus, one way to achieve both credibility and legitimacy is either to acquire a luxury brand from those nations or be integrated into a conglomerate. For example, to be considered a luxury watch brand, association with the Swiss Watchmaking industry is a must and the brand has to build an affinity with the host culture. The first Modular Connected Tag Heuer 45 smartwatch had to face this dilemma as it was made in collaboration with Google and Intel. It was not made in Switzerland. For the subsequent versions, 60% of the manufacturing costs of the watch were incurred in Switzerland, to receive the official "Swiss Made" label.

Third, the emerging brands need to be positioned in the mind of the consumers. There may be more than one way to do this. Due to the geographic spread of emerging market countries, a critical parameter is the distribution strategy. This requires considerable investment in directly operated stores in order to establish themselves as legitimate brands abroad. For example, Coach, an American brand, grew by the power of association with its stores with the main luxury brands in the US, Japan, and Asia. Early in the last decade, it was not present in Europe, but it launched its Paris store in Printemps just adjacent to Dior and LV and its flagship on rue Saint Honoré.

Fourth, brand awareness and clear communication of its DNA are key. A stated long-term and shared strategic vision that moves from fragmented marketing activities to totally aligned branding activities is mandatory. Brand awareness and brand building is perhaps the most critical element for a new emerging market luxury brand. The right marketing mix is almost mandatory. Companies usually tap into these specific details and incorporate them in their brand personalities and identities so that customers can be offered an authentic experience. This has especially been observed in the Chinese market where any adverse or geopolitical event causes mass reaction.

It becomes more sensitive for both new and heritage brands as China is expected to lead the recovery of the luxury industry, and the industry is geared to attribute particular importance to the Chinese customer base, notably in terms of e-commerce. Local digital giants, such as Alibaba and JD.com, or even smaller tech companies like Douyin and Kuaishou, control a large share of worldwide digital shares, while keeping in mind the geopolitical tensions based on cultural, class, and religious nuances. It is beyond doubt that China will continue to be a key market for luxury brands, especially as the digital development allows an increasing part of the population to gain access to luxury brands online. Studies are predicting that, based on how fast the region is growing, Asia Pacific will be by far the largest region in the world for luxury goods by 2025.

In conclusion, it is difficult to precisely predict the future of frontier markets and brands arising from those markets. Today China is maturing, Russia and Brazil are emerging, and India is a longtime promising market for European brands. Although it might seem surprising, even the US can be considered an emerging market for luxury brands as American consumers represent a large untapped potential for personal luxury goods.

Moreover, it is assumed that luxury brands will discover the potential of Iran, Nigeria, and South Africa, followed by several other African countries. In Asia, Vietnam and Mongolia will soon join the club of fast-growing South East Asian countries such as Indonesia, Thailand, Cambodia, and Malaysia. Thus, the frontier market story is here to stay, though it may shift to other locations in the future.

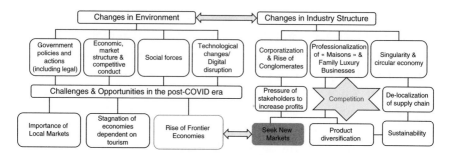

Figure 14.1 Globalization and the Luxury Industry

Figure 14.1 shows an overview of how globalization affects the market strategy of luxury companies.

Research Design, Methodology, and Data Collection

The aim of this book was to examine the evolution of the luxury industry from the lens of management principles without losing the focus on business reality. It aimed to analyze the luxury phenomenon through several academic frameworks as applied to numerous practical examples. This book has attempted to look at what the luxury industry has been, is, and will be.

Given the primary objective of the present study, to examine the relevance and applicability of time-tested management principles within an evolving and constantly changing industry, exploratory research was conducted. Qualitative research is usually recommended for studying such process-related issues, and also when the phenomenon being studied is not to be de-linked from its context.

Qualitative research—that is, case studies—gave a thorough grounding and a feel for real-life situations, especially where theory development and research were at an early stage. To develop a clear understanding of the interlinked phenomena in an ever-changing industry landscape, there was a need to look at varied data from multiple sources and study the phenomenon in its own context. The case

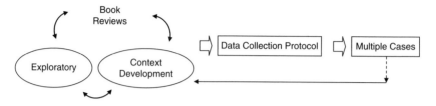

Figure R.1   Research Design

study method permitted a holistic analysis of a wide range of variables, open-ended and descriptive data, and multiple data sources and data collection techniques within the research setting. Figure R.1 shows the research design.

Methodology

The methodology of the study that was the basis for this book involved focusing on a wide number of organizations covering different sectors of the personal luxury goods business, documenting their creation, their historical evolution, and the processes that these organizations followed, especially during the pandemic. A deliberate choice was made to focus on breadth, keeping in mind that it is unrealistic to try to attempt both detailed, in-depth analyses of organizations, while also viewing a large sample of firms at the same time.

In order to understand the contingent effects of the environment, both archival and primary data were collected through interviews. Longitudinal data was necessary, to capture changes in context and to observe any processes of evolution.

The method used in writing this book included three distinct phases. First, an in-depth analysis of archival data was undertaken, analyzing articles and documents concerning each organization, including analysts' and consultants' reports, changes in organization structure, annual reports (when available), industry reports, and more. Second, longitudinal case studies were written about the organizations. Third, primary data were collected from interviews, discussions, and by participation at conferences on the luxury industry.

Data Collection and Analysis

The data required during this study called for top management involvement and the opinions of industry experts. That was because the information needed involved strategic decisions taken by the family houses and the multibrand conglomerates. This data was available by attending industry conferences, such as the New York Times Luxury Conference, the Conde Nast Luxury Conference and the Financial Times Luxury Conference over a period of five years, and taking notes while CEOs spoke. This gave me the scope of interacting with top management on a one-to-one basis. The data required were mostly post hoc. To reconstruct an accurate account of the strategies, the informant also needed to have knowledge of events and to have observed them closely. Interviewing a range of informants enabled cross-checking of the data and yielded multiple perspectives and varieties of opinion within the business houses and family-held firms.

Constant effort was undertaken to increase the reliability and validity of the study. Multiple respondents provided reliability and validity by cross-checking the data, and fostering insights into the evolution of the industry and its business houses. The interview data was cross-checked with press reports. The study undertook several measures, such as informal solicitation, personal viewpoints, alumni feedback, and others, in obtaining accurate and tangible information. Before starting the fieldwork, an interview protocol was prepared that was improved and revised after discussion with experienced professionals. The interview protocol consisted of various questions broadly related to different categories of variables, such as the changing dynamics of luxury environment, the logic of the business, the global financial crisis and its effect on luxury, marketing vis-à-vis branding, the nature of people, their management styles, the skills of luxury brands working in this industry, distribution, and more. The data was collected over a 17-year period from 2004 onward.

The open-ended nature of questions gave the informants leeway in giving their responses. The interview protocol was strictly followed at all times and no constraints were imposed on the choice of responses.

The use of multiple informants also helped in identifying multiple perspectives and any differences of opinion within an organization.

The notes resulting from these interviews were transcribed into categories and used as raw data. Multiple case studies were undertaken.

The data were analyzed through a variety of measures. The case analysis of each firm summarized the formal aspects of each organization. Results were compared and contrasted across multiple correspondents and functions. Emergent themes were further pursued to extract leads to understand in-depth the evolution process of the industry.

These are some of the important questions that were asked during the interview process:

- How do you define today "the logic of luxury"? What does "luxury" mean to you? What is your prediction during and after the pandemic for this industry?
- How will the COVID-19 pandemic affect the luxury industry? Is the crisis positive or negative for luxury? What is its impact?
- Going by this trend, do you think that family businesses (focused and reactive) are more equipped to succeed vis-à-vis financial corporate groups? Or not?
- What is the definition of the classic sense of "marketing" in the luxury world? Does it exist or not?
- Who is the typical luxury consumer today? Describe. What is your assessment of the elasticity of prices in the luxury world? Does it exist?
- How would you define the characteristics of the leadership and leaders in the luxury world?
- Do you think that the fact that the role of the *chefs des maisons* has been replaced by managers has changed the way luxury groups are managed today? For example, has the business changed from being based on craftsmanship to being shareholder-value driven?
- How do you assess the potential or the feasibility of newcomers in the luxury world? Is it feasible or not? And where will they come from—the United States, India, Japan, China, Africa, or Europe?
- We are talking about innovation in products. What is the role of innovation in service and what types of service innovation are you thinking of?
- What is the role of digitization, the social media market place, e-commerce, and the phygital experience in the distribution of luxury goods?

- What is your take on sustainability? What about reselling and renting? What do you think of certified pre-owned (CPO) goods and circularity? Will consumers adapt to the notion of singularity?
- How did you make your brand a success in such a short time? How did you turn the brand around? What, in your opinion, is the logic of the magic in creating and nurturing a brand to success?

Index